D1445761

Corporate
Capital Structures
in the
United States

A National Bureau
of Economic Research
Project Report

Corporate Capital Structures in the United States

Edited by Benjamin M. Friedman

The University of Chicago Press

Chicago and London

BENJAMIN M. FRIEDMAN is professor of economics at Harvard University and program director for financial markets and monetary economics at the National Bureau of Economic Research. His other books include *The Changing Roles of Debt and Equity in Financing U.S. Capital Formation*, also published by the University of Chicago Press.

The University of Chicago Press, Chicago 60637
The University of Chicago Press, Ltd., London

© 1985 by the National Bureau of Economic Research
All rights reserved. Published 1985
Printed in the United States of America
94 93 92 91 90 89 88 87 86 85   54321

Library of Congress Cataloging in Publication Data
Main entry under title:

Corporate capital structures in the United States.

(A Project report / National Bureau of Economic
Research)
    Includes bibliographies and indexes.
    1. Corporations—United States—Finance. I. Friedman,
Benjamin M.   II. Series: Project report (National Bureau
of Economic Research)
HG4061.C66   1985   338.7'4'0973   84-16138
ISBN 0-226-26411-4

Relation of the Directors to the
Work and Publications of the
National Bureau of Economic Research

1. The object of the National Bureau of Economic Research is to ascertain and to present to the public important economic facts and their interpretation in a scientic and impartial manner. The Board of Directors is charged with the responsibility of ensuring that the work of the National Bureau is carried on in strict conformity with this object.

2. The President of the National Bureau shall submit to the Board of Directors, or to its Executive Committee, for their formal adoption all specific proposals for research to be instituted.

3. No research report shall be published by the National Bureau until the President has sent each member of the Board a notice that a manuscript is recommended for publication and that in the President's opinion it is suitable for publication in accordance with the principles of the National Bureau. Such notification will include an abstract or summary of the manuscript's content and a response form for use by those Directors who desire a copy of the manuscript for review. Each manuscript shall contain a summary drawing attention to the nature and treatment of the problem studied, the character of the data and their utilization in the report, and the main conclusions reached.

4. For each manuscript so submitted, a special committee of the Directors (including Directors Emeriti) shall be appointed by majority agreement of the President and Vice Presidents (or by the Executive Committee in case of inability to decide on the part of the President and Vice Presidents), consisting of three Directors selected as nearly as may be one from each general division of the Board. The names of the special manuscript committee shall be stated to each Director when notice of the proposed publication is submitted to him. It shall be the duty of each member of the special manuscript committee to read the manuscript. If each member of the manuscript committee signifies his approval within thirty days of the transmittal of the manuscript, the report may be published. If at the end of that period any member of the manuscript committee withholds his approval, the President shall then notify each member of the Board, requesting approval or disapproval of publication, and thirty days additional shall be granted for this purpose. The manuscript shall then not be published unless at least a majority of the entire Board who shall have voted on the proposal within the time fixed for the receipt of votes shall have approved.

5. No manuscript may be published, though approved by each member of the special manuscript committee, until forty-five days have elapsed from the transmittal of the report in manuscript form. The interval is allowed for the receipt of any memorandum of dissent or reservation, together with a brief statement of his reasons, that any member may wish to express; and such memorandum of dissent or reservation shall be published with the manuscript if he so desires. Publication does not, however, imply that each member of the Board has read the manuscript, or that either members of the Board in general or the special committee have passed on its validity in every detail.

6. Publications of the National Bureau issued for informational purposes concerning the work of the Bureau and its staff, or issued to inform the public of activities of Bureau staff, and volumes issued as a result of various conferences involving the National Bureau shall contain a specific disclaimer noting that such publication has not passed through the normal review procedures required in this resolution. The Executive Committee of the Board is charged with review of all such publications from time to time to ensure that they do not take on the character of formal research reports of the National Bureau, requiring formal Board approval.

7. Unless otherwise determined by the Board or exempted by the terms of paragraph 6, a copy of this resolution shall be printed in each National Bureau publication.

(Resolution adopted October 25, 1926, as revised through September 30, 1974)

Contents

In Memoriam
John Lintner

John Lintner, an outstanding economist and one of the creators of modern financial theory, participated in the NBER conference that provided the basis for this book, but died before the book went to press.

John was a scholar and a teacher, and to many he was also a colleague and a friend. Because of his special blend of intellectual vigor and personal warmth, of interest in the subject matter for its own sake and concern for others' individual development, of energy for his work and generosity with his time, in his case these often disparate roles were really one. The attitudes and efforts with which he advanced the frontiers of economics and finance were inseparable from those with which he contributed to the lives of those who knew him.

John's approach to both his scholarship and his teaching had as its foundation a tripod built from a faith in the theory of economics and finance, a keen interest in the actual working of financial markets, and a concern for issues of public policy. He believed that what happens in financial markets can and does importantly affect nonfinancial economic activity. He also believed that the institutional setting of the financial markets, including legal and regulatory restrictions as well as elements of business organization and practice, can and does importantly affect financial behavior and the resulting market outcomes.

The chief consequence of these central beliefs was an astonishing breadth of intellectual scope in the approach he took to any question of positive economics or economic policy. Matters for him were not just not simple; they were complex in infinitely varied and interesting ways. Factors seemingly peripheral to the issue at hand might turn out, on closer inspection, not to be so peripheral after all. The corollary of such an open (and open-minded) approach to intellectual inquiry, of course, is appropriate caution about accepting at face value even carefully buttressed conclusions. In this, too, John was consistent. Always eclectic, never dogmatic, he combined an infectious enthusiasm for new thinking, both his own and others', with a healthy reluctance to be persuaded that anyone's work, either his own or others', had ever provided the last word.

It is no coincidence that many of the papers published in this volume strongly reflect these fundamental perspectives, both in substance and in style. John Lintner's impact on the thinking of an entire generation of scholars has been profound and far-reaching.

John's influence on the fields of economics and finance grew not just from the force and appeal of his intellectual approach, as conveyed in his published work, but also from his extraordinary generosity in taking time with and for others. This was especially the case with his students and younger colleagues, and with younger scholars more generally. One part of this interaction, to be sure, was simply his love of conversation about all aspects of economics and finance, at both the scientific and the practical levels. In the case of younger scholars, however, John gave even more of himself. His willingness to discuss research plans and read drafts of papers, and to provide, in his uniquely gentle and encouraging way, insightful comments on issues ranging from the basic goals of the research to the smallest details of its execution, reflected a more intensive dedication of himself not often found in today's rushed and overcommitted academic environment.

John devoted this time and effort not only because of his interest in the subjects on which younger people were working but also because of his concern for their personal development, both as scholars and as individuals. Younger people's lives mattered very much to him. He rejoiced with them at their advances, and he cared for them in adversity.

From the late 1960s until his death, John was also a great friend and advisor—formal and informal—to the National Bureau of Economic Research. For many years he was a research associate of the NBER, and he directed the NBER project on Inflation and Financial Markets. Toward the NBER, too, he was characteristically generous of himself, always available for advice, always willing to help.

With a heavy sadness, but also a warm remembrance and great gratitude for it, I dedicate this book to the memory of my friend.

B.M.F.

Acknowledgments

This volume, which consists of papers and discussions presented at a conference held at Palm Beach, Florida, 6–7 January 1983, presents research carried out within the National Bureau of Economic Research project, "The Changing Roles of Debt and Equity in Financing U.S. Capital Formation." The NBER has undertaken this project—including the conference, the research described in this volume, and the publication of the volume itself—with the support of the American Council of Life Insurance.

The many people whose advice and assistance have helped to make this volume possible include NBER directors George T. Conklin, A. Gilbert Heebner, and Roy E. Moor; NBER research associates Roger Hall Gordon and Edward J. Kane; NBER staff members Mark Fitz-Patrick, Kirsten Foss, Susan Jannone, Cynthia Nelson, and Annie Spillane; and Kenneth M. Wright of the American Council of Life Insurance.

The opinions expressed in this volume are those of the respective authors. They do not necessarily reflect the views of the National Bureau of Economic Research, the American Council of Life Insurance, or any other organization.

Benjamin M. Friedman

Corporate Capital Structures in the United States: An Introduction and Overview

Benjamin M. Friedman

In recent years questions about U.S. capital formation have increasingly become a major focus of both public and private concern. Such questions inevitably deal in large part with the economy's corporate sector. Since World War II, business corporations consistently have accounted for about three-quarters of all investment in plant and equipment in the United States. As a result, corporate behavior—including corporations' physical investment decisions and their corresponding financial decisions—constitutes a primary determinant of the economy's overall capital formation process and performance.

The research reported in this volume represents the second stage of a wide-ranging National Bureau of Economic Research effort to investigate "The Changing Roles of Debt and Equity in Financing U.S. Capital Formation." The first group of studies sponsored under this project, which have been published individually and summarized in a 1982 volume bearing the same title (Friedman 1982), addressed several key issues relevant to corporate sector behavior along with such other aspects of the evolving financial underpinnings of U.S. capital formation as household saving incentives, international capital flows, and government debt management. In the project's second series of studies, presented at a National Bureau of Economic Research conference in January 1983 and published here for the first time along with the commentaries from that conference, the central focus is the financial side of capital formation undertaken by the U.S. corporate business sector. At the same time, because corporations' securities must be held, a parallel focus is on the behavior of the markets that price these claims.

Benjamin M. Friedman is professor of economics at Harvard University and program director for financial markets and monetary economics at the NBER.

This focus on both the corporate sector and the financial environment which it confronts is valuable, not only because of corporations' large role in undertaking the economy's capital formation but also because the corporate sector context itself helps to define more sharply, and render more operational for purposes of empirical research, key elements of the debt and equity financing process. A major advantage at the theoretical level, for example, is that business corporations, unlike households (and, by extension, unincorporated businesses for some purposes), do no direct consumption. A variety of research strategies can therefore conceptually connect corporate financing to firms' capital formation objectives without at the same time having to deal with issues affecting consumption-saving decisions. Major advantages of the corporate sector context at the empirical level include the more formally explicit nature of corporate debt and equity claims, the superior availability of data summarizing central elements of corporate financial behavior, and, of course, the availability of observable market prices for claims that are publicly traded.

The financial capital structure of an economy's business corporations, either individually or in the aggregate, is the joint product of decisions taken by claim-issuing corporations on one side and by claim-holding investors—collectively, "the market"—on the other. The capital structure existing at any one time reflects the cumulative result of the entire prior history of corporate decisions on what kind of claims to issue, and how much of each, in response to the associated history of market prices. Changes in the capital structure over time in turn reflect corporate responses either to changing nonfinancial influences or to changes in the financial market environment, which in turn stem from investors' responses to a wide variety of further economic and noneconomic factors. The main goals motivating the research presented here are not only to advance understanding of the basic behavior connecting debt and equity financing to physical capital formation in the United States but also, and more specifically, to assess how the roles in this process of debt and equity have changed over time.

Within this overall direction, three sets of questions about corporate sector and financial market behavior emerge as the direct objects of the research undertaken in these papers. First, what has been the actual experience of the use of debt and equity financing by U.S. business corporations in recent years? Have corporate capital structures changed significantly? It is well known that the use of debt has increased in some ways, but has the debt component of capital structures actually increased after allowance for erosion due to the secular upward trends in price inflation and in nominal interest rates?

Second, what is the relationship (if any) between firms' real investment decisions and their financial decisions? Does the external environment that firms face in the product markets help shape their debt and equity decisions? How important are specific institutional factors like taxes, or arrangements for monitoring performance and contract compliance? Do firms have individually optimal capital structures? If so, what determines them? Does the entire corporate sector, or even the entire economy, have an optimal aggregate capital structure? If so, can identifiable movements in the factors determining it account for the changes in capital structures that have taken place in recent years?

Third, what factors drive the financial markets' pricing of—that is, the setting of terms on which investors are willing to hold—debt and equity securities? Are single-factor models of market pricing behavior adequate? Are securities markets "efficient" in the familiar sense? Are debt and equity securities substitutes or complements in investors' portfolios? Have significant changes taken place in recent years in the structure of equilibrium market prices? If so, can identifiable changes in market risks or other objective factors, or in investors' assessments of risks, account for them?

In addition to these substantive questions of economic behavior at the individual firm and market levels, the work presented here inevitably addresses several methodological issues, including some that frequently arise in empirical economic research regardless of its subject, as well as some that are more specific to the study of corporate capital structures. What standards are useful for evaluating formal models of behavior? Is the appropriate use of such models limited to the explanation of observed behavior, or is prediction also warranted? If the latter, then under what circumstances? How can empirical research discriminate among competing hypotheses when key explanatory variables are unobservable, and the best available proxies for them not only are highly collinear but could each be proxying for more than one concept? Is it useful to assume that the market is always "correctly" pricing assets? In what contexts are market values versus replacement values more relevant? What is the best way to infer market participants' unobservable assessments from magnitudes that are observable? What is the best way to make operational models relying centrally on aspects of the exchange of information, including such examples as agency costs and signaling phenomena?

The first three of these ten papers establish the basic empirical facts of the changes that have (and, in some cases, have not) taken place in U.S. corporate capital structures and in the financial price and yield relationships that U.S. corporations have faced in recent years.

Robert A. Taggart's paper, "Secular Patterns in the Financing of United States Corporations," sets the stage for the entire series of studies. In it Taggart develops a conceptual framework for thinking about changes in corporate capital structures and assembles and analyzes relevant time-series data going back in many cases to the beginning of the twentieth century. He begins by using available aggregate time-series data to document the main features of the changes that have occurred over time. He shows that the use of debt by U.S. corporations has increased considerably since World War II, but he leaves open the question of whether current debt levels are high by prewar standards. The postwar surge in corporate debt certainly appears less dramatic when viewed in the context of the whole century's experience. Taggart also documents several other changes that have occurred, including the increasing importance of short-term relative to long-term debt and the declining importance of new issues of either common or preferred stock relative to internally generated equity.

In the paper's theoretical sections, Taggart reviews several basic explanations of the determination of firm and/or aggregate corporate capital structures, including those relying on the trade-off between bankruptcy costs and tax savings from deductibility of interest, on the relative agency costs of debt and equity, on information transfer problems and signaling, and on the differential between personal and corporate tax rates. Taggart lays out the relationships among these four classes of theories and uses them to examine a series of (at least potentially) measurable influences on corporate capital structures including tax factors, price inflation, supplies of competing securities, and the physical characteristics of corporate investment.

Taggart then asks which among these different explanations could plausibly account for the changes that have taken place. He concludes that tax factors in conjunction with inflation have played an important role but not one sufficient to explain the main trends that have occurred over long periods of time. He argues that, in addition, supplies of competing securities like government bonds, along with the secular development of the nation's financial intermediary system, may also be important determinants of long-run corporate financing patterns.

John H. Ciccolo and Christopher F. Baum's paper, "Changes in the Balance Sheet of the U.S. Manufacturing Sector, 1926–1977," takes a closer look at an important slice of the corporate sector's capital structure on the basis of new data series developed as part of this NBER project and now available to other researchers. Ciccolo and Baum describe a micro-level dataset that they developed for a rolling sample of approximately fifty manufacturing firms, spanning a half century and including for each firm a large number of balance sheet and income account items. A major contribution of this dataset is the ready availability, for the first time, of accurate information on the market value of corporations' publicly traded liabilities. In addition, the dataset Ciccolo and Baum developed provides estimates of the replacement value of firms' physical assets as well as computations of rates of return based on both market and replacement values.

Ciccolo and Baum show that the chief aggregate features exhibited by this dataset over time are broadly consistent with the principal developments documented at the aggregate level by other researchers. The data show an increasing importance of external funds, and especially of debt, in financing corporations' physical capital formation. On the asset side, the data show a substantial decline in corporations' holdings of cash and short-term marketable securities. Rates of return have declined on balance within the post–World War II period, but not from the perspective of a longer time frame. In the latter half of the postwar period, market valuations of corporations' net assets have declined dramatically in relation both to replacement values and to realized rates of return.

As an illustration of its potential micro-level applications, Ciccolo and Baum use the 1927–35 and 1966–77 panels of their dataset to test a simple portfolio model relating the movements of corporations' key balance sheet items to changes in their net cash flow and to changes in the ratio of market to replacement value of their net assets. The principal idea underlying their model is that firms face different constraints, and therefore behave differently, when they are attempting to increase their stock of physical capital than when they are trying to reduce it. The empirical results generally support their model for the later period but not the earlier one.

Patric H. Hendershott and Roger D. Huang's paper, "Debt and Equity Yields, 1926–1980," provides a parallel review and analysis of the market prices (yields) that U.S. corporations have faced in deciding on their capital structures. Hendershott and Huang first document the principal movements of and interrelationships among debt and equity yields in the United States over a half century, including both secular and cyclical movements, and then go on to test several familiar propositions about yield relationships.

Hendershott and Huang focus in the first instance on corporate bond and equity yields, the market prices most directly relevant to capital structure decisions, but for purposes of analysis and comparison their work also includes the yields on both short- and long-term U.S. Treasury securities. A familiar result, which their review of the experience of these yields reinforces, is the contrast between the patterns that have dominated the post–World War II period and the events of the 1930s. A significant but less familiar result is the appearance of strong regularities in security yield movements over the business cycle, including systematic differences in the cyclical movements of ex post returns on bonds and equities. The strength of equity returns during the year surrounding business cycle troughs stands out especially clearly.

Hendershott and Huang also investigate several familiar hypotheses about the determination of debt and equity yields. The principal conclusion of their work here is that unanticipated price inflation, which they represent by the difference between the actual inflation experience and the corresponding estimate in the Livingston survey, is a major determinant of these yields. Other factors also emerge from their analysis as bearing on the determination of yields, however, including in particular measures of real economic activity like industrial production and capacity utilization.

Against the background of this general review of the experience of both the quantities and the prices associated with changes in corporate capital structures in the United States, the next four papers address more directly the market mechanism determining the prices (yields) of debt and equity securities. The first two of the four focus on general aspects of the behavior of investors in debt and equity securities; the next two examine the market pricing mechanism in contexts specifically related to actual or potential changes in corporate capital structures.

Zvi Bodie, Alex Kane, and Robert McDonald's paper, "Inflation and the Role of Bonds in Investor Portfolios," explores both theoretically and empirically the role of nominal (that is, not indexed) bonds of various maturities in the portfolios of U.S. investors. A principal goal of their analysis is to determine whether an investor constrained to hold bonds only in the form of a single portfolio of nominal debt instruments—as is the case, for example, in employer-sponsored saving plans offering a choice between a common stock fund and a single bond fund—will suffer a serious welfare loss. For this purpose Bodie et al. take as their measure of the welfare gain or loss due to a given change in the investor's opportunity set the increment to current wealth needed to offset that change. A second goal of their analysis is to study the desirability and feasibility of introducing a market for indexed bonds, offering a riskless real return, in the United States.

A novel feature of the empirical approach of Bodie et al. is their method of deriving equilibrium risk premia on the various asset classes they study. They employ the variance-covariance structure of real returns computed from historical data for 1953–81, in combination with assumptions about net asset supplies and about the economy's overall average degree of risk aversion, to derive estimates of these risk premia. By using this procedure they circumvent the problems that would be associated with estimating risk premia on the basis of historical *mean* returns, which are sometimes negative.

Bodie et al. conclude that a substantial loss in welfare can be associated with participation in a saving plan offering a choice only between a diversified common stock fund and an intermediate-term bond fund. They argue that it is possible to eliminate most of this loss, however, by introducing, as a third option in such plans, a fund consisting of short-term money market instruments. Bodie et al. also conclude that the potential welfare gain from introducing explicitly indexed bonds in the U.S. financial market is probably not large enough to justify the costs of innovation by private issuers. The major reason the gain would be so small is that one-month U.S. Treasury bills, with their small variance of real returns, already constitute an effective substitute for indexed bonds in investors' portfolios.

My own paper, "The Substitutability of Debt and Equity Securities," investigates empirically the degree of substitutability between debt and equity securities in the United States. The analysis first applies fundamental relationships connecting portfolio choices with expected asset returns to infer key asset substitutabilities directly from the observed variance-covariance structure of U.S. asset returns, using quarterly data for 1960–80. It then compares these implied substitutabilities with the corresponding econometrically estimated portfolio behavior of U.S. households.

The resulting evidence provides little ground for any conclusion about even the sign, much less the magnitude, of the substitutability of short-term debt and equity. Although the implied optimal behavior indicates that these two assets are substitutes, the observed behavior indicates that households have treated them as complements. By contrast, the evidence consistently indicates that long-term debt and equity are substitutes. Moreover, with a few exceptions the empirical estimates of the associated substitution elasticity are quite closely clustered around the value − .035.

The conclusion that long-term debt and equity are substitutes with elasticity − .035 bears mixed implications for broader economic and financial questions. At one level, the finding that the two assets are indeed substitutes validates the standard assumption underlying a variety of familiar models in both corporate finance and monetary economics. At the same time, if the absolute magnitude of the elasticity of substitution is so small, then many of these models' more important substantive conclusions do not follow.

E. Philip Jones, Scott P. Mason, and Eric Rosenfeld's paper, "Contingent Claims Valuation of Corporate Liabilities: Theory and Empirical Tests," addresses the specific question of how the financial markets value the complicated securities, encumbered by numerous covenants and indenture provisions, that U.S. corporations typically issue. The central tool in their analysis is the familiar contingent claims models, which applies to the pricing of corporate liabilities the fundamental insight that every corporate security is a contingent claim on the value of the underlying firm. Hence it is possible to model the financial markets' pricing of these securities via an arbitrage logic that is independent of the specific equilibrium structure of risk and return. If this model is correct, then the price of every security depends in a formally quantifiable way on the rate of return on riskless assets and on the issuing firm's market value and the volatility of that value.

Jones et al. lay out the basic theory of the contingent claims model, extend it to cover such practically relevant special cases as multiple debt issues of a single firm and debt issues with sinking funds (with and without an option to double the associated payment schedule), and then test the expanded theory using monthly 1975–82 data on the actual market prices of 177 bonds issued by 15 U.S. corporations. Even though they restrict their sample to corporations with relatively simple capital structures, the numerical solution of the model to derive predicted securities prices is complex. The required data include interest rates, volatility of firms' market values, and specific aspects of the bonds' indentures including principal amount outstanding, coupon rate, call price schedule and deferment period, and sinking fund schedule and associated options.

Jones et al. conclude that their empirical results do not warrant using the model, in its conventional form, as a practical basis for valuing corporate securities. Although there is almost no systematic bias in the pricing errors that the model makes for the sample as a whole, the model does systematically over- or underprice bonds with specific characteristics. In particular, the model tends to underprice less risky bonds and overprice more risky bonds. This failure leads Jones et al. to suggest that several of the standard assumptions underlying contingent claims analysis in its usual form are inconsistent with the actual workings of the U.S. financial markets.

Wayne H. Mikkelson's paper, "Capital Structure Change and Decreases in Stockholders' Wealth: A Cross-sectional Study of Convertible Security Calls," examines the financial markets' pricing of corporate securities in the specific context of the changes in common stock values that occur when firms call outstanding convertible debt or preferred stock. The goals of the paper are to investigate the potential determinants of the usually observed negative common stock price reaction to the announcement of a convertible security call forcing conversion and, on the basis of this analysis, to draw inferences about the pricing of corporate securities and hence about the determination of corporate capital structures more generally.

Mikkelson's empirical work relates the observed changes in common stock prices following 164 convertible security calls made by U.S. corporations during 1962–78 to several quantifiable effects associated with these calls, including the change in interest expense tax shields, the potential redistribution of wealth from common stockholders to holders of debt or preferred stock, the decrease in value of the conversion option held by owners of the convertible securities, the increase in the number of common shares outstanding, and the change in earnings per share.

Among these various effects, only the reduction in interest expense tax shields exhibits a significant relationship to the change in common stock price.

Mikkelson argues that this result is consistent with systematic reductions in common stock prices due not only to reductions in interest expense tax shields, as would be implied by theories relating optimal capital structure to tax factors, but also to the negative information about corporations' earnings prospects conveyed by convertible security calls. He therefore concludes that this evidence is also consistent with theories which relate capital structure to earnings prospects and hence which imply that reductions in leverage convey unfavorable information about firm value.

The last three papers examine directly the observed capital structures of U.S. corporations, emphasizing in particular the question of the relationship (if any) of capital structure decisions to corporations' real-sector behavior.

Alan J. Auerbach's paper, "Real Determinants of Corporate Leverage," focuses on one of the key factors underlying several familiar theories of optimal corporate capital structures: the role of taxes. Auerbach argues that the U.S. corporate income tax distorts corporations' real-sector behavior, via the variation in depreciation allowances and investment tax credit provisions across different types of physical investments, and also distorts financial behavior via the differential treatment of debt and equity returns. The object of his analysis of corporations' real and financial decisions is to determine the extent to which these biases offset one another.

Auerbach's model connecting firms' real and financial behavior rests on the idea that corporations prefer to finance different physical investments in different ways. Such behavior would be important in this context because the conclusion that tax effects bias investment choices is necessarily valid only if a separation prevails between real and financial decisions. For example, if a corporation's optimal capital structure depends on a tax advantage to debt financing which is dissipated by risk-related costs as the firm's leverage increases, and if these risk-related costs in turn depend on the firm's investment mix, then the resulting financial bias in favor of investing in structures could offset the initial tax bias in favor of investing in equipment.

Auerbach's empirical work, based on 1958–77 data for a panel of 189 U.S. corporations, suggests that observed patterns of real and financial behavior are only partially consistent with familiar theories of optimal capital structure based on tax factors and costs connected to agency considerations and risks of bankruptcy. The effect of firms' growth rates on their borrowing is inconsistent with the predictions of models based on agency costs. In addition, although the effect of the tax loss carry-forward is consistent with models based on tax shields, the effect of earnings variance is not. Auerbach also concludes that there is no obvious financial offset to the tax bias against investment in structures since, on the whole, firms do not appear to borrow more to invest in structures than in equipment.

Michael S. Long and Ileen B. Malitz's paper, "Investment Patterns and Financial Leverage," focuses on another of the major elements underlying familiar theories of corporate capital structures: the role of investment opportunities. Here, too, an important implication of such models is that corporations' real and financial decisions are connected. In this case the connection takes the form of a systematic bias toward underinvestment when firms with risky debt outstanding act in the interest of their shareholders. One potential role of complex covenants in debt contracts is to alleviate this problem.

Long and Malitz argue that, because growth opportunities that are firm-specific and intangible (and hence unobservable) reduce the effectiveness of debt covenants, corporations with a high proportion of their investment opportunities in intangible form can limit the agency costs of their debt only by limiting the amount of risky debt that they have outstanding. Conversely, corporations with a high proportion of their investment opportunities in the form of tangible assets like capital equipment can support a greater level of debt. Hence a key determinant of optimal corporate capital structure is the specific type of investment opportunity that the firm faces.

Long and Malitz present empirical results, based on 1978–80 data for a sample of 545 U.S. corporations, that provide evidence in support of such a relationship between real and financial behavior. In particular, their results show that corporations which invest heavily in intangibles—research and development, for example, or advertising—systematically rely less on debt than do corporations which invest largely in tangibles. These results also stand up in the presence of other variables like tax factors that represent alternative explanations of capital structure decisions, although there is evidence that the most important single determinant of corporations' borrowing decisions remains the availability of internal funds.

Finally, A. Michael Spence's paper, "Capital Structure and the Corporation's Product Market Environment," examines the question of a relationship between corporations' real and financial behavior from a different perspective. Spence argues that, if choosing an optimal capital structure is a way for a corporation to reduce its costs in some relevant sense, then corporations facing greater competitive pressure in their product markets will have a greater incentive, and hence a greater tendency, to do so than will corporations enjoying more sheltered competitive environments. Alternatively, if theories treating financial structure as irrelevant are correct, then there will be no observed connection between competitive product markets and observed patterns of corporate capital structures.

Spence tests this hypothesis by relating the observed interfirm variance of capital structures to measures of product market competitive pressure for 1,183 U.S. corporations in 403 four-digit industries. His measures of competitiveness include returns earned by firms as well as variables directly and indirectly reflecting entry barriers and potential oligopolistic consensus. Spence also includes in the empirical work measures of product market diversification for each firm, so as to be able to distinguish results based on the full sample from results based on a smaller sample of relatively undiversified firms.

Spence finds that, although industry product market environments help explain the returns that firms earn and also bear systematic relationships to firms' actual capital structures, they apparently do not much influence intra-industry deviations of firms' capital structures from the respective implied industry optima. One possible explanation for this negative result, of course, is that capital structure does not strongly influence corporations' costs or hence their total value—in other words, that there exists no optimal capital structure. The positive results that emerge seem inconsistent with this view, however. An alternative explanation is that, while optimal capital structures do exist, the factors that give rise to them simply do not become significantly more influential in more competitive environments.

Reference

Friedman, Benjamin M., ed. *The Changing Roles of Debt and Equity in Financing U.S. Capital Formation.* Chicago: University of Chicago Press, 1982.

1 Secular Patterns in the Financing of U.S. Corporations

Robert A. Taggart, Jr.

Developments in the financing of corporations are often traced by look-ing at financial ratios for the corporate sector as a whole. For many years, in both academic and business publications, patterns in these ratios have been observed, interpreted, and sometimes decried.[1] There is little con-sensus on what these patterns mean, however, and even some disagree-ment over what the patterns have been. Some studies, for example, argue that corporate debt ratios have increased sharply over the past two to three decades, and they point to such factors as inflation and the tax system to explain this trend.[2] Other studies assert that the corporate debt-equity mix has exhibited remarkable secular stability.[3]

Several factors have contributed to this lack of consensus. First, finan-cial ratios can be measured in a variety of different units, such as book value versus market value or stocks versus flows. Different measure-ments are subject to different biases and thus present different pictures of the trends in corporate finance. Second, different time periods have been used to trace the behavior of these ratios. Studies emphasizing increased use of corporate debt, for example, focus generally on the post–World War II period, while those arguing for debt ratio stability typically encompass a longer period overall but do not include the most recent years' experience. Third, attempts to interpret financing trends have been hampered by the lack of a theoretical framework. With few excep-

Robert A. Taggart, Jr., is professor of finance at Boston University and a research associate of the NBER. The author is grateful to the NBER for financial support and to Michael Burda, Leslie Edison, and Wing Woo for research assistance. Helpful comments on earlier drafts were provided by Fischer Black, Benjamin Friedman, John Lintner, Terry Marsh, Robert McDonald, Stewart Myers, William Sahlman, and participants in the Finance Workshops at Harvard University, MIT, McGill University, and the University of Minnesota.

tions, previous studies have discussed these trends without reference to a detailed model.[4] Although this may seem odd in view of corporate capital structure's place among the central theoretical issues in finance, it should be kept in mind that many of the academic studies of aggregate financing trends came before theoretical work had progressed very far. More fundamentally, theoretical work that has been conducted has been largely aimed at the individual firm, and, until very recently, little analysis has been explicitly devoted to the determinants of corporate finance at the aggregate level.[5] Much of existing theoretical work, then, has not made it clear what to look for in attempting to explain secular financing patterns for the corporate sector as a whole.

In view of these difficulties, the purpose of the current study is to broaden existing perspectives on both the measurement and theory of corporate financing trends. One premise of this effort is that stepping back and looking at the longest possible period with different types of data will resolve some of the controversy over what these trends have been. A second premise is that the determinants of these trends can be further illuminated by examining current capital structure theories with the specific aim of drawing out their implications for aggregate financing patterns.

The paper consists of four sections. In section 1.1, the measurement issue is addressed. Observations from a number of previous studies are gathered and updated in order to present the broadest possible view of corporate financing trends from the beginning of this century to the present. Section 1.2 undertakes the first step in interpreting these trends by reviewing available capital structure theory. The major aim of this review is to identify the determinants of aggregate supplies and demands for corporate securities relative to competing securities in the capital market. In section 1.3, a very preliminary test is presented of existing theory's ability to explain the capital structure trends described in section 1.1. This is done by comparing trends in capital structure determinants, as predicted by existing theory, with the capital structure trends themselves. Finally, in section 1.4, some suggestions are offered for improving the ability of capital structure theory to explain the evolution of aggregate corporate financing patterns over time. These suggestions center around providing a fuller description of the role of corporate financing activities in the context of the financial system as a whole.

To preview some of the major conclusions, it is found that there has been an undeniable trend toward greater use of debt financing by corporations in the post–World War II period. Nevertheless, the relative level of corporate debt was unusually low around the time of World War II, and current debt levels are not unprecedented when viewed in the context of the twentieth century as a whole. The tax system, in conjunction with inflation, has probably played an important role in the postwar increases in corporate debt, but these factors appear insufficient to explain the trends over longer periods of time. In particular, it is argued that supplies of competing securities, such as federal government bonds, as well as the secular development of the financial intermediary system, may also be important determinants of long-run corporate financing patterns.

1.1 Measurement of Capital Structure Trends

Attempts to identify the secular trends in corporate financing encounter a variety of measurement problems. Comparable data series often are not available over long periods of time. Accounting conventions are subject to change, and fluctuations in economic conditions, especially the rate of inflation, may destroy the comparability of accounting numbers between periods. Market value numbers may be used in their stead, but these must be estimated with some error, and it is unclear to what extent market values reflect the actual financing decisions of corporations and to what extent they reflect other exogenous factors.

The approach taken here will be to present a variety of different measures of corporate financing trends and then to try to infer the common patterns that emerge. Four different types of data have been used in previous studies of corporate financing, and all four will be presented sequentially in the sections that follow. These include book value, market value, replacement cost, and flow-of-funds data. Each type of measurement has its problems and advantages, and these will be discussed as the data are presented.

Throughout the ensuing discussion, primary attention is devoted to corporations' relative use of debt and equity financing. This has been the focal point of most previous attempts to trace patterns in corporate financing and of capital structure theory as well. Where possible, however, trends in preferred stock, external versus internal equity, and short-term versus long-term debt will also be noted.

1.1.1 Book Value Balance Sheet Data

Perhaps the simplest approach to assessing corporate financing patterns is to examine changes in the composition of the liability side of the corporate balance sheet. This was the approach adopted by Miller (1963), for example, in a study undertaken for the Commission on Money and Credit. The Internal Revenue Service compiles balance sheet data both for U.S. corporations in the aggregate and for U.S. manufacturing corporations, and Miller's study examined these data for the period 1926–56. Using data through 1979, table 1.1 presents a variety of balance sheet ratios from this source, including the ratios of long-term debt and preferred stock to total capital. These data are plotted in figure 1.1.

As Miller pointed out in his study, the ratios of long-term debt to total

Table 1.1   **Selected Book Value Balance Sheet Ratios, All U.S. Corporations and U.S. Manufacturing Corporations**

	All U.S. Corporations			Manufacturing Corporations		
Year	LD/TC (1)	P/TC (2)	D/A (3)	LD/TC (4)	P/TC (5)	D/A (6)
1926	.21	.11	—	.09	.14	—
1927	.22	.11	—	.09	.14	—
1928	.23	.10	—	.10	.13	—
1929	.23	.09	—	.09	.12	—
1930	.24	.09	—	.10	.12	—
1931	.25	.10	—	.10	.13	—
1932	.26	.11	—	.11	.13	—
1933	.26	.11	—	.10	.14	—
1934	.26	.10	—	.10	.14	—
1935	.26	.11	—	.10	.14	—
1936	.26	.10	—	.10	.13	—
1937	.26	.10	.53	.10	.12	.26
1938	.27	.10	.54	.11	.13	.25
1939	.27	.09	.55	.11	.12	.25
1940	.26	.09	.57	.11	.11	.27
1941	.26	.08	.58	.11	.10	.31
1942	.24	.08	.61	.10	.10	.35
1943	.23	.08	.63	.09	.09	.36
1944	.23	.08	.64	.09	.09	.34
1945	.21	.08	.65	.09	.09	.30
1946	.21	.07	.64	.10	.09	.30
1947	.22	.07	.63	.11	.08	.31
1948	.23	.06	.62	.12	.07	.32
1949	.23	.06	.62	.12	.07	.28
1950	.23	.05	.63	.11	.06	.31
1951	.23	.05	.63	.13	.06	.35
1952	.24	.05	.65	.15	.05	.36
1953	.25	.04	.65	.15	.05	.36
1954	.25	.04	.65	.15	.05	.34
1955	.24	.04	.66	.15	.04	.35
1956	.25	.04	.65	.16	.04	.36
1957	.26	.04	.65	.17	—	.38
1958	.26	.03	.65	.17	—	.37
1959	.27	.03	.66	.17	—	.38
1960	.27	.03	.66	.17	.03	.38
1961	.28	.03	.66	.18	.03	.43
1962	—	—	—	—	—	—
1963	.28	—	.68	.17	—	.38
1964	.28	—	.68	.18	—	.39
1965	.28	—	.69	.19	—	.40
1966	.29	.02	.69	.21	.02	.43
1967	.29	—	.69	.21	—	.42
1968	.30	—	.70	.23	—	.45

Table 1.1 (continued)

Year	All U.S. Corporations			Manufacturing Corporations		
	LD/TC (1)	P/TC (2)	D/A (3)	LD/TC (4)	P/TC (5)	D/A (6)
1969	.31	—	.70	.23	—	.45
1970	.32	—	.71	.26	—	.49
1971	.33	—	.72	.27	—	.49
1972	.33	—	.72	.26	—	.49
1973	.34	—	.73	.26	—	.51
1974	.34	—	.74	.27	—	.53
1975	.34	—	.74	.28	—	.52
1976	.34	—	.74	.28	—	.53
1977	.34	—	.74	.27	—	.53
1978	.34	—	.75	.28	—	.54
1979	.33	—	.74	.28	—	.55

Source: Internal Revenue Service, *Statistics of Income*.
Note: LD = long-term bonds and notes; P = preferred stock; TC = total long-term capital = long-term debt + preferred stock + common equity; D = total debt; A = total assets.

long-term capital fluctuate but exhibit virtually no trend through the mid-1950s. The ratios of total debt (including liabilities of all kinds) to total assets show some tendency to rise in the late 1930s and early 1940s but exhibit no trend thereafter until at least the late 1950s.[6] The use of preferred stock, on the other hand, exhibits a steady secular decline through the early 1960s.[7]

Data that were not available to Miller at the time of his study, however, suggest that debt ratios have tended to drift steadily upward since the late 1950s. This may indicate a fundamental change in corporate financial policy, although Miller (1977) has warned that at least some of this apparent trend may be spurious. Liberalized depreciation allowances since the early 1960s, for example, would tend to depress reported equity values and would automatically tend to increase debt ratios. Inflation in the 1960s and 1970s has also caused distortions in book value measures of debt ratios. Such measures do not reflect inflation-induced transfers of value from bondholders to equityholders, for example. By the same token, inflation causes reported asset values to be understated, thus giving a misleading impression of the size of corporate debt relative to assets.[8]

If capital markets are efficient, investors should see through these accounting changes and should also adjust for the effects of inflation. Some of the problems described above may be circumvented, then, by the use of market value balance sheet ratios, and it is to these that we now turn.[9]

Fraction of Total
Capitalization

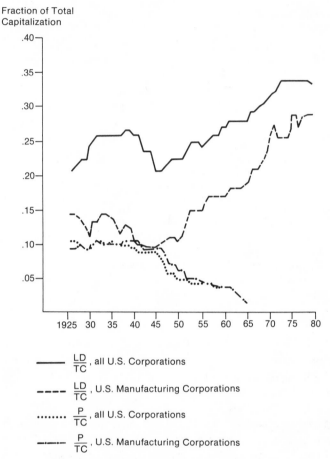

Fig. 1.1   Plot of book value financial ratio data from table 1.1.

1.1.2   Market Value Balance Sheet Data

Since market value data are not available for the nonfinancial corporate sector as a whole, they must be estimated. A variety of estimates using somewhat different techniques are presented in table 1.2. Several of these measures are also plotted in figure 1.2.

The most common approach is to take dividend and interest payments reported by corporations and to capitalize these at appropriate rates to obtain estimates of the market values of equity and debt, respectively. This approach has been followed by Holland and Myers (1979), using the dividend yield on the Standard and Poor's Composite Index and Moody's Baa corporate bond rate as capitalization rates. Their estimates, updated through 1981 are shown in column 1 of table 1.2. Like the accounting numbers in table 1.1, these estimates suggest that there has been a considerable increase in corporate debt ratios since the late 1950s. A major portion of this increase has apparently occurred during the decade of the 1970s. The increase is not nearly as smooth as the accounting numbers suggest, however, as dips occur in the early and late 1960s, and again in the early and late 1970s. Furthermore, although the 1930s and 1940s hardly could be characterized as a normal period, the estimates at least suggest that the debt ratios occurring in the 1970s are by no means unprecedented.

The estimates in columns 2 and 3 of table 1.2 are from von Furstenberg (1977), and they differ in two respects. First, dividend payments for common and preferred stock have been separated and capitalized at different rates. Second, von Furstenberg argued that the weighted average rating of corporate bonds outstanding has tended to be A or slightly better. He thus capitalized interest payments using the A-rated bond yield and also attempted to take into account the maturity composition of corporate debt. His estimates give consistently higher values for corporate debt ratios than those in Holland and Myers (1979), partly because of the lower capitalization rate for corporate debt and partly because the higher dividend yield on preferred stock gives a lower estimate for the combined market value of common and preferred stock. Nevertheless, the two series move in unison, with von Furstenberg's estimates also suggesting a considerable rise in corporate debt ratios since the mid-1950s. The estimates also reveal that the relative value of preferred stock has remained low throughout and has generally tended to decline, with the exception of a modest comeback in the mid-1970s.

A third approach has been followed by Gordon and Malkiel (1981), who use the sample of nonfinancial corporations for which data are reported on the Standard and Poor's COMPUSTAT Tapes. Market values of common equity can be observed directly for these companies. Market values of debt and preferred stock have been estimated using methods similar to von Furstenberg's but with the estimates derived from bond and preferred stock prices sampled at the two-digit industry level. Again, the estimated debt ratios, shown in column 4 of table 1.2, move in parallel with the other two series, with their absolute magnitudes generally falling between the other two. The estimates suggest the same increase in debt ratios, particularly since the late 1950s. Since both the von Furstenberg and the Gordon and Malkiel estimates range over a shorter period than those of Holland and Myers, however, they may give the impression that current debt ratios are higher by historical standards than is really the case.

The last approach to estimating market values, followed by Ciccolo (1982), uses observed market values for all securities for samples of roughly fifty U.S. manufacturing firms. Ciccolo has reported market

Table 1.2 Market Value Balance Sheet Ratios

Year	Holland & Myers (1) D/(D+P+E)	von Furstenberg (2) D/(D+P+E)	von Furstenberg (3) P/(D+P+E)	Gordon & Malkiel (4) D/(D+P+E)	Ciccolo (5) D/(D+P+E)	Ciccolo (6) P/(D+P+E)
1926	—	—	—	—	.085	.102
1927	—	—	—	—	—	—
1928	—	—	—	—	—	—
1929	.13	—	—	—	—	—
1930	.18	—	—	—	.057	.097
1931	.25	—	—	—	—	—
1932	.39	—	—	—	—	—
1933	.37	—	—	—	—	—
1934	.32	—	—	—	—	—
1935	.36	—	—	—	.042	.120
1936	.24	—	—	—	—	—
1937	.27	—	—	—	—	—
1938	.41	—	—	—	—	—
1939	.32	—	—	—	—	—
1940	.33	—	—	—	—	—
1941	.38	—	—	—	.069	.155
1942	.44	—	—	—	—	—
1943	.28	—	—	—	—	—
1944	.28	—	—	—	—	—
1945	.25	—	—	—	—	—
1946	.16	—	—	—	—	—
1947	.17	—	—	—	.082	.091
1948	.17	—	—	—	—	—
1949	.23	—	—	—	—	—

Year						
1950	.18	—	—	—	—	—
1951	.19	—	—	—	—	—
1952	.21	.29	.04	—	—	—
1953	.21	.30	.04	—	.133	.058
1954	.22	.26	.04	—	—	—
1955	.16	.22	.03	—	—	—
1956	.15	.24	.03	—	—	—
1957	.17	.21	.03	.21	—	—
1958	.17	.25	.03	.17	—	—
1959	.16	.23	.02	.16	.084	.016
1960	.18	.26	.02	.17	—	—
1961	.16	.23	.02	.16	—	—
1962	.21	.27	.02	.18	—	—
1963	.18	.24	.02	.17	—	—
1964	.17	.22	.02	.16	—	—
1965	.17	.22	.02	.16	.080	.018
1966	.22	.28	.02	.19	—	—
1967	.19	.25	.02	.18	—	—
1968	.18	.23	.02	.18	—	—
1969	.22	.27	.02	.21	—	—
1970	.27	.32	.02	.22	—	—
1971	.26	.32	.02	.23	.132	.017
1972	.24	.30	.02	.23	—	—
1973	.31	.35	.02	.28	—	—
1974	.38	.45	.03	.36	—	—
1975	.32	.40	.03	.32	—	—
1976	.32	.38	.03	.29	.230	.150
1977	.34	—	—	.32	—	—
1978	.35	—	—	.33	—	—
1979	.36	—	—	—	—	—
1980	.32	—	—	—	—	—
1981	.28	—	—	—	—	—

Sources: Cited in text.

Fraction of Total
Capitalization

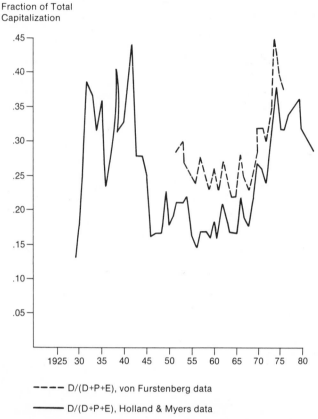

---- D/(D+P+E), von Furstenberg data

—— D/(D+P+E), Holland & Myers data

Fig. 1.2   Plot of market value debt ratios from table 1.2.

value balance sheet ratios for the aggregate of his sample firms for selected years, and these are shown in the last two columns of table 1.2. The debt ratios are generally much lower than those in the other series and do not move in parallel with the Holland and Myers estimates for the early years. The fact that the debt ratios are so much lower for all years raises the possibility that the sample may not be representative of the nonfinancial corporate sector as a whole. Nevertheless, Ciccolo's figures reveal the same increase in debt ratios since the 1960s that the other series do. Moreover, the preferred stock figures confirm the secular decline in the importance of preferred stock that appears in the accounting data of table 1.1.

1.1.3   Replacement Cost Data

Another ratio that has been used in previous studies to measure corporate leverage is that of the market value of debt to the replacement value of total assets. Like the market value data, replacement values are subject to substantial estimation error. However, replacement cost asset measures alleviate the overstatement in book value debt ratios during inflationary periods resulting from both the understatement of corporate assets and the overstatement of debt in real terms. Moreover, as we shall see in section 1.2, the replacement value of assets may have some theoretical advantages as a measure of debt capacity.[10] In any case, estimates of the ratio of the market value of debt to the replacement value of assets are available over a long period.

Two series of these ratios are available. One is from von Furstenberg's (1977) study and runs annually from 1952 to 1976, while the other is from Goldsmith's (Goldsmith et al. 1963) study of national balance sheets. Goldsmith's estimates are available for selected years from 1900 to 1945 and annually from 1945 to 1958. The two series are shown in table 1.3 and are plotted in figure 1.3. The figures from Goldsmith et al. suggest that nonfinancial corporations' use of debt financing relative to the replacement value of their assets was markedly lower in the decade following World War II than it had been earlier in the century. The figures from von Furstenberg indicate that corporate debt ratios then rose in the postwar period. Little trend is apparent after the early 1960s, however, suggesting that trends in the book value ratios in figure 1.1 may reflect inflationary distortions.

It can be seen from the years of overlap in the 1950s that there are some discrepancies between the two series. The ratios derived from Goldsmith's data, for example, are consistently somewhat lower than von Furstenberg's.[11] Moreover, Goldsmith's series itself may not give comparable data between prewar and postwar periods. Balance sheets from the prewar period are from Goldsmith (1958) while the annual data from 1945 to 1958 are from Goldsmith et al. (1963). Some changes in sectoral definitions and estimation methods occurred between these two studies, and the only year of overlap, 1945, indicates that these changes may have caused some differences in the debt ratios.

Nevertheless, some tentative conclusions can be drawn. Between 1952 and 1958, Goldsmith's and von Furstenberg's series move quite closely together, and it may be that they would exhibit similar trends throughout the whole period 1900–1978. If so, it appears that even though corporate debt ratios increased substantially in the postwar period, particularly from the mid-1950s to the mid-1960s, the debt ratios of recent years are not unusual by historical standards. Even if it is argued on the basis of the two 1945 estimates that the prewar figures are overstated by a third, the debt ratios of the 1960s and 1970s would still represent a return to roughly the levels that prevailed over the prewar period. The replacement value data, then, provide some further support for the impression gained from market value data that, while debt ratios have increased in recent de-

Table 1.3   Balance Sheet Ratios with Debt and Preferred Stock Measured at Market Value, Assets at Replacement Cost

Year	Goldsmith (1) D/A	von Furstenberg (2) D/A	von Furstenberg (3) P/A
1900	.32	—	—
1912	.42	—	—
1922	.28	—	—
1929	.28	—	—
1933	.35	—	—
1939	.33	—	—
1945	(.15)[a].10	—	—
1946	.13	—	—
1947	.14	—	—
1948	.14	—	—
1949	.14	—	—
1950	.13	—	—
1951	.14	—	—
1952	.15	.17	.02
1953	.15	.17	.02
1954	.15	.18	.03
1955	.15	.17	.03
1956	.16	.18	.03
1957	.17	.19	.02
1958	.17	.20	.02
1959	—	.19	.02
1960	—	.21	.02
1961	—	.22	.02
1962	—	.23	.02
1963	—	.24	.02
1964	—	.24	.02
1965	—	.25	.02
1966	—	.25	.02
1967	—	.24	.02
1968	—	.23	.02
1969	—	.23	.02
1970	—	.23	.02
1971	—	.24	.02
1972	—	.26	.02
1973	—	.27	.02
1974	—	.25	.02
1975	—	.24	.02
1976	—	.26	.02
1977	—	.27[b]	—
1978	—	.28	—

Sources: Cited in text.

[a]Figure in parentheses is from Goldsmith (1956). Other figure is from Goldsmith et al. (1963).

[b]Gordon and Malkiel (1981) update von Furstenberg's figures, using the same estimation method, through 1978. They do not report figures for preferred stock, however.

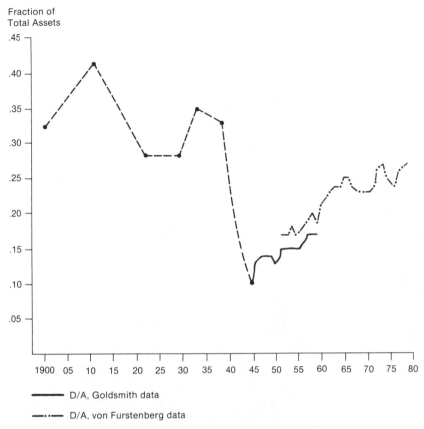

Fig. 1.3   Ratios of market value of debt to replacement cost of assets
                from table 1.3.

cades, after a relatively flat period in the 1940s and 1950s, they are
nevertheless not unusual by prewar standards.

1.1.4   Flow of Funds Data

The final method for measuring corporate financing patterns makes use
of flows of funds over periods of time as opposed to stocks at particular
dates. While this method does not take into account inflation-induced
valuation changes, as market value and replacement value estimates do,
it may nevertheless come closest to recording the actual decisions made
by corporations. Furthermore, since capital consumption allowances are
included as a component of internal equity financing, this method is not
subject to Miller's criticisms about understatement of equity financing in
the wake of changes in depreciation accounting.[12]

Between Goldsmith's *Study of Saving* data, which run from 1900 to
1945, and the Federal Reserve *Flow of Funds Accounts* which cover the
period 1946 to the present, it is possible to put together a fairly lengthy

Table 1.4 Flow of Funds Data: Proportions of Total Financing Accounted for by Particular Sources of Funds

Period	Total Debt Total Sources (1)	Long-Term Debt Total Sources (2)	Short-Term Liabilities Total Sources (3)	Internal Funds Total Sources (4)	New Stock Issues Total Sources (5)
1901–12	.31	.23	.08	.55	.14
1913–22	.29	.12	.17	.60	.11
1923–29	.26	.22	.04	.55	.19
1930–39	negative	negative	negative	1.14	.19
1940–45	.15	negative	.20	.80	.05
1946–59	.30	.16	.14	.64	.05
1960–69	.36	.18	.18	.62	.02
1970–79	.45	.21	.24	.52	.03

Sources: Goldsmith et al. (1963) and Federal Reserve *Flow of Funds Accounts*.

record of corporate financing flows. The data are shown in table 1.4. Since the emphasis of this paper is on secular patterns in corporate financing, the flows are divided into periods covering roughly a decade each.

The same data have previously been examined by Kuznets (1961), Sametz (1964), and Friedman (1980). Kuznets and Sametz were limited to the period from 1900 through the late 1950s. Both were struck by the sharp decline in the use of stock issues as a financing source, and both argued that internal funds, disregarding the aberrant years of the Depression and World War II, had shown at least a modest upward trend relative to other financing sources. Both authors also pointed out that, although short-term liabilities fluctuated considerably, they generally increased relative to both total financing sources and total debt through the late 1950s. Finally, Sametz emphasized that, despite trends in internal funds and external equity and in short-term and long-term debt, the use of total debt financing relative to total equity financing appeared to have remained roughly constant over long periods of time.

Friedman, confining his attention to the postwar period, pointed out that internal funds first increased relative to total sources in the 1950s and then decreased in the 1960s and 1970s. He also emphasized the continued decline in stock issues, an increased use of debt, and, in the late 1960s and 1970s, an increase in the use of short-term debt.

Looking at the whole period, as shown in the data in table 1.4, the trends discussed by all three authors are evident, and at the same time some longer-run trends come into sharper focus. It is clear, for example, that the use of debt financing has increased in the 1960s and 1970s after recovering in the years following World War II to pre-Depression levels. Use of long-term debt, however, is by no means unusual, even after steady postwar increases, relative to the levels prevailing in the first decade of the century and in the 1920s. The increased use of debt, then, seems largely attributable to an increase in short-term liabilities. It should also be noted that short-term liabilities have shown considerable fluctuations over time, with substantial increases occurring in the 1913–22 period and again during the World War II years. Although it cannot be denied that short-term liabilities have been much higher in the postwar period than in the prewar years, it is not clear if the recent surge represents a temporary phenomenon or the continuation of a trend. In addition, it is likely that inflationary distortions account for some portion of the most recent increases in debt proportions generally.

On the equity side, the greatly diminished use of stock issues appears to be a long-term trend. Stock issues staged a modest comeback in the 1970s, compared with the 1960s, but they remain very low by prewar standards. Furthermore, much of the increase in the 1970s is accounted for by public utility preferred stock issuance (Friedman 1980). Because utilities are required to meet the demand for service, their investment and financing decisions reflect special factors that may not be present in the decisions of other nonfinancial corporations. As has been widely noted, internally generated funds have also declined relative to total sources during the postwar period. The data indicate, however, that the depressed levels of internal funds experienced in the 1970s are not unusually low relative to the levels of the first decade of the century and the 1920s. It might be inferred, instead, that the use of internal funds was unusually high during the period 1930–60 and that the past two decades have witnessed a return to roughly the levels experienced during the pre-Depression era.

1.1.5   Common Trends

Viewing the different measures of corporate financing patterns simultaneously, some common threads appear. First, the use of debt financing has increased considerably in the postwar period. Despite the presence of inflationary distortions in some of the data, this trend emerges regardless of the method of measurement employed. There is considerably more doubt, however, as to whether current debt levels are unusually high relative to those of the prewar period. The accounting-based data of tables 1.1 and 1.4 suggest that they are, but the measures that make some attempt to correct for valuation changes, as shown in tables 1.2 and 1.3, indicate that this may not be true. At the very least, the trend in corporate debt ratios has not been unidirectional. Rather, these ratios appear to have been somewhat low in the 1920s and especially in the years surrounding World War II. Thus, the postwar surge in corporate debt does not appear to be as dramatic when viewed in the light of the whole century's experience as it does when the postwar period is considered in isolation.

Second, some changes have occurred within the debt and equity components of corporate finance. Although it is traceable only in the sources- and uses-of-funds data, there appears to be little doubt that short-term liabilities have increased in importance over time. Again, however, the trend is not unidirectional. Within the equity component, there is no doubt that issues of both preferred and common stock have declined considerably in relative importance. Internally generated equity, on the other hand, is currently low relative to the previous few decades, but whether it is unusually low when a longer-run view is taken is far less clear.

1.2   Implications of Existing Theory for the Determinants of the Aggregate Corporate Capital Structure

Before the trends observed in the preceding section can be interpreted, a theory is needed to predict the causal factors underlying them. Existing capital structure theories are capable of identifying a number of such factors, although this has not been recognized as explicitly as it might be. In this section, the major capital structure theories are reviewed with an eye toward drawing out more explicitly the determinants of aggregate financing trends.

To facilitate this process, some of the theories will be recast in terms of their implications for the aggregate supply and demand for corporate securities. This analysis of aggregate supply and demand is carried out in section 1.2.1, while the determinants of aggregate capital structure trends are discussed in section 1.2.2. In the diagrams accompanying the text, the aggregate amount of corporate debt, B, will be measured along the horizontal axis, and since investment will be held fixed, movements along this axis represent substitutions of corporate debt for equity. On the vertical axis will be measured the certainty-equivalent yields on corporate debt, r, and on corporate equity, r_e.

In keeping with most previous literature, corporate capital structure will be taken to represent the mix of debt and common equity financing. The framework employed is more general than that, however, and could also be used to include preferred stock and a variety of other hybrid financing instruments.

1.2.1   A Brief Review of Existing Capital Structure Theories

Modigliani and Miller's (1958) analysis of corporate capital structure is the logical place to begin, both because it remains the classic paper on the topic and because it is a special case of most subsequent theories. In the context of a "complete" capital market, the Modigliani-Miller theorem implies that the aggregate supply and demand for corporate debt coincide and that both are perfectly elastic, as depicted in figure 1.4. Supply is perfectly elastic because corporations can costlessly transform their financing mixes from all equity to any degree of leverage. Thus they are willing to freely substitute one form of financing for the other as long as

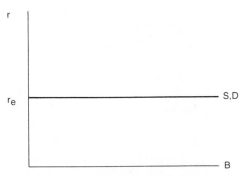

Fig. 1.4   Supply, S, and demand, D, for corporate debt implied by Modigliani and Miller (1958).

both have the same certainty-equivalent cost. But demand is likewise perfectly elastic because households can costlessly perform the same transformations on their own account, and thus they will be unwilling to accept any yield differential between the two securities.[13]

This configuration of supply and demand implies that corporate capital structure is indeterminate not only at the individual firm level but also at the level of the corporate sector as a whole, since corporate and household financial transformation are perfectly substitutable.[14] While this analysis emphasizes the important fact that corporations face competition from other sectors in their financial transformation activities, however, it also does not tell us much about factors that would cause the aggregate corporate financing mix to change over time. As long as equilibrium in the capital market is continuously maintained, such changes are largely random events.

Following Modigliani and Miller's (1963) correction for corporate taxes, a theory that gained considerable support took the trade-off between bankruptcy costs and tax savings from the deductibility of interest to be the primary determinant of corporate capital structure.[15] Under this theory the demand for corporate debt is still perfectly elastic, because investors are willing to substitute debt for equity freely as long as their certainty-equivalent yields are equal.[16] The supply of debt is no longer perfectly elastic, however. Because of the tax deductibility of interest, corporations would be willing to pay a certainty-equivalent yield on the first dollar of debt equal to $(1/1 - t_c)$ times the certainty-equivalent yield on equity, where t_c is the corporate tax rate. As more debt is issued, the probability of bankruptcy increases, and if bankruptcy imposes costs on firms, the premium rate that they are willing to pay to issue debt decreases. Thus the supply curve for corporate debt is downward sloping, as depicted in figure 1.5. Equilibrium is reached when the corporate sector has issued an amount of total debt that drives the certainty-equivalent yields on debt and equity into equality. Furthermore, since bankruptcy costs are firm specific, the optimal capital structure is determinate at the individual firm level as well as at the aggregate level. The aggregate supply curve for corporate debt may be thought of as a horizontal sum of individual firm supply curves, and the optimal capital structure for any firm is determined by the point at which r_e cuts its individual debt supply curve. As will be seen in section 1.2.2, the primary determinants of changing patterns in the aggregate corporate financial structure are changes in corporate tax rates and changing perceptions of bankruptcy costs.

The agency theory of Jensen and Meckling (1976) is diagrammatically similar to the tax savings–bankruptcy costs theory, but some of its implications are different. Again, the demand curve for corporate debt is perfectly elastic at the level r_e. Likewise the supply curve has its intercept

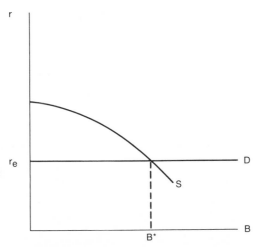

Fig. 1.5   Supply and demand for corporate debt implied by the tax-saving-bankruptcy costs theory.

at a point above r_e, because, starting from all-equity financing, the firm can reduce total agency costs associated with outside financing by substituting a dollar of debt for a dollar of outside equity. Thus the firm would be willing to pay a higher certainty-equivalent yield on debt to reflect this advantage. As more debt is issued, however, its ability to reduce agency costs at the margin declines and eventually turns negative, so the supply curve is downward sloping as depicted in figure 1.6.[17] As with the previous theory, the costs that cause this downward slope are firm specific, so equilibrium determines an optimal capital structure at the individual firm as well as at the aggregate level.

The difference between this theory and the previous one is that in the agency theory, the supply curve's vertical intercept lies above r_e even in the absence of taxes. In the tax savings–bankruptcy costs model, eliminating taxes would shift the intercept of the debt supply curve down to r_e. Under the agency cost theory, by contrast, the possibility of economizing on agency costs makes the firm willing to offer a premium rate on the first dollar of debt, even if it could realize no tax saving. Without specific knowledge of the nature of the agency costs, however, the vertical intercept of the debt supply curve cannot be identified as precisely in figure 1.6 as it can in figure 1.5.

Shifts in the relative agency costs of debt and equity would be the primary determinants under this theory of changing patterns in the aggregate corporate financial structure. In addition, there is an interaction in the agency cost theory between financing and investment. Certain types of assets may be more amenable than others to reducing the agency costs associated with either form of financing. Some types of assets may

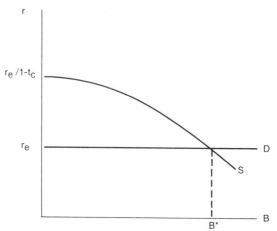

Fig. 1.6   Supply and demand curves for corporate debt implied by the agency cost theory of Jensen and Meckling (1976).

be more suitable for use as collateral, for example, and may facilitate the use of more debt. In the aggregate, then, changes in the characteristics of the corporate sector's capital stock may also influence changes in the aggregate financing mix.

As an aside, it might be mentioned that the Ross (1977) signaling model can be viewed for our purposes as very similar to the agency cost model. Corporate capital structures are determined by a combination of information and managerial incentive problems in the Ross model, and these would lead to a similar downward-sloping debt supply curve. For each firm in Ross's model, there is some amount of debt that maximizes its perceived value, subject to the equilibrium condition that investors' perceptions be correct. Because of the way their incentive compensation scheme is set up, the firm's managers would be willing to pay a premium yield to substitute debt for equity up to this optimal point, but a negative premium beyond that point. The signaling model is thus diagrammatically identical to the agency cost model. As in the agency cost model, asset characteristics would play an important role in secular financing patterns, since firms' optimal capital structures depend on the range of asset qualities across firms and on investors' ability to distinguish among them.

The only theory explicitly aimed at the capital structure of the corporate sector as a whole is Miller's (1977) "debt and taxes" model. Here, the supply curve is horizontal since, apart from tax considerations, corporations can costlessly split their return streams into debt and equity portions. Furthermore, because of the tax deductibility of interest they are willing to pay a premium yield, $r_e/1 - t_c$, to issue debt. Unlike the three theories discussed above, however, personal taxes are considered, and the demand curve is upward sloping, starting from r_e.[18] This is because investors are arrayed in groups subject to successively higher personal tax rates and because tax arbitrage restrictions make it costly for them to mitigate the differing tax consequences of different securities. Thus, since returns on corporate debt are taxed more heavily at the personal level than returns on corporate equity, investors in successively higher tax brackets must be enticed with successively higher yields to buy these bonds. As depicted in figure 1.7, equilibrium occurs when enough bonds have been issued to drive the corporate bond rate up to $r_e/1 - t_c$.

In contrast to the tax savings–bankruptcy costs theory and the agency cost theory, however, corporate capital structure is determinate only at the aggregate level, not at the individual firm level. As in the original Modigliani-Miller model, corporations and households compete with one another to perform financial transformations, but here they do not all compete on equal terms. Corporations that issue debt reap tax savings at the rate t_c per dollar of interest, and thus they have a comparative advantage in borrowing over those investors with personal tax rates lower than t_c. It will thus pay corporations to keep on borrowing until the marginal shareholder is just indifferent between buying levered shares and borrowing on his own account to buy unlevered shares. This will occur when the marginal shareholder's tax rate is just equal to t_c. Nevertheless, this comparative advantage applies to the corporate sector as a whole, but not to any individual firm. One corporation's debt is as good as any other's, and thus, in equilibrium, capital structure is of no consequence at the firm level.

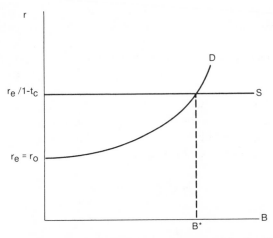

Fig. 1.7   Supply and demand for corporate debt implied by Miller (1977).

Determinants of changes in the aggregate capital structure in Miller's model include corporate and personal tax rates and the relative supplies of taxable and tax-exempt securities. The specific effects of these factors will be brought out in more detail in section 1.2.2.

The four theories reviewed above are primarily distinguished, then, by their implications for the shapes and positions of the aggregate supply and demand curves for corporate debt. A salient characteristic of these theories is that all of them imply perfect elasticity for the demand curve, the supply curve, or both. It should also be noted that the theories are not necessarily mutually exclusive. It is possible to combine corporate taxes with the agency cost model, for example, resulting in a diagram that looks qualitatively similar but has the debt supply curve shifted upward to reflect its tax advantage.[19] Similarly, agency or bankruptcy costs could be grafted onto Miller's model, imparting a downward slope to the debt supply curve.[20]

We now turn to a comparative statics analysis of the effects of various factors, such as tax rates and security supplies, on the equilibrium financial structure in these models. Since there is no equilibrium financial structure in the original Modigliani-Miller model, the discussion will center largely on the other three models.

1.2.2   Determinants of Secular Trends in Corporate Finance

Tax Factors. A prominent factor affecting the equilibrium financial structure in both the tax savings–bankruptcy costs and Miller models is the corporate tax rate. An increase in the corporate tax rate in the tax savings–bankruptcy costs model simply shifts the debt supply curve upward. Investors would still be willing to freely substitute debt for equity securities as long as their certainty-equivalent yields were equal, however, and thus, abstracting from any wealth effects that might change the absolute level of security yields, the demand curve for corporate debt would be unaffected.[21] The net result of the increased corporate tax rate, therefore, would be an increased amount of corporate debt relative to equity.

In the Miller model, the effect of an increase in the corporate tax rate is somewhat less straightforward. Recalling that the certainty-equivalent return on equity in Miller's model is equal to the tax-exempt bond yield, r_0, the equilibrium condition can be written as

(1) $$1 - \frac{r}{r_0}(1 - t_c) = 0.$$

This condition can in turn be thought of as an implicit function, $H(B^*, f)$ $= 0$, of the optimal amount of corporate debt, B^*, and a vector of exogenous factors, f, such as tax rates. The effect of an increase in t_c, holding all other factors constant, for example, is found by implicit differentiation to be

$$\text{(2)} \qquad \frac{\partial B^*}{\partial t_c} = -\frac{\partial H/\partial t_c}{\partial H/\partial B} = \frac{\left[\dfrac{r}{r_0} - (1 - t_c)\partial\left(\dfrac{r}{r_0}\right)/\partial t_c\right]}{-(1 - t_c)\partial\left(\dfrac{r}{r_0}\right)/\partial B}.$$

The denominator is negative, since an increase in B increases the supply of taxable relative to tax-exempt securities and thus increases r relative to r_0. The whole expression will thus be positive, and an increase in corporate tax rates will increase the equilibrium amount of corporate debt, if the numerator is positive. An increase in t_c, holding all security supplies constant, decreases the availability of tax-exempt income from shares, and this will induce high tax bracket investors to bid down r_0 relative to r. The sign of the numerator in (2), therefore, depends on the relative magnitudes of the two terms. It is argued in Appendix A, however, that the net effect of t_c on B^* will be positive unless the adjustment in relative interest rates to t_c, the second term in the numerator, is unreasonably large. This exercise is represented diagrammatically in figure 1.8. The increase in the corporate tax rate from t_c to t_c' shifts the supply curve upward. The effect of t_c on the relative yields, r/r_0, however, also causes the demand curve to rotate upward. Comparing this case with the effect of increased corporate taxes in the tax savings–bankruptcy costs model, the upward shifts of the supply curves are similar. The upward slope of

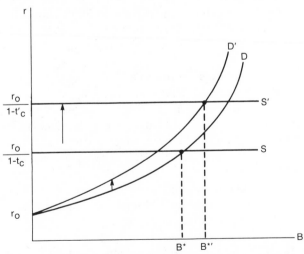

Fig. 1.8   Change in equilibrium quantity of corporate debt caused by an increase in the corporate tax rate.

the demand curve in Miller's model, as well as its upward rotation resulting from the increase in t_c, though, makes the net increase in corporate debt smaller in Miller's model than in the tax savings–bankruptcy costs model.

Another tax factor that can affect equilibrium corporate leverage is the set of personal tax rates, t_p. These rates play no role in either the tax savings–bankruptcy costs or agency costs models, but in Miller's model they are an important determinant of the corporate sector's comparative advantage in borrowing over different segments of the investing public. If an increase in the corporate tax rate is accompanied by an increase in personal tax rates, for example, analysis similar to that carried out in the previous exercise indicates that the resulting change in corporate debt is given by

$$
(3) \qquad \frac{\partial B^*}{\partial t_c} = - \frac{\left[\frac{r}{r_0} - (1 - t_c) \left(\frac{\partial \left(\frac{r}{r_0} \right)}{\partial t_c} + \frac{\partial \left(\frac{r}{r_0} \right)}{\partial t_p} \frac{dt_p}{dt_c} \right) \right]}{- (1 - t_c) \frac{\partial \left(\frac{r}{r_0} \right)}{\partial B}}.
$$

Since increases in t_p increase the value of tax-exempt income to investors, r/r_0 would be expected to increase with t_p and hence any increase in B^* would be smaller than in the previous case where only t_c increased. It is possible, of course, that B^* may even decline.[22]

Diagrammatically, this exercise is similar to that shown in figure 1.8. The only difference is that the demand curve rotates upward by an even greater amount, thus dampening further or even offsetting any upward pressure on corporate debt caused by the upward shift in the supply curve.

The models' predictions about the effects of extreme changes in tax rates can also be examined. If all tax rates are driven to zero, for example, the supply curve in the tax savings–bankruptcy costs model shifts downward until its vertical intercept is at r_e. Since the demand curve is unchanged, this implies that equilibrium corporate leverage goes to zero. In the Miller model, by contrast, elimination of all taxes shifts the supply curve down to r_e ($= r_0$) and flattens out the demand curve at the same level since taxable and tax-exempt securities are now perfect substitutes. This reduces, then, to the original Modigliani-Miller model and equilibrium corporate leverage is indeterminate.

An Aside on Taxes and Preferred Stock. Similar analysis can be applied to different types of securities, such as preferred stock. The supply curve for preferred stock in the Miller model would be horizontal at the level r_e.

That is, preferred stock and common equity receive the same tax treatment at the corporate level, and thus corporations would regard them as perfect substitutes at the same certainty-equivalent yield. If we ignore any inflexibilities from the cumulation of omitted dividends, preferred stocks entails no bankruptcy costs, and thus the supply curve would also be horizontal at r_e in the tax savings–bankruptcy costs model. The demand curve in both models would be horizontal in the absence of taxes. The imposition of personal taxes would make this demand curve slope upward in Miller's model.[23]

If we start from a no-tax situation and then impose both corporate and personal taxes with no tax deductibility of preferred stock dividends, the Miller model offers no prediction of what would happen to the amount of preferred stock outstanding. This amount was indeterminate in the absence of taxes and some preferred stock could still be issued to tax-exempt investors and corporations at a yield of r_e in the presence of taxes. Thus, the model does not predict preferred stock's disappearance or even, necessarily, its decline. The tax savings–bankruptcy costs model does not even have the upward slope in demand and hence it likewise offers no firm prediction about the equilibrium amount of preferred stock when taxes are imposed.

If the Miller model is combined with the agency costs model, a determinate amount of preferred stock could exist, even in the absence of taxes, because of its agency cost-reducing properties. That is, corporations might be willing to pay a premium yield to issue some amount of preferred stock, whereas investors would demand no premium. The supply curve will also slope downward because additional issues of preferred stock would create agency problems of their own, similar to those posed by debt. If taxes are then imposed, the demand curve will bend upward, leaving the supply curve unchanged, and the equilibrium quantity of preferred stock will thus be reduced. This effect is illustrated in figure 1.9.

Inflation. Inflation is often mentioned in popular discussions as a determinant of corporate financing trends. While financial economists would reject the notion that debt financing is advantageous under inflation because it can be repaid in "cheaper dollars," there is, nevertheless, some basis in capital structure theory for an inflation-induced effect on aggregate financing patterns. This effect generally stems from the interaction between inflation and tax factors.

In the tax savings–bankruptcy costs model, for example, an increase in anticipated inflation will increase all interest rates by (approximately) the increase in the expected inflation rate. Looking at figure 1.5, and letting Δi denote the increase in expected inflation, the demand curve for corporate debt will shift upward by Δi. The supply curve, on the other hand,

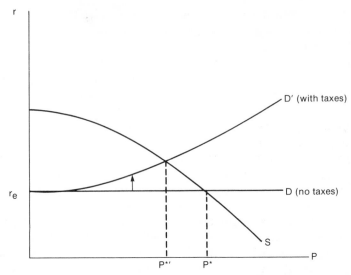

Fig. 1.9   Effect on equilibrium amount of preferred stock from imposing taxes (Miller model with agency costs).

shifts up by $\Delta i/1 - t_c$. Since the supply curve shifts up by more than the
demand curve, the equilibrium amount of corporate debt must increase,
and this can be interpreted as occurring because inflation increases the
real value of the interest tax deduction on debt.

In the Miller model, by contrast, the inflation premium in interest rates
is taxed at the personal level and this has offsetting effects. An increase in
expected inflation of Δi, for example, will increase the tax-exempt bond
rate demanded by investors by approximately Δi. Investors in taxable
securities, however, will demand that nominal rates rise sufficiently to
maintain real after-tax yields. This implies that for the marginal investor,
whose personal tax rate is t_{pm}, the taxable bond rate must rise by approximately $\Delta i/(1 - t_{pm})$.[24]

The change in equilibrium corporate debt resulting from a change in
expected inflation is given by

$$(4) \qquad \frac{\partial B^*}{\partial i} = -\frac{-(1 - t_c)\partial\left(\dfrac{r}{r_0}\right)/\partial i}{-(1 - t_c)\partial\left(\dfrac{r}{r_0}\right)/\partial B}.$$

The numerator may, in turn, be expressed as

$$(5) \qquad -(1 - t_c)\partial\left(\frac{r}{r_0}\right)/\partial i = -(1 - t_c)\left(\frac{r_0\dfrac{\partial r}{\partial i} - r\dfrac{\partial r_0}{\partial i}}{r_0^2}\right).$$

But, letting $\partial r/\partial i = 1/(1 - t_{pm})$ and $\partial r_0/\partial i = 1$ and recognizing that in equilibrium the marginal investor will be just indifferent between taxable and tax-exempt bonds, this numerator reduces to zero.

Diagrammatically, as shown in figure 1.10, the increase in expected inflation shifts the supply curve for debt upward by $\Delta r_0/(1 - t_c) = \Delta i/(1 - t_c)$. The demand curve, however, shifts upward by different amounts for investors in different tax brackets. At the intercept, which corresponds to the demand for taxable bonds by tax-exempt investors, the demand curve shifts upward by $\Delta r_0 = \Delta i$. At other points, corresponding to the demand for bonds by investors in tax bracket j, the demand curve will shift upward by $\Delta i/(1 - t_{pj})$. In particular, in the initial equilibrium an amount, B^*, of corporate debt had been issued such that the personal tax bracket, t_{pm}, of the marginal bondholder was equal to the corporate tax bracket, t_c. At B^*, then, the increase in expected inflation causes the demand curve to shift upward by $\Delta i/(1 - t_c)$, which is exactly the same amount by which the supply curve shifts upward. The new supply and demand curves, S' and D', must therefore intersect at B^*, and hence equilibrium corporate debt remains unchanged.[25]

This result is altered, however, when Miller's model is combined with the agency cost model. As depicted in figure 1.11, agency costs impart a downward slope to the debt supply curve, and the initial equilibrium occurs at B_a^*. As long as agency costs cause equilibrium debt to be less than it would be if supply were perfectly elastic (that is, as long as B_a^* is less than B^* in fig. 1.10), the personal tax bracket, t_{pm}, of the marginal bondholder at B_a^* will be less than the corporate tax rate.

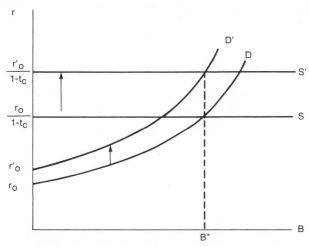

Fig. 1.10   Effect of an increase in expected inflation in Miller model with no agency costs.

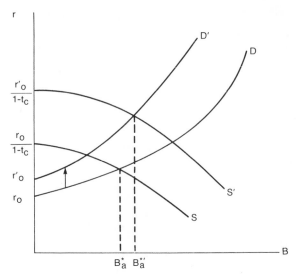

Fig. 1.11   Effect of an increase in expected inflation in Miller model with agency costs.

When an increase in expected inflation occurs, the supply curve in figure 1.11 shifts up by $\Delta i/(1 - t_c)$ assuming that inflation is neutral with respect to the agency cost function. At B_a^*, however, the demand curve shifts up by $\Delta i/(1 - t_{pm}) < \Delta i/(1 - t_c)$, and, given the slopes of the two curves, the new intersection point must occur to the right of B_a^*. Hence, in the presence of agency costs, an increase in expected inflation encourages substitution of debt for equity financing and increases equilibrium corporate leverage.[26] This result emerges, however, not from some "debtor-creditor" hypothesis, as has sometimes been argued, but from inflation's interaction with the tax system and agency costs.[27]

Supplies of Competing Securities. A special feature of Miller's model is its prediction that exogenous changes in the supplies of other securities will induce changes in corporate leverage. An increase in the supply of tax-exempt bonds, B_0, for instance, will result in the following change in corporate debt:

$$(6) \qquad \frac{\partial B^*}{\partial B_0} = - \frac{- (1 - t_c)\partial\left(\dfrac{r}{r_0}\right)/\partial B_0}{- (1 - t_c)\partial\left(\dfrac{r}{r_0}\right)/\partial B}.$$

Since an increase in B_0 increases r_0 relative to r, expression (6) will be positive. From a personal tax standpoint, tax-exempt bonds are substitutes for equity in Miller's model, and thus an increase in the supply of tax exempts encourages corporations to shift their financing mix more toward debt. Graphically, the increase in the supply of tax exempts results in a downward rotation of the demand curve for corporate debt. Since there are now more tax-exempt bonds, the marginal investor at any given level of corporate debt will be in a lower personal tax bracket than was previously the case. Hence, the equilibrium amount of corporate debt increases.

An increase in the supply of competing taxable bonds, on the other hand, has the opposite effect on B^*. If the supply of federal government bonds, G, increases, for example, the effect on corporate debt is given by

(7)
$$\frac{\partial B^*}{\partial G} = - \frac{-(1 - t_c)\, \partial\left(\frac{r}{r_0}\right)/\partial G}{-(1 - t_c)\, \partial\left(\frac{r}{r_0}\right)/\partial B}.$$

Since the increase in G must increase r relative to r_0, expression (7) is negative. From a personal tax standpoint, taxable government bonds are a substitute for corporate debt, and an increase in the supply of debt substitutes induces corporations to shift their financing mix more toward equity. Graphically, the demand curve for corporate debt rotates upward, and this results in a decrease in equilibrium corporate debt. It should also be pointed out that an increase in the supply of any other type of taxable debt instrument, such as mortgages, would have the same effect on the corporate financing mix.[28]

In sharp contrast to Miller's model, exogenous changes in security supplies would have no effect on relative yields in any of the other capital structure models. The perfectly elastic demand curves in each of the other models imply that investors are willing to freely substitute one type of security for another in their portfolios, as long as the certainty-equivalent yields on these securities are equal. Any changes in portfolio risk resulting from such substitutions can be offset costlessly because investors can create perfect substitutes for corporate (or any other) securities, either on their own account or through financial intermediaries acting on their behalf. In such an environment, then, changes in relative security supplies will have no effect on relative yields and hence no effect on the optimal corporate financing mix.

In the Modigliani-Miller world, it is true in a general equilibrium sense that an increase in the supply of substitutes for corporate debt might result in a decrease in the amount of corporate debt outstanding. In equilibrium, the supply of some debt security (e.g., personal debt, financial intermediary debt, corporate debt) must fall in order to make room for any increased amount of substitute securities, and the one that falls could just as well be corporate debt as any other. But since it could also just as well be some other security, the Modigliani-Miller model offers no strong prediction of a decline in corporate debt. In the agency costs or tax savings–bankruptcy costs models, moreover, the downward-sloping supply curve determines the equilibrium amount of corporate debt, and if both relative yields and the position of the supply curve are unchanged, corporate debt is unchanged. Hence these models offer a strong prediction that corporate debt will not change in response to competing security supplies.

Miller's model, on the other hand, is the only one of the capital structure models that has an imperfectly elastic demand curve for corporate debt. Because of tax arbitrage restrictions (or at least the costly nature of tax arbitrage), investors are unable to create perfect substitutes for securities with different tax treatment. Such securities are imperfect substitutes, therefore, and the terms on which investors are willing to substitute one type of security for another differ across investors in different tax brackets. In such an environment, changes in the relative supplies of different types of securities will cause changes in relative yields and these will, in turn, induce changes in the corporate financing mix.

Agency Costs and the Characteristics of Corporate Investment. A final determinant of aggregate corporate financing patterns that can be drawn from existing capital structure theories is the costs associated with corporate debt. These include bankruptcy costs or, more generally, agency costs of all kinds. It is clear from figures 1.5 and 1.6, for instance, that increases (decreases) in the magnitude of these costs will tilt the debt supply curve more (less) sharply downward and thus decrease (increase) the equilibrium amount of corporate debt. Moreover, the important aspect of these costs is corporate managers' and investors' perceptions of their magnitude. If the risk of bankruptcy is perceived to increase because it is felt that the economy generally has become less stable, this will induce corporations to reduce their leverage.

It should also be noted that the costs associated with debt create an interaction between financing and investment. Even if the functional relationship among assets, financing sources, and agency costs does not change, a change in asset characteristics can alter the optimal financing mix. If the corporate sector's investment shifts more toward assets that are less risky, that are more easily used as collateral, or that lend themselves more readily to perquisite consumption by owner-managers, the aggregate corporate financing mix will shift away from outside equity and more toward debt. In addition, as suggested by Myers's (1977) analysis, the relationship between future investment opportunities and assets in place will also influence the corporate financing mix. The greater these future opportunities are, the more debt financing will exacerbate the problem of potential underinvestment and hence the less heavily debt will be used.

This influence that asset characteristics and other factors specific to individual firms have on the financing mix is a unique feature of the capital structure models that exhibit downward-sloping debt supply curves. In the Modigliani-Miller and Miller (without agency costs) models, this supply curve is perfectly elastic and hence firms are willing to substitute debt and equity financing indefinitely on the same terms. Asset characteristics are incapable of altering this terms of trade, and no firm is unique in the terms it is willing to offer to substitute one form of financing for another. Hence, firm-specific factors play no role in capital structure determination.

Summary. The results of the comparative statics exercises in this section are summarized in table 1.5. These exercises are intended to accomplish

Table 1.5   **Summary of Effects on Corporate Debt of Various Factors in Different Capital Structure Models**

Effect on Corporate Debt of an Increase in	Model			
	Tax Savings–Bankruptcy Costs	Agency Costs	Miller	Miller with Agency Costs
Corporate tax rate	More debt	Taxes not applicable	Probably more debt	Probably more debt
Corporate & personal tax rates combined	Personal taxes not applicable	Taxes not applicable	Ambiguous	Ambiguous
Inflation	More debt	No effect	No effect	More debt
Supply of tax-exempt bonds	No effect	No effect	More debt	More debt
Supply of noncorporate taxable bonds	No effect	No effect	Less debt	Less debt
Costs associated with corporate debt	Less debt	Less debt	Debt costs not applicable	Less debt
Future investment opportunities relative to assets-in-place	No effect	Less debt	No effect	Less debt

two purposes. First, they are intended to identify those causal factors that capital structure theory suggests might be useful in explaining corporate financing patterns. The left-hand column of table 1.5 provides a list of such factors. Second, table 1.5 lists a set of predictions that can be used to test the different capital structure theories. A finding that changes in expected inflation are systematically associated with changes in corporate financing, for example, would be consistent with the tax savings–bankruptcy costs or Miller-cum–agency costs models, but not with the simple versions of either the Miller or agency costs models. Similarly, the finding of a relationship between noncorporate security supplies and the corporate financing mix would weigh in favor of one of the versions of Miller's model, or perhaps in favor of the Modigliani-Miller model, but against both the tax savings–bankruptcy costs and the agency costs models. It is unfortunate, however, that none of the rows of table 1.5 contain direct sign contradictions. It may be more difficult to distinguish empirically between an effect and the absence of an effect than between effects in opposite directions.

Looking at the results in table 1.5 in general terms, two additional points emerge. The first is that the determinants of corporate financing patterns suggested by existing capital structure theories rest heavily on tax considerations. Apart from tax rates themselves, any effect of inflation depends on its interaction with the tax system, while the effect of noncorporate security supplies rests on the fact that the tax system renders security demands less than perfectly elastic. The only factors entirely unrelated to the tax system, in fact, are agency cost considerations.

The second point is that the extreme assumptions made by most of these models about the elasticity of either demand or supply severely limit the range of factors that might influence corporate financing patterns. As we have seen, if demand is perfectly elastic, supplies of noncorporate securities can have no effect on the corporate financing mix. If supply is perfectly elastic, firm-specific factors can have no effect. The column headed "Miller with Agency Costs," the only model in which neither demand nor supply is perfectly elastic, is the only column in table 1.5 that does not contain several "no effect" entries.

1.3   Interpretation of Capital Structure Trends

The task of this section is to link the theories described in the preceding section with the financing trends observed in section 1.1 in an attempt to interpret these trends. This will be done by comparing the trends in capital structure's determinants, as outlined in table 1.5, with the capital structure trends themselves.

This attempt must be regarded as preliminary, since neither the available data nor the available theory is sufficiently rich to allow very powerful tests. Nevertheless, some distinctions can be made among the abilities of different theories to explain these trends. Furthermore, it is hoped that the empirical regularities discussed here will stimulate further refinement of an aggregate corporate capital structure theory.

1.3.1 Corporate and Personal Tax Rates

As was seen in the preceding section, tax considerations are an important element of capital structure determination in both the tax savings–bankruptcy costs and Miller models. Movements in marginal corporate and personal tax rates from 1913 to the present are shown in table 1.6. Personal tax rates for those investors in the lowest and highest marginal brackets are shown in columns 1 and 2, respectively, while the corporate tax rate is shown in column 3.

The corporate tax rate has moved sharply upward, particularly in the 1940s and early 1950s. This trend is consistent, under either the tax savings–bankruptcy costs or Miller models, with the postwar increase in corporate leverage, although one may well ask why more of the increase in debt did not come earlier when corporate tax rates were rising most steeply. One might also ask why corporate leverage seems to have decreased during at least the first decade of the tax code's existence, at the same time that corporate tax rates increased dramatically in percentage terms, albeit from a small base.

Part of the answer could lie with the parallel increases in personal tax rates, which as we saw in the subsection "Tax Factors" in section 1.2.2 could dampen the leverage effects of corporate taxes. Some additional insight into the relationship between personal and corporate tax rates can be gained if we think in terms of the "clientele" version of Miller's model. In this version, low-tax-bracket investors hold shares in highly leveraged firms while the reverse is true for high-tax-bracket investors. In effect, low-tax-bracket investors prefer to borrow through corporations so as to maximize the tax advantage of debt, while high-tax-bracket investors prefer to borrow on their own account. A very rough measure of the strength of these preferences is what Grier and Strebel (1980) have referred to as the "net debt incentive tax ratio." This ratio, δ, is defined as

$$(8) \qquad \delta = 1 - \frac{1 - t_c}{1 - t_{pB}},$$

where t_c is the corporate tax rate and t_{pB} is the personal tax rate on ordinary income. Columns 4 and 5 of table 1.6 give time series for δ_L, the debt incentive tax ratio for investors in the lowest tax bracket, and δ_H, the ratio for investors in the highest bracket. These ratios measure the value

Table 1.6   **Corporate and Personal Tax Rates and Debt Incentive Tax Ratios**

Year	Lowest Value of t_{pB} (1)	Highest Value t_{pB} (2)	t_c (3)	δ_L (4)	δ_H (5)
1913–15	.010	.070	.010	.00	− .06
1916	.020	.150	.020	.00	− .15
1917	.020	.670	.060	.04	− 1.85
1918	.060	.770	.120	.06	− 2.83
1919–21	.040	.730	.100	.06	− 2.33
1922	.040	.560	.125	.09	− .99
1923	.030	.560	.125	.10	− .99
1924	.015	.460	.125	.11	− .62
1925	.011	.250	.130	.12	− .16
1926–27	.011	.250	.135	.12	− .15
1928	.011	.250	.120	.11	− .15
1929	.004	.240	.110	.11	− .17
1930–31	.011	.250	.120	.11	− .17
1932–35	.040	.630	.138	.10	− 1.33
1936–37	.040	.790	.150	.11	− 3.05
1938–39	.040	.790	.190	.16	− 3.86
1940	.044	.811	.240	.21	− 3.02
1941	.100	.810	.310	.23	− 2.63
1942–43	.190	.880	.400	.26	− 2.47
1944–45	.230	.940	.400	.22	− 9.00
1946–47	.190	.865	.380	.23	− 3.60
1948–49	.166	.821	.380	.26	− 2.47
1950	.174	.910	.420	.30	− 5.44
1951	.204	.910	.508	.38	− 4.47
1952–53	.222	.920	.520	.38	− 5.00
1954–63	.200	.910	.520	.40	− 4.33
1964	.160	.770	.500	.41	− 1.17
1965–67	.140	.700	.480	.40	− .73
1968	.140	.753	.480	.40	− 1.10
1969	.140	.770	.480	.40	− 1.26
1970	.140	.718	.480	.40	− .84
1971–78	.140	.700	.480	.40	− .73
1979–	.140	.700	.460	.37	− .80

Source: Pechman (1977).

of the marginal return stream to investors in these tax brackets, when firms in which they hold shares substitute an additional dollar of debt for equity financing.[29]

Ideally, of course, we would like to have a measure of the strength of investor's demand for corporate leverage under different tax rate configurations, and this would necessitate knowing the distribution of wealth, and particularly shareholdings, across the spectrum of true marginal tax rates. Without such knowledge it is perilous to infer too much from the values of δ_L and δ_H.[30] Nevertheless, if it can reasonably be assumed that personal tax rates between the highest and lowest values move in concert and that the underlying wealth distribution does not shift radically over time, movements in δ will give at least a rough idea of the strength of demand for corporate leverage by low-tax-bracket investors and of the aversion to corporate leverage by high-tax-bracket investors. If δ values tend to increase over time for both high- and low-tax-bracket investors, for example, the demand for corporate leverage should also increase. In addition, during times when δ values are small, even for low-tax-bracket investors, one would expect that any tax advantage to corporate debt would be more easily offset by such factors as bankruptcy and agency costs.

Turning to the values of δ in table 1.6, the tax code apparently gave little or no incentive for corporate leverage in the early years of its existence. Until the early 1920s, even investors in the lowest tax brackets had little incentive, purely from a tax standpoint, to hold shares in levered firms, while high-tax-bracket investors often incurred a substantial tax disadvantage from corporate leverage. During the 1920s this tax disadvantage for high-tax-bracket investors grew much smaller, but at the same time the tax advantage for low-bracket investors remained small. It was not until the 1940s, when corporate tax rates rose dramatically, that the δ value grew very much for low-tax-bracket investors. From 1940 to 1954, these δ values for low-tax-bracket investors approximately doubled, whereafter they have remained essentially unchanged to the present. Since top-bracket personal tax rates were very high in the 1940s and 1950s, the δ values for high-bracket investors were also very negative during this period. These δ values have become less negative in the 1960s and 1970s.

Overall, then, it can be inferred that the tax system should have given rise to a demand for corporate leverage on the part of at least a segment of the investing population. This demand should have shown particular growth, moreover, between the 1920s and the early 1950s. In addition, the less negative values of δ_H from the mid-1960s to the present may indicate an atmosphere more conducive to corporate debt in recent years.

Comparing these trends with those discussed in section 1.1, however, it is apparent that tax considerations cannot be the sole determinant of patterns in corporate sector financing. Although the values of δ_L were small immediately following the advent of the income tax system, they roughly doubled in the 1920s, again in the 1930s, and again in the 1940s. Despite the apparent increase in the demand for corporate leverage, however, the tables in section 1.1 indicate that corporate debt usage fell for at least the first two decades following 1913 and that it remained low at least through World War II. The increases in both δ_L and δ_H that have occurred since the 1940s are broadly consistent with increased corporate leverage that has occurred since that period, but the two trends are not closely synchronized.[31] According to tables 1.2 and 1.4, the largest increases in corporate debt financing appear to have occurred during the 1970s, for example, whereas the debt tax incentive ratios have been relatively flat during that time.

1.3.2 Inflation

Another potential explanatory factor is the inflation rate. As discussed in the subsection "Inflation" in section 1.2.2, inflation can enhance the real tax advantage to debt, and thus the interaction between taxes and inflation may produce an explanation of corporate financing patterns that is superior to that of taxes alone.

Some idea of inflation trends can be gained from the yearly percentage changes in the implicit GNP price deflator, shown in table 1.7 for the years 1901 to the present.[32] From these it might be concluded that the relatively high inflation rates of the late 1960s and the 1970s interacted with relatively high debt tax incentive ratios to produce an increase in corporate debt financing during this period (although, as we have seen, inflationary distortions in the data raise some doubts as to just how much debt usage increased in the 1970s). There was also a temporary increase in corporate debt usage coinciding with both the increase in debt tax incentive ratios and the inflationary burst of the immediate post–World War II years.[33] Earlier, however, the years surrounding World War I were also years of relatively high inflation rates coupled with rising debt tax incentive ratios (at least for investors in low tax brackets). The data in section 1.2 indicate, though, that corporate debt financing was lower in that decade than in the one preceding it. Again, therefore, although the interaction between taxes and inflation may have contributed to increased debt usage in recent years, it does not appear to be the sole determinant of corporate financing patterns.

1.3.3 Supplies of Noncorporate Securities

Since the demand for corporate debt is less that perfectly elastic in the Miller model, relative supplies of noncorporate securities can affect corporate financing patterns. Some idea of the relative position of corporate debt in the economy may be gained from table 1.8, which shows the total liabilities of the nonfinancial corporate, federal government, and state and local government sectors as well as the mortgage liabilities of the household sector, all expressed as percentages of total liabilities of the domestic nonfinancial sectors. Data are available from Goldsmith et al. (1963) for selected years from 1900 to 1945 and annually from 1945 to 1958. Annual data are also available from the Federal Reserve *Flow of*

Table 1.7   **Yearly Changes in Implicit GNP Price Deflator**

Year	% Change in Deflator	Year	% Change in Deflator	Year	% Change in Deflator
1901	−.8	1929 ⎫		1957	3.4
1902	3.3	1930 ⎪		1958	1.7
1903	1.2	1931 ⎬ −2.1		1959	2.4
1904	1.2	1932 ⎪		1960	1.6
1905	2.4	1933 ⎭		1961	.9
1906	2.3	1934 ⎫		1962	1.8
1907	4.1	1935 ⎪		1963	1.5
1908	−.7	1936 ⎪ −.8		1964	1.5
1909	3.6	1937 ⎬		1965	2.2
1910	2.8	1938 ⎪		1966	3.2
1911	−1.0	1939 ⎭		1967	3.0
1912	4.1	1940	2.2	1968	4.4
1913	−.7	1941	7.5	1969	5.1
1914	2.0	1942	9.9	1970	5.4
1915	4.6	1943	5.3	1971	5.0
1916	12.1	1944	2.4	1972	4.2
1917	24.2	1945	2.4	1973	5.7
1918	12.5	1946	15.7	1974	8.7
1919	14.1	1947	12.9	1975	9.3
1920	13.9	1948	6.9	1976	5.2
1921	−16.7	1949	−.9	1977	5.8
1922	−8.1	1950	2.1	1978	7.3
1923	2.4	1951	6.6	1979	8.5
1924	−.2	1952	1.4	1980	9.0
1925	1.4	1953	1.6	1981	9.1
1926	−1.5	1954	1.2		
1927	−2.2	1955	2.2		
1928	1.6	1956	3.2		

Source: Historical Statistics of the United States and Economic Report of the President.

Funds Accounts for the years 1945–78. The series for U.S. government debt and household mortgage debt are intended to reflect supplies of securities that might act as close substitutes for corporate debt in investor's portfolios.[34]

The data suggest that in the post–World War II years, corporate liabilities have been much smaller relative to total liabilities than in the pre-Depression era. There has also been little if any trend in the share of corporate liabilities since the 1950s. While the data in tables 1.2–1.4 indicate that corporate debt financing has increased relative to equity since that time, therefore, corporate debt has still only kept pace with the postwar expansion in liabilities for the economy as a whole. The share of corporate liabilities dropped sharply during the Depression and World War II before recovering somewhat during the years 1945–50. Since that

Table 1.8   Ratios of Sectoral Liabilities Outstanding to Total Liabilities of Domestic Nonfinancial Sectors

Year	Nonfinancial Corporation Liabilities		Federal Government Liabilities		State and Local Government Liabilities		Household Mortgage Liabilities	
	Goldsmith (1)	Flow of Funds (2)	Goldsmith (3)	Flow of Funds (4)	Goldsmith (5)	Flow of Funds (6)	Goldsmith (7)	Flow of Funds (8)
1900	.49	—	.04	—	.07	—	.15	—
1912	.54	—	.02	—	.07	—	.12	—
1922	.44	—	.17	—	.07	—	.11	—
1929	.47	—	.09	—	.08	—	.18	—
1933	.45	—	.15	—	.10	—	.17	—
1939	.34	—	.30	—	.10	—	.14	—
1945	.20	.18	.64	.66	.05	.04	.07	.05
1946	.22	.21	.60	.60	.05	.04	.08	.06
1947	.24	.23	.57	.55	.05	.04	.09	.09
1948	.24	.24	.54	.51	.05	.05	.10	.09
1949	.24	.23	.53	.50	.06	.05	.11	.09
1950	.26	.26	.49	.46	.06	.05	.12	.09
1951	.27	.27	.46	.43	.06	.06	.13	.10
1952	.27	.27	.45	.42	.06	.06	.14	.11
1953	.27	.26	.44	.41	.06	.06	.14	.12
1954	.27	.26	.43	.40	.07	.07	.15	.13

Year								
1955	.28	.27	.40	.36	.07	.07	.16	.14
1956	.29	.28	.37	.34	.07	.08	.17	.15
1957	.30	.28	.36	.32	.07	.08	.18	.16
1958	.30	.28	.35	.32	.07	.08	.18	.16
1959	—	.28	—	.30	—	.08	—	.17
1960	—	.28	—	.30	—	.08	—	.17
1961	—	.28	—	.29	—	.09	—	.18
1962	—	.28	—	.28	—	.09	—	.19
1963	—	.28	—	.25	—	.09	—	.19
1964	—	.28	—	.24	—	.09	—	.19
1965	—	.29	—	.22	—	.09	—	.20
1966	—	.30	—	.21	—	.09	—	.20
1967	—	.31	—	.21	—	.09	—	.19
1968	—	.32	—	.20	—	.09	—	.19
1969	—	.33	—	.19	—	.09	—	.19
1970	—	.33	—	.18	—	.09	—	.19
1971	—	.33	—	.19	—	.09	—	.19
1972	—	.33	—	.17	—	.09	—	.19
1973	—	.35	—	.16	—	.09	—	.19
1974	—	.33	—	.15	—	.09	—	.20
1975	—	.32	—	.17	—	.09	—	.20
1976	—	.31	—	.18	—	.08	—	.20
1977	—	.31	—	.18	—	.08	—	.21
1978	—	.31	—	.17	—	.08	—	.21
1979	—	.32	—	.16	—	.07	—	.21

Sources: Goldsmith et al. (1963) and Federal Reserve *Flow of Funds Accounts*.

time a modest upward trend seems to have occurred at least through the mid-1970s.

Liabilities of the federal government, by contrast, were quite small at the beginning of the century and remained so until the Depression, even including the increase surrounding World War I. During the Depression and especially during World War II, however, federal government debt mushroomed relative to that of the other sectors of the economy. Thereafter, it declined steadily before reaching an apparent plateau in the 1970s.

On the whole, state and local government and household mortgage liabilities have been smaller than those of the corporate and federal government sectors. State and local government debt has remained relatively small throughout, with little apparent trend. Household mortgage debt hovered around 15% of total liabilities in the pre-Depression era, before falling somewhat by the end of World War II. Since then it has increased to a plateau of about 20%, beginning in the 1960s.

If we focus on the relationship between corporate debt and federal government debt, the prediction that corporate debt responds inversely to supplies of close substitute securities appears to receive some support from the data in table 1.8. A similar relationship has also been noted by Friedman (1982). Particularly in the first half of this century, the share of corporate liabilities has tended to move in the opposite direction from that of federal government liabilities. At the same time that federal government debt was taking its great upward leap during the Depression and World War II, for example, the share of corporate liabilities declined dramatically, as did the share of debt in total corporate financing. Similarly, corporate debt financing has generally increased relative to equity during the postwar years at the same time that the share of federal government liabilities has fallen.

At other points, however, the predictions from Miller's model and the data in table 1.8 do not seem to coincide exactly. Little can be inferred, for example, about the relationship between corporate financing patterns and movements in state and local government liabilities or household mortgage liabilities. If anything, the share of corporate liabilities seems to have moved in the same direction as that of household mortgages.[35] Moreover, corporate leverage, as measured by tables 1.2 and 1.4 at least, shows large increases in the 1970s when the relative supply of government securities is essentially flat.

1.3.4 Perceived Costs Associated with Corporate Debt

A final determinant of corporate financing trends that is suggested by existing capital structure theory is shifts in the perceived magnitude of bankruptcy and agency costs. The greater these costs are perceived to be, the smaller will be the share of debt in total corporate financing. Unfortunately, while the theory's prediction is straightforward, these costs are impossible to measure with any precision.

One factor related to agency costs that can be measured at least roughly is the relationship between corporations' future investment opportunities and their assets in place. As was seen in the subsection "Agency Costs and the Characteristics of Corporate Investment" in section 1.2.2, Myers (1977) has argued that the availability of future investment opportunities exacerbates the moral hazard problem between current bondholders and shareholders and weighs against the use of debt financing for existing assets.

Since future investment opportunities are theoretically reflected in the market value of firms' securities, movements in Tobin's q, or the ratio of the market value of firms' assets to their reproduction cost, provide a rough measure of the changing relationship between these future opportunities and existing assets. It is true that a marginal, rather than an average, q is the best measure of the prospective profitability of a firm's next dollar of investment. But in long-run competitive equilibrium, firms will have adjusted their investment until both marginal and average q values are equal to unity. Changes in average q values provide signals for this adjustment process by indicating changes in the perceived profitability of future investment.[36]

Estimates of q covering the period 1929–80 for U.S. nonfinancial corporations as a whole are shown in table 1.9. The agency cost theory would predict that q and corporate debt usage should move inversely, but comparing the data in table 1.9 with those in tables 1.1–1.3, the evidence in favor of this prediction is somewhat mixed. Through World War II, the market value debt ratios generally moved inversely with the q values in table 1.9.[37] Similarly, the Goldsmith data in table 1.3 suggest that debt ratios rose during the early years of the Depression as q was falling and then fell in the later years of the Depression as q was rising. Both the Holland and Myers and the Goldsmith data indicate sharply lower debt ratios by the end of World War II than had prevailed during the 1930s, however, and it is less clear if this can be explained by any consistent increases in q values around this time. In the postwar years, the early increase in corporate debt is consistent with the depressed q values prevailing during the 1950s. Debt usage should then have fallen in the 1960s, though, when q values soared, but there is no evidence that it did so. Similarly, although increased debt in the early 1970s is consistent with lower q values, debt usage should have continued to rise in the mid-1970s as q values fell further, but it seems instead to have fallen.

This facet of the agency cost theory, then, seems to show a modest degree of explanatory power in interpreting capital structure trends. In fairness to the theory, it should be kept in mind that its predictions have been made at the individual firm level, and aggregation problems may

Table 1.9   **Estimates of q (Ratio of Market Value of U.S. Nonfinancial Corporations to Replacement Cost of Assets)**

Year	Holland & Myers Estimates	Council of Economic Advisers Estimates
1929	1.93	—
1930	1.69	—
1931	1.09	—
1932	.57	—
1933	1.14	—
1934	1.46	—
1935	1.44	—
1936	2.34	—
1937	1.95	—
1938	1.06	—
1939	1.53	—
1940	1.27	—
1941	1.10	—
1942	.89	—
1943	1.19	—
1944	1.19	—
1945	1.31	—
1946	1.44	—
1947	1.00	—
1948	.84	—
1949	.68	—
1950	.76	—
1951	.70	—
1952	.70	—
1953	.70	—
1954	.76	—
1955	.95	.85
1956	.98	.84
1957	.90	.78
1958	.89	.81
1959	1.12	.98
1960	1.08	.95
1961	1.26	1.06
1962	1.21	1.00
1963	1.35	1.10
1964	1.45	1.18
1965	1.52	1.26
1966	1.38	1.13
1967	1.36	1.14
1968	1.35	1.18
1969	1.27	1.06
1970	.94	.87
1971	1.08	.94
1972	1.15	1.02
1973	1.12	.93
1974	1.04	.67

Table 1.9 (continued)

Year	Holland & Myers Estimates	Council of Economic Advisers Estimates
1975	.81	.66
1976	.88	.75
1977	—	.66
1978	—	.61
1979	—	.56
1980	—	.53

Source: Holland and Myers (1979) and *Economic Report of the President.*

weaken its predictive power at the level of the corporate sector as a whole.[38]

Another factor related to agency and bankruptcy costs that can be measured at least roughly is the general stability of business, or "business risk." The less stable are economic conditions, the greater is the overall chance of business failures and the greater will be the weight of bankruptcy costs on corporate financing decisions. Similarly, as the chance of bankruptcy increases, the agency problems associated with debt are exacerbated. As business conditions become less stable, therefore, corporate leverage should fall.

A possible measure of perceived stability is the standard deviation of stock price changes or stock market returns. These measures, derived from monthly changes in the Standard and Poor's Composite Index, are shown in table 1.10 for the years 1890–1981. A crude measure of the standard deviation of returns on total assets, which is perhaps a better indicator of business, as opposed to financial, risk is also shown in column 3 of table 1.10.[39]

On the basis of these figures, it might be plausible to argue that increased tax incentives for corporate debt in the late 1930s and early 1940s were overwhelmed by greater perceived instability in the wake of the Depression. One could similarly make a case, as Gordon and Malkiel (1981) do, that increased instability since 1974 has contributed to a decline, or at least a leveling off, of corporate leverage since that time.

Nevertheless, it is difficult to isolate any general trends in the data in table 1.10. The increased instability surrounding the Depression does not seem to have been inordinately long-lived, for example, relative to the apparent inertia in the recovery of corporate debt ratios. Moreover, the decline in corporate leverage between 1912 and 1929 does not seem to coincide with any general increase in economic instability. Overall, then, the data again appear to grant some explanatory power to agency and bankruptcy cost notions, but these factors do not seem capable of standing alone as determinants of corporate financing trends.

A possible avenue for further study of the effects of agency costs is the

Table 1.10   Annualized Standard Deviations of Monthly Stock Market Returns

Year	S.D. of % Stock Price Changes (1)	S.D. of Total Returns on Stock (2)	S.D. of Returns on Total Assets (3)	Year	S.D. of % Stock Price Changes (1)	S.D. of Total Returns on Stock (2)	S.D. of Returns on Total Assets (3)
1890	9.87	—	—	1930	21.30	26.3	21.6
1891	10.74	—	—	1931	28.02	43.9	32.9
1892	4.26	—	—	1932	61.31	68.0	41.5
1893	15.87	—	—	1933	37.59	56.1	35.3
1894	7.97	—	—	1934	16.45	22.2	15.1
1895	10.32	—	—	1935	15.73	16.3	10.4
1896	13.89	—	—	1936	11.33	14.4	10.9
1897	11.09	—	—	1937	21.93	23.4	17.1
1898	11.40	—	—	1938	24.60	41.2	24.3
1899	12.78	—	—	1939	17.60	29.5	20.1
1900	11.85	—	—	1940	17.46	26.7	17.9
1901	16.04	—	—	1941	12.16	14.3	8.9
1902	7.72	—	—	1942	12.37	14.7	8.2
1903	11.40	—	—	1943	11.78	15.6	11.2
1904	9.39	—	—	1944	7.38	7.9	5.7
1905	8.52	—	—	1945	7.59	13.1	9.8
1906	10.01	—	—	1946	17.29	18.7	15.7
1907	16.28	—	—	1947	11.02	9.6	8.0
1908	10.12	—	—	1948	13.48	19.9	16.5
1909	6.27	—	—	1949	10.15	10.2	7.9
1910	10.15	—	—	1950	11.02	10.8	8.9
1911	9.39	—	—	1951	9.84	12.2	9.9
1912	6.17	—	—	1952	7.34	11.3	8.9

Year	Column 1	Column 2	Column 3
1913	—	7.55	—
1914	—	13.96	—
1915	—	9.63	—
1916	—	7.79	—
1917	—	10.50	—
1918	—	8.45	—
1919	—	12.78	—
1920	—	15.55	—
1921	—	12.09	—
1922	—	9.63	—
1923	—	10.29	—
1924	—	9.66	—
1925	—	6.44	—
1926	11.7	10.98	—
1927	13.2	6.86	—
1928	17.4	11.95	—
1929	31.0	31.94	27.0
1953	9.4	8.76	7.4
1954	13.0	3.81	10.1
1955	12.4	12.06	10.4
1956	14.8	10.60	12.6
1957	12.6	11.29	10.5
1958	6.3	3.74	5.2
1959	8.0	8.00	6.7
1960	13.4	8.49	11.0
1961	8.9	7.21	7.5
1962	20.1	17.22	15.9
1963	9.8	6.34	8.0
1964	4.0	5.47	3.3
1965	8.5	6.89	7.1
1966	10.9	11.05	8.5
1967	12.1	6.58	9.8
1968	13.0	10.22	10.7
1969	13.0	10.05	10.1
1970	20.3	15.93	14.8
1971	13.7	11.22	10.1
1972	6.6	6.96	5.0
1973	13.9	10.98	9.6
1974	23.9	17.11	14.8
1975	17.9	15.90	12.2
1976	13.7	10.57	9.3
1977	9.6	4.19	6.3
1978	16.6	12.44	10.8
1979	12.8	8.66	8.2
1980	17.5	25.39	11.9
1981	12.3	18.19	8.9

Sources: Column 1 = Annualized standard deviations of monthly percentage changes in Standard & Poor's Composite Index. Derived from Standard & Poor's *Trade and Security Statistics, Security Price Index Record.*

Column 2 = Annualized standard deviations of monthly total returns (dividends plus capital gains) on Standard & Poor's Composite Index stocks. From Ibbotson and Sinquefield (1982).

Column 3 = Column 2 multiplied by [1 − (D/D + P + E)] from table 1.2, col. 1.

changing industry composition of the corporate sector. Jensen and Meckling (1976) suggest, for example, that firms in different industries will have different optimal capital structures because they face agency problems of varying magnitudes. As industries rise and fall in relative importance, then, the aggregate corporate capital structure could change even if agency cost functions remain perfectly stable. Interpretation of such trends, however, requires a better understanding of industry effects on capital structure than is currently available from existing theory. Thus this avenue of inquiry will not be pursued further here.

1.3.5   The Ability of Existing Theory to Explain Aggregate Patterns in Corporate Finance

Taking the results of this section as a whole, we can distinguish the relative abilities of existing theories to explain the data. The primary conclusion is that the simplest capital structure models, based on one or two explanatory factors, do not seem fully consistent with the data. To the extent that the analysis in this section has favored any of the models in table 1.5, then, it is the Miller model with agency costs.[40]

Despite the caveats noted in section 1.3.1, for example, this model is broadly consistent with the parallel trends in debt ratios and tax factors, particularly in the post–World War II years. In addition, the model is consistent with the parallel increases in inflation and debt usage of the late 1960s and 1970s. To the extent that the interaction between inflation and the tax system is important, this may explain why, by market value measures at least, much of the postwar increase in debt ratios did not occur until this time, even though corporate tax rates and debt tax incentive ratios increased earlier. Moreover, a relationship between inflation and debt ratios would weigh against the simpler version of the Miller model, since that version predicts no such relationship.

It might be argued that the tax savings–bankruptcy costs model is also consistent with these trends. Several other factors, however, would favor the Miller model with agency costs over the tax savings-bankruptcy costs model. The initial existence and then secular decline of preferred stock financing, for instance, cannot be explained by the latter model, whereas it can by the former. The simple version of the Miller model would also have difficulty explaining this phenomenon. An additional factor favoring the Miller model with agency costs over the tax savings–bankruptcy costs model is the apparent inverse relationship between federal government debt and corporate debt. At the same time, such a relationship would weigh against the pure agency cost model. Finally, to the extent that there is at least some relationship between debt ratios and future investment opportunities, this would tend to favor a capital structure model with an agency cost component.

One potential cloud hangs over the Miller model with agency costs, however, and that is its behavior in the complete absence of taxes. In that case the model simply reverts to the pure agency cost model. It is entirely possible that agency cost considerations alone can account for corporate financing trends prior to the imposition of the U.S. tax code in 1913, or in the years immediately following that when tax considerations may not have been very important. Looking at tables 1.3 and 1.4, though, it is difficult to pinpoint agency cost factors that would explain the decreases in corporate debt usage surrounding that time. As pointed out in section 1.3.4, for example, there is no apparent trend toward greater economic instability during this period. In addition, table 1.8 suggests that the inverse relationship between corporate and federal government debt may have existed even in the early years before tax factors had a very strong limiting influence on the substitutability among different types of securities. The pure agency cost model would be unable to explain such an inverse relationship.

There are some grounds for suspecting, therefore, that even the Miller model with agency costs does not provide an entirely satisfying explanation for the secular patterns in corporate finance. In the next section, some suggestions are offered for augmenting the theory so as to enhance its explanatory power.

1.4   Some Suggestions for an Augmented Theory of the Aggregate Corporate Capital Structure

As was seen in the subsection "Supplies of Competing Securities" of section 1.2.2, the demand curve for corporate debt distinguishes Miller's model from other existing capital structure theories. In all of the competing theories, this demand curve is perfectly elastic.

In general, perfect elasticity on the demand side indicates a well-developed capital market, that is, one in which trading is competitive, transaction costs are low, investors are not subject to trading restrictions, and a full range of securities is available.[41] In such an environment, changes in relative security supplies need not change relative prices because investors can engage in costless portfolio transactions that will completely offset any effects of the change in security supplies. If the corporate sector substitutes debt for equity financing, for example, investors holding equity would then have riskier portfolios on the average because of the increased corporate leverage. This change could be completely offset, however, if investors simply reduced their personal borrowing by an equivalent amount, and thus the increased corporate debt could be absorbed without any change in the relative prices of debt and equity securities.

While the vision of a well-developed capital market that has pervaded modern finance theory has proved to be a highly useful abstraction, it may be more appropriate for analyzing snapshots of equilibrium than for examining longer historical eras. The primary suggestion offered in this section, therefore, is that a better understanding of corporate financing trends over such eras requires a broader understanding of the corporate sector's evolving role in the development of the financial system. Over long periods, economic forces work toward making the capital market more perfect and more complete. Such forces will shape the corporate sector's financing choices, but at the same time corporate financing patterns themselves can serve as a force in the development process.[42]

1.4.1 The Place of the Corporate Sector in the Overall Financial System

Suppose we step back to get a broader perspective on the place of the corporate sector's financial structure in the context of the financial system generally. In order to reconcile the desires of its ultimate wealthholders (households) with the characteristics of its ultimate wealth (tangible assets), the economy develops a financial structure, consisting of non-financial corporations, securities markets, and financial institutions. Corporations specialize in holding and managing tangible assets and issue debt and equity claims against them. Financial institutions hold some of these corporate securities and in turn issue their own claims with different liquidity characteristics and patterns of return. Some of these institutions also purchase claims on households, thus affording individuals further financial transformation opportunities on their own account.

What determines the breakdown of these transformation activities among the corporate, financial institution, and household sectors? If the process of transforming asset characteristics were costless, then, as the Modigliani-Miller theorem implies, the allocation of these activities across sectors would be indeterminate. If the process is costly, on the other hand, agents in the various sectors may have access to different transformation technologies, and the scope and allocation of these activities will be determined by the principles of comparative advantage and cost minimization.

If we think of the supply and demand for substitutions of corporate debt for equity, as discussed in conjunction with the diagrams of section 1.2, the shapes and locations of the curves will be determined by the nature of these financial transformation technologies. The supply curve, for example, represents the corporate sector's technology for transforming the returns on its assets from equity claims into debt. If this technology is costless, the supply curve is flat at the level of the certainty-equivalent return on equity, as in the Modigliani-Miller model. If there is a constant corporate tax advantage per dollar of debt, the supply curve is flat at the higher level $R_e/(1 - t_c)$, as in the Miller model. In effect, the corporate sector's transformation technology exhibits constant returns to scale in this case, and thus the equilibrium corporate financing mix is determinate at the sectoral level but not at the individual firm level. Moreover, both the agency costs and tax savings–bankruptcy costs models can be viewed in this light as simply descriptions of the transformation technology on the supply side.

The demand side of the market reflects the competition that corporations face from both financial institutions and households themselves in performing these transformation activities. The more highly developed the financial intermediary system and the broader and less costly the range of transformation opportunities possessed by households on their own account, the less likely it is that corporate debt will possess unique characteristics and the more elastic the demand for this debt will be. In most existing capital structure theories, it is implicit either that investors can costlessly create perfect substitutes for corporate debt on their own account or that financial intermediaries can create such substitutes for them at no cost to the investors. Hence, corporate debt can be substituted for equity without limit at the same terms of trade. It is only in the Miller model that households face a costly transformation technology because of the costs of tax arbitrage activities.[43]

Existing capital structure theories, then, frequently adopt asymmetric views of the relationship between the corporate sector's financial transformation technology and the technologies faced by other sectors in the economy. In both the tax savings–bankruptcy costs and the agency costs models, for example, financial transformation is costly for corporations and the cost varies with the amount of transformation performed. For investors, on the other hand, such transformation activities are costless.

One could argue that any asymmetry in the costs of financial transformation faced by the corporate and household sectors might more plausibly go in the other direction. If there are economies in monitoring one large borrower rather than a number of smaller ones, for instance, or if investors face such restrictions as margin limits, financial transformation might be more costly for households than for the corporate sector. To see how corporate capital structure might be determined under these conditions, we next examine a simple model of such an environment.

1.4.2   A Model of Capital Structure Determination When Transformation Is Less Costly for Corporations Than for Households

To take an extreme case for illustrative purposes, let us suppose that borrowing is prohibitively costly for the household sector but that it entails no costs at all, other than interest, for corporations. In order to highlight the effect of these transformation costs, we will assume away all taxes. We will also ignore, for the time being, the possible existence of financial intermediaries, and we will assume that corporations start out relying exclusively on equity financing.

Initially, then, the only savings vehicle available to individuals is holdings of (risky) corporate shares. They will trade until all individuals place the same marginal valuation on these shares. As shown in Appendix B, these marginal valuations consist of two components: the marginal value of a dollar of certain future income plus an adjustment for risk. Because there is no separate trading in risk-free securities, however, these separate components need not be equal across individuals.

The yield on equity securities, r_e, thus reflects an average of investors' valuations of certain prospects plus an average of their required risk adjustments. But if part of corporations' return streams could be split off and sold separately as riskless securities, these could be sold at a premium price (lower certainty-equivalent yield) to the most risk-averse segment of the investing public.[44]

Corporations might try to profit from this repackaging activity, but competition would eliminate any gains in equilibrium. Since financial transformation has been assumed to be costless for corporations, the supply curve of corporate debt would be perfectly elastic at the level r_e. That is, corporations would be willing to freely substitute debt for equity financing as long as their certainty-equivalent yields were the same. Investors, on the other hand, would demand progressively higher yields to purchase additional increments of debt, since this additional debt would have to be sold to progressively less risk-averse segments of the investing population. Just as in Miller's model, then, restrictions on investors' transformation opportunities cause the demand curve for corporate debt to be upward sloping. As is depicted in figure 1.12, equilibrium is reached in this model when corporations have issued that amount of debt, B^*, that is sufficient to drive the cost of debt, r, into equality with r_e.

As in Miller's model, corporate capital structure is determinate at the aggregate level here, but not at the level of the individual firm. Because of trading restrictions on investors, there is a demand for the corporate sector's transformation services, and firms compete with one another to supply these services. Since all firms compete on equal terms, however, profits from financial transformation are squeezed out, and the most risk-averse investors reap a "bondholders' surplus," just as those investors in the lowest tax brackets do in Miller's model.

In addition, we might suppose that a government suddenly sprang up and issued an amount of government bonds, G, that were perfect substitutes for corporate debt. Since these bonds would tend to drive up the relative yields on corporate bonds above r_e, corporations would start substituting equity for debt and equilibrium corporate leverage would be

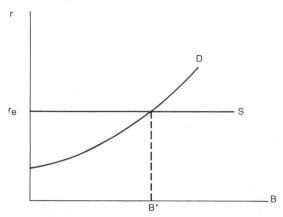

Fig. 1.12   Equilibrium when investors face costly financial transformation but firms do not.

reduced. Costly financial transformation in the household sector, then, is capable of yielding the same kind of substitution relationship between corporate securities and other sectors' securities that occurs in Miller's model. This relationship occurs here, moreover, in the complete absence of taxes.

The transaction costs that impart positive slope to the demand curve in this model are, of course, unrealistically severe. In practice, one would expect firms to face competition in their efforts to overcome transaction costs through financial transformation. Overcoming such costs and helping to satisfy divergent investor demands, in fact, is one of the primary rationales given for the existence of financial intermediaries.

In general, then, not only the corporate sector but also the financial intermediary and household sectors will have access to financial transformation technologies. To the extent that the corporate sector's technology exhibits cost advantages over those of other sectors, the corporate sector will tailor its financing mix to exploit these advantages. Demand curves for corporate securities will be upward sloping in this case because the financial transformations of the corporate sector cannot be duplicated at comparable cost. Exogenous shifts in the supplies of noncorporate securities, moreover, will shift these demand curves and thus cause changes in the equilibrium corporate financing mix.

To the extent that financial intermediaries or investors themselves can transform return streams at relatively low cost, on the other hand, demand curves for corporate securities will be highly elastic. Shifts in relative security supplies, in this case, can be easily accommodated in investors' portfolios, and thus they necessitate no changes in the corporate sector's financing mix. In addition, it might be reasonable to expect that the progression from the first case, in which demand curves for corporate securities are relatively less elastic, to the second case, in which these curves are highly elastic, would bear some relationship to the development of the capital market over time. In less developed periods, when investors face a less plentiful array of financial transformation opportunities, one would expect the intermediation role of corporate finance to be relatively important. As the capital market develops, however, and as investors come to rely less on the corporate sector for financial transformation, this role would be expected to diminish.

1.4.3 Conclusion

The foregoing discussion, of course, need not rule out such factors as tax considerations and the agency costs of corporate finance. The essential point is simply that such costs should be recognized on both sides of the market, particularly if one is interested in interpreting corporate financing patterns over long periods of time.

In general, then, both the demand and supply curves for corporate securities may exhibit less than perfect elasticity. The shape and position of the supply curve for corporate debt will reflect such aspects of the corporate sector's transformation technology as agency costs, the costs of issuing and servicing securities, and corporate taxes. The shape of the demand curve reflects the transformation technology available to investors, either on their own account or through financial intermediaries. In short, it reflects the range of portfolio opportunities open to investors and the costs of switching among them.

In principle, this augmented version of the Miller model with agency costs is capable of offering a richer interpretation of the capital structure trends discussed in section 1.1. The analysis there confirmed previous studies' findings of greater corporate debt financing in the post–World War II period. Nevertheless, the evidence further suggested that corporate reliance on debt financing was unusually low around World War II and that current debt proportions are not entirely out of line with those experienced in the earlier decades of the century.

Since the study has encompassed periods when the current tax system did not exist, tax considerations alone do not explain these overall trends. Instead, the augmented theory described here would suggest the following interpretation: In the early decades of the century, corporations may have played a more substantial intermediary role than has been true in recent decades. Investors' demands for relatively safe, fixed-dollar claims were not met to such a degree in the earlier decades by either the government or financial institutions as has been the case in more recent times. These factors may help account for the relatively high proportion of debt in total corporate financing and for the relatively high proportion of corporate debt in total domestic liabilities in the early part of the century. In the years following the Depression, however, this intermediary role of corporate debt has probably been reduced, both by increased relative supplies of federal government and household mortgage debt and by the increased extent of financial intermediation.[45]

By the present time, the markets both for corporate debt and for corporate stock have become heavily institutionalized, and it would be much more difficult to describe convincingly an overt intermediary role played by these securities. Nevertheless, tax rates and inflation in the postwar years have combined with the declining relative size of federal government debt to stimulate corporate debt financing again. Although corporate debt has never approached its earlier importance relative to total domestic liabilities, corporations' reliance on debt financing relative to equity has returned, by some measures at least, to roughly the proportions experienced in the early part of the century.

The augmented theory of the aggregate corporate capital structure described in this section has several points in its favor. First, it is consistent with the apparent inverse relationship between supplies of federal government and corporate debt, even in the absence of taxes. Second, it is capable of describing the interaction between the corporate sector's financing patterns and the secular development of the capital market and its institutions. The growth of pension funds, for example, would be expected to have alleviated some of the lack of substitutability between debt and equity securities induced by personal tax considerations. Development of these institutions, therefore, may have caused the demand curve for corporate debt to become more highly elastic. Finally, this theory is capable of explaining more corporate financing patterns than just the debt-equity mix. It is widely held, for instance, that recent interest rate volatility has made it increasingly dangerous for financial institutions to intermediate between long-term financial assets and short-term liabilities. This may account in part, then, for the shift in corporate liabilities toward increasingly short maturities.[46]

It is clear that many details still remain to be filled in. In particular, if the costs of financial transformation are an important element in the corporate sector's financing behavior, one would like a better understanding of these costs and of where, specifically, corporations might be expected to possess a comparative advantage over financial institutions and individual investors. In addition, hypotheses should be developed about the ways in which technological and regulatory changes alter these comparative advantages.[47] On the basis of the data examined in this paper, however, further development of an aggregate capital structure theory along the lines suggested here appears to offer some promise for explaining the secular patterns in corporate finance.

Appendix A

The Net Effect of an Increase in Corporate Tax Rates
on Equilibrium Corporate Debt

The numerator of expression (2) in the text can only be less than or
equal to zero if

(A1) $$\partial\left(\frac{r}{r_0}\right)/\partial t_c \geq \frac{r/r_0}{1 - t_c}.$$

Note, however, that if X represents the annual, certainty-equivalent,
pretax operating cash flow for the corporate sector as a whole, then the
aggregate market value, S, of corporate equity is given by

(A2) $$S = \frac{(X - rB)(1 - t_c)}{r_0} = \left(\frac{X}{r} - B\right)\frac{r}{r_0}(1 - t_c).$$

Discounting in expression (A2) is done at the tax-exempt rate since in
Miller's model corporate equity is tax exempt by assumption.

If we then increase t_c and abstract from any changes in the absolute
level of security yields, the resulting change in the aggregate value of
corporate equity is given by

(A3) $$\Delta S = -\left(\frac{X}{r} - B\right)\frac{r}{r_0}\Delta t_c$$
$$+ \left(\frac{X}{r} - B\right)(1 - t_c)\left(\partial\left(\frac{r}{r_0}\right)/\partial t_c\right)\Delta t_c.$$

If condition (A1) holds, however, ΔS must be nonnegative. Therefore, if
an increase in t_c fails to increase the equilibrium amount of corporate
debt, it will also fail to reduce the aggregate market value of corporate
equity. It seems unlikely, though, that an increase in corporate taxes
would increase the value of corporate equity. Thus, as long as the change
in relative yields is small enough that the value of equity declines, an
increase in the corporate tax rate will also increase equilibrium corporate
leverage in the Miller model.

Appendix B

Investors' Valuation of Corporate Stock
When No Riskless Asset Is Traded

Individuals, i, have initial endowments of cash, y_1^i, as well as initial
fractional shareholdings, $\bar{\alpha}^i$, in the aggregate market value of corporate
equity, V. There is no second-period endowment, so individuals must

make a consumption-saving decision that maximizes the expected utility, $E^i(U^i)$, of first- and second-period consumption, C_1^i and C_2^i. As noted in the text, the only available savings vehicle is holdings of corporate shares.

Firms in the aggregate are assumed to be subject to the same uncertainty, and thus the shares of one firm are viewed as perfect substitutes for those of any other firm. We will ignore distinctions among firms, then, and simply think of the corporate sector in the aggregate. The aggregate net income of firms in the second period is $\tilde{\Theta}\bar{X}$, where $\tilde{\Theta}$ is a random variable. In general, individuals may differ in their views of the distribution of $\tilde{\Theta}$ and their subjective probability density functions will be denoted by $f^i(\tilde{\Theta})$.

A representative individual's consumption-saving problem is

(B1) $$\max_{\alpha^i} \int U^i(C_1^i, \tilde{C}_2^i) f^i(\Theta) d\Theta,$$

where

(B2) $$C_1^i = Y_1^i + (\bar{\alpha}^i - \alpha^i)V,$$

and

(B3) $$\tilde{C}_2^i = \alpha^i \tilde{\Theta}\bar{X}.$$

The first-order condition is

(B4) $$\frac{\partial U^i}{\partial \alpha^i} = \bar{X} E^i(\tilde{U}_2^i \tilde{\Theta}) - V E^i(\tilde{U}_1^i) = 0,$$

where

$$E^i(U_2^i \tilde{\Theta}) = \int \tilde{\Theta}(\partial U^i/\partial C_2^i) f^i(\tilde{\Theta}) d\Theta,$$

and

$$E^i(U_1^i) = (\partial U^i/\partial C_1^i) f^i(\tilde{\Theta}) d\Theta.$$

Using the fact that $\operatorname{cov}(\tilde{A}\tilde{B}) = E(\tilde{A}\tilde{B}) - E(\tilde{A})E(\tilde{B})$, where $\tilde{A}$ and $\tilde{B}$ are any two random variables, (B4) may be written as

(B5) $$V = \bar{X}\left(\frac{E^i(\tilde{U}_2^i)\,E^i(\tilde{\Theta})}{E^i(\tilde{U}_1^i)} + \frac{\operatorname{cov}(\tilde{U}_2^i\theta)}{E^i(\tilde{U}_1^i)}\right).$$

That is, each individual buys or sells shares until his personal valuation of corporate equity is exactly equal to the market's valuation, V.

As indicated by the right-hand side of (B5), however, the individual's personal valuation has two components, which need not be equal separately for all individuals. If we assume away differences in expectations for the moment and let $E^i(\tilde{\Theta}) = 1$ for all individuals, the first component, $E(U_2^i)/E(U_1^i)$, can be thought of as a personal discount factor for certain prospects, and the second component can be thought of as a personal risk-adjustment factor. From (B5), those investors with higher certainty discount factors (that is, those who place a higher value on certain future consumption) must have correspondingly larger (i.e., more negative) risk-adjustment factors.

If we aggregate by summing (B5), weighted by individual shareholdings, over all individuals, the result is

$$(B6) \qquad \sum_i \alpha^i V = V = \bar{X}\left(\sum_i \alpha^i \frac{E(U_2^i)}{E(U_1^i)} + \sum_i \alpha^i \frac{\text{cov}(U_2^i \tilde{\Theta})}{E(U_1^i)}\right)$$

and the cost of equity financing to the corporate sector may be expressed as

$$(B7) \qquad \frac{\bar{X}}{V} = \frac{1}{\sum_i \alpha^i \dfrac{E(U_2^i)}{E(U_1^i)} + \sum_i \alpha^i \dfrac{\text{cov}(U_2^i \tilde{\Theta})}{E(U_1^i)}}.$$

That is, the cost of equity is determined by weighted averages of investors' certainty discount factors and risk-adjustment factors. Furthermore, since the second term in the denominator of (B6) can be thought of as the overall market risk–adjustment factor, the market certainty–equivalent cost of equity, r_e, is given by

$$(B8) \qquad r_e = \frac{1}{\sum_i \alpha^i \dfrac{E(U_2^i)}{E(U_1^i)}}.$$

If firms were now to begin substituting some risk-free debt financing for equity, those investors with the highest certainty discount factors (that is, those placing the highest personal value on this debt) would be the first to buy it. Since these investors would have higher-than-average certainty discount factors relative to the market as a whole, (B8) indicates that they would be willing to accept a yield lower than r_e on at least an initial increment of risk-free corporate debt.

Notes

1. Academic studies of aggregate corporate financing patterns include Goldsmith (1958, 1963), Lintner (1960), Kuznets (1961), Miller (1963), Sametz (1964), Friedman (1980), and Gordon and Malkiel (1981). Business journalists have also surveyed trends in aggregate financial ratios, particularly in conjunction with the "capital shortage" discussions that were popular in the mid-1970s. See, for example, *Business Week* (1974).

2. Examples include Friedman (1980) and Gordon and Malkiel (1981). Discussions in the business press have also tended to emphasize deterioration in corporation balance sheets. *Business Week* (1974) is a good example.

3. Studies emphasizing stability in debt-equity proportions include Lintner (1960), Miller (1963), and Sametz (1964). Updated versions of these arguments also appear in Miller (1977) and Sametz and Keenan (1981).

4. Among the exceptions are Miller (1977) and Gordon and Malkiel (1981).

5. Miller's (1977) paper was perhaps the first to provide a theory explicitly aimed at the aggregate corporate capital structure.

6. The total-debt-to-total-assets ratio was not examined by Miller.

7. After 1961, the IRS generally stopped reporting separate figures for preferred stock.

8. Distortions in the opposite direction can also occur, however. For example, book-value debt ratios may be understated by the omission of such "off-balance-sheet" financing sources as leases and unfunded pension liabilities. The use of these sources is believed to have grown tremendously in the 1960s and 1970s. One indication of the possible magnitude of this understatement is given in Gordon and Malkiel (1981). They calculate the ratio of debt to debt plus equity for the aggregate of firms included on the Compustat tape. Since 1973 the data on the tape include lease and pension liabilities. The ratios with and without these liabilities are as follows:

	Debt Ratio without Leases and Pensions	Debt Ratio including Leases and Pensions
1973	.367	.497
1974	.381	.511
1975	.374	.499
1976	.362	.485
1977	.358	.473
1978	.358	.462

9. See Modigliani and Cohn (1979), however, for an argument that the market does not properly adjust for inflation in determining equity values. By their argument, market-value debt ratios would be substantially overstated in recent years.

10. Myers (1977), for example, has argued that a firm's capacity to issue debt is closely related to its assets-in-place. The total market value of assets, on the other hand, reflects not only assets-in-place, but also future investment opportunities, and Myers points out that firms may not find it advantageous to borrow against these opportunities. Thus the replacement value of assets, which reflects only assets-in-place, may be a better measure of debt capacity. However, assets-in-place will be overstated to the extent that replacement value figures include assets that firms would not be willing to replace.

11. One problem is that von Furstenberg's measure of debt is different from Goldsmith's. In von Furstenberg, non-interest-bearing liabilities have been netted out against the asset side of the balance sheet, while interest-bearing financial assets have been netted out against the liability side in computing this ratio. To make the figures as closely comparable as possible, the same procedure has been used in calculating debt ratios from Goldsmith's data. Nevertheless, the detail in Goldsmith's data is not the same as that in the *Flow of Funds Accounts*, from which von Furstenberg worked, and thus we would not expect the ratios to be identical.

12. To the extent that some investment expenditures, such as research and development, are expensed immediately, however, the extent of equity financing may still be understated somewhat. There are also other problems inherent in Flow of Funds data. Von Furstenberg and Malkiel (1977) discuss the distortions resulting from failure to recognize the reduction in the real value of previously outstanding debt caused by inflation. In addition, the *Flow of Funds Accounts* published by the Federal Reserve System lump preferred stock financing together with common equity financing.

13. It could be argued that this interpretation of Modigliani-Miller is excessively literal

and that we should view it as an equilibrium tendency rather than as a law that holds instant by instant. Brealey and Myers (1981), for example, conclude their chap. 17 with an equilibrium tendency version of the Modigliani-Miller argument. Nevertheless, the more stringent version depicted in figure 2.4 is representative, I believe, of the way the Modigliani-Miller argument is usually interpreted in formal finance theory. It is certainly the version that is consistent with a complete market model. See Litzenberger and Sosin (1977) for a discussion of related points.

14. The financial institution sector is introduced in Stiglitz's (1974) generalization of Modigliani-Miller. Even if financial transformation were costly for households on their own account, their demand for corporate debt would still be perfectly elastic if financial intermediaries could costlessly perform these services.

15. Examples of this theory may be found in Robichek and Myers (1966), Kraus and Litzenberger (1973), and Kim (1978).

16. Implicitly, there are no personal taxes, or at least corporate debt and equity securities are subject to identical tax treatment at the personal level. When the model is discussed in the analysis that follows, it will be assumed that there are no personal taxes.

17. Certainty-equivalent returns on debt here are net of those agency costs (such as monitoring expenses) borne directly by bondholders. The downward slope in the debt supply curve reflects increases in both these agency costs (which are passed back to firms' owner-managers) and in those (such as bonding expenses or opportunities forgone) borne directly by the owner-managers. See Jensen and Meckling (1976) for further discussion.

18. In the simplest version of Miller's model, equity is assumed to be free from personal taxation. Thus r_e, the certainty-equivalent return on equity, is the same as the certainty–equivalent return, r_0, on tax-exempt bonds.

19. An example of such a model is Myers (1977), in which debt is subject to an agency cost but equity is not. In the absence of taxes, the supply curve for debt would slope downward starting from r_e, and in equilibrium no debt would be issued. When corporate taxes are introduced, however, the supply curve shifts upward and there is a positive equilibrium quantity of debt.

20. See, for instance, DeAngelo and Masulis (1980) or Barnea et al. (1981). The models of Gordon and Malkiel (1981) and Modigliani (1982) can also be interpreted in this vein. It is a semantic nicety, in fact, whether such models are classified as "Miller models with agency costs" or tax savings–bankruptcy costs models adjusted for personal taxes. For simplicity, the former label will be applied in the ensuing discussion.

21. All of the comparative statics exercises in this section are of the partial equilibrium variety in that they concentrate on changes in r relative to r_e but do not consider changes in the absolute level of security yields induced by changes in aggregate wealth.

22. It is easily verified that an increase in t_p alone reduces B^*.

23. As in Miller's model, the presence of tax-exempt investors would lead to an initial horizontal segment (at the rate r_e) in the demand curve for preferred stock. In addition, because of the 85% intercorporate dividend exclusion, corporate investors would demand the same certainty-equivalent return on preferred stock that they would on dividend-paying common stock. Corporate demand for preferred stock, then, would further extend the horizontal segment of the demand curve. Eventually, however, additional preferred stock would have to be purchased by taxable investors, and this would impart an upward slope to the demand curve.

24. This effect is discussed by Modigliani (1982), who labels it "Super Fisher's Law."

25. McDonald (1983) has derived a similar result by somewhat different means.

26. The Gordon-Malkiel (1981) model, which combines tax considerations with bankruptcy costs, reaches a similar conclusion. This finding is also consistent with Modigliani's (1982) analysis.

27. A further interaction between inflation and the tax system has been pointed out by DeAngelo and Masulis (1980). They argue that such items as depreciation provide substi-

tute tax shelters and thus limit the firm's ability to benefit from the tax deductibility of interest. Since an increase in inflation reduces the real value of depreciation and other tax shields, however, the firm is then encouraged to substitute debt for equity financing in order to further shelter its real income.

28. Results similar to those in both of these exercises have been derived independently by McDonald (1983).

29. See Kim et al. (1979) and Taggart (1980) for discussions of how investors in different tax brackets sort themselves into clienteles with respect to their preferences for corporate leverage. At Miller's equilibrium, the marginal investor will have $t_{pB} = t_c$ and $\delta = 0$. Furthermore, this investor will be just indifferent between holding taxable and tax-exempt bonds, so for him $r(1 - t_{pB}) = r_0$. In equilibrium, then, $\delta = 1 - (1 - t_c)/(1 - t_{pB}) = 1 - r(1 - t_c)/r(1 - t_{pB}) = 1 - r(1 - t_c)/r_0 = 0$, and thus expression (8) is consistent with expression (1).

30. In 1973, for example, investors who paid taxes at marginal rates greater than the statutory corporate rate accounted for just 3.57% of the economy's taxable income (Pechman 1977, App. B). If taxable income is at all related to wealth (another treacherous assumption), this may suggest that the aversion to corporate leverage on the part of high-tax-bracket investors was not very important. The presence of tax-exempt investors could also add to the demand for corporate leverage.

31. The upward trend in corporate tax rates is also broadly consistent with the secular decline in preferred stock financing, at least in terms of the Miller model with agency costs, as was seen in the subsection "An Aside on Taxes and Preferred Stock" in section 1.2.2.

32. In principle, expected rates of inflation would be preferred. Over long periods, one might expect at least a rough correspondence between expected and realized inflation rates. Another potential measurement problem stems from the possibility that higher inflation rates may be associated with greater uncertainty about relative price changes. To the extent that this is in turn associated with increased business risk, there may be an offsetting influence on corporate debt usage.

33. This increase in debt financing is particularly apparent if one examines yearly Flow of Funds data. In 1946 and 1947, for example, the years of greatest inflation around that period, total debt accounted for 52% and 49%, respectively, of total sources of funds for the corporate sector. In large part this increased debt financing was accounted for by heavy reliance on short-term liabilities, which made up 33% and 29%, respectively, of total sources.

34. The supply of government debt might reasonably be viewed as exogenous to the system. Observed amounts of household mortgages, on the other hand, will presumably be more affected by prevailing capital market yields.

35. To the extent that tax considerations and their interaction with inflation have affected corporate liabilities and household mortgages in the same direction, this may not be surprising.

36. See Holland and Myers (1979) for a good discussion of the pitfalls in interpreting measured q values.

37. Use of the same data for q and for the financing ratios may entail some spurious correlation, however.

38. Williamson (1981) has had some success in using this theory to explain observed capital structures of individual firms.

39. Column 3 of table 1.10 is derived by multiplying the standard deviation of stock returns by one minus the market-debt-to-value ratio. This is a good measure of business risk or the standard deviation of unlevered asset returns if (i) debt is risk-free, (ii) preferred stock is negligible in magnitude, and (iii) leverage has no effect on overall firm value. All three assumptions are questionable here, and thus the measure is very rough. See Hamada (1972) for a discussion of the problem of measuring business risk.

40. It would be tautological, of course, to say that the model with the most explanatory

variables has the greatest explanatory power. What is being asserted here is that there are economically significant trends that the simpler models are incapable of explaining.

41. The widely used "complete" market model would be one in which these conditions are satisfied. Weaker conditions than market completeness (the "spanning" assumption, for example) would also be sufficient to generate perfectly elastic demands for securities if corporate financing choices were confined to traditional debt and equity securities.

42. A considerable literature exists, tracing this process of capital market development with particular emphasis on the role of financial institutions. See, for example, Davis and North (1971), Silber (1975), and James (1978).

43. See Barnea et al. (1981) for further elaboration on the role of tax arbitrage restrictions in making this demand curve imperfectly elastic.

44. Differences in investor expectations could play a similar role. Firms could try to gain by selling riskless securities to the most pessimistic segment of investors.

45. In the immediate post-Depression years, investors probably also became increasingly skeptical about the safety of corporate debt.

46. Ultimately, this involves a shift in the bearing of interest rate risk from shareholders and other owners of financial institutions and from liability insurance agencies to the shareholders of nonfinancial corporations. A more complete explanation would detail the mechanism by which such a shift might take place. In particular, the stance of financial institution regulators might be an important factor.

47. See Greenbaum and Haywood (1971) for a discussion of the role of technology and regulation in circumscribing the intermediate possibilities open to financial institutions.

References

Barnea, Amir; Haugen, Robert A.; and Senbet, Lemma W. 1981. An equilibrium analysis of debt financing under costly tax arbitrage and agency problems. *Journal of Finance* 36:568–81.

Brealey, Richard, and Myers, Stewart. 1981. *Principles of corporate finance.* New York: McGraw-Hill.

Business Week. 1974. The debt economy. Special Issue. October 12.

Ciccolo, John C., Jr. 1982. Changing balance sheet relationships in the U.S. manufacturing sector, 1926–77. In *The changing roles of debt and equity in financing U.S. capital formation,* ed. Benjamin M. Friedman. Chicago: University of Chicago Press.

Davis, Lance E., and North, Douglas C. 1971. *Institutional change and American economic growth.* Cambridge: Cambridge University Press.

DeAngelo, Harry, and Masulis, Ronald W. 1980. Optimal capital structure under corporate and personal taxation. *Journal of Financial Economics* 8:3–29.

Friedman, Benjamin M. 1980. Postwar changes in the American financial markets. In *The American economy in transition,* ed. M. Feldstein. Chicago: University of Chicago Press.

———. 1982. Debt and economic activity in the United States. In *The changing roles of debt and equity in financing U.S. capital formation,* ed. Benjamin M. Friedman. Chicago: University of Chicago Press.

Goldsmith, Raymond W. 1956. *A study of saving in the United States*. 3 vols. Princeton: Princeton University Press.

————. 1958. *Financial intermediaries in the American economy since 1900*. Princeton: Princeton University Press.

Goldsmith, Raymond W.; Lipsey, Richard E.; and Mendelson, Morris. 1963. *Studies in the national balance sheet of the United States*. 2 vols. Princeton: Princeton University Press.

Gordon, Roger H., and Malkiel, Burton G. 1981. Corporation finance. In *How taxes affect economic behavior*, ed. H. J. Aaron and J. A. Pechman. Washington, D.C.: Brookings Institution.

Greenbaum, Stuart E., and Haywood, Charles F. 1971. Secular change in the financial services industry. *Journal of Money, Credit and Banking* 3:571–89.

Grier, Paul, and Strebel, Paul. 1980. The empirical relationship between taxation and capital structure. *Financial Review* 15:45–57.

Hamada, Robert R. 1972. The effect of the firm's capital structure on the systematic risk of common stocks. *Journal of Finance* 27:435–52.

Holland, Daniel M., and Myers, Stewart C. 1979. Trends in corporate profitability and capital costs. In *The nation's capital needs: three studies*, ed. R. Lindsay. New York: Committee for Economic Development.

Hai Hong. 1977. Inflation and the market value of the firm: theory and tests. *Journal of Finance* 32:1031–48.

Ibbotson, Roger G., and Sinquefield, Rex A. 1982. *Stocks, bonds, bills and inflation: the past and the future*. 1982 ed. Charlottesville, Va.: Financial Analysts' Research Federation.

James, John A. 1978. *Money and capital markets in postbellum America*. Princeton: Princeton University Press.

Jensen, Michael C., and Meckling, William H. 1976. Theory of the firm: managerial behavior, agency costs and ownership structure. *Journal of Financial Economics* 3:305–60.

Kim, E. Han. 1978. A mean-variance theory of optimal capital structure and corporate debt capacity. *Journal of Finance* 33:45–63.

Kim, E. Han; Lewellen, Wilbur G.; and McConnell, John J. 1979. Financial leverage clienteles: theory and evidence. *Journal of Financial Economics* 7:83–109.

Kraus, Alan, and Litzenberger, Robert. 1973. A state-preference model of optimal financial leverage. *Journal of Finance* 28:911–23.

Kuznets, Simon. 1961. *Capital in the American economy: its formation and financing*. Princeton: Princeton University Press.

Lintner, John V. 1960. The Financing of Corporations. In E. S. Mason, ed., *The Corporation in Modern Society*. Cambridge, MA: Harvard University Press.

Litzenberger, Robert H., and Sosin, Howard B. 1977. The theory of recapitalizations and the evidence of dual purpose funds. *Journal of Finance* 32:1433–65.

McDonald, Robert. 1983. Government debt and private leverage: an extension of the Miller theorem. *Journal of Public Economics* 22: 303–25.

Miller, Merton H. 1963. The corporation income tax and corporate financial policies. In *Stabilization Policies*, by Commission on Money and Credit. Englewood Cliffs, N.J.: Prentice-Hall.

———. 1977. Debt and taxes. *Journal of Finance* 32:261–75.

Modigliani, Franco. 1982. Debt, dividend policy, taxes, inflation, and market valuation. *Journal of Finance* 37:255–73.

Modigliani, Franco, and Cohn, Richard A. 1979. Inflation, rational valuation, and the market. *Financial Analysts Journal* 35:24–44.

Modigliani, Franco, and Miller, Merton H. 1958. The cost of capital, corporation finance, and the theory of investment. *American Economic Review* 48:261–97.

———. 1963. Corporate income taxes and the cost of capital—a correction. *American Economic Review* 53:433–43.

Myers, Stewart C. 1977. Determinants of corporate borrowing. *Journal of Financial Economics* 5:147–75.

Pechman, Joseph A. 1977. *Federal tax policy.* 3d ed. Washington, D.C.: Brookings Institution.

Robichek, Alexander A., and Myers, Stewart C. 1966. Problems in the theory of optimal capital structure. *Journal of Financial and Quantitative Analysis* 1:1–35.

Ross, Stephen A. 1977. The determination of financial structure: the incentive—signalling approach. *Bell Journal of Economics* 8:23–40.

Sametz, Arnold W. 1964. Trends in the volume and composition of equity finance. *Journal of Finance* 19:450–69.

Sametz, Arnold W., and Keenan, W. Michael. 1981. Business investment demand. In *Financial institutions and markets* by M. E. Polakoff, T. A. Durkin, et al. 2d ed. Boston: Houghton Mifflin.

Senbet, Lemma W., and Taggart, Jr., Robert A. 1984. Capital structure equilibrium under market imperfections and incompleteness. *Journal of Finance* 39:93–103.

Silber, William B., ed. 1975. *Financial innovation.* Lexington, Mass.: D. C. Heath.

Stiglitz, Joseph E. 1974. On the irrelevance of corporate financial policy. *American Economic Review* 64:851–66.

Taggart, Jr., Robert A. 1980. Taxes and corporate capital structure in an incomplete market. *Journal of Finance* 35:645–59.

Von Furstenberg, George M. 1977. Corporate investment: does market valuation matter in the aggregate? *Brookings Papers on Economic Activity* 2:347–97.

Von Furstenberg, George M., and Malkiel, Burton G. 1977. Financial analysis in an inflationary environment. *Journal of Finance* 32:575–88.

Williamson, Scott H. 1981. The moral hazard theory of corporate financial structure: empirical tests. Ph.D. thesis, Massachusetts Institute of Technology.

Comment   John Lintner

The first section of this paper provides a very useful overview and synthesis of the evidence regarding the secular patterns in the relative use of debt and equity financing by corporations developed in the classic studies of Goldsmith, von Furstenberg, Holland and Myers, and others. These earlier studies have used book or market or replacement cost valuations to measure the relative stocks of debt and equity securities, or have turned to flow-of-funds data. Each of these individual series measures a different aspect of the underlying reality and raises its own problems of possible bias and measurement error. Taggart's convenient tables also remind us that the levels of corporate leverage reported in different studies using the same concepts for overlapping dates frequently differ substantially. The issues raised by these observations would have required much further detailed investigation if the author had intended to develop econometric tests of the adequacy of any (or of any combination) of our models to explain the year-to-year levels and fluctuations in corporate leverage. But Taggart's objectives in this paper are more broad-brush and qualitative. His focus is on using the available evidence simply to identify the broader trends and stronger tides in the relative use of corporate debt and equity over the eight decades for which estimates are available—the trends and tides which theory should be able to explain in terms of a comparative static analysis.

In spite of the imperfections and differences in the various separate series, Taggart is able to show that there is often, if not always, substantial agreement regarding the general stability or the relative increase or decrease in the use of corporate leverage over various intervals of five or ten years or more.[1] The agreement among all the series in showing a massive increase in the relative use of debt over the last fifteen or twenty years is simply the most dramatic and best known of the instances of common broad movements (or stability) he points out. Taggart also adds useful perspective on this recent experience by observing that equally high levels of leverage measured in market values (or relative to the

Until his death, John Lintner was George Gund Professor of Economics and Business Administration at Harvard University.

replacement cost of assets) were common in the 1930s, and that Gold-smith's data show even higher levels early in this century when inflation was mild and there were no income taxes. While readers familiar with the underlying literature may not be especially surprised at any of the conclusions, this survey and summary of the available evidence will serve to sharpen our perspectives on what the longer-term patterns in the financing of corporate assets and investments have been.

The rest of the paper summarizes, reinterprets, tests, and finally extends the existing body of corporate financial theory in an effort to understand and explain the various stabilities and secular movements in the relative use of debt financing identified in the first section. Of the many models of corporate capital structure which have been developed in recent years, only Miller's "debt and taxes" and its successors directly provide a determinate equilibrium for the aggregate capital structure of the corporate sector as a whole. Optimal debt-to-equity ratios in the original Modigliani-Miller models were of course indeterminate at both the firm and the corporate sector levels. The numerous other theories have all concentrated on deriving the optimal mix of financing for individual firms under different sets of conditions in a partial equilibrium setting. For expositional convenience, along with the original Miller macro model, Taggart groups the rich set of micro models which have been developed in recent years into three generic types: the union of tax savings and bankruptcy cost theories, agency cost theories, and Miller's model combined with agency costs. Taggart then handles the aggregation problems involved in deriving the implications of these various micro theories for the equilibrium values of sector-wide totals of debt and equity financing by recasting the theories in terms of supply and demand curves expressed as functions of what are described as certainty-equivalent rates of return.

On careful examination, however, this description of the functions as certainty equivalents is inappropriate and potentially misleading. In the presence of a riskless asset, the marginal certainty-equivalent rate of return on all risk assets is equal to the riskless rate.[2] In particular, this is true for all outstanding issues of debt and equity securities, regardless of their relative volumes for each firm or for the corporate sector as a whole. Rather than certainty equivalents, Taggart's supply and demand functions are denominated in terms of required expected rates of return throughout. They are simply normalized relative to the rate of return required on outstanding equity in the limiting case of an all-equity capitalization, or alternatively normalized on the rate which borrowers would just be willing to pay (or lenders would just be willing to accept) on the first dollar of debt issued, as the case may be. Each generic theory specifies the all-equity intercept of either the supply or demand function as its primary benchmark. It then derives the intercept of the other function relative to this point by allowing for the initial impact of the factors, such as taxes or agency or bankruptcy costs, which are being analyzed. Once the two intercepts have been located, the shapes, slopes, and derivatives of both the supply and demand functions as more debt is added under the specified conditions are inferred and the sector-wide equilibrium at their point of intersection or equality is determined. At each stage, all measurements are in terms of expected rates of return rather than certainty equivalents.

When properly described and understood in this way, Taggart's recasting of the major micro theories brings out interesting and useful comparisons between them both in his text and in his summary diagrams. It also handles the aggregation problem in a very convenient way,[3] and it facilitates the derivation of the predictions of each theory regarding the qualitative comparative static effects on aggregate debt-to-equity ratios of changes in various contextual factors.

The predictions of each of Taggart's generic model types for the broad effects on corporate financial ratios of changes in corporate and personal tax rates, in inflation, in the costs associated with corporate debt, in the supplies of tax-exempt or of noncorporate taxable bonds, and in growth opportunities relative to assets in place are derived in the second section and conveniently summarized in table 1.5. The simpler types of models focus on only one or two of these determining factors and ignore the others, but, as would be expected, whenever any two models include a common determining factor, they are in complete agreement regarding the impact of a change in that factor. While the separate discussions of the location and shapes of the sectoral supply and demand functions in each model are instructive and nicely set the stage for Taggart's own "augmented theory" in the final section of the paper, these generic models are seen to be quite compatible and complementary.

The third section examines the ability of existing theory to explain the secular movements in corporate capital structures, drawing on many decades of annual data on corporate and personal tax rates, "net debt incentive tax ratios," inflation rates, Tobin's q values, yearly standard deviations of monthly stock market returns, and the relative supplies of corporate and noncorporate securities. Taggart carefully and informatively compares the fluctuations in each series with the observed secular trends in corporate financial patterns. Not surprisingly, he finds that secular fluctuations in corporate debt-to-equity ratios are not adequately explained by any of these factors. Each factor is associated with debt ratios in the way theory predicts over parts of the record, but in each case the expected association is not found during other periods. But however convenient and constructive this one-on-one analysis may be, this part of the paper generally has the character of an examination of the time-series residuals in a series of simple regressions. The important interactions of tax rates and inflation are recognized, but the other causal factors are considered separately. Further research to explain these secular trends will have to move on to examine the net effects of each of the causal factors while appropriately taking into account the simultaneous effects of others. In addition, there are important interactions between these other factors which will have to be analyzed and allowed for—notably those between different risk and agency costs and tax rates.

Even though Taggart did not explicitly carry through this further analysis, he must have done so implicitly and judgmentally, for he clearly believes that all of the factors listed in his table 1.5 are important, though partial, determinants of corporate debt-to-equity ratios. This is the basis for his further conclusion that the Miller model combined with agency costs explains the broad fluctuations in these financial ratios more adequately than any of the three other generic models considered. The original Miller or agency cost models, and even the popular tax savings and bankruptcy cost models, all leave out various factors which appear to be empirically significant, while the Miller-cum–agency cost model in effect is treated as the union of all the elements in the others.

But Taggart regards even this inclusive model as not fully adequate to explain the historical record. He observes that the demand function for corporate debt will become more elastic as capital markets become more fully developed and competitive and as transactions costs and trading restrictions are reduced. Similarly, the position and curvature of this demand function over time will reflect changes in the structure of the set of financial intermediaries and financial instruments available to investors in the economy. He shows that variations in all these major aspects of the broader institutional context of corporate financial decisions, as well as exogenous changes in the relative supplies of noncorporate securities, will affect the equilibrium debt-to-equity ratios for the corporate sector, other things equal, even in the complete absence of taxes and agency and bankruptcy costs. When the latter factors are reintroduced, the resulting augmented version of the Miller-cum–agency costs model helps to explain several important but otherwise rather puzzling features of the historical trends in corporate capital structures, which are discussed in the final section.

As I studied the paper, I was somewhat surprised that Taggart did not explicitly identify and develop some additional determinants of corporate debt-to-equity ratios. Some of these are implicitly suggested in his text, while others are not. In particular, Taggart properly recognizes that the absence of complete markets and the presence of agency and bankruptcy costs make investment and financing decisions interdependent. The optimal debt ratio for any ongoing firm similarly depends on the unsystematic (as well as the systematic) risks of its assets in place.[4] To at least a rough approximation, these risks will depend on the industries within which the firm operates, and it is well known that there are clear and remarkably persistent patterns in the relative use of debt financing by firms in different industries. All this clearly suggests that a considerable part of the variation in aggregate corporate debt-to-equity ratios may have reflected shifts in the relative volumes of total financing required by different industries—due for instance to shifts in the relative growth in demands for their output—rather than to shifts in economy-wide factors such as tax rates or inflation. During a period when the total capitalization of such heavily levered industries as hotels and electric utilities increases relative to that of such industries as soft drink manufacturers or industrial chemicals, the overall corporate debt-to-equity ratio will rise even if nothing else is happening.

Similarly, just as the distribution of income and the pattern of progression in personal tax rates affect the elasticity of the demand for corporate debt in the original Miller model, it is clear from Taggart's analysis that shifts in the distribution of wealth as well as of income among individual investors will shift this demand curve in his augmented model. While the available data on the distributions of income and wealth are rather rough, they may help explain debt usage over time by way of various clientele effects. The data on nondebt corporate tax shields are much more solid, and the direction of their net effect is quite clear. The depressing impact on equilibrium debt ratios of the veritable explosion in these other tax shields over the last decade or so clearly needs to be allowed for in assessing the true explanatory power of other factors. The excess profits taxes imposed during World War II and the Korean War should also be mentioned and taken into account. Finally, it should be observed that Taggart generally discusses the adequacy of each explanatory factor by comparing the contemporaneous movements in corporate debt-to-equity ratios and the series in question. It is becoming increasingly clear that corporations have *target* (equilibrium) debt-to-equity ratios, just as they have target dividend payout ratios, and that as conditions change they progressively but partially adjust their immediate position toward the equilibrium value.[5] This suggests that in future work, even that intended to explain only the secular trends and broader movements in debt ratios, it would be advisable to allow for appropriate lags between the explanatory series and the debt ratios being investigated.

These various observations, however, are in the nature of suggestions for further refinements and extensions in future research on these issues, building on what is already a very broad-ranging, insightful, and commendable piece of work. In particular, Taggart's review and augmentation of our received theory has been very constructive and useful, and the paper as a whole has considerably enriched our understanding of the major trends in corporate financing over the last century.

Notes

1. The major exceptions are of course found in comparisons between series based on book values with those based on either market values or replacement costs.

2. This property is explicitly derived in Lintner (1969, p. 356) and shown to hold when investors have differing (as well as common) probability assessments. When there is no riskless asset (as when inflation is uncertain), the marginal certainty-equivalent real rates of return on all assets in every investor's portfolio again have a common value equal to the shadow value of his wealth constraint—i.e., his marginal real certainty-equivalent of ending wealth (pp. 373–77). This is of course true even when short-selling constraints are effective (pp. 389 ff.). Alternatively, when the objective function is expressed as the utility of a stream of consumption, the marginal certainty-equivalent real rate of return is the ratio of the utility of an added dollar of certain future real consumption to that of a dollar of current consumption. In both formulations, the marginal certainty-equivalent return in the absence of a riskless asset will vary from investor to investor (even when probability assessments are homogeneous), and the market value will involve weighted averages across investors.

3. The lateral summation of rising, horizontal or falling micro supply or demand functions will produce macro functions with qualitatively the same characteristic. Similarly, the displacement of any aggregated function will be qualitatively the same as that of its component micro functions in response to the change of any common factor such as tax rates or inflation.

4. This position is advanced, and some of its further implications are developed, in Lintner (1982), esp. pp. 135–40.

5. The speed of adjustment of debt-to-equity ratios may of course be different than that for dividends. This combined model was originally proposed in Lintner (1967).

References

Lintner, John. 1967. Corporation finance: risk and investment. In *Determinants of investment behavior*, ed. Robert Ferber. New York: National Bureau of Economic Research.

——. 1969. The aggregation of investor's diverse judgments and preferences in purely competitive securities markets. *Journal of Financial and Quantitative Analysis* (December), pp. 347–400.

——. 1982. Some new perspectives on tests of CAPM and other capital asset pricing models and issues of market efficiency. In *Economic activity and finance*, ed. Marshall E. Blume et al. Cambridge, Mass.: Ballinger.

2   Changes in the Balance Sheet of the U.S. Manufacturing Sector, 1926–1977

John H. Ciccolo, Jr., and Christopher F. Baum

This paper reports the results of a research project which involves the collection and organization of income account and balance sheet data, at the individual firm level, for the years 1926–77. The primary data source for the study is *Moody's Industrial Manual*.

By working at the level of the individual firm, it is possible to obtain more accurate information on the market values of traded securities and more detailed information on the structure of firms' balance sheets than is typically available at the aggregate level. Accurate data on the income accounts and balance sheets of firms over a substantial period of time can provide researchers with a rich source of information against which specific hypotheses regarding corporate financing and investment decisions can be tested. The data collected for this study, and software necessary to manage them efficiently, are available from the authors in either IBM or VAX formats at a nominal fee. An NBER Technical Paper is also available which describes the dataset and software in detail.

Section 2.1 briefly describes the manner in which the data were collected and organized. A more detailed presentation of the characteristics of the dataset and accompanying computer software can be found in the Appendix. Section 2.2 considers the aggregate characteristics of the sample. In particular, firm average data on the sources and uses of funds, market valuations, and rates of return are presented for the 1926–77 period. Section 2.3 reports on the results of utilizing some firm-level data to estimate a simple portfolio model which attempts to explain changes in balance sheet flows.

John H. Ciccolo, Jr., is an economist with the Capital Market Group at Citibank Corporation and a research affiliate of the NBER. Christopher F. Baum is associate professor of economics at Boston College.

2.1   Collection and Organization of the Data

Our primary goal in this research project was to construct a micro dataset covering a substantial period of time for use in testing specific hypotheses regarding firm financing and investment decisions and the financial markets' valuations of these activities. A secondary goal was to organize and present the data in a manner that would allow other researchers conveniently to access, verify, and extend the basic dataset. To that end, the project also involved the creation of computer software to provide easy access to and retrieval of the data.

The sample of firms for the period 1926–77 is actually composed of nine separate subsamples, drawn periodically from various issues of *Moody's Industrial Manual.* The composition of these subsamples is outlined in table 2.1. The goal was to obtain nine overlapping subsamples of 50 subject firms each. Subject to restrictions on fiscal year, degree of consolidation, decipherability of complex transactions, and natural resource intensiveness, 52 firms were initially selected using a set of random numbers spanning the number of pages in each *Moody's* edition. Referring to table 2.1, 28 firms in subsamples 1–7 were deleted ex post because closer examination revealed inconsistencies with the initial selection criteria. For subsamples 8 and 9, only 77 of the 104 firms initially selected survived, due primarily to changes in accounting policies (typically resulting from acquisitions) which could not be reconciled without resort to additional data sources such as annual reports or form 10-K's.

For each firm in a subsample, the values for 52 data items are recorded annually. These items are listed and described in the Appendix. About thirty of the data items can be transcribed directly from the income account and balance sheet tables of the *Moody's* volume corresponding to the subsample (see the third column of table 2.1). For most of the remaining data items, it was generally necessary to read the additional

Table 2.1   **Sample Characteristics**

Subsample Number	Panel Number	Volume of *Moody's* (Data Source)	Number of Firms in Subsample	Years of Coverage
1	31	1931	48	5 (1926–30)
2	36	1936	46	6 (1930–35)
3	42	1942	48	7 (1935–41)
4	48	1948	47	7 (1941–47)
5	54	1954	50	7 (1947–53)
6	60	1960	50	7 (1953–59)
7	66	1966	47	7 (1959–65)
8	72	1972	37	7 (1965–71)
9	78	1978	40	7 (1971–77)

information provided in *Moody's* and to employ issues of the *Manual* from several years of the subsample. For instance, multiple issues of the *Manual* were necessarily referenced when firms retired a debt or preferred stock issue during the subsample interval. In cases where information on the outstanding amounts of individual debt issues for particular years were missing, the sinking fund terms were used to interpolate for the missing values.

The replacement value figures reported for firms' inventories (data item 45) are generally available for the firms of subsample 9 from footnotes in *Moody's* for the years 1976 and 1977. Also, a substantial fraction of firms increased the amount of inventories carried on a LIFO basis in 1974 and also reported the replacement values. To fill in data for missing years, 20 industry-level price indices were used to construct estimates in the manner suggested by Lindenberg and Ross (1981). For subsamples 7 and 8, book values of inventories were converted to replacement values using indices for the aggregate manufacturing sector. For all subsamples, book values of plant and equipment were converted to replacement values using Census Bureau deflators for the manufacturing sector. One way in which the quality of these data clearly could be improved would be to gather replacement values from form 10-K's for recent years and use industry deflators computed by other researchers for earlier years. The existing software would allow these new deflators to be integrated easily into the main body of data.

2.2   Aggregate Characteristics of the Sample

Several aspects of the recent performance of U.S. nonfinancial corporations have attracted widespread attention. Since the mid-1960s there has been a dramatic decline in the securities markets' valuations of these firms relative to the replacement costs of their assets and also relative to the returns generated by these assets (Brainard et al. 1980; Feldstein 1980). At the same time, nonfinancial corporate businesses have become more reliant on debt securities in financing their growth (Friedman 1980, pp. 21–26). The inflationary environment of the past 15 years has provided a powerful incentive for those with taxable incomes to increase their indebtedness. Additionally, as Friedman (1980) points out, the postwar trend away from internal sources of funds toward debt financing represents, at least partially, an adjustment toward more normal pre-Depression debt levels.

To place these issues in perspective, this section documents the sources and uses of funds, market valuations, and rates of return for the 1926–77 period using our sample of manufacturing firms. To present the general characteristics of the sample, a substantial amount of aggregation is performed. The balance sheets of the sample firms are consolidated as

Table 2.2   Typical Firm's Balance Sheet

Net Assets	Liabilities
Cash Items	Short-term debt
Accounts Receivable	Traded long-term debt
Inventories (replacement)	Nontraded long-term debt
Net Property (replacement)	Preferred stock
− Current Liabilities (excluding short-term debt, including accounts payable)	Common stockholder's equity
Miscellaneous items (net)	

described in table 2.2. For each firm, variables of interest—such as new debt or equity issues—are measured relative to net assets. Then firm data are averaged for each year to provide a time series for a hypothetical firm with the mean characteristics of its subsample. Table 2.3 shows the results of performing such calculations on the components of net assets for the overlapping years of the subsamples, as well as the years 1926–27 and the years 1976–77.

An interesting feature of the results presented in table 2.3 is the rather dramatic decline in the cash items variable, which is composed primarily of cash and short-term marketable securities. Considered in conjunction with the recent increase in the role of debt in corporate capital structures, the decline is even more striking. Closer inspection reveals that, at least since the mid-1960s, the fall in the share of cash items in net assets has been accompanied by an increase in the share of physical capital. The

Table 2.3   Composition of Net Assets, Selected Years

	Cash Items	Accounts Receivable	Inven- tories	Net Property	Current Liabilities & Accounts Payable	Miscel- laneous
1926–27	15.3	14.4	25.4	47.7	−7.4	4.8
1930	18.1	11.3	22.0	48.0	−5.9	6.5
1935	22.6	11.0	22.3	42.7	−7.3	9.2
1941	22.8	16.2	31.3	42.7	−20.5	7.7
1947	22.0	16.4	32.7	45.6	−21.3	6.0
1953	24.5	16.0	33.6	47.5	−26.0	4.3
1959	16.9	17.5	31.8	48.0	−19.1	5.5
1965	14.8	20.1	33.2	47.0	−21.9	6.6
1971	10.1	20.6	31.6	49.5	−19.2	7.1
1976–77	9.1	19.4	31.4	53.7	−19.3	5.5

Note: Column entries are percentages of net assets. Rows may not sum to 100% because of rounding.

drastic increase in current liabilities in 1941 was due primarily to increased corporate taxation.

2.2.1   Sources and Uses of Funds

Figure 2.1 illustrates the relative importance of internal and external funds in financing the "average" firm, while figure 2.2 depicts the role of debt among external sources of finance. In both figures, the large spikes appearing above the years 1937, 1941, 1947, 1951, 1956, and 1974 coin-

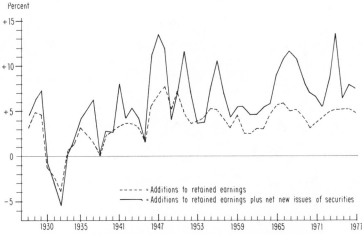

Fig. 2.1   Sources of funds as a percentage of net assets, 1927–77.

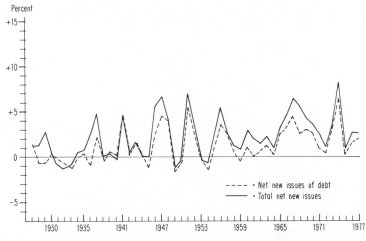

Fig. 2.2   Sources of external funds as a percentage of net assets, 1927–77.

cide with periods of unusual inventory accumulation and apparently represent a demand for external funds to finance unplanned inventories. However, this is not true for the broad spike that appears above the years 1965–68. During this period there was an unusually large demand for funds for capital expenditures and for takeovers.[1]

To highlight the longer-run trends, data on sources and uses of funds have been averaged over the individual years of the subsamples, and the results are presented in table 2.4. According to these results, net issues of debt securities remained quite constant from the 1936–41 period through the mid-1960s, when a large shift toward external sources of funds occurred. In fact, the percentage of total sources accounted for by net debt issues since 1965 is about 20, slightly more than double that in the pre-1965 period. The results of table 2.4 also clearly illustrate the increased demand for funds to finance nonfinancial activities that has occurred since the mid-1960s. Virtually all of the increase in total uses is

Table 2.4   **Sources and Uses of Funds as a Percentage of Net Assets**

	Sources						
	Total Sources	Debt Issues	Debt Retire.	Stock Issues[a]	Stock Retire.	Undis-tributed Profits	CCA
1927–30	7.3	2.4	−2.3	2.1	−.8	2.8	3.1
1931–35	2.6	.9	−1.5	.9	−.9	−.1	3.3
1936–41	7.5	2.4	−1.4	1.6	−.6	2.2	3.3
1942–47	10.3	2.8	−1.5	2.0	−.7	4.1	3.6
1948–53	11.0	2.9	−1.2	.7	−.7	5.4	3.5
1954–59	10.6	2.4	−1.4	1.5	−.5	4.4	4.2
1960–65	10.6	2.6	−1.5	1.6	−.4	3.6	4.7
1966–71	13.9	4.5	−1.5	2.1	−.3	4.6	4.6
1972–77	12.5	4.8	−2.4	1.5	−.6	4.9	4.3

	Uses						
	Total Uses	Plant/ Equip-ment	Cash Items	Inven-tories	Receiv-ables	Miscel-laneous (Net)	Current Liabilities
1927–30	6.4	5.2	1.0	−.2	−.6	.7	.3
1931–35	2.5	2.5	.3	.1	−.1	.0	−.3
1936–41	7.2	4.7	1.0	2.9	1.6	.1	−3.1
1942–47	10.6	7.8	2.6	3.2	.9	−1.8	−2.1
1948–53	10.9	7.4	2.1	2.7	1.3	−.1	−2.5
1054–59	10.4	7.1	.6	1.8	1.6	.2	−.9
1960–65	10.4	7.6	.7	1.8	1.7	.4	−1.8
1966–71	13.7	8.7	.7	3.2	2.1	1.0	−2.0
1972–77	12.7	8.6	1.4	3.1	2.4	.2	−3.0

[a]Both preferred and common shares.

accounted for by increased expenditures on physical assets. The gradual trend toward external (relative to internal) sources of funds during the earlier postwar years reflects primarily a decline in undistributed profits relative to net assets.

Several features of the 1927–30 and 1931–35 periods require comment. First, during 1927–30 there were virtually no retirements of common stock, and the -0.8 figure under stock retirements is due solely to retirements of preferred stock. Net issues of common equity were negligible except for the years 1928 and 1929. Furthermore, the plant/equipment data for the years prior to 1935 were estimated as depreciation allowances plus the change in net property account and are thus not comparable with the figures presented for later years. This latter feature accounts for the relatively large discrepancy between total uses and total sources for 1927–30. Also, the relatively low figure for undistributed profits for the 1927–30 period, 2.8% of net assets, is not indicative of low profitability, as 70% of funds available for common stock were paid out as dividends during this period.

2.2.2   Market Valuations

Securities markets provide a continuing valuation of corporations and their earnings streams and therefore, indirectly of their net assets. The ratio of market value, as determined in financial markets, to the replacement value of tangible assets has been dubbed Tobin's q, and this section investigates how q has behaved over the 1926–77 period.

Figure 2.3 plots q for the average firm in each of the nine overlapping

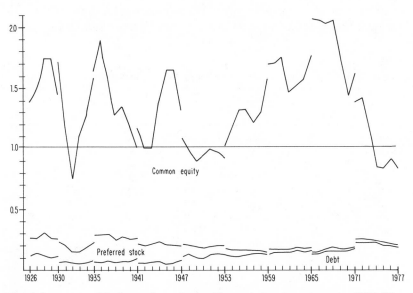

Fig. 2.3   Market value of securities, relative to net assets, 1926–77.

subsamples and also indicates the composition of the ratio as between debt, equity, and preferred stock components. For instance, the distance between the horizontal axis and the first broken line represents the market valuation of debt securities relative to net assets. To assist in interpreting the figure, table 2.5 provides the average values for the overlapping years of the subsamples, as well as for 1926–27 and 1976–77.[2] A complete listing of the data used to construct figure 2.3 appears as table 2.6.

Both table 2.5 and figure 2.3 clearly indicate the increasing importance of debt in the capital structure of the "average" corporation. It is somewhat surprising that the sum of debt and preferred stock, relative to net assets, has remained virtually constant over the entire 50-year period, suggesting that the increase in debt has come primarily at the expense of preferred stock. Another feature of figure 2.3 that clearly stands out is the sharp fall and subsequent rapid recovery of the common equity component of the ratio during the 1930–34 period. This is even more dramatic when one considers that capital goods prices were falling and thus reducing net assets and moving the ratio in the opposite direction. The figure also shows plainly the substantial decline of equity values that began in 1968. This slide in the ratio of the market value of equity relative to net assets is steeper and more prolonged than any previous decline illustrated in the diagram.

Because of significant sampling differences between the subsamples, figure 2.3 has several substantial jumps which hinder interpretation. This is especially true for the most recent years. Figure 2.4 and table 2.7 present data on q for the period 1965–77 which have been spliced to eliminate the discrete jump for 1971. The numbers for the period 1965–71 preserve their percentage changes over time but are constrained to meet

Table 2.5   **Market Value of Securities Relative to Net Assets**

	Debt	Pre-ferred	Common	Total	Debt Relative to Preferred + Common
1926–27	.120	.146	1.195	1.46	.089
1930	.089	.153	1.353	1.59	.059
1935	.068	.194	1.351	1.61	.044
1941	.076	.170	.853	1.10	.074
1947	.099	.110	1.001	1.21	.089
1953	.131	.057	.793	.98	.154
1959	.138	.026	1.474	1.64	.092
1965	.156	.015	1.775	1.95	.087
1971	.202	.028	1.275	1.51	.155
1976–77	.213	.014	.615	.84	.339

Table 2.6 Tobin's q and Its Components, 1926–77

Year	Debt Ratio	Preferred Ratio	Common Ratio	Tobin's q
1977	.211	.012	.566	.789
1976	.215	.015	.664	.894
1975	.219	.017	.597	.833
1974	.234	.025	.584	.843
1973	.230	.036	.860	1.125
1972	.225	.043	1.121	1.389
1971	.225	.044	1.076	1.345
1971	.178	.011	1.474	1.663
1970	.169	.011	1.276	1.456
1969	.165	.013	1.606	1.784
1968	.169	.017	1.793	1.978
1967	.170	.009	1.780	1.959
1966	.153	.011	1.816	1.980
1965	.144	.015	1.944	2.103
1965	.167	.016	1.606	1.789
1964	.162	.020	1.414	1.596
1963	.166	.022	1.352	1.540
1962	.161	.022	1.311	1.493
1961	.161	.022	1.601	1.784
1960	.159	.025	1.540	1.725
1959	.154	.027	1.543	1.724
1959	.122	.025	1.404	1.550
1958	.137	.030	1.125	1.291
1957	.133	.031	1.036	1.200
1956	.129	.036	1.157	1.322
1955	.114	.050	1.150	1.314
1954	.116	.048	1.003	1.166
1953	.128	.049	.857	1.033
1953	.134	.064	.730	.928
1952	.144	.066	.769	.978
1951	.128	.071	.814	1.012
1950	.098	.077	.784	.959
1949	.111	.081	.718	.910
1948	.129	.085	.776	.990
1947	.115	.103	.871	1.089
1947	.083	.116	1.132	1.330
1946	.062	.148	1.465	1.675
1945	.052	.162	1.456	1.671
1944	.066	.159	1.170	1.394
1943	.066	.150	1.033	1.250
1942	.055	.143	.821	1.018
1941	.061	.158	.965	1.185
1941	.091	.181	.744	1.015
1940	.065	.188	.960	1.212

Table 2.6 (continued)

Year	Debt Ratio	Preferred Ratio	Common Ratio	Tobin's q
1939	.069	.204	1.088	1.361
1938	.061	.197	1.028	1.286
1937	.071	.215	1.315	1.601
1936	.059	.231	1.624	1.913
1935	.071	.220	1.350	1.642
1935	.065	.168	1.353	1.587
1934	.057	.134	1.089	1.280
1933	.049	.104	.958	1.111
1932	.055	.099	.608	.762
1931	.065	.131	1.004	1.201
1930	.071	.159	1.488	1.718
1930	.107	.147	1.219	1.473
1929	.100	.157	1.514	1.771
1928	.113	.192	1.463	1.769
1927	.126	.140	1.245	1.511
1926	.114	.152	1.146	1.412

the 1971 values of the 1971–77 subsample. These adjusted results indicate that the ratio of the market value of debt to the replacement value of net assets increased moderately over the 1965–77 period.

Finally, this spliced series on q is compared, in table 2.8, with alternative estimates reported in the literature.

2.2.3   Rates of Return

This subsection presents calculations of several measures of the returns experienced by firms in the sample. Figure 2.5 compares the rate of

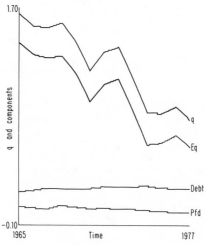

Fig. 2.4 q and components, 1965–77.

return on common stockholders' equity with the total rate of return on net assets, both rates of return measured on a replacement-cost basis. In computing both rates, an adjustment is made to place depreciation charges on a replacement-cost basis. Stockholders' equity is defined as net assets (replacement) minus the market values of debt and preferred

Table 2.7   Tobin's q and Its Components, 1965–77

Year	Debt Ratio	Preferred Ratio	Common Ratio	Tobin's q
1965	.060	.182	1.419	1.661
1966	.045	.193	1.326	1.564
1967	.035	.215	1.299	1.549
1968	.069	.213	1.309	1.591
1969	.054	.209	1.172	1.435
1970	.043	.214	.931	1.188
1971	.044	.225	1.076	1.345
1972	.043	.225	1.121	1.389
1973	.036	.230	.860	1.126
1974	.026	.234	.584	.844
1975	.017	.219	.597	.833
1976	.015	.215	.664	.894
1977	.012	.211	.566	.789

Table 2.8   Alternative Estimates of Tobin's q, 1965–77

Year	Ciccolo-Baum	Brainard-Shoven-Weiss	Economic Report of the President	Lindenberg & Ross
1965	1.661	1.740	1.360	1.960
1966	1.564	1.390	1.210	1.620
1967	1.549	1.580	1.220	1.820
1968	1.591	1.560	1.260	1.840
1969	1.435	1.300	1.120	1.610
1970	1.188	1.200	.910	1.480
1971	1.345	1.260	1.000	1.580
1972	1.389	1.370	1.080	1.630
1973	1.126	1.070	1.020	1.280
1974	.844	.690	.760	.960
1975	.833	.740	.730	1.000
1976	.894	.830	.830	.980
1977	.789	.720	.770	.880

Sources: Ciccolo-Baum: Calculations by the authors based on a sample of firms from the PANEL database; Brainard-Shoven-Weiss: *Brookings Papers on Economic Activity* 2 (1980): 466; Economic Report of the President: January 1979, table 30, p. 128; Lindenberg-Ross: in "Tobin's Q Rates and Industrial Organization," *Journal of Business* 54:1–32.

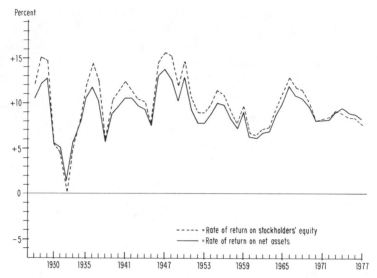

Fig. 2.5   Net rates of return, 1927–77.

stock; analogous calculations using book values yield similar figures. An inventory valuation adjustment (IVA) was not included in the figure 2.5 data because the database at present does not contain the information necessary to compute IVA prior to 1960. However, an IVA is presented in table 2.9, which compares various rates of return for the 1961–70 and 1971–77 periods. Coupled with the information presented in figure 2.3 and table 2.5, these results confirm the significant decline which has recently occurred in the securities markets' valuation of assets relative to the returns generated by those assets. When we consider the differences in sampling procedures, the rates of return (inclusive of IVA) presented in this study are close to those reported by Brainard et al. (1980, table 1, p. 463). Their estimates for the rate of return on net assets are 7.8% and 6.9% for the 1961–70 and 1971–77 periods, respectively, compared with the estimates of 8.7% and 7.5% presented in table 2.9.

The rates of return reported in table 2.9 ignore the effects of both actual and expected inflation upon the real value of the firms' financial

Table 2.9   **Rates of Return (%)**

	Rates of Return on Stockholders' Equity		Rates of Return on Net Assets	
	With IVA	Without IVA	With IVA	Without IVA
1961–70	9.3	9.7	8.7	9.1
1971–77	6.3	8.6	7.5	9.0

assets and liabilities. In particular, the component of the rate of return on net assets which reflects the tax deductibility of the inflation premium contained in nominal interest rates is not included in the calculations. Also, no allowance is made for the distributional effects of realized inflation versus anticipated inflation between creditors and stockholders. However, because the difference between paper assets and paper liabilities, relative to total net assets, is only $+0.02$ for 1961–70 and -0.055 for 1971–77, one would expect these effects to be small.

2.2.4 Conclusion

This section has presented some of the aggregate characteristics of the sample of manufacturing firms for the years 1926–77. The results, as regards the postwar period, are broadly consistent with those obtained by other researchers. That is, the data illustrate the increasing importance of external financing—particularly debt—as a source of funds for firms' real investment expenditures. The results also illustrate the dramatic decline that has occurred in the past 15 years in the securities markets' valuation of net assets relative to replacement values, and also relative to rates of return.

2.3 Balance Sheet Flows, 1966–77 and 1927–35

This section of the paper presents a simple portfolio model explaining the responses of nine balance sheet items to changes in firms' net cash flow, defined as additions to retained earnings plus depreciation allowances, and Tobin's q. The idea underlying the model is that firms face different constraints, and behave differently, when attempting to increase their stock of physical capital than when trying to reduce it. The framework for the investment model is the familiar flexible accelerator model of investment behavior which relates investment to the discrepancy between a desired and actual capital stock.

In the special case where the elasticity of the marginal product of capital with respect to the desired stock is unity, the market value of the existing capital stock provides an estimate of the desired stock. This is the rationale for relating the ratio of fixed investment to capital stock to Tobin's q. However, fixed investment expenditures represent only one use of a firm's resources, and thus only one part of the portfolio decision. The flows of other assets and liabilities must be considered simultaneously, if for no other reason than that the investment expenditures must be financed. The approach taken here is that firms simultaneously determine all asset and liability flows given a desired firm size—as represented by q—and given their cash flow, which is assumed exogenous to the portfolio decision.

The final feature to be incorporated into the model is an allowance for asymmetric behavior in expansionary and contractionary regimes. For the simplest case of a firm for which the speed of capital accumulation is limited by variable adjustment costs and for which decumulation is limited by the rate of physical depreciation, the structural parameters of the investment function would reflect the adjustment costs when net investment is positive and would be zero otherwise. Again, if there is an asymmetric response of investment to changes in the independent variables depending on whether further investment is profitable or not, then there must be an asymmetric response in at least one other balance sheet flow. To estimate such a model, then, it is necessary to classify firm observations into these two regimes. An effective way to jointly classify the observations and estimate the model's parameters is by means of a switching regression (Day 1969). We now outline this procedure.

For the two-variable case, the estimation procedure can be described as follows. Given T observations on a dependent variable y_t and an independent variable x_t, we desire to estimate for each observation the probability, p_t, that the observation is generated by one regime or the other. Let

Regime I $\qquad y_t p_t^{1/2} = \beta_1 x_t p_t^{1/2} + \epsilon_{1t} p_t^{1/2}$

Regime II $\quad y_t(1 - p_t)^{1/2} = \beta_1 x_t (1 - p_t)^{1/2} + \epsilon_{2t}(1 - p_t)^{1/2}, \; t = 1, \ldots, T,$

$$E(\epsilon_{jt}) = 0, \; E(\epsilon_{jt}^2) = \sigma^2, \; j = 1, 2 \,.$$

If we assume that a fixed proportion of the population, λ, is generated by Regime I, the likelihood of an observation can be expressed as

$$L(\beta_1, \beta_2, \lambda, \sigma^2) = \lambda L_1(\beta_1, \sigma^2) + (1 - \lambda)L_2(\beta_2, \sigma^2) \,.$$

Further assuming the ϵ_{jt} to be normal and independently distributed, the likelihood of a sample is

$$L(\beta_1, \beta_2, \lambda, \sigma^2) = \left(\frac{1}{2\pi\sigma^2}\right)^{T/2} \prod_{t=1}^{T} \left\{ \lambda \exp\left[-(y_t - \beta_1 x_t)^2/2\sigma^2\right] \right.$$

$$\left. + (1 - \lambda) \exp\left[-(y_t - \beta_2 x_t)^2/2\sigma^2\right] \right\} \,.$$

Maximizing the logarithm of this latter expression with respect to its four arguments,

$$\hat{\beta}_1 = \frac{\Sigma y_t x_t \hat{p}_t}{\Sigma x_t^2 \hat{p}_t}, \; \hat{\beta}_2 = \frac{\Sigma y_t x_t (1 - \hat{p}_t)}{\Sigma (1 - \hat{p}_t) x_t^2}, \; \hat{\lambda} = \frac{1}{T} \Sigma \hat{p}_t,$$

$$\hat{\sigma}^2 = \frac{1}{T} \Sigma[(y_t - \hat{\beta}_1 x_t)^2 \hat{p}_t + (y_t - \hat{\beta}_2 x_t)^2 (1 - \hat{p}_t)] \,.$$

Let $\text{pr}\,(I, y_t) = \hat{\lambda} \exp\left[(y_t - \hat{\beta}_1 x_t)^2/2\hat{\sigma}^2\right]$, the joint probability of Regime I and y_t, $\text{pr}\,(y_t) = \text{pr}\,(I, y_t) + (1 - \hat{\lambda}) \exp\left[(y_t - \hat{\beta}_2 x_t)^2/2\sigma^2\right]$, the marginal probability of y_t; then $\hat{p}_t = \text{pr}\,(I,\,y_t)/\text{pr}\,(\,y_t)$, the conditional probability of Regime I given y_t.

To obtain the empirical results presented below, a switching regression relating investment to q and net cash flow is estimated iterating on the four first-order conditions as described by Kiefer (1980). Given these estimated parameters, the $\hat{p}_t$ are computed and used to weight the observations in the regressions which explain changes in other balance sheet items.

2.3.1   Data

To apply the procedure outlined above, data from the first two panels, 1931 and 1936, and the last two panels, 1972 and 1978, were combined to give 9 annual observations (1927–35) for the earlier period and 12 (1966–77) for the later period. To make the data in two neighboring panels more compatible, information on firms that overlap was used to adjust the means of the nonoverlapping firms in each separate period. This is done assuming, for each variable, that had a nonoverlapping firm been represented in both panels, its mean would have changed between panels in the same way as for the average overlapping firm. For the earlier period there are 12 overlapping firms, and 11 in the later period.

Tobin's q is adjusted and redefined for each firm as the ratio of observed q to the mean value of q over the particular sample period. This is done to correct for persistent deviations of q above unity due to the capitalization of monopoly rents. The q variable enters the regressions with a lag of 1 year, while the net cash flow variable enters contemporaneously. All variables are measured as deviations around firm means.

2.3.2   Balance Sheet Flow Definitions

The nine dependent variables of interest, measured in current period prices, are

1. Investment: additions at cost.
2. Δcash assets: Δ[total current assets minus inventories minus accounts receivable].
3. Δinventories: Δ[FIFO inventories] minus capital gains (estimated residually for 1927–35).
4. Δnet accounts receivable: [accounts receivable minus accounts payable].
5. Δother long-term assets: Δ[book value of plant and equipment minus additions at cost plus excess of cost over book value of acquisitions] (estimated residually for 1966–77).
6. Δshort-term debt: Δ[debt due in less than one year].
7. Δlong-term debt: long-term debt issues minus retirements.
8. Δcommon equity: [equity issues minus equity retirements].
9. Δother short-term liabilities: Δ[total current liabilities minus accounts payable].

These variables are all measured relative to total net assets, lagged 1 period. Due to the balance sheet constraint, an unit increase in cash flow will result in a unit increase in the difference between the sum of the asset flows and the sum of the liability flows, whereas a unit increase in q will leave this difference unchanged.

2.3.3 Results for 1966–77

The results of estimating the investment switching regression, computing the regime probabilities, and employing them in estimating equations for the other eight balance sheet flow items for the 1966–77 period appear in table 2.10. The estimate of the mixing parameter, λ, is 0.302, which indicates that about 30% of the observations are classified into Regime I (expansion) and about 70% into Regime II (contraction). The parameter estimates indicate substantial differences in balance sheet flows, resulting from changes in both q and cash flow (CF), between regimes. With the exception of net accounts receivable, the Regime I coefficients for q are larger for all flow items than those for Regime II, and, with the exception of cash assets, the same is true for the CF coefficients.

The Regime I results indicate that substantial portfolio reallocations take place in response to increases in q and CF. On the asset side of the balance sheet, the largest responses to changes in both q and CF are in

Table 2.10   **Balance Sheet Flows Due to Unit Increase in q or Net Cash Flow (CF) (Manufacturing Firms, 1966–77)**

Assets			Liabilities		
Flows	q	CF	Flows	q	CF
A. Regime I ($\lambda = .302$):					
Investment	.038	1.75	Δshort-term debt	.035	.386
Δcash assets	−.006	−.015	Δlong-term debt	.098	1.44
Δinventories	.028	.840	Δcommon equity	.024	.779
Δnet accounts receivable	.009	.170	Δother short term	.001	.324
Δother long term	.083	1.19			
Sums	.152	3.93	Sums	.158	2.92
B. Regime II ($[1 - \lambda] = .698$):					
Investment	.019	.237	Δshort-term debt	.017	.018
Δcash assets	−.014	.204	Δlong-term debt	.061	.203
Δinventories	.017	.494	Δcommon equity	.001	.177
Δnet accounts receivable	.012	.138	Δother short term	−.007	.284
Δother long term	.036	.574			
Sums	.070	1.65	Sums	.072	.682

Note: The difference between asset and liability column sums may not add to zero or one due to rounding.

real assets: plant and equipment, inventories, and other long-term assets. Recalling that other long-term assets primarily represent acquisitions, it is not surprising that its q coefficient is larger than that reported for investment expenditures. On the liability side, this increase in fixed assets is accompanied primarily by increases in long-term debt and common equity.

Contrary to prior expectations, cash flow is a more important variable in classifying observations between regimes than q, the respective standard deviations of CF and q being 0.02 and 0.30.

Figures 2.6–2.9 plot the results of aggregating the variables of the investment equation across firms, by regime, using the estimated classification probabilities as weights. That is, the label p^*q is $\Sigma_i \hat{p}_{it} q_{it}$. Given the underlying model, the appropriate variables to include in equations explaining aggregate balance sheet flow variables would be P^*q, $(1 - P)^*q$, P^*CF, and $(1 - P)^*CF$. This procedure would account for the changing distribution of firms by regime.

For example, it can be seen from figure 2.8 that while aggregate q was falling during 1973, the proportion of firms classified into Regime I increased dramatically, actually increasing P^*q. This provides a possible explanation for the fact that investment was increasing during a period when aggregate q was falling.

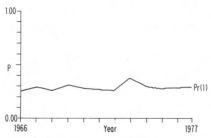

Fig. 2.6   Regime proportions, 1966–77.

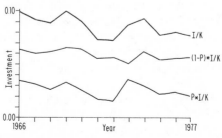

Fig. 2.7   Investment/assets, 1966–77.

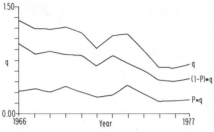

Fig. 2.8 q and its components, 1966–77.

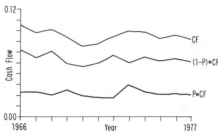

Fig. 2.9   Cash flow/assets, 1966–77.

2.3.4   Results for 1927–35

The same set of regression equations was estimated for the years 1927–35, but for this earlier period the sample is split into durable-goods and nondurable-goods firms. For the 1966–77 period the difference in results due to this disaggregation was sufficiently minor to warrant pooling the firms. For the earlier period, there are significant timing differences in the peaks and troughs of many of the variables. The 1927–35 results appear in table 2.11 (durables) and table 2.12 (nondurables). Figures 2.10–2.17 plot the results of aggregating the variables of the investment equation across firms, by regimes, using the estimated classification probabilities as weights.

For both durable and nondurable goods samples the observations are about evenly divided between regimes. Qualitatively, the results for the durable-goods sample are very similar to the results reported for 1966–77, but quantitatively unit changes in q and CF do not induce such large portfolio reallocations. This can be explained, at least in part, by firms' greater reliance on internal sources of funds in the earlier period.

On the other hand, the results for the nondurable-goods sample indicate that the data are inconsistent with our underlying model. While there is some difference in the coefficient estimates across regimes, these

Table 2.11   **Balance Sheet Flows Due to Unit Increase in q or Net Cash Flow (CF) (Durable-Goods Firms, 1927–35)**

	Assets			Liabilities	
Flows	q	CF	Flows	q	CF
A. Regime I ($\lambda = .487$):					
Investment	.038	.388	Δshort-term debt	.003	.038
Δcash assets	−.013	.131	Δlong-term debt	.009	.079
Δinventories	.003	.641	Δcommon equity	.011	.093
Δnet accounts receivable	−.008	.164	Δother short term	−.014	.092
Δother long term	−.004	−.006			
Sums	.016	1.31	Sums	.009	.303
B. Regime II ($[1 - \lambda] = .513$):					
Investment	.018	.085	Δshort-term debt	.008	.007
Δcash assets	−.026	.186	Δlong-term debt	.008	−.065
Δinventories	.026	.663	Δcommon equity	.009	.032
Δnet accounts receivable	−.006	.067	Δother short term	−.014	.055
Δother long term	−.002	.028			
Sums	.010	1.03	Sums	.011	.029

Note: The difference between asset and liability column sums may not add to zero or one due to rounding.

Table 2.12   **Balance Sheet Flows Due to Unit Increase in q or Net Cash Flow (CF) (Nondurable-Goods Firms, 1927–35)**

	Assets			Liabilities	
Flows	q	CF	Flows	q	CF
A. Regime I ($\lambda = .546$):					
Investment	.016	.238	Δshort-term debt	−.008	.067
Δcash assets	−.014	.068	Δlong-term debt	−.002	.088
Δinventories	−.043	.984	Δcommon equity	−.008	.185
Δnet accounts receivable	−.004	.111	Δother short term	−.018	.069
Δother long term	.010	.021			
Sums	−.035	1.42	Sums	−.036	.409
B. Regime II ($[1 - \lambda] = .454$):					
Investment	.017	.032	Δshort-term debt	−.008	.041
Δcash assets	−.023	.142	Δlong-term debt	.003	−.054
Δinventories	−.038	.931	Δcommon equity	−.011	.216
Δnet accounts receivable	−.002	.101	Δother short term	−.016	.061
Δother long term	.008	.057			
Sums	−.038	1.26	Sums	−.032	.264

Note: The difference between asset and liability column sums may not add to zero or one due to rounding.

differences do not provide much discriminatory power because of relatively large standard errors of estimate.

Examining the figures which plot the aggregate variables for the 1927–35 period, one can see that the timing, at turning points, between our independent variables and investment is not very supportive of the underlying model. Figures 2.12, 2.13, and 2.14 clearly show, for instance, that investment started its long decline at least one year before q and CF. Also, investment bottomed out in 1932, while q reached its minimum in 1933.

2.4   Summary and Conclusions

This paper has reported the results of a research project which involved collecting and organizing income account and balance sheet data, at the firm level, for the years 1926–77. Aggregate characteristics of the sample, including sources and uses of funds, financial market valuations, and rates of return, were presented and discussed. Another section of the paper presented the results of estimating a simple portfolio model, explaining a number of balance sheet flows using the firm-level data.

The dataset should provide other researchers with a rich source of information against which specific hypotheses regarding corporate financing and investment decisions can be tested.

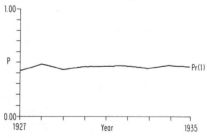

Fig. 2.10   Regime proportions, durables.

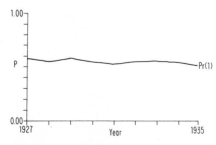

Fig. 2.11   Regime proportions, nondurables.

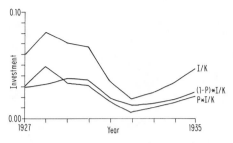

Fig. 2.12   Investment/assets, durables.

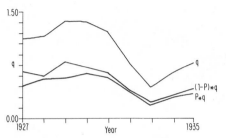

Fig. 2.13 q and its components, durables.

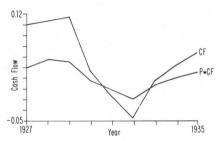

Fig. 2.14a   Regime I, cash flow/assets, durables.

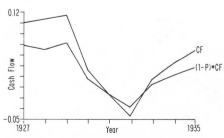

Fig. 2.14b   Regime II, cash flow/assets, durables.

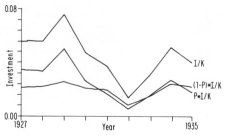

Fig. 2.15   Investment/assets, nondurables.

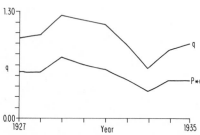

Fig. 2.16a   Regime I, q and its components, nondurables.

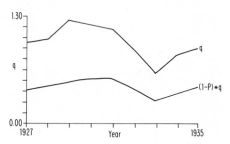

Fig. 2.16b   Regime II, q and its components, nondurables.

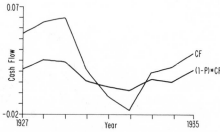

Fig. 2.17a   Regime I, cash flow/assets, nondurables.

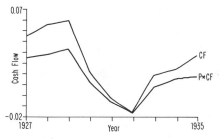

Fig. 2.17b   Regime II, cash flow/assets, nondurables.

Appendix

Description of the PANEL Data Set

The PANEL Data System provides income and balance sheet data on a sample of manufacturing firms for the years 1926–77. The sample of firms is actually composed of nine separate subsamples (panels) drawn periodically from various editions of *Moody's Industrial Manual*. The general composition of the sample is outlined in table 2.1.

The goal was to obtain randomly drawn subsamples of size 50, but this was not possible for all panels given our requirements regarding accounting procedures. These criteria involve fiscal year, degree of consolidation, and, in the cases of firms purchasing other firms, accounting based on a pooling of interest. Also, natural-resource-intensive firms are excluded.

The large quantity and several dimensions of these data necessitate a second component of the PANEL Data System—an integrated set of computer programs which enable the user to access the data in each of several modes and manipulate it for research purposes.

This section of the Appendix describes the data available in each of the nine panels. Section A.1 describes the original, or raw, data and section A.2 describes the transformations that are currently contained in the PANEL Data System.

A.1   Raw Data

Fifty-two items of raw data are available for each firm in each panel. The first line is a firm header card giving the year of the panel (e.g., 1972), an eight-letter firm identification code, the firm's name, a durable/nondurable classification, the bond rating of the most recently issued debt security, and the page number from *Moody's* from which the firm's data was generated. The bond rating symbol NR indicates that the firm's debt is unrated. An example of a header card from the 1954 panel of data is

PANEL 1954 BRISTOL-MYERS CO. [n A p. 1362.]

Following each header card, there are 51 lines of raw numerical data. For instance, the line following the header card listed above is

01 55462,56611,61617,52266,42778,45308,44655 .

Item 01 is sales and the data are in thousands of dollars, for years 1953, 1952, . . . , 1947. Thus, in 1953 Bristol-Myers had sales of $55,462,000. In 1947, sales were $44,655,000.

Section A.3 of the Appendix lists the variable symbols as they appear on printed output, along with a brief description of each of the 52 data items.

Most of the 52 raw data items listed are self-explanatory. However, some of the data items require additional explanation, and this is done below. Also, some of the data items are not available for each of the nine panels. These exceptions are also discussed below.

Data Item 23, SPLIT V.

This variable records information on the stock splits and stock dividends. For a firm which splits its stock two for one, SPLIT V would equal two. If the firm pays a 10% stock dividend, this V variable would take on the value 1.10. The main use of SPLIT V is in allowing one to distinguish between issues and retirements of common equity, on the one hand, and splits and stock dividends on the other. Thus, this variable must be used in computing new issues and retirements of equity.

Data Item 24, PF NONT.

PF NONT is the amount of preferred dividends associated with a firm's nontraded preferred stock. To value nontraded preferred stock, PF NONT is capitalized by a preferred dividend-price ratio which is user supplied. Currently, the PANEL Data System contains a preferred dividend price ratio corresponding to *Moody's* "medium grade industrials."

Data Items 38 and 42.

These items give the coupon, maturity date, date of issue, date on which sinking fund begins, amount authorized, and amount outstanding for the traded debt issues number 1 and 2, respectively.

Data Item 45.

This data item gives an estimate of the replacement value of a firm's inventories. The estimates in many cases are actually provided by the firms themselves in footnotes to the *Moody's* tables. When the only information available is the proportion of inventories in LIFO and the length of time LIFO has been used, one of 20 available price indices is used to estimate the replacement value of LIFO inventories. FIFO inventories are assumed to equal replacement value.

Data Item 46.

This variable is the reported proportion of a firm's inventories that is under the LIFO accounting method.

Data Item 47.

This is the price index associated with a firm's FIFO inventories. It is used to compute an IVA. It is not necessarily the same price index that is used in constructing a replacement estimate for the LIFO portion of inventories.

Availability of Data Items.

All 52 data items are not available for all panels. Items 45–51 are available only for the 1978 panel (years 1971–77). Item 19, additions at cost, and item 1, sales, are not reported for the 1931 and 1936 panels. Data item 1 for the 1931 and 1936 panels is replaced with the variable "income taxes."

A.2   Variable Transformations

The PANEL Data System permits the user to define up to 76 variable transformations. The current version of subroutine AGGREG contains 53 transformations. In performing transformations the user can introduce external data via the data file AGGREG. Currently, a capital stock deflator (DEFL), preferred stock dividend-price ratio (PDIV), inventory deflator (PIN), and bond price index (BONDP) are present in the AGGREG file. DEFL is used to convert firms' capital stock (data item 14), which is measured on a historical cost basis, to a replacement cost basis; PIN serves a similar function for inventories. PDIV is the (medium-grade industrial) preferred dividend-price ratio used to capitalize the dividends paid on the nontraded preferred stock. BONDP is a bond price index.

The transformations currently programmed are listed in section 4 of the Appendix.

The PANEL data system software provides access to the data, computation of various averages, and regression of PANEL variables. The PANEL software and data set is available from the authors in either an IBM 370 or VAX 11/780 format for a nominal fee.

A.3   Listing of the PANEL Data Items

1 : SALES   Net sales
2 : OPER INC   Income from operations
3 : TOT PFT   Total income before interest and taxes
4 : INT EXP   Interest expense
5 : DEPREC   Depreciation (as reported in property acc'ts.)
6 : NET INC   Net income (avail. for pref/common
                        dividends)
7 : PREF DIV   Preferred dividends
8 : COMM DIV   Common dividends
9 : MAINT   Expenditures for Maintenance and repairs
10 : ACC RECV   Accounts receivable
11 : INVENTRY   Inventory, book value
12 : TOT C.A.   Total current assets
13 : GROS PLT   Gross property account, book value
14 : NET PLT   Net property account, book value
15 : TOT ASST   Total assets (excluding intangibles)
16 : 1YR LIAB   Short-term debt and debt due in one year
17 : ACC PAY   Accounts payable
18 : TOT C.L.   Total current liabilities
19 : ADD COST   Additions at cost (gross P + E expenditures)
20 : HI PRICE   High price of common stock for year
21 : LO PRICE   Low price of common stock for year
22 : NR COMMN   Number of common shares at year end
23 : SPLIT V   Variable to adjust for stock splits, dividends
24 : PF NONT   Dividends on nontraded preferred stock
25 : PFD 1 HI   High price, first traded preferred stock issue
26 : PFD 1 LO   Low price, first traded preferred stock issue
27 : NR PFD 1   Number of shares, first traded preferred issue
28 : PFD 2 HI   High price, second traded preferred issue
29 : PFD 2 LO   Low price, second traded preferred issue
30 : NR PFD 2   Number of shares, second traded preferred
                        issue
31 : CV NONT   Nontraded convertible debt, book value
32 : CV TRAD   Traded convertible debt, book value
33 : CV 1 HI   High price of traded convertible debt
34 : CV 1 LO   Low price of traded convertible debt
35 : DET 1 HI   High price, first traded debt issue
36 : DET 1 LO   Low price, first traded debt issue
37 : DET VAL   Book value, first traded debt issue
38 : ITEM 38   (See text)
39 : DET 2 HI   High price, second traded debt issue
40 : DET 2 LO   Low price, second traded debt issue
41 : ITEM 41   Book value, second traded debt issue

42 : ITEM 42   (See text)
43 : NT LDEBT   Book value, nontraded debt
44 : TOT LTD   Total book value of all long-term debt
45 : ITEM 45   Inventory at replacement value
46 : ITEM 46   Proportion of inventories in LIFO
47 : ITEM 47   Price index for FIFO portion of inventories
48 : ITEM 48   Deferred taxes
49 : ITEM 49   Deferred compensation (incl. unfunded
                       pensions)
50 : ITEM 50   Minority interest
51 : ITEM 51   Other long-term liabilities
52 : Durable   Durable / nondurable indictor

A.4   Listing of the PANEL Transformations

# 1 (Firmavg # 53) : TOT NASS	Total net assets (TA)
# 2 (Firmavg # 54) : MV DEBTR	Mkt. value debt/TA
# 3 (Firmavg # 55) : MV PREFR	Mkt. value preferred/TA
# 4 (Firmavg # 56) : MV EqtyR	Mkt. value equity/TA
# 5 (Firmavg # 57) : Q	Tobin's q (#1 + #2 + #3)
# 6 (Firmavg # 58) : CASH R	Cash assets/TA
# 7 (Firmavg # 59) : MISC R	Misc. net assets/TA
# 8 (Firmavg # 60) : INVT R	Inventories/TA
# 9 (Firmavg # 61) : Liab R	S.T. liabilities/TA
# 10 (Firmavg # 62) : RECV R	Net receivables/TA
# 11 (Firmavg # 63) : REPL R	Plt. + equip.(repl.)/TA
# 12 (Firmavg # 64) : INV/CAP	Inventory(book)/TA
# 13 (Firmavg # 65) : DEF TAX	Deferred taxes/TA
# 14 (Firmavg # 66) : Oth Liab	Other liabilities/TA
# 15 (Firmavg # 67) : MIN INT	Minority interest/TA
# 16 (Firmavg # 68) : CFLO R	(Internal use)
# 17 (Firmavg # 69) : PF ISSUE	Value new pref. issues/TA
# 18 (Firmavg # 70) : PF RETIR	Cost retirements, pref./TA
# 19 (Firmavg # 71) : Eq Issue	Value new equity issues/TA
# 20 (Firmavg # 72) : EQ RETIR	Cost retirements, equity/TA
# 21 (Firmavg # 73) : DET NEW	Value new debt issues/TA
# 22 (Firmavg # 74) : DET RETR	Cost retirements, debt/TA
# 23 (Firmavg # 75) : RE	Add. to retained earnings/TA
# 24 (Firmavg # 76) : CF	Cash flow/TA
# 25 (Firmavg # 77) : GG	(Internal use)
# 26 (Firmavg # 78) : GN	(Internal use)
# 27 (Firmavg # 79) : IG	Additions to plant + equipment/TA
# 28 (Firmavg # 80) : DEPR	Depreciation/TA
# 29 (Firmavg # 81) : ACQ	(Internal use)

# 30 (Firmavg # 82) : IGA	(Internal use)
# 31 (Firmavg # 83) : DC	Change in cash assets/TA
# 32 (Firmavg # 84) : DM	Change in misc. assets/TA
# 33 (Firmavg # 85) : DINV	Change in inventory/TA
# 34 (Firmavg # 86) : DCL	Change in current liabs./TA
# 35 (Firmavg # 87) : DREC	Change in net. acct.recv./TA
# 36 (Firmavg # 88) : XGG	(Internal use)
# 37 (Firmavg # 89) : YGG	(Internal use)
# 38 (Firmavg # 90) : DVR	Dividend/price ratio, common
# 39 (Firmavg # 91) : CG	Capital gain on common share
# 40 (Firmavg # 92) : DK	Common dividends/TA
# 41 (Firmavg # 93) : PFK	Preferred dividends/TA
# 42 (Firmavg # 94) : INK	Interest payments/TA
# 43 (Firmavg # 95) : FG1	(Internal use)
# 44 (Firmavg # 96) : NtDt Rat	Nontraded debt/TA
# 45 (Firmavg # 97) : ZGG	(Internal use)
# 46 (Firmavg # 98) : STDT RAT	Short-term debt/TA
# 47 (Firmavg # 99) : BOND IND	Bond index
# 48 (Firmavg # 100) : FIFO PR	Proportion of inventories FIFO
# 49 (Firmavg # 101) : I V A	Inventory valuation adjustment
# 50 (Firmavg # 102) : Aggr 50	(Internal use)
# 51 (Firmavg # 103) : Aggr 51	(Internal use)
# 52 (Firmavg # 104) : Aggr 52	(Internal use)
# 53 (Firmavg # 105) : Aggr 53	(Internal use)

Notes

1. Takeovers show up on the balance sheet in miscellaneous items as this variable contains the difference between the actual cost of an acquisition and its book value. Generally, acquisitions exceeding 10% of the purchasing firm's net assets disqualified the firm from the sample.

2. Debt due in less than 1 year is valued at book. Nontraded long-term debt is valued using a bond price index generated for each year for each subsample.

References

Brainard, William C.; Shoven, J. B.; and Weiss, L. 1980. The financial valuation of the return to capital. *Brookings Papers on Economic Activity* 2:453–502.

Day, N. E. 1969. Estimating the components of a mixture of normal distributions. *Biometrika* 56:463–74.

Feldstein, Martin. 1980. Inflation and the stock market. *American Economic Review* 70:839–47.

Friedman, Benjamin M. 1980. Postwar changes in American financial markets. In *The American economy in transition*, ed. Feldstein, Martin. Chicago: University of Chicago Press.

Kiefer, Nicholas M. 1980. A note on switching regressions and logistic discrimination. *Econometrica* 48:1065–69.

Lindenberg, Eric B., and Ross, S. 1981. Tobin's *q* and industrial organization. *Journal of Business* 54:1–32.

Comment   Franco Modigliani

In this paper, Ciccolo and Baum report on their endeavor to collect income accounts and balance sheet data for a sample of industrial firms over the span from 1926 to 1977. They also give a number of results based on the analysis of these data. I will first comment briefly on their sampling procedure and their method of estimating various components of the balance sheet and of the income statement. The rest of my comments will deal with section 2.2, in which they report information on the structure of the balance sheet and its changes over the period, and on the composition of the sources and uses of funds and its changes. I will focus particularly on their discussion of the changing structure of the liability side.

The essence of Ciccolo and Baum's approach is to collect the basic data for each firm with utmost care. But given limited resources, in order to achieve this goal, they had to confine themselves to a rather modest sample of firms. Their target was a sample of 52 firms, but some of the firms had to be discarded for various reasons, and that left them with samples mostly just below 50.

Given the smallness of the sample, one might have expected that Ciccolo and Baum would have tried to oversample large firms—for instance, by sampling dollar of sales or dollar of assets, rather than firms. However, one gathers that in effect they sampled pages of *Moody's*. This procedure would give, presumably, more chance to larger firms to appear in the sample, but only to the extent that larger firms usually occupy more space in *Moody's*. On the whole, one has a feeling that their sample may be somewhat thin in the sense of being subject to significant sampling fluctuations.

Ciccolo and Baum's sampling design makes it possible to throw some light on this conjecture. In fact, their procedure consists in changing the

Franco Modigliani is Institute Professor and professor of economics and finance at the Massachusetts Institute of Technology.

sample of firms every 5 years, but with 1-year overlap. For instance, the first sample covers the years 1926–30, while the second covers the years 1930–35. Thus, for the year 1930, for 1935, and for every seventh year thereafter, we have information available from two different samples. In figure 2.3, one can compare some statistics for the outgoing and incoming samples. The top graph exhibits the ratio of the market value of all securities to the value of net of assets, at reproduction cost (basically, Tobin's q). In the two lower graphs, the numerator of the ratio is, respectively, debt plus preferred stock and debt only. It is apparent that there are nonnegligible differences in the value of these ratios at points of overlap. This fact raises some questions about the reliability of the statistics computed from the sample and creates further problems on appropriate methods of "splicing" the various samples. The authors seem generally to handle this problem by using, for every year of overlap, the mean of the two samples. Unfortunately, this procedure is very questionable, and possibly very misleading, raising serious problems in the interpretation of the results, as I shall point out shortly.

In table 2.2, the authors analyze the structure of the assets for the years of overlap (where the sample is roughly twice as large as in other years), plus the end points. I would like to remark on the classification of assets and liabilities in the table. Specifically, I have some qualms about the treatment of net current liabilities (except short-term debts) as a deduction from assets (a negative use) rather than as a source of funds. This practice is appealing in the sense that it leaves, on the sources side, only market instruments: debt, preferred stock, and equity. However, this procedure does tend to produce a distorted picture of the importance of individual assets and its change in time, at least when, as in the case of table 2.2, the share of "net current liabilities" has almost tripled early in the period. I note that many of the apparent movements in asset composition in table 2.2—some of them stressed by the authors—largely disappear when the shares are corrected by excluding "current liabilities." This holds for the overall trend of net property and much of the trend in net receivables. Even the large rise and fall in the cash items share is considerably flattened, though the decline over the postwar period as a whole remains impressive. This trend may, at least partly, reflect more efficient cash management induced by higher interest rates and computer technology. A part of this decline shows up as a rise in the net property share, but only in the last decade; over the entire period, on the other hand, this share has changed remarkably little.

Let me now come to the issue of leverage and its behavior during the recent period of rising inflation. This is an issue that is central both to the Ciccolo and Baum and the Taggart papers. The former cite Friedman's statement (1980) as an undisputed fact that since the mid-1960s "nonfinancial corporate businesses have become more reliant on debt securities in financing their growth" and that the "inflationary environment of the past 15 years has provided a powerful incentive for those with taxable incomes to increase their indebtedness." Similarly, Taggart states that "corporations' use of debt has undeniably increased in the post–World War II"—although both sets of authors do mention that current leverage is not out of line—and indeed may be low—in comparison with prewar and, more particularly, pre-Depression periods.

Now, I completely agree with the authors that all models of rational behavior, except possibly the recent model of Miller, do suggest that, under the present structure of the corporate and personal tax system, inflation gives a strong incentive to increase leverage if management is concerned with maximizing the market value of the firm and if at the same time markets behave rationally. In my view, however, markets have not behaved rationally during the last inflationary decade; they have tended to underestimate the profitability of levered corporations by failing to adjust profits adequately for the inflationary premium incorporated in nominal interest rates (see Modigliani and Richard Cohn 1979). As a result, levered firms have tended, on the whole, to be undervalued in the market, and that has counteracted the tax incentives to leverage. I would not, therefore, be surprised to find that, despite the inflation-induced increases in the gain, leverage has not appreciably increased over the last decade. Previous contributions have suggested that the evidence is consistent with this view (see e.g., references in the above paper). What I would like to argue is that, despite Ciccolo and Baum's statements, neither their evidence nor Taggart's supports the conclusion that leverage has significantly increased in the course of the inflation which began in the mid-1960s.

In the case of both papers, the evidence is of two kinds: stocks and flows. With respect to stocks, they measure the proportion of total financing that takes the form of debt, or debt plus preferred stock. With respect to flows, they examine the share of total sources of funds which consists of net new issues of debt instruments.

In the case of the stock analysis, one faces the issue of what is the aggregate amount to be financed against which the outstanding debt should be compared. As is well known, the three alternative measures are the book value of assets, the market value of assets as measured by the market value of the liabilities, and the reproduction costs of assets. These three measures would coincide in an ideal world of no inflation, no significant technological change, and no significant oligopolistic profits. Taggart actually gives all three measures even though the book value measure is, in my view, totally worthless and misleading in an economy which has experienced inflation as high, and for as long, as the American economy. It is certain to underestimate, on the average, the true value of assets as measured by any sensible economic measure, and to do so more and more as inflation increases. It is therefore not surprising, but also totally uninformative, that when one uses this measure, one finds that the ratio of debt to the book value of assets has risen during the recent inflation.

The relevant choice, therefore, is between reproduction cost and market valuation. In the long run, of course, these two measures should tend to coincide—that is, Tobin's q (or at least marginal q) should tend to unity. But the problem with reproduction cost, aside from the difficulties of estimating it, lies in the fact that assets may, to some extent, be obsolete and that, therefore, no one would want to reproduce them—that is, their true economic value falls below reproduction costs. One might expect that this true value would tend to be captured by market valuation, and in this sense, the ratio of debt to market valuation may appear to be the most effective way of measuring leverage. On the other hand, what we are interested in measuring is leverage policy, or the desired financial structure which, one hopes, is only changing slowly over time. It is questionable that this desired structure can be reflected adequately in the ratio of debt to market valuation, which is swayed by the volatile market valuation of equity. On the other hand, the ratio of debt to reproduction cost should provide relevant information on leverage policy in the sense that current financial decisions must bear on the composition of funds needed to finance the current acquisition of assets which, clearly, must be at (re)production cost. So, insofar as firms do tend to have a consistent and stable policy with respect to financing of assets, then that ought to be reflected in the balance sheet at reproduction cost. To be sure, the reproduction cost measure will also be subject to a certain noise. But there is no reason to suppose that it will be systematically biased as a measure of target leverage—at least when this measure is more stable than the ratio based on market value.

Ciccolo and Baum's data are set forth in table 2.5, which gives the ratios of debt preferred and common stock at market value to the reproduction cost of net assets. The first impression that one may gather from this table (which is reinforced by the authors' comments) is that the debt ratio rose steadily from a low point in 1935 up to 1965—more than doubling—and that, since 1965, it has risen further, by another third, in the course of the recent inflation, to reach a peak in 1976–77.

One must first note that there are many features of their table that appear quite puzzling. One is the behavior of Tobin's q given in column 4. It would appear that the ratio of market value to reproduction cost was higher in both 1930 and 1935 than it was in 1926 and 1927, as well as in just about every other year except 1965 and marginally in 1959. Another puzzle is that the debt ratio in column 1 is a good deal lower, at least through 1959, than is suggested by other data, such as those reported by Taggart in his table 1.3. On the other hand, the preferred stock ratio is amazingly high, at least until 1953. On the whole, the sum of debt and preferred appears to behave more reasonably than either of its components and also is a good deal more stable. But, even if one confines oneself to the behavior of the debt ratio, one can see, by comparing table 2.4 and figure 2.3, that the systematic rise in leverage, beginning with 1965, which is exhibited in the first column of table 2.4, is largely the result of the doubtful procedure adopted in splicing together overlapping samples. Specifically, the higher ratio reported for 1971 and 1976–77 over 1965 reflects the shift in 1971 to a new sample which had a larger debt ratio (as well as a very much larger preferred stock ratio). To be sure, the 1965 sample does indicate a modest rise in leverage until 1971. But then the 1971 sample shows a roughly equal decrease between 1971 and 1977. For the sum of preferred and debt, the stability of the share is even greater; it was roughly the same at the end of the period as it was in 1965 on the basis of the 1959 sample. On the whole, there does seem to be a substantial rise in leverage between the war period and 1965, that is, during the period of relative price stability. This rise could be accounted for by a gradual return toward the pre-Depression target leverage which had been greatly reduced by the fiscal and financial policies of the war period. But, from that time on, there is no more systematic growth in leverage through 1976. This picture is supported by Taggart's data on the ratio of debt to assets at replacement cost reported in his table 1.3. The figures of columns 2 and 3 show that the debt ratio did rise somewhat from the low point at the end of the war through the 1950s and the first half of the 1960s. To be sure, his data do show a rise in the last 2 years, but, since that estimate comes from another source which is available for just 2 years, I would hesitate to make much of this small rise.

The picture is rather different if we look at the ratio of debt to market value. Taggart's estimates in table 1.2 reveal a rather substantial rise from 1965 through the late 1970s, especially if for the First War period one relies on the von Furstenberg's estimates in columns 2 and 3. Similar results were reported by Ciccolo and Baum in a table which has been dropped from the final version.

However, as pointed out earlier, the ratio of debt to the market value of the firm can not be regarded as a reliable measure of target leverage because it is largely swayed by movements in the market value of equity. This is particularly true for the more recent period since 1965. In particular, comparing the leverage measured at market value with the leverage measured at production cost suggests that the rise in the market value measure reflects to a large extent the depressing effect of inflation on the stock market, which by now is well documented, even if there still may be some disagreement as to the best way of explaining it.

When one comes to the evidence provided by the source of fund flows, the situation is very different. Taggart's table 1.4 shows an enormous rise, roughly a doubling, in the ratio of total debt to total sources from the war years to the 1950s, and another 50% rise from the 1950s to 1970s. Ciccolo and Baum's figures in table 2.4 also show a very substantial rise in net issues of debt, at least since the mid-1960s. But I was amazed to discover that both sets of figures are meaningless because they are not adjusted for inflation. We know, in fact, that with rational markets (and nondistorting taxes) Fisher's law holds, increasing the interest bill by pD. Hence, the after-interest cash flow goes down by pD, which amount, in turn, represents a compensation to lenders, because the real debt decreases to that extent. Thus, in order to maintain the initial flow of (real) investment, and dividends, and an *unchanged* real debt and leverage, firms have to increase their debt by pD more than without inflation. Or, equivalently, to find out whether leverage is changing, one has to adjust the change in nominal debt by subtracting pD, which amount must, at the same time, be added back to measured gross internal funds, because true profits, and hence retained profits, are underestimated by pD. (The same result should roughly hold, even under the current [distorting] American tax system, except that Fisher's law has to be replaced by a generalization sometimes labeled "Super Fisher's" law).

The size of the bias in relative share of debt financing generated by failure to make the proper inflation corection depends on the rate of inflation, the size of leverage, and the rate of real growth. While I have not attempted to make that correction, rough calculation sugests that both for Taggart and for Ciccolo and Baum, much of the apparent growth in the share of debt financing since 1965 would disappear with the proper adjustment.

I conclude, therefore, that there is no convincing evidence that target leverage has changed appreciably since the beginning of inflation in the second half of the 1960s, even though most theories would suggest that inflation does increase the tax avoidance benefits that can be reaped from leverage. As I suggested earlier, one possible explanation for the discrepancy between what one should expect and what happened could be inflation fallacies, in the guise of confusion between nominal and real interest rates. To be sure, Miller's model could also be consistent with this evidence since, in that model, leverage would presumably have no value, in equilibrium, independently of the rate of inflation. But I find that model unacceptable in terms of explaining observed facts. For, if the total market value of firms were, in fact, independent of leverage, then investors in low tax brackets would have an advantage in acquiring more levered firms and unlevering them on personal account, which is inconsistent with the value of firms being unaffected by leverage.

It is less clear how Taggart's eclectic model would be affected by growing inflation. But, one would presume that even, in his view, given the current tax structure, a rise in inflation should produce some increase in demand and, hence, presumably, induce a higher supply of leverage.

Let me finally conclude by noting that the empirical data on the behavior of financial structure of both the Ciccolo and Baum and Taggart papers are taken entirely from the history of the U.S. corporate sector. There is, however, another set of data which could be very useful in assessing the explanatory power of alternative theories. It consists of data bearing on the financial structure prevailing in other industrial countries. Anyone who has had an opportunity to look at the experience of foreign countries cannot fail to be impressed by the fact that, almost everywhere in the rest of the world, leverage is far greater than in this country, and is frequently of a size that would be considered here absolutely unsound, no matter what kind of firm one is dealing with. The only exception I know is Canada, presumably because of the contagion from the United States. But high leverage seems to prevail in most of Europe, from France and Italy to Germany, England, Sweden, and the other Scandinavian countries, and it probably is even greater in the case of Japan. These countries differ from each other and from the United States in many important ways, such as in terms of the structure of taxes, the structure of intermediation, the nature of the relation between banks and industry, and also in the structure of wealth holding, and perhaps in its concentration; also, in attitudes toward risk, and in the extent of credence placed on information provided by corporate accounting. It would be fascinating to see which, if any, of the models which have been developed to account for leverage in the United States could explain differences between countries.

Reference

Modigliani, Franco, and Cohn, R. 1979. Inflation, rational valuation, and the market. *Financial Analysts Journal* (March/April).

3 Debt and Equity Yields, 1926–1980

Patric H. Hendershott and Roger D. Huang

An important companion to a study of how corporations have issued and investors have purchased debt and equity securities during the past half century is an examination of how these securities have been priced in this interval. Both resource utilization and inflation have varied widely in the American economy, causing sharp changes in security prices and thus enormously diverse ex post returns on corporate equities and bonds. Even if we limit ourselves to the post-Accord (1951) years, the variation in returns is huge. To illustrate, equities earned positive *real* returns in 1954, 1958, and 1975 of 54%, 41%, and 30%, respectively, but had −24% and −38% returns in 1973 and 1974. Variations in real returns on high-quality corporate bonds were smaller, but in the double-digit range nonetheless (14% in 1970 and 1976 and −13% to −16% in 1969, 1974, 1979, and 1980). The primary purpose of this study is to increase our understanding of the determinants of these variations.

The study is divided into four broad parts. We begin with an exploratory analysis of the data for the 1926–80 period. It makes good analytical sense to examine the data for any regularities without the imposition of too much structure before studying the data in the confines of a particular

Patric H. Hendershott is John W. Galbreath Professor of Real Estate and professor of finance at Ohio State University and a research associate of the NBER. Roger D. Huang is assistant professor of finance at the University of Florida, Gainesville. Research assistance was provided by Peter Elmer and Randy Brown. Comments by John Carlson, Benjamin Friedman, Stewart Myers, and Jess Yawitz have been incorporated in this revision. Reactions of participants at seminars given at Arizona State University, Boston College, Ohio State University, and the Kansas City and San Francisco Federal Reserve Banks have also been useful.

model. In section 3.2, we estimate the relationships between one-month ex post returns on corporate bonds and equities and variations in Treasury bill rates, economic activity, and other variables. The major other variable is unanticipated changes in new issue coupon rates on long-term Treasury bonds. Sections 3.3 and 3.4 contain econometric investigations of the determinants of one-month Treasury bill rates and unanticipated changes in long-term Treasury coupon rates, respectively. These parts perform two functions: they extend the analysis of section 3.2 by explaining variables that determine ex post corporate bond and equity returns, and they provide evidence on the determination of new issue yields on short- and long-term default-free debt. The first part of the study differs from the others in that it consists of simple numerical analysis (plots, calculation of means, etc.) rather than formal econometrics, and considers data from the entire 1926–80 period rather than the 1953–80 span.

A number of important issues are addressed in the econometric parts of the paper. These include the validity of the Modigliani-Cohn valuation-error hypothesis, the measurement of Merton's "excess return on the market," the relationship between real new-issue debt rates and real economic activity, and the usefulness of the Livingston survey data in explaining financial returns.

Three general datasets are analyzed. First, the ex post returns on bills, bonds, and equities are those compiled by Ibbotson and Sinquefield (1980); causality tests of relationship among these returns and inflation are reported in Appendix A. Second, changes in the coupon rate on long-term, new-issue-equivalent Treasury bonds and unanticipated changes in this rate are based upon the work of Huston McCulloch and are described in Appendix B. Third, unanticipated inflation and industrial production growth are derived from the Livingston survey data, and they and the entire semiannual dataset utilized in the analysis of unanticipated changes in new-issue coupon rates are presented in Appendix C.

3.1 Exploratory Data Analysis

This part of the study contains sections dealing with (1) inflation and Treasury bill rates; (2) inflation and relative returns on equities, bonds, and bills; and (3) the business cycle and returns on equities and bonds.

Before turning to the analysis, a few words about the data are in order. First, all of the underlying yield data compiled by Ibbotson and Sinquefield—equities, corporate bonds, Treasury bonds, and Treasury bills—are roughly representative of returns on economy-wide "market" portfolios and are available monthly for the 1926–80 period. These yields are realized, rather than expected, returns, except for those on Treasury bills which are both expected and realized because their one-month maturity equals the period over which the returns are calculated. Second, the returns—income plus capital gains (except for bills)—are before-tax returns. They are not truly representative of what either highly taxed or tax-exempt investors actually earned after tax (both investor groups presumably would have opted for portfolios with relative income and capital gains components different from the market average, and the former group, of course, paid taxes). Hopefully, differential returns, at least, are roughly representative of those earned by most investors.

The inflation rate is the rate of change in the consumer price index for the 1926–46 period and the rate of change in the consumer price index net of the shelter component after 1946. The latter circumvents the erroneous treatment of housing costs (especially mortgage interest) in the construction of the basic CPI (see Blinder 1980; Dougherty and Van Order 1982).

3.1.1   Inflation and Treasury Bill Returns

During the 1926–80 period there was a single episode of significant deflation, 1930–32. In those three years the inflation rate ranged from -6% to -10%. Modest deflation also occurred in 1926–27, 1938, and 1949. In contrast, there have been three significant bursts of inflation—the beginning of World War II (9% in 1941 and 1942), the postwar surge (18% in 1946 and 9% in 1947), and the Korean War scare (6% in 1950 and 1951)—and the prolonged post-1967 inflationary era. The current inflation has ranged from slightly over 4% (adjusting for the impact of price controls in 1971–72) to double-digit inflation in 1974 and again in 1979–80.

The above overview of the 1926–80 period suggests that division of these years into four subperiods might be useful. These are 1926–40 (which includes the Depression and all years of even modest deflation except 1949), 1941–51 (which includes the inflationary spurts of World War II, its aftermath, and the outbreak of the Korean conflict), 1952–67 (the era of stable prices), and 1968–80 (the present inflationary period). The first two columns of table 3.1 present the mean and standard deviations for the annual inflation rate for these and overlapping periods. The great differences in the mean inflation rate and its variability are obvious.

The next four columns list means and standard deviations for both the nominal and real one-month Treasury bill rate. As can be seen, there is an enormous difference in the variability of the real bill rate between 1926–51 and 1952–80. In the latter period the standard deviation of the real bill rate, 1.5%, is only three-fifths of that of the nominal bill rate, 2.6%; in the earlier period, the former, 6.4%, is over five times the latter, 1.2%. Division of the earlier interval into 1926–40 and 1941–51 reveals enormous variability in the real bill rate (and stability in the nominal rate). The mean real bill rate was a full 2.8% in 1926–40 and an incredible -5.4% in 1941–51. The negative real rate in the 1940s was due to the

Table 3.1   **Annual Inflation and Nominal and Real One-Month Treasury Bill Rates**

	Inflation Rate		Nominal Bill Rate		Real Bill Rate	
	Mean	S.D.	Mean	S.D.	Mean	S.D.
1926–40	−1.5	4.0	1.3	1.5	2.8	4.5
1941–51	6.0	5.3	.6	.4	−5.4	5.5
1952–67	1.5	1.2	2.7	1.0	1.2	0.8
1968–80	7.1	3.1	6.7	2.2	−0.4	1.8
1926–51	1.7	5.9	1.0	1.2	−0.6	6.4
1952–80	4.0	3.6	4.5	2.6	0.5	1.5

Note: The real bill rate is the nominal rate less the inflation rate. Annual rates are geometric averages of the 12 monthly rates during calendar years.

monetary authorities' policy of pegging nominal interest rates at low levels during a period of significant inflation. The high real rate in the 1930s is largely attributable to the combination of the general nonnegativity constraint on the nominal rate and the existence of significant deflation. However, it is noteworthy that the real bill rate exceeded 4% in all years in the 1926–30 period during which the nonnegativity constraint was not binding (the nominal bill rate ranged from 2.4% to 4.7%).

Figure 3.1 illustrates the marked difference between the 1926–51 and 1952–80 periods in the volatility of both the nominal and real bill rates. In the former period, the nominal rate declines in the early 1930s and is then

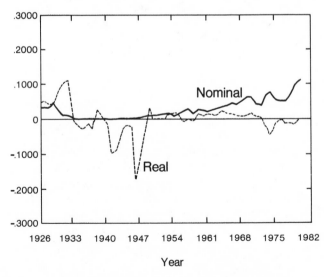

Fig. 3.1   Real and nominal Treasury bill rates, 1926–80.

flat; in the latter period this rate cycles around a sharply rising trend (the 1980 average bill rate of almost 12% disguises variations in monthly rates between less than 7% and over 16%). In contrast, the real bill rate varied between +12% in 1931 and 1932 and −18% in 1946. Its often-cited stability clearly refers to the post-1951 period only.[1]

3.1.2 Inflation and Relative Returns on Equities, Bonds, and Bills

The first two columns in table 3.2 repeat the same columns in table 3.1. The third and fourth columns record the mean and standard deviation of the difference between the annual returns on equities and corporate bonds. As can be seen, the premiums equities have earned over bonds have varied widely. The premium was much greater in the 1940s, 1950s, and 1960s than in the 1930s and 1970s.[2] It would appear from these data that there is no simple relationship between the premium and either the mean or the standard deviation of the inflation rate.[3]

The last two columns in table 3.2 report the mean standard deviation of the difference between the annual returns earned on U.S. government bonds and one-month bills. The difference was extraordinarily large, 3.8%, in the 1926–40 period, and small, −2.5%, in the 1968–80 period. These differences are due to apparently unanticipated movements in interest rates.[4] To illustrate, if yields fall unexpectedly, then prices of long-term bonds will rise unexpectedly, and the one-year return on bonds will be large. This was apparently the case in the 1930s (the one-month bill rate declined from an average of over 3.0% in 1926–30 to less than 0.5% in the 1933–40 period). In contrast, if yields rise unexpectedly, then prices of long-term bonds will fall unexpectedly, and the one-year return on bonds will be low. This apparently has happened in the post-1952 period (the one-month bill rate rose from 1.5% in 1952–55 to 5% in 1967–69 to over 10% in 1979–80).[5]

It is important to note that only unanticipated movements in interest rates have such impacts on the difference in realized returns on bonds and bills. For example, if long-term bond rates were expected to rise during the year, then bonds would be priced at the beginning of the year such

Table 3.2   **Annual Inflation and the Returns on Equities (Relative to Bonds) and Bonds (Relative to Bills)**

	Inflation Rate		Corporate Equities Less Bonds		Treasury Bonds Less Bills	
	Mean	S.D.	Mean	S.D.	Mean	S.D.
1926–40	−1.5	4.0	2.2	28.7	3.8	5.3
1941–51	6.0	5.3	13.2	14.8	1.5	4.0
1952–67	1.5	1.2	12.6	19.7	−1.1	5.8
1968–80	7.1	3.1	4.0	16.2	−2.5	7.8

that a high income return would offset the anticipated capital loss. In this case, the difference in ex post returns on bonds and bills would be independent of observed changes in new-issue bond yields.

3.1.3 The Business Cycle and Returns on Equities and Treasury Bonds

In this section, we explore the presence of a business cycle effect on returns earned on investment in corporate bonds and stocks. The reference dates of the National Bureau of Economic Research are employed as a general guide to the stages of the business cycle. In the 1926–80 period, 10½ cycles have occurred (see table 3.3). Excluding the 43-month depression, contractions have ranged from 6 to 16 months and have had an average duration of 11 months. Excluding the 80- and 106-month wartime (World War II and Viet Nam) expansions, upswings have varied from 21 to 59 months in duration and have averaged 39 months.

Annualized differences in ex post equity and bond returns over different phases of the business cycle have been compared.[6] For contractions, the first and last 5 months (which overlap for contractions of less than 10

Table 3.3   **Business Cycle Reference Dates: 1926–80**

		Duration in Months	
Business Cycle Reference Dates		Contraction (Previous Peak to Trough)	Expansion (Trough to Peak)
Trough	Peak		
November 1927	August 1929	13	21
March 1933	May 1937	43	50
June 1938	February 1945	13	80
October 1945	November 1948	8	37
October 1949	July 1953	11	45
May 1954	August 1957	10	39
April 1958	April 1960	8	24
February 1961	December 1969	10	106
November 1970	November 1973	11	36
March 1975	January 1980	16	59
July 1980		6	—
Average, all cycles:			
11 cycles, 1926–1980		14[a]	50[b]
5 cycles, 1926–1953		18[a]	47[b]
6 cycles, 1953–1980		10	53[b]

Source: National Bureau of Economic Research.
Notes:
[a]11 months, excluding the Great Depression.
[b]39 months, excluding the World War II and Vietnam cycles.

months duration) were examined. For expansions, the first, second, third, and last 6 months were studied (the last two periods overlap during the 21 month upswing in the late 1920s). The cycles were divided into the 1926–52 and 1953–80 subperiods, and means and standard deviations of the differences in equity and bond returns were calculated for the 5 pre-1953 cycles, the 5½ post-1952 cycles, and all 10½ cycles. A cursory examination of the data revealed that equities tend to earn a relatively superior return (i.e., greater than the average 7% by which equity returns exceeded bond returns throughout the entire 1926–80 period) late in contractions and early in expansions and a relatively inferior return late in expansions and early in contractions.

A systematic comparison of the return data is reported in table 3.4. We first divided the months between January 1926 and December 1980 into three types of periods: those around troughs (in which equity returns appear to be superior), those around peaks (in which equity returns appear to be relatively inferior), and the remainder. The inferior periods are defined as the last 6 months of every expansion and the first half (dropping fractions) or first 6 months, whichever is less, of every contraction. The superior periods are defined as the last half (dropping fractions) or last 6 months, whichever is less, of every contraction and the first 6 months of every expansion. In the second step in this comparison, the total 1926–80 period is partitioned into 11 overlapping intervals that contain single adjoining peaks and troughs and all the surrounding months that do not overlap with adjacent superior and inferior periods. That is, the intervals extend from 6 months after a trough to 6 months before the second following peak. These 11 overlapping intervals are listed at the left in table 3.4. Also listed are the geometric mean returns (annualized) during the superior periods within the interval, the inferior periods, and all months excluding such periods. The mean in the latter months is the "normal" return to which the mean returns around the trough and peak are compared.[7]

Columns 4 and 5 are the differences between the superior and inferior returns, respectively, and the normal returns. The extraordinary annual net returns on equities around troughs average 26% (no net return is less than 18%), and the standard deviation is only 11%. In contrast, the extraordinary annual net returns on equities are negative around most peaks, and these net returns average −13%. Here, however, the standard deviation is a relatively large 17%.

These results indicate that investors could devise superior trading schemes involving transactions between equities and government bonds to the extent that they were able to forecast the turning points of business cycles, particularly the recession trough. Given the brevity of the post–World War II recessions, this would not appear to be difficult; when a recession is clearly upon us, the trough is just around the corner. Unfor-

Table 3.4   **Geometric Difference between Returns on Equities and Treasury Bonds, Near Troughs, Near Peaks, and in Other Periods (%)**

	Near Troughs	Near Peaks	Other Months	Excess Near Troughs	Excess Near Peaks
January 1926–February 1929	37	19	17	20	2
June 1928–November 1936	24	−12	−6	30	−6
October 1933–August 1944	26	−32	8	18	−40
January 1939–May 1948	31	17	1	30	16
May 1946–January 1953	35	−10	12	23	−22
May 1950–February 1957	43	−4	20	23	−24
December 1954–October 1959	46	−10	16	30	−26
November 1958–June 1969	32	−14	8	24	−22
September 1961–May 1973	27	−11	6	21	−17
June 1971–July 1979	27	−10	3	24	−13
October 1975–December 1980	56[a]	13[b]	4[c]	51	9
Mean	35	−5	8	26	−13
S.D.	10	15	8	11	17

Note:
[a]Covers the period May 1980–December 1980.
[b]Covers the period August 1979–April 1980.
[c]Covers the period October 1975–July 1979.

tunately, such a trading rule will lead to incredibly negative returns if the early 1930s are ever repeated.

3.2 Ex Post Returns and the Interest Rate and Business Cycles

Our next task is to explain ex post monthly returns on corporate bonds and equities. The analytical framework, which follows Mishkin (1978, 1981), is first developed and then empirical results for bonds and equities are reported.

3.2.1 The Analytical Framework

The ex post after-tax return on an asset equals the expected or required return plus the difference between the ex post and expected returns. With the required return equal to the after-tax return on one-month Treasury bills plus a risk/liquidity premium, we have

(1) $(1 - \tau^j)R_{t+1}^j = (1 - \tau)R_{t+1} + \rho^j + \mathrm{UNEX}_{t+1}^j,$

where ρ^j is the premium required on the jth asset and UNEX_{t+1} is the difference between the ex post and anticipated after-tax return on asset j that occurs because of unexpected changes in variables relevant to the return on asset j. Next ρ^j and $UNEX_{t+1}$ are replaced by a constant plus a set of responses to proxies for them (X_i^j) and an error term (η^j) to obtain

$$(2) \qquad R_{t+1}^j = \beta_0^j + \beta_1^j R_{t+1} + \sum_{i=2}^{u} \beta_i^j X_{i,t+1}^j + \eta_{t+1}^j,$$

where $\beta_1 = (1 - \tau)/(1 - \tau^j)$. The difficult problem is, of course, specification of the $X_i's$.

Unanticipated Changes in Treasury Coupons. In section 3.2, it was suggested that changes in new-issue-equivalent 20-year Treasury bond yields have been largely unanticipated during the 1952–80 period. This proposition can be tested with data compiled by Huston McCulloch. For the 1947–mid-1977 period, McCulloch (1977) has meticulously constructed monthly series for both (1) new-issue-equivalent (par value) long-term Treasury bond yields and (2) cumulative unanticipated changes in these yields.[8] A regression of the monthly change in the 20-year new-issue yield $(\Delta R20)$ on the unanticipated change $(UN\Delta)$ over the January 1953–June 1977 period results in

$$\Delta R20 = 1.27 + .999 \, UN\Delta, \qquad R^2 = .882, \text{ D-W} = 2.88,$$
$$\quad (.34) \quad (.021) \qquad\qquad \text{SEE} = 5.9 \text{ basis points,}$$

where the yields are at annual rates. The positive constant reflects the generally upward slope of yield curves, and the response to unanticipated changes is clearly one for one. The adjusted R^2 indicates that 88% of monthly changes other than the constant are explained by the unanticipated change.

In equation estimates reported below, variables based on both $\Delta R20$ and UN will be employed (the latter in equations excluding data after June 1977). The specific form of the variables depends on how an unexpected change in the bond rate should affect the price of (capital gain on) the specific security being analyzed. The percentage capital gain on a portfolio of n-year bonds (CG_b) is related to changes in the yield on the n-year bond, ΔR_n, by

$$CG_b = -\frac{\Delta R_n [(1 + R_n)^n - 1]}{R_n (1 + R_n)^n}.$$

In the regressions reported below, n is set equal to 20. With CG_b defined in this way, its coefficient is expected to be near unity.

For equities, the relationship between the capital gain component of the yield and the unanticipated change in the new-issue coupon rate is more complicated. The perpetual dividend growth valuation model says that the value of equities (V) equals current after-tax dividends $[(1 - \tau_d)D]$ divided by the required after-tax nominal return on equities (R_e^a) less the expected rate of appreciation in dividends (g):

(3)
$$V = \frac{(1 - \tau_d)D}{R_e^a - g}.$$

Taking derivatives, the percentage capital gain on equities, dV/V, is related to changes in the 20-year coupon rate by

$$CG_e = -\frac{d(R_e^a - g)}{dR20}\frac{\Delta R20}{R_e^a - g}.$$

The issues are, How should $R_e^a - g$ be measured, and what is the likely value of the derivative of $R_e^a - g$?

Portfolio equilibrium requires that

(4) $R_e^a = (1 - \tau_d)R20 + \rho,$

where bonds and dividends are assumed to be taxed equivalently and ρ is a required risk premium. Thus

$$R_e^a - g = (1 - \tau_d)R20 + \rho - g,$$

and

(4')
$$\frac{d(R_e^a - g)}{dR20} = 1 - \tau_d - \frac{dg}{dR20}.$$

Equation (4') suggests the following. First, if all changes in $R20$ are due to changes in expected inflation which are, in turn, reflected in $g(dg/dR20 = 1)$, then $d(R_e^a - g)/dR20$ equals $-\tau_d$ and CG_e is positive. Second, for low values of τ_d, $R_e^a - g$ is roughly constant. This joint hypothesis suggests the use of $\Delta R20/0.06$ as a regressor, with an expected positive coefficient of τ_d.[9] On the other hand, if x percent of changes in $R20$ are due to changes in the real rate of interest and thus $dg/dR20 = 1 - x$, then the coefficient on the regressor would be $-(x - \tau_d)$. Ideally, one would separate changes in interest rates into nominal and real components and enter these in the regressions separately. Such a separation of monthly changes would seem to be nearly impossible and is not attempted here.

An alternative view of equity valuation exists. Equation (4) assumes that investors rationally compare nominal returns on debt and equities. In contrast, Modigliani and Cohn (1979) have contended that investors compare real equity returns with nominal debt returns and that this error has been the cause of the dismal performance of equities during the 1966–80 period of rising inflation. To test this hypothesis, (4) is replaced with

(4a) $R_e^a - \pi = (1 - \tau_d)R20 + \rho.$

In this case

$$R_e^a - g = (1 - \tau_d)R20 + \rho - g + \pi.$$

Taking derivatives,

(4a') $$\frac{d(R_e^a - g)}{dR20} = 1 - \tau_d - \frac{dg}{dR20} + \frac{d\pi}{dR20} \sim 1 - \tau_d.$$

If Modigliani and Cohn are correct, then the appropriate regressor is $\Delta R20/[(1 - \tau_d)R20 + .04]$—we take the real component of g to be 0.02—and the expected coefficient is $-(1 - \tau_d)$. Whether changes in interest rates are perceived to be real or nominal is irrelevant (g and π change equally in any event) to investors and thus to equity prices. In the empirical work reported below, both the rational and Modigliani and Cohn views will be tested. In these tests, we shall set $\tau_d = 0.3$ (see n. 17 for results with other values of τ_d).

Of course, $R20/.06$ and $R20/[(1 - \tau_d)R20 + .04]$ are closely correlated, being dominated by their numerators. Thus, if one "works," so will the other. If neither works, then we will accept the rationality hypothesis with $x = \tau_d$. If both work positively, then the Modigliani-Cohn hypotheses will be rejected. If both work negatively, we will choose between the rationality and Modigliani-Cohn hypotheses on the basis of the plausibility of the implied estimates of x and τ_d.

Other Variables. In section 3.1.3, it was established that equities earned extraordinarily large returns relative to bonds around recession troughs, very likely because of a turnaround in expectations regarding the growth of the economy. We would expect this to generate capital appreciation on equities and possibly bonds (if default premia decline). Based on the earlier analysis, a turnaround dummy variable is defined as:[10]

$$\text{TURN} = \begin{cases} 1 & \text{last half (dropping fractions) or last 6 months,} \\ & \text{whichever is less, of every contraction and first} \\ & \text{6 months of every expansion} \\ 0 & \text{elsewhere.} \end{cases}$$

A final proxy is unexpected inflation. This variable is measured as the difference between actual and expected inflation where the latter is based on the Livingston survey data.[11] More specifically, the variable is the difference between the actual average monthly inflation rate between the survey date and the date forecast and the Livingston forecasted 6-month inflation rate converted to a monthly basis. Because the forecasts are available only semiannually, our proxy changes value only every 6 months.[12] Because price surprises appear to lead declines in real economic activity—there is a strong negative correlation between our unanticipated inflation variable and the growth rate of industrial production in the following year—the surprises should be expected to depress equity returns (and possibly bond returns if default premia rise).[13]

3.2.2 The Results for Bonds

The results for corporate bonds are reported in table 3.5. Equations (T1) and (T2) are for the 1953–mid-1977 period and differ only in that (T1) includes the capital gains variable based on the unexpected change in the 20-year Treasury rate as a regressor while the variable in (T2) is based on the total change.[14] Given our earlier evidence that changes in the 20-year rate are largely unanticipated, it is not surprising that the results are quite similar. The bill rate coefficients are close to their expected value of unity. On the other hand, the capital gain coefficients are only about 70% of their expected unity value. The unanticipated inflation and superior dummy variables enter with the expected signs, but only the coefficient on the former is significantly different from zero at the .05 level.

Equation (T3) contains estimates for the entire 1953–80 period. The coefficient on the bill rate is now quite close to the expected unity value, and the explanatory power of the equation increases sharply (R^2 rises from .56 to .68). The coefficient on the capital gain variable, .76, is closer to unity, but still significantly below, and the other coefficients, while continuing to have the expected signs, are not significantly different from zero. These coefficients are not small, however. Bond returns tend to be 2.3% less than normal in a year of 2.5% unanticipated inflation and 2.3% more in the year surrounding business cycle troughs.

3.2.3 The Results for Equities

Hendershott and Van Horne (1973, pp. 304–5) observed that the new-issue bond yield and Standard and Poor's dividend-price ratio moved in opposite directions throughout the 1950s (they conjectured that a sharp decline in the relative risk premium required on equities occurred) but were positively correlated in the 1960s and early 1970s. Consequently, the 1953–80 period is divided into the 1953–60 and 1961–80 subperiods and results are reported for these.

Equation (T1) in table 3.6 illustrates the familiar, but hardly explicable, result that ex post equity returns were strongly negatively correlated with expected inflation in the 1950s.[15] The point estimate is an astounding −16, indicating that a one-percentage-point increase in the bill rate (expected inflation?) induced a 16-percentage-point decline in equity returns. Equation (T2) indicates the expected negative relationship with our unanticipated inflation variable (the average monthly inflation rate between the date the Livingston survey was taken and the date forecast less the Livingston forecasted 6-month inflation rate) and positive relationship with the turnaround cycle dummy variable, but neither relationship is statistically significant. Equations (T3) and (T4) include current and lagged one-month values of the variables based upon changes in the long-term Treasury coupon rate. The variables in equations (T3) and (T5) are the Modigliani-Cohn nominal rate versions defined as $\Delta R20/(.7$

Table 3.5   **Explanation of Monthly Realized Returns on Corporate Bonds**

Period	Constant	Bill Rate	Capital Gain Variable[a]	Turnaround Dummy	Unanticipated Inflation	R^2 (SEE)
(T1) 1953–mid-1977	.00020 (.00168)	1.230 (.523)	.720 (.038)	.00257 (.00178)	-1.162 (.638)	.577 (.0117)
(T2) 1953–mid-1977	.00113 (.00172)	1.276 (.532)	.659 (.036)	.00284 (.00182)	-1.321 (.651)	.560 (.0119)
(T3) 1953–1980	.00216 (.00141)	.898 (.388)	.764 (.029)	.00191 (.00169)	-.908 (.582)	.677 (.0119)

[a]The variable entered in eq. (T1) is based on the unexpected change in the 20-year, new-issue rate; in the other equations the variable is based on the total change.

Table 3.6 Explanation of Monthly Realized Equity Returns, 1953–60

Eq.	Constant	One-Month Bill Rate	Unanticipated Inflation	Turnaround Dummy	Changes in Coupon Rate[a] Current	Changes in Coupon Rate[a] Lagged	$\bar{R}^2$ (SEE)
(T1)	.0410 (.0086)	−16.005 (4.494)	—	—	—	—	.108 (.0336)
(T2)	.0315 (.0112)	−10.752 (5.528)	−3.457 (3.410)	.0139 (.0096)	—	—	.115 (.0335)
(T3)	.0263 (.0112)	−8.173 (5.452)	−4.069 (3.410)	.0154 (.0095)	.397 (.173)	−.282 (.176)	.173 (.0323)
(T4)	.0262 (.0112)	−8.125 (5.467)	−4.084 (3.418)	.0155 (.0095)	.362 (.163)	−.262 (.165)	.167 (.0324)
(T5)	.0095 (.0051)	1.0	−5.606 (3.318)	.0244 (.0079)	.421 (.174)	−.285 (.177)	.163 (.0327)
(T6)	.0095 (.0052)	1.0	−5.628 (3.323)	.0245 (.0079)	.384 (.164)	−.268 (.167)	.163 (.0327)

[a]This variable equals $\Delta R20 / (.7\ R20 + .04)$ in the odd-numbered equations and $\Delta R20 / .06$ in the even-numbered equations.

$R20 + 0.04$); the variables in equations (T4) and (T6) are the real rate versions defined as $\Delta R20/0.06$. A one-month lag was tested because equities and new-issue bonds are not as close substitutes as are corporate and Treasury bonds. Recall that the coefficients in (T3) are expected to be negative and sum to -0.7 if investors make the Modigliani-Cohn valuation error (and the tax rate on dividends is 0.3), and the coefficients in (T4) can be interpreted as $-(x - \tau_d)$, where x is the portion of changes in $R20$ due to changes in real coupon rates and τ_d is the tax rate on dividends. A positive relation between equity returns and the concurrent change in the bond yield is indicated, although the effect is largely reversed the following month.[16] This is inconsistent with the Modigliani-Cohn hypothesis and supports the rationality hypothesis. The implied dividend tax rate, assuming that changes in interest rates are perceived as nominal ($x = 0$), is 0.1 (when the lagged term is taken into account) to 0.36.

While the bill rate coefficient is still a startling -8 in equations (T3) and (T4), it is not significantly different from the expected unity value. In equations (T5) and (T6) this coefficient has been constrained to unity. As anticipated, the decline in explanatory power is minor. The impact of changes in Treasury coupon rates is unchanged from equations (T3) and (T4), but the coefficients on unanticipated inflation and the turnaround dummy rise in absolute value and statistical significance (the t-ratios are 1½ and 3, respectively).

Equations for the 1961–80 period are listed in table 3.7. While the Treasury bill rate enters negatively in equation (T1), the coefficient is only a tenth as large as that in equation (T1) of table 3.6. Moreover, when unanticipated inflation and the turnaround dummy variable are included, the bill rate coefficient is close (given its standard error) to unity. The coefficients on unanticipated inflation and the turnaround dummy have the expected signs and are significantly different from zero. Equations (T3) and (T4) contain the change in coupon rate variables. The coefficients in equation (T3) sum to -0.6, very close to the expected value of -0.7 in the Modigliani-Cohn framework (further lagged values of the variable have essentially zero coefficients), and the variables add substantially to the explanatory power of equation (T2).[17] The coefficients in equation (T4) sum to -0.33, implying that most of changes in long-term coupon rates (one-third plus the dividend tax rate) have been perceived by rational investors (not Modigliani-Cohn investors) as changes in real rates. The rationality of this perception, during a period of rising inflation, is questionable.

When the bill rate coefficient is constrained to unity (see eq. [T5] and [T6]), the other coefficients are little affected except for that on unanticipated inflation which falls by a quarter in absolute value. Because its

Table 3.7   Explanation of Monthly Realized Equity Returns, 1961–80

Eq.	Constant	One-Month Bill Rate	Unanticipated Inflation	Turnaround Dummy	Changes in Coupon Rate[a]		$\bar{R}^2$ (SEE)
					Current	Lagged	
(T1)	.0147 (.0066)	−1.575 (1.352)	—	—	—	—	.001 (.0417)
(T2)	.0025 (.0071)	2.162 (1.906)	−6.437 (2.491)	.0253 (.0071)	—	—	.085 (.0399)
(T3)	.0020 (.0069)	2.770 (1.877)	−6.062 (2.425)	.0215 (.0070)	−.326 (.099)	−.272 (.101)	.149 (.0385)
(T4)	.0005 (.0070)	3.173 (1.907)	−6.479 (2.441)	.0222 (.0070)	−.178 (.060)	−.156 (.062)	.141 (.0387)
(T5)	.0075 (.0036)	1.0	−4.445 (1.714)	.0227 (.0069)	−.333 (.098)	−.254 (.099)	.156 (.0385)
(T6)	.0073 (.0036)	1.0	−4.507 (1.723)	.0237 (.0069)	−.181 (.060)	−.139 (.060)	.147 (.0387)

[a]This variable equals $\Delta R20/(.7\ R20 + .04)$ in the odd-numbered equations and $\Delta R20/.06$ in the even-numbered equations.

standard error falls proportionately, the statistical significance of the coefficient is unaltered.

Comparisons of equations (T5) and (T6) in table 3.6 with their counterparts in table 3.7 indicates a close similarity of all coefficients except those on the current change in the Treasury coupon rate. Given this similarity, equations for the entire 1953–80 period have been estimated and are reported as equations (T1) and (T2) in table 3.8. The estimates are, of course, close to those of the subperiods. The coefficients in equation (T2) can be interpreted in the following way. First, the constant term, which is 0.102 on an annual basis, represents Merton's excess expected return on the market. Second, the bill rate contributed an average 4½% return over the period, rising steadily from under 2% in the early 1950s to over 10% in 1979–80. Third, the continuing climb in the Treasury coupon rate lowered stock returns by nearly 2% per annum on average during the 1953–80 period. More important, the change in this rate has had large impacts in particular years. To illustrate, the percentage increase in the coupon rate from 9% to 12½% between March 1979 and March 1980 generated a 15% ex post decline in stock returns in that year, other things being equal. Fourth, the coefficient on the turnaround dummy variable suggests that equities have earned a 34% greater return in the year roughly surrounding business cycle troughs than during other periods. Fifth, stocks have earned sharply negative returns, ceteris paribus, during periods of unanticipated inflation. More specifically, the roughly 4½ percentage point unanticipated inflation in 1973–74 and 1979 translates into a 22% lower annual return on equities than would otherwise be the case. Our interpretation of this negative relation between equity returns and unanticipated inflation is that the latter generates expectations of tighter monetary policy and thus both higher interest rates and sluggish economic activity.[18]

It is well known that equity returns follow a strong political cycle. For example, during the 1953–80 period equity returns averaged 3½% in the 2 years following presidential elections, but 20% in the 2 years leading up to the elections. Because the political cycle is so readily predictable, such differences in returns must certainly be attributable to other factors which, it just happens, have been correlated with the business cycle in the past but might well not be in the future. Likely candidates for these other factors are the interest rate and business cycles as reflected in our change-in-coupon, turnaround, and unanticipated inflation variables. To determine whether our equations have captured the observed political cycle impact, we have computed the annual errors from equation (T2) in table 3.8 and averaged them over the first and second pairs of years of presidential terms. Much to our surprise, the difference in these averages was a full 13%. That is, our equation accounts for only 3% of the 16½%

Table 3.8   Explanation of Monthly Realized Equity Returns, 1953–80

Eq.	Constant	One-Month Bill Rate	Unantic-ipated Inflation	Turnaround Dummy	Change in Coupon Rate[a] Current	Change in Coupon Rate[a] Lagged	Presidential Term Dummies Year 2	Presidential Term Dummies Year 3	Presidential Term Dummies Year 4	$\bar{R}^2$ (SEE)
(T1)	.0084 (.0030)	1.0	−5.082 (1.501)	.0238 (.0054)	−.189 (.086)	−.264 (.087)	—	—	—	.139 (.0374)
(T2)	.0081 (.0030)	1.0	−4.948 (1.502)	.0244 (.0053)	−.131 (.055)	−.155 (.055)	—	—	—	.140 (.0374)
(T3)	.0022 (.0048)	1.0	−3.695 (1.564)	.0264 (.0055)	−.200 (.085)	−.260 (.086)	−.0040 (.0059)	.0115 (.0050)	.0088 (.0058)	.153 (.0371)
(T4)	.0016 (.0048)	1.0	−3.521 (1.566)	.0271 (.0055)	−.138 (.055)	−.152 (.055)	−.0038 (.0059)	.0117 (.0058)	.0094 (.0058)	.156 (.0370)

[a]This variable equals $\Delta R20/(.7\ R20 + .04)$ in the odd-numbered equations and $\Delta R20/.06$ in the even-numbered equations.

average difference in average returns between the 2 years preceding presidential elections and the 2 following years.

The last two equations in table 3.8 include political cycle dummy variables that equal one in months which fall in the second/third/fourth year of presidential terms and zero in all other months. As can be seen, their inclusion raises the explanatory power of the equations. Moreover, the hypothesis that the coefficients on the three political-cycle dummy variables are jointly zero can be rejected at the .05 level. Inclusion of these variables does not affect the interest rate coefficients, but it does alter the others by one-half (the turnaround dummy and the constant terms) to a full (unanticipated inflation) standard error.[19]

3.3 Treasury Bill Returns and the Inflation Rate

3.3.1 Theory

Definitionally, the real rate of interest is the nominal interest rate less the inflation rate. If we let r_{t+1} and R_{t+1} be the real and nominal interest rates earned over the holding period t to $t + 1$, respectively, and I_{t+1} be the inflation rate over the same time span, then

$$(5) \qquad r_{t+1} \equiv R_{t+1} - I_{t+1} .$$

Taking expectations of both sides of (5) contingent on information available at t, so that expectations are formed rationally, (5) becomes

$$(6) \qquad {}_t r_{t+1} \equiv R_{t+1} - {}_t \pi_{t+1} ,$$

where ${}_t r_{t+1}$ is the real rate expected at time t to exist in period $t + 1$, ${}_t \pi_{t+1}$ is the inflation rate expected at time t to exist in period $t + 1$, and (6) utilizes the fact that the expected nominal interest rate is the ex post rate because R_{t+1} is known at time t. In a world where lenders are required to pay an income tax rate τ on their nominal interest receipts and borrowers can deduct τ percent of their nominal interest payments,

$$(6a) \qquad {}_t r_{t+1}^a \equiv (1 - \tau)R_{t+1} - {}_t \pi_{t+1} ,$$

where ${}_t r_{t+1}^a$ is the expected after-tax real short-term rate.

The expected inflation rate is the difference between actual and unanticipated inflation: ${}_t \pi_{t+1} \equiv I_{t+1} - \mathrm{UNINF}_{t+1}$. With this substitution in (6a), one can obtain

$$(7) \qquad I_{t+1} \equiv {}_t r_{t+1}^a + (1 - \tau)R_{t+1} + \mathrm{UNINF}_{t+1} .$$

If the expected after-tax real short-term rate and τ are constants and the unanticipated rate of inflation is white noise, then it is appropriate to regress I_{t+1} on R_{t+1} and a constant. The equation is estimated with inflation as the dependent variable and the interest rate as the independent because the latter is predetermined while the former develops during the period. Unfortunately, a large body of evidence rejects the assumption of a constant real rate (see Garbade and Wachtel 1978; Mishkin 1981 and references cited in the latter), and the Livingston inflation survey data indicate systematic inflation forecast errors. The purposes of our estimation are to provide evidence on the determinants of the real short-term rate and to test for the presence of systematic errors in inflation forecasts.

3.3.2   Problems with the Inflation and Interest Rate Data

Fama (1975) regressed inflation on the bill rate on data from the January 1953–July 1971 period. He ruled out the data from World War II and its aftermath owing both to the low quality of the CPI prior to 1953 and to the Federal Reserve's pegging of nominal interest rates. Given constant nominal rates and highly variable inflation, the real bill rate varied widely. Our earlier examination of the 1926–39 period suggests that there, too, nominal bill rates were relatively stable (near zero in the 1930s) and real bill rates relatively volatile. Thus we also restrict ourselves to the post-1952 data.

Fama did not extend his analysis beyond July 1971 because the CPI was contaminated beginning in August 1971 by the Nixon price controls. Because "true" inflation is relevant to the nominal bill rate, regressions of recorded inflation on the nominal bill rate may give misleading results when true and recorded inflation rates differ. Subsequently, many investigators, including Fama, have proceeded to analyze data from the control period with no adjustments. In order to utilize post-July 1971 data in our tests, we include a proxy for the difference between recorded and true inflation in our regressions. In constructing this proxy, we utilize the results of Blinder and Newton (1981). More specifically, we use the change in their Model 1 measure of the impact of the controls on the nonfood, nonenergy consumer price index as our proxy for the difference between recorded and true inflation.[20] Their results suggest that the controls reduced the price *level* by 3 percentage points by early 1974, a reduction which was completely offset when the controls were lifted in 1974.

A more general problem with the consumer price index is the treatment of housing costs (especially mortgage interest) in the construction of the index (see Blinder 1980; Dougherty and Van Order 1982). To circumvent this problem, the inflation rate employed in this paper is the consumer price index net of the shelter component. Such an adjustment is particularly important in analyzing data after 1978.

A final possible data problem follows from a phenomenon documented by Cook (1981). He notes that in 1973 and 1974 short-term bill rates became far "out of line" relative to short-term rates on large CDs, commercial paper, and bankers acceptances. During this period market interest rates rose sharply relative to ceiling-constrained yields on deposits. According to Cook, the bill market was segmented from markets for private short-term securities. Because only bills were available in smaller denominations, many households were able to shift deposit funds only into bills. Corporations did not have sufficient bill holdings to arbitrage between the bill and private security markets (they drew their holdings down to zero in 1974), and commercial banks and municipalities had nonyield reasons for maintaining bill holdings. Thus bill rates fell relative to other yields. As a result, expected inflation was not fully reflected in bill rates. In fact, the enormous disparity between private and Treasury short-term yields in 1974 was the driving force behind the creation of the money market fund, an entity that, in the absence of other government regulations, should prevent such disparities from recurring.[21]

During the 156-month 1965–77 period, the spread between one-month prime CDs and one-month Treasury bills was generally within the 30–80 basis point range.[22] Two major exceptions occurred. During the 20 months from April 1969 to November 1970, the spread exceeded 90 basis points in 17 months and was at a maximum of 189 basis points in July 1969. During the 24 months from April 1973 to March 1975, the spread exceeded 90 basis points in 23 months, the maximum being 431 basis points in July 1974. In the 4 years prior to April 1969, the spread was above 80 basis points in only 4 of 48 months and never exceeded 110 basis points. In the 28 months between November 1970 and April 1973, the spread exceeded 81 basis points only once (85 basis points in July 1972). Finally, in the 39 months between April 1975 and June 1978, the spread never exceeded 90 basis points.

In the empirical estimates, then, we specify the inflation rate as the CPI net of shelter, the price control variable CONT is included in regressions using data from the August 1971–December 1974 period, and both the observed one-month Treasury bill rate and an adjusted rate that moves with the CD rate when the bill rate is out of line are utilized as regressors.

3.3.3 The Estimates

Table 3.9 contains the regression coefficients (and their standard errors, below them in parentheses), the coefficient of determination (and the equation standard error, under it in parentheses), and Durbin-Watson ratio for equations explaining the rate of change in the CPI net of shelter over the January 1953–December 1980 span.[23] In the first two equations, it is assumed that the real after-tax bill rate is either a constant or a linear function of the nominal after-tax bill rate and unanticipated inflation is white noise. As can be seen, the bill rate coefficient is significantly above unity. This result is similar to that obtained by Fama and Gibbons (1981, table 1) in their study of data from the 1953–77 period.

Table 3.9   Regressions of the Inflation Rate on the Treasury Bill Rate, 1953–80

Eq.	Constant	Bill Rate[a]	Price Controls Variable	Capacity Util. − .834	Unanticipated Inflation	R^2 (SEE)	Durbin-Watson
(T1)	−.00120 (.00029)	1.220 (.069)	—	—	—	.484 (.00260)	1.47
(T2)	−.00109 (.00029)	1.190 (.069)	.539 (.194)	—	—	.495 (.00258)	1.50
(T3)	−.00099 (.00028)	.920 (.080)	.231 (.191)	—	.744 (.124)	.545 (.00245)	1.61
(T4)	−.00095 (.00027)	.857 (.075)	.215 (.190)	−.00909 (.00295)	.879 (.123)	.555 (.00243)	1.64
(T5)	−.00133 (.00018)	1.0	.222 (.190)	−.00862 (.00295)	.753 (.104)	.158 (.00244)	1.64
(T6)	−.00082 (.00027)	.863 (.076)	1.0	−.00889 (.00302)	.744 (.121)	.504 (.00249)	1.58
(T7)	−.00090 (.00026)	.846 (.073)	.029 (.188)	−.00933 (.00293)	.782 (.126)	.559 (.00241)	1.63

[a]Except eq. (T7) where adjusted bill rate series is used. See the text for the adjustment.

Because tax rates cannot be negative, this estimate implies that the after-tax real bill rate is negatively related to expected inflation (and thus to the after-tax nominal rate).[24] To illustrate, if $r_{t+1}^a = \alpha - \beta_t \pi_{t+1}$, then the use of (6a) and the inflation identity (inflation is the sum of its expected and unexpected components) yields

$$(8) \qquad I_{t+1} = -\frac{\alpha}{1 - \beta} + \frac{1 - \tau}{1 - \beta} R_{t+1} + \text{UNINF}_{t+1}.$$

The coefficient on the nominal rate will be greater than unity if $\beta > \tau$.[25] A negative relation between real after-tax debt rates and expected inflation is hardly surprising when the use of historic depreciation and FIFO inventory accounting erodes after-tax real earnings of firms during periods of rising inflation. Because firms are unable to pay constant real after-tax returns to debtors and shareholders in the aggregate, the returns to each would be expected to decline (Hendershott 1981, pp. 913–14).

Examination of the residuals from equation (T2) reveals that they tend to be negative in the 1950s and 1960s and positive in the 1970s. That is, the equation overpredicts inflation in the early years and underpredicts it later. Two possible explanations come to mind. First, the real bill rate may have fallen between the 1960s and 1970s by even more than is captured by the high coefficient on the bill rate and the increase in this rate. If real interest rates are positively correlated with real economic activity, then the relatively sluggish activity in the 1970s would suggest a decline in the real rate.[26]

Second, possibly more of the higher inflation in the 1970s was unanticipated than was the case in the 1950s and 1960s. Comparison of actual 6-month inflation rates with the forecasts computed from the Livingston survey data suggests that this was the case (see Appendix C). Four periods of prolonged unanticipated inflation (four consecutive large 6-month forecasting errors) occurred: the four surveys from June 1956 to December 1957, January 1969 to June 1970, January 1973 to June 1974, and June 1978 to December 1979. Not only did two of these come during the shorter period of large positive residuals, but the average degree of unanticipated inflation was 4½% (at an annual rate) in these two compared to 2½% for the earlier episodes.

Equation (T3) is the result of including a proxy for unanticipated inflation. Of course, if the real bill rate were a constant and the proxy for unanticipated inflation were perfect, then we would be estimating an identity whose usefulness could be easily questioned. What is being tested in equation (T3) is whether an unanticipated inflation variable based on the Livingston survey data improves on the assumption of white noise. The proxy enters with the anticipated positive sign and yields a marked improvement in explanatory power. Moreover, the coefficient on the bill rate is lowered below unity, although not significantly so.

Equation (T3) is consistent with the joint hypotheses that the real Treasury bill rate was constant during the 1953–80 period (at a 1.2% annual rate) and that the Livingston survey data are slightly high estimates of unanticipated inflation.

In equation (T4) we test the hypothesis that real bill rates are related to real economic activity. As a proxy for real activity, we follow Carlson (1979) and Hendershott and Hu (1981) in using the Federal Reserve's capacity utilization rate for manufacturing. Because this rate is available only quarterly, we assign this value to the middle month of the quarter and interpolate linearly between mid-quarter months. This series, lagged one month and divided by 100, less its mean value over the 1953–80 period of 0.834 is the regressor. This variable enters with the expected negative sign and has a t-ratio of 3.[27] The coefficient on unanticipated inflation rises to within a standard error of unity and that on the bill rate falls to nearly two standard errors below unity.[28]

Fama and Gibbons (1981), among others, have provided evidence that expected real bill returns behave like random walks. If this is true of real bill returns even after allowing for their positive relationship with real economic activity, then the nominal bill rate is correlated with the error term and thus its estimated coefficient is biased downward. Equation (T5) provides estimates of the other coefficients when that on the bill rate is arbitrarily constrained to unity. The standard error of the equation rises ever so slightly, and the coefficient on unanticipated inflation falls to 0.75. The adjusted R^2 indicates that one-sixth of the variation in inflation after allowing for variations in the bill rate is explained by variations in unanticipated inflation and capacity utilization.

To this point, the coefficient on the price controls variable has not been discussed. In equation (T2), the coefficient is statistically different from both its maximum plausible value of unity and its minimum plausible value of zero. In subsequent equations, the coefficient is about 0.2 or only one standard error from zero. Although the controls variable is nonzero in only the August 1971–December 1974 period, its coefficient could affect the coefficients on the other variables because all variables move sharply in this period. To test this sensitivity, equation (T4) was rerun with the controls coefficient arbitrarily constrained to unity. Equation (T6) indicates that only the coefficient on unanticipated inflation is affected, declining to 0.75.

Our last experiment tests an adjusted bill rate variable which takes into account the fact that bill rates were out of line relative to private open market rates during much of the April 1969–March 1975 period. In April 1975, the first month after bill rates returned to the normal relationship with private rates, the one-month bill rate was 0.004347. The bill rate was almost precisely the same in November 1968, shortly before it got out of line. In this month, the one-month CD rate exceeded the bill rate by

0.00047. The adjusted bill rate series is defined as the CD rate less 0.00047 during the November 1968–March 1975 period and the bill rate otherwise. This adjusted series replaces the observed bill rate in equation (T7). Relative to equation (T4), the coefficients on the price controls and unanticipated inflation variables decline by a standard error, and the explanatory power of the equation rises slightly.

3.3.4 Summary

Three findings should be emphasized. First, the existence of price controls and out-of-line bill rates in the early and middle 1970s do not have an important impact on the estimates. Inclusion of the price controls variable or adjustment of the bill rate improve the explanation of inflation slightly, but the values of the important regression coefficients are largely unaffected.

Second, the real bill rate is shown to be systematically related to the level of real activity as measured by the capacity utilization rate. With the coefficient of the latter equal to -0.009, the real bill rate is 2½ percentage points higher (at an annual rate) when the utilization rate is 90% than when it is 70%.

Third, the estimated responses of actual inflation to both expected inflation (as reflected in the bill rate) and unanticipated inflation (based on the Livingston survey data) are close to unity. The bill rate coefficient point estimate is 0.85, while that of the unanticipated inflation varies between 0.74 and 0.88. Although the lowest of these coefficients is two standard errors below unity, we do not emphasize this because there is reason to believe that the coefficients may be biased downward. Unfortunately, the tax rate of the representative investor cannot necessarily be inferred from the bill rate coefficient. For example, an estimate of unity implies a zero tax rate if the real bill rate is independent of the expected inflation rate, but a positive tax rate if the real bill rate is negatively related to expected inflation, a relationship that would be reflected in the estimated bill rate coefficient. The significance and empirical importance of the unanticipated inflation measure suggest that the Livingston survey data, which indicate a significant underestimate of 6-month inflation throughout much of the 1969–80 period, may well have accurately reflected the expectations of market participants. This underestimate of expected inflation explains why nominal bill rates failed to move one for one with actual inflation during the 1952–80 period.

3.4 The Determinants of Unanticipated Changes in Treasury Coupon Rates

In section 3.2, ex post returns on corporate bonds and equities were shown to be strongly influenced by unanticipated changes in long-term new-issue Treasury coupons (or by total changes which were shown to be largely unanticipated). The last stage of our study is an investigation of the determinants of these unanticipated changes.[29] We begin with the analytical framework and then report some equation estimates.

3.4.1   Framework

Unanticipated changes in long-term Treasury rates are caused by changes in long-run expected inflation, which are unanticipated by definition, and unanticipated changes in the long-term real rates. Of course, neither of these is observable. Thus the problem is to specify proxies for expected inflation and the expected real rate and, for the latter, to distinguish between anticipated and unanticipated changes.

The results of sections 3.2 and 3.3 give us some guidance here. From the Livingston survey, we have estimates of expected short-run inflation. While the validity of this survey data is questioned by some, the empirical significance of the measure of unanticipated inflation based on these data in both the equity-return and inflation regressions suggests that the data have empirical content. It seems reasonable that long-run inflationary expectations would be revised upward in response to unanticipated short-run inflation.

The inflation equations also implied that real Treasury bill rates are related positively to the capacity utilization rate. Short-run changes in this rate, in turn, must be closely correlated with the growth rate of industrial production. As a consequence, it is reasonable to hypothesize that unanticipated changes in long-term rates are positively correlated with deviations between actual and expected growth rates in industrial production. Fortunately, the Livingston survey also contains forecasts of industrial production 6 months ahead.

Because the Livingston survey data are available only semiannually (June and December), the analysis of unanticipated changes in Treasury coupon rates is conducted in a 6-month time frame. That is, changes from December of one year to June of the next, from that June to the next December, and so on, are the dependent variable in the analysis (the specific data are discussed and listed in Appendix C). We denote the change from $t - 1$ to t as $UN\Delta_t$. This change is hypothesized to depend on unanticipated industrial production growth, $UNIP_t$ and unanticipated inflation, $UNINF_t$, between $t - 1$ and t. These variables are defined more precisely as

$$UNIP_t = [IP_t - E_{t-1}(IP_t)]/IP_{t-1}$$
$$UNINF_t = I_t - E_{t-1}(I_t),$$

where IP is the level of industrial production, I is the inflation rate (the subscript t denotes inflation from $t - 1$ to t), and E is the expectations operator.

Policy surprises must also be accounted for because they may provide information beyond that incorporated in the above defined variables. This would likely be true to the extent that policy surprises affect prices and real income with a lag; if the full impact occurred instantaneously, it would be reflected in the unanticipated inflation and industrial production growth variables. The most obvious surprise in the 1955–80 period was the imposition and removal of price controls in the early 1970s. To proxy this surprise, we specify a controls dummy variable that assumes the value − 1 in the second half of 1971 when the controls were imposed, + 1 in the first half of 1974 when the controls were removed, and zero in all other periods. To the extent that the imposition and removal of controls, respectively, lowered and raised expected long-run inflation, this variable, PCDUM, should have a positive impact on the change in coupon rate.

The fiscal surprise variable employed is that computed by von Furstenberg (1981). This variable is defined as the difference between the actual and "normal" surpluses of federal, state, and local governments, divided by net national product. The normal surplus takes into account not only the stage of the business cycle but also regular (forecastable) discretionary policy actions taken over the course of the business cycle (regular tax cuts during recessions, for example). This variable is denoted by FSUR. The variable exceeds 1½% in absolute value in only three periods: 1960, mid-1966–mid-1968 (the Vietnam buildup), and the second quarter of 1975 (the extraordinary tax rebate). A positive fiscal surprise (unusually large surplus) would be expected to lower interest rates. The decline would be relatively minor if the surprise does not lead to a revision in the "fiscal policy" rule. Von Furstenberg argues persuasively that this was the case in the 1955–78 period.

The monetary surprise variable tested is the difference between the rate of growth in the adjusted monetary base computed by the Federal Reserve Bank of St. Louis and the growth rate in recent periods (say the previous 2 years). The impact of this variable on interest rates is unclear. Unanticipated monetary growth would tend to depress real rates (Milton Friedman's "liquidity effect") but would lead to an upward revision in the inflation premia.[30] Because the estimated coefficient on variance of this variable never had a t-ratio greater than one or an estimated impact greater than a few basis points, equation estimates with this variable are not reported below.

We would expect that the coupon rate would be linearly related to the unanticipated inflation and price control variables as constructed. Because the unanticipated industrial production and fiscal surprise variables are real ratios, we would expect them to affect the percentage change in the new-issue coupon rate. To reflect these considerations, the unanticipated change in the coupon rate, unanticipated inflation, and the price controls variable have all been deflated by the lagged value of the 20-year Treasury coupon rate. Thus the estimated equations are of the form:

$$(9) \quad UN\Delta/R20_{-1} = \theta_0 + \theta_1 UNIP + \theta_2 UNINF/R20_{-1} - \theta_3 FSUR + \theta_4 PCDUM/R20_{-1},$$

where $\theta_0 \sim 0$ and $\theta_i > 0$ for $i > 0$.

3.4.2   The Estimates

The first equation in table 3.10 is estimated over the 1955–78 period, the span for which von Furstenberg calculated his fiscal surprise variable. All variables enter significantly with the expected signs, the constant term is within a standard error of zero, and the equation explains a third of the variance in the dependent variable. The sources of the cumulated 6 percentage point rise in the new issue coupon rate over the 1955–78 period are unanticipated 6-month inflation and industrial production growth; both averaged 1.3 percentage points per period in this span. Multiplication of 1.3 by 48 semiannual periods and the relevant regression coefficient yields 3.3 percentage points for the cumulative effect of unanticipated inflation. To obtain the impact of unanticipated industrial production growth, we multiply 1.3 by 48, the regression coefficient (.0082), and the mean value of the 20-year Treasury coupon in this period, 5.4. The result is 2.8 percentage points. A single 4½ percentage point inflation error, which occurred during 1973–74 and again in 1979, is accompanied by a quarter of a percentage point rise in the coupon rate. The production growth forecasting errors exceeded ±0.06 in six semiannual periods between 1955 and 1978 but were never larger than ±0.092; the 0.0082 coefficient implies that a 0.08 underforecast of industrial production growth is associated with a two-thirds percentage point increase in the new issue coupon when it is at the 10% level. A relatively

Table 3.10   **Determination of Semiannual Percentage Unanticipated Changes in the New Issue Coupon Rate[a]**

Period	Constant	Unanticipated Individual Product Growth	Unanticipated Inflation	Fiscal Surprise	Price Controls Dummy	$\bar{R}^2$ (SEE)
1955–78	−.0107	.0082	.0535	−.0129	.660	.340
	(.0109)	(.0020)	(.0281)	(.0066)	(.268)	(.0519)
1955–80	−.0074	.0093	.0578	−.0128	.646	.331
	(.0115)	(.0021)	(.0292)	(.0071)	(.287)	(.0557)

[a]The dependent variable, unanticipated inflation, and the price controls dummy are deflated by the beginning-of-period, 20-year, new-issue coupon rate.

large negative fiscal surprise, such as the 2½ percentage point surprise during the mid-1966–mid-1968 Vietnam buildup, is accompanied by a 15 basis point per period rise in the coupon rate. Finally, the imposition of price controls appears to have lowered long-run inflation expectations by nearly two-thirds of a percentage point.

The second equation in table 3.10 contains estimates for the full 1955–80 period. In this equation the fiscal surprise variable was arbitrarily set equal to zero (the variable was 0.404 in the fourth quarter of 1978 and averaged −0.187 during the 1955–78 period). Beause there were not any obvious surprises in the last 2 years of the Carter administration, this is probably a reasonable approximation. The estimated coefficients are close to those of the first equation with the exception of the response to unanticipated growth which rises by half a standard error. The actual and predicted percentage changes from this equation are plotted in figure 3.2. As can be seen, the equation seems to underpredict a number of large changes (except those associated with price controls) but does capture major swings in the new issue coupon (except possibly the most recent one).

With the fiscal surprise variable still maintained at zero, our equation significantly overpredicts the level of the Treasury coupon rate in 1981 and 1982, even allowing for the sharp decline in late 1982. This is to be expected for two reasons. First, a substantial fiscal surprise has undoubtedly occurred. While taxes are normally cut during recessions and the 1982 full employment deficit is not large by historical standards, the combination of the July 1983 tax cut, the indexation of taxes in future years, and the difficulties of controlling many expenditures leads to large "out year" full employment deficits. This "permanent" surprise could have had a quite large impact on interest rates. Second, the sharp 1981 cut in the taxation of returns from business capital would be expected to raise real interest rates by a percentage point or two (Hendershott and Shilling 1982).

3.5 Summary

This study began with an examination of data for the 1926–80 period on returns earned on one-month Treasury bills, long-term Treasury and corporate bonds, and corporate equities. Relationships among the returns and between them and inflation and the business cycle were identified. We then turned to econometric investigations of the relationships between ex post monthly returns on corporate securities and bill rates and other variables, principally the unanticipated change in the coupon on new-issue Treasury bonds. We concluded with an investigation of the determinants of the bill rate and the unanticipated change in long-term Treasury coupon rates.

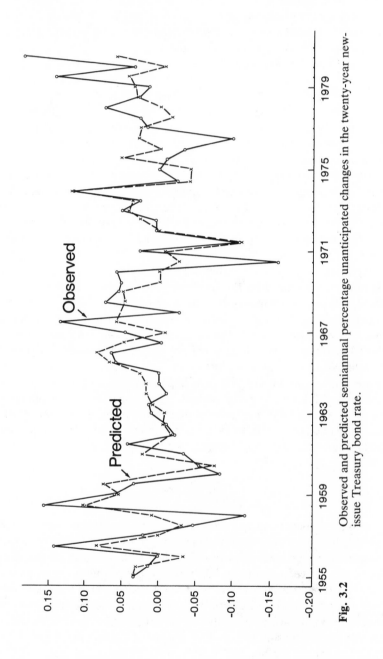

Fig. 3.2 Observed and predicted semiannual percentage unanticipated changes in the twenty-year new-issue Treasury bond rate.

The most general theme of the econometric work is the usefulness of the Livingston survey data in explaining financial returns. Unanticipated inflation, defined as the difference between short-run observed inflation and the Livingston forecast, enters the equity-returns, inflation-rate, and change-in-new-issue-coupon equations significantly. (When unanticipated inflation is not included as a regressor in the inflation equation, the estimates imply that real [bill] interest rates are negatively related to expected inflation; when unanticipated inflation is included this negative relationship does not appear to exist.) In addition, changes in new-issue coupon rates are positively related to unanticipated growth in industrial production, defined as the difference between observed growth and the Livingston forecast.

The latter result is part of a secondary theme, a positive relationship between real interest rates or returns and real economic activity. Ex post equity returns ("the market") are strongly related to expectations of future economic activity. In every business cycle since at least 1926, the market has risen sharply around cycle troughs (the last half or 6 months, whichever is shorter, of recessions and first 6 months of expansions); other things being equal, equity returns are 34 percentage points higher during this key year of turnaround in expectations than these returns are at other times. In addition, unanticipated inflation, which appears to lead to expectations of lower real economic activity, depresses equity values (by as much as 22% in 1973–74 and 1979), other things being equal. The investigation of new-issue debt yields lends supporting results. The real Treasury bill rate is positively related to the capacity utilization rate with the real rate being 2½ percentage points higher when utilization is at 90% than when it is at 70%. Because more rapid growth in industrial production leads to higher capacity utilization, the relationship between changes in new issue rates on long-term Treasuries and this growth is implicitly a relationship between the level of Treasury bond rates and capacity utilization.

Unanticipated changes in new Treasury coupon rates (and 88% of monthly changes during the 1953–77 period were unanticipated) are the dominant determinant of ex post monthly coporate bond returns and also strongly influence equity returns. Regarding the latter, a 2½ percentage point increase in new-issue Treasury coupon rates is estimated to lower the market by 10%. More generally, for the 1961–80 period the data are consistent with the Modigliani-Cohn valuation error model and a dividend tax rate of about 0.4. Finally, a third of semiannual percentage unanticipated changes in new-issue coupon rates over the 1955–80 period can be explained by unanticipated 6-month inflation and industrial production growth, fiscal policy "surprises," and the imposition and removal of price controls in the early 1970s.

The analysis of the present study can usefully be extended in two ways. First, a switch to a semiannual data base for all parts of the empirical work is called for in order to utilize the Livingston survey data more appropriately. This switch might also allow some differentiation in the effects of real and purely nominal unanticipated bond rate changes on equity returns. Our analysis was not able to distinguish between Modigliani-Cohn irrationality (there is no need to differentiate between changes in real rates and in inflationary premia because investors only care about their sum) and rationality (with much of nominal rate changes being real changes) because it is nearly impossible to identify inflationary premia in long-term bond rates on a monthly basis. Second, the stability of the estimated relationships over time should be tested. It would, of course, be useful to know if the relationships have been altered by the change in Federal Reserve operating procedures and the resulting increased volatility in financial markets since October 1979. Preliminary examination of the movement in long-term Treasury coupons indicates that a change has likely occurred.

Appendix A
Granger Causality Tests

The purpose of this Appendix is to investigate the information content of past returns on bonds (equities) in determining equity (bond) yields after accounting for past yields on equities (bonds). The role of the inflation rate is examined in this context both by introducing it as a determining factor for asset yields and by comparing the behavior of nominal and real asset yields.

The statistical tool we use here corresponds to a statistical test for exogeneity commonly known as the Granger causality test. It should be emphasized that the word 'causality' is used here only in the restrictive sense of predictability. More specifically, we say that a time series X_t Granger causes another time series Y_t if we are able to better predict Y_t in the sense of a lower mean squared prediction error by using the past values of both X_t and Y_t than by employing only the past values of Y_t.

Specifying the predictor to be a linear one, the test involves regressing Y_t on lagged Y_t's and X_t's, that is,

(A1) $$Y_t = \sum_{i=1}^{k_1} \alpha_i Y_{t-1} + \sum_{i=1}^{k_2} \beta_i X_{t-i}.$$

If the parameters β_i, $i = 1, \ldots, k_2$, are significantly different from zero, then X_t Granger causes or is informative in the prediction of Y_t. In order to test the predictive content of Y_t in determining X_t, the roles of Y_t and X_t in (A1) are reversed.

If, contrary to (A1), the relevant information set contains variables other than X_t and Y_t, then the above regression test may show spurious causality between X_t and Y_t if the other variable leads both X_t and Y_t. Given the results of the previous section, it is therefore highly probable that a test of the predictive relationship between corporate bonds and stocks will reveal Granger causality; the causality being the result of shocks that are common to both stocks and bonds.

In our tests, we specify $k_1 = k_2 = 6$. It is felt that 6 months is long enough to reflect any price adjustments. A constant term and time trend are added to (A1) in the estimation to capture the presence of deterministic components.

In table 3.A.1 we report the results of the tests of the bivariate relationships between equity and debt returns. The overlapping sample periods reported are the entire sample 1926–80, the pre–Treasury

Table 3.A.1   **Granger Causality Tests**

$$Y_t = c + \sum_{i=1}^{6} \alpha_i Y_{t-i} + \sum_{i=1}^{6} \beta_i X_{t-i} + \delta t$$

Variables		Sample Period	$F_{m,n}$-Statistic:		m, n
Y	X		Nominal	Real	
CS	CB	1926–	3.130*	4.172*	6,640
CB	CS	1980	1.273	1.653	6,640
CS	CB	1926–	2.596	2.444	6,304
CB	CS	1952	6.199*	6.276*	6,304
CS	CB	1932–	1.413	1.852	6,220
CB	CS	1952	.913	1.093	6,220
CS	CB	1953–	2.950*	3.512*	6,316
CB	CS	1980	3.452*	3.260*	6,316
CS	GB	1926–	2.203	3.104*	6,640
GB	CS	1980	1.267	.686	6,640
CS	GB	1926–	1.131	1.038	6,304
GB	CS	1952	.443	.630	6,304
CS	GB	1933–	.215	.691	6,220
GB	CS	1952	.491	.328	6,220
CS	GB	1953–	3.337*	3.808*	6,316
GB	CS	1980	2.478	2.113	6,316
CS	TB	1926–	1.871	2.414	6,640
TB	CS	1980	2.427	1.530	6,640
CS	TB	1926–	.945	1.352	6,304
TB	CS	1952	.771	1.085	6,304
CS	TB	1933–	1.138	2.493	6,220
TB	CS	1952	.954	1.808	6,220
CS	TB	1953–	1.398	2.187	6,316
TB	CS	1980	1.716	1.239	6,316

Note: The following notations are used: CS for common stocks, CB for corporate bonds, TB for Treasury bills. X and Y variables refer to the same variables in eq. (A1) in the text.
*Significant at the 5% level.

Accord period 1926–52, the pre–Treasury Accord period after the Great Depression 1933–52, and the post-Accord span of 1953–80. Reported are the F-statistics for tests of the null hypothesis that all the β's in (A1) are zero. The tests are performed for both the nominal and real rates of return.

With one exception, returns on government bonds or bills contain no informative content in the prediction of equity returns. The reverse is also supported. The sole exception is the informativeness of government bonds in predicting stock returns during the post-Accord period. As for common stocks and corporate bonds, the latter Granger-caused the former when the whole sample is utilized. However, when subperiods of

Table 3.A.2   Granger Causality Tests with Past Inflation Included

$$Y_t = c + \sum_{i=1}^{6} \alpha_i Y_{t-i} + \sum_{i=1}^{6} \beta_i X_{t-i} + \sum_{i=1}^{6} \gamma_i I_{t-i} + \delta t$$

Y	X	Sample Period	$F_{m,n}$-Statistic	m, n	$F_{m,n}$-Statistic	m, n
CS	CB	1926–	1.751	6,634	2.451*	12,634
CB	CS	1980	.542	6,634	.905	12,634
CS	CB	1926–	1.141	6,298	1.872	12,298
CB	CS	1952	.884	6,298	3.534*	12,298
CS	CB	1933–	1.845	6,214	1.646	12,214
CB	CS	1952	1.704	6,214	1.317	12,214
CS	CB	1953–	1.573	6,310	2.277*	12,310
CB	CS	1980	1.548	6,310	2.518*	12,310
CS	GB	1926–	1.685	6,634	1.784	12,634
GB	CS	1980	.465	6,634	1.440	12,634
CS	GB	1926–	.999	6,298	.972	12,298
GB	CS	1952	.431	6,298	.597	12,298
CS	GB	1933–	2.206	6,214	1.690	12,214
GB	CS	1952	.887	6,214	.919	12,214
CS	GB	1953–	2.277	6,310	1.854	12,310
GB	CS	1980	3.465*	6,310	2.630*	12,310
CS	TB	1926–	1.576	6,634	1.895	12,634
TB	CS	1980	.303	6,634	.781	12,634
CS	TB	1926–	.935	6,298	1.033	12,298
TB	CS	1952	.445	6,298	.442	12,298
CS	TB	1933–	1.872	6,214	1.046	12,214
TB	CS	1952	1.573	6,214	1.036	12,214
CS	TB	1953–	1.367	6,310	2.364*	12,214
TB	CS	1980	1.634	6,310	2.071	12,310

Note: The following notations are used: CS for common stocks, CB for corporate bonds, TB for Treasury bills, and I is the inflation rate. X and Y variables refer to the same variables in eq. (A1) in the text.

*Significant at the 5% level.

the entire sample are examined, the causality is in the opposite direction with corporate bonds leading stocks for the 1926–52 period. When the Depression years are excluded from the 1926–52 period, no causality in either direction was observed. Finally, both equity and corporate bonds appear to be valuable in predicting one another in the post-Accord period. These observations are virtually unchanged whether real or nominal returns are used.

In 3.A.2, we reexamine the results of table A1 by focusing on nominal returns but with past inflation rates (I_{t-i}) added as a possible additional source of information. The results indicate that past inflation rates by themselves do not contain information content. Moreover, the same conclusions drawn from table 3.A.1 with respect to common stocks and corporate bonds can be drawn from table 3.A.2 when the null hypothesis tested is that both past X_t and I_t have no informative content in predicting Y_t once one has accounted for past values of Y_t. Also, as in table A1, in general no distinct causal patterns emerges when government bonds or bills are used in place of corporate bonds.

To summarize, the results indicate the usefulness, in the post-Accord period, of past corporate bonds (stock) returns in predicting current corporate stock (bond) returns even after allowing for the presence of past corporate stock (bond) returns. This result is observed when either nominal or real returns are used as well as when past inflation rates are added as additional sources of information. As for government bonds or bills when examined with stocks, no consistent lead or lag relationships were uncovered. It may very well be that the Granger causalities observed for corporate bonds and stocks are due to variables other than the inflation rate that affect both the variables being examined.

Appendix B
The McCulloch Data

Our analysis of ex post bond and equity returns employed changes in the long-term, new-issue-equivalent Treasury bond rate and the unanticipated change in this rate as regressors. Both of these variables have been computed by Huston McCulloch (1975, 1977) who developed a technique of curve-fitting the term structure of interest rates from security prices so as to determine implicit forward interest rates as precisely as possible. At each point in time for which Treasury security prices are available, a discount function is estimated, using a cubic spline tax-adjusted technique, to give the value at these points of a promise to repay a dollar at alternative future dates. Before-tax equivalent instantaneous forward rates, single payment yields, and par bond yields were calculated from the parameters of the spline discount curve for maturities sufficiently close to allow linear interpolation to all desired intermediate points. The tax adjustment was especially important in the late 1960s and early 1970s when all long-term Treasury bonds were selling at substantial discounts owing to effective restrictions against new issues between 1965 and 1973 and the sharp rise in interest rates after the mid-1960s (see Cook and Hendershott 1978).

Except for tax-exempt and selected flower bonds (those whose prices were determined by the flower bond characteristic), virtually all U.S. Treasury bills, notes, and bonds have been analyzed monthly since January 1974 (McCulloch updates the file a number of times per year). The data presented in columns 4 and 3 of table 3.A.3 are the level and change in the new-issue-equivalent semiannual coupon yields on 20-year Treasury bonds or on the longest possible maturity computable with McCulloch's technique. During the 1952–81 period the longest maturity was below 19 years only in the 1970–72 period.

Column 2 of table 3.A.3 contains McCulloch's measure of unanticipated monthly changes in the longest-term Treasury rates, ignoring liquidity premia (McCulloch 1977, app. 3). This is the difference between the one-month forward par bond yield and the observed corresponding spot par bond yield one month later.

In our analysis of semiannual changes in long-term interest rates, we have updated McCulloch's data on a semiannual basis. Here, we compute the difference between 6-month forward par bond yields (b^*) and the observed corresponding spot par bond yield 6 months hence ($R20_{+1}$). The unanticipated change ($UN\Delta$) is thus $UN\Delta = R20_{+1} - b^*$, where b^* is the semiannual coupon rate that will make the value of a bond in 6 months, evaluated at the current term structure, just equal to par, discounted to the present using the current term structure. To make the calculations, we use as inputs McCulloch's semiannual coupons (y) on 6-month (0.5 years) and 20½-year bonds and continuous single-point par discount yields (d) on the same maturity bonds. First, the semiannual coupons are converted to continuous equivalents

$$c = 2 \log_e(1 + y/2)$$

for maturities 0.5 and 20.5.

Second, the continuous forward par bond yield is computed as

$$b = \frac{e^{-0.5d}0.5 - e^{-20.5d}20.5}{[1 - e^{-20.5d}20.5]/c_{20.5} - [1 - e^{-0.5d}0.5]/c_{0.5}}.$$

Finally, this continuous yield is converted to a semiannual coupon equivalent: $b^* = 2(e^{b/2} - 1)$.

Unanticipated changes for the first half of 1977 (December 1976—

average of beginning and end of month values—to June 1977) through the first half of 1982 are listed in Appendix C.

The percentage changes in yields employed in the stock return equations are the changes ($\Delta R20$ or $UN\Delta$) divided by the end of period value of $R20$.

Table 3.A.3   McCulloch's Data

Date	$U\Delta R20$	$\Delta R20$	$R20$	Date	$U\Delta R20$	$\Delta R20$	$R20$
5212	—	—	2.76	5604	.056	.13	3.02
5301	.072	.08	2.84	5605	.098	.05	3.07
5302	.009	.01	2.85	5606	−.087	−.12	2.95
5303	.080	.08	2.93	5607	−.037	.01	2.96
5304	.020	.03	2.96	5608	.105	.15	3.11
5305	.162	.18	3.14	5609	.120	.17	3.28
5306	.029	.11	3.25	5610	−.074	−.08	3.20
5307	−.074	−.19	3.06	5611	.131	.08	3.28
5308	.081	.05	3.11	5612	.066	.09	3.37
5309	.012	.05	3.16	5701	.153	.22	3.59
5310	−.154	−.21	2.95	5702	−.268	−.43	3.16
5311	−.043	.04	2.99	5703	.045	.14	3.30
5312	.004	.04	3.03	5704	−.004	−.06	3.24
5401	−.137	−.18	2.85	5705	.137	.13	3.37
5402	−.042	−.03	2.82	5706	.030	.07	3.44
5403	−.177	−.21	2.61	5707	.094	.09	3.53
5404	−.013	.02	2.63	5708	.019	−.01	3.52
5405	−.047	−.03	2.60	5709	.022	.02	3.54
5406	.054	.08	2.68	5710	.058	.15	3.69
5407	−.118	−.12	2.56	5711	.057	.06	3.75
5408	−.051	−.03	2.53	5712	−.136	−.04	3.71
5409	.010	.02	2.55	5801	−.463	−.46	3.25
5410	.005	.00	2.55	5802	.050	.05	3.30
5411	.022	.05	2.60	5803	−.091	−.04	3.26
5412	.051	.08	2.68	5804	.000	.01	3.27
5501	−.019	.01	2.69	5805	−.126	−.13	3.14
5502	.125	.13	2.82	5806	−.063	.02	3.16
5503	.052	.05	2.87	5807	.085	.10	3.26
5504	−.038	−.03	2.84	5808	.275	.28	3.54
5505	−.020	.03	2.87	5809	.184	.22	3.76
5506	−.012	−.04	2.83	5810	.070	−.01	3.75
5507	.004	.06	2.89	5811	−.076	−.04	3.71
5508	.056	.10	2.99	5812	−.042	−.01	3.70
5509	.019	−.03	2.96	5901	.095	.14	3.84
5510	−.025	−.03	2.93	5902	.119	.21	4.05
5511	−.036	−.06	2.87	5903	−.005	−.05	4.00
5512	.041	.08	2.95	5904	−.002	.02	4.02
5601	−.051	−.02	2.93	5905	.027	.08	4.10
5602	−.018	−.07	2.86	5906	.031	.02	4.12
5603	.011	.03	2.89	5907	.030	.06	4.18

Table 3.A.3 (continued)

Date	$U\Delta R20$	$\Delta R20$	$R20$	Date	$U\Delta R20$	$\Delta R20$	$R20$
5908	−.035	−.01	4.17	6309	.000	−.01	4.05
5909	.053	.05	4.22	6310	.078	.05	4.10
5910	−.018	.01	4.23	6311	.027	.06	4.16
5911	−.035	−.04	4.19	6312	−.001	.00	4.16
5912	.066	.09	4.28	6401	.025	.07	4.23
6001	.172	.18	4.46	6402	−.025	−.02	4.21
6002	−.064	−.02	4.44	6403	.004	.02	4.23
6003	−.144	−.17	4.27	6404	.029	.04	4.27
6004	−.212	−.18	4.09	6405	−.009	−.02	4.25
6005	.195	.23	4.23	6406	−.049	−.05	4.20
6006	−.110	−.08	4.24	6407	−.017	−.02	4.18
6007	−.224	−.23	4.01	6408	.039	.05	4.23
6008	−.201	−.23	3.78	6409	−.003	.02	4.25
6009	.096	.07	3.85	6410	−.008	−.02	4.23
6010	.002	.03	3.88	6411	−.024	−.02	4.21
6011	−.004	.05	3.93	6412	.014	.03	4.24
6012	.039	.08	4.01	6501	.007	.02	4.26
6101	−.125	−.16	3.85	6502	−.013	−.02	4.24
6102	.078	.09	3.94	6503	.007	.01	4.25
6103	−.125	−.10	3.84	6504	−.002	−.01	4.24
6104	−.016	.03	3.87	6505	−.003	.00	4.24
6105	−.066	−.05	3.82	6506	.004	.02	4.26
6106	−.016	.01	3.83	6507	−.012	−.02	4.24
6107	.151	.12	3.95	6508	.017	.02	4.26
6108	.015	.04	3.99	6509	.036	.04	4.30
6109	.098	.03	4.02	6510	.059	.08	4.38
6110	−.016	−.04	3.98	6511	.005	.02	4.40
6111	−.038	−.04	3.94	6512	.075	.10	4.50
6112	.019	.06	4.00	6601	.097	.10	4.60
6201	.026	.05	4.05	6602	.070	.05	4.65
6202	.010	.05	4.10	6603	.226	.22	4.87
6203	.029	.03	4.13	6604	−.167	−.16	4.71
6204	−.155	−.12	4.01	6605	.034	.07	4.78
6205	−.029	−.02	3.99	6606	.065	.05	4.83
6206	.003	−.01	3.98	6607	.072	.13	4.96
6207	.033	.04	4.02	6608	.012	.00	4.96
6208	.179	.09	4.11	6609	.269	.30	5.26
6209	−.150	−.08	4.03	6610	−.250	−.25	5.01
6210	−.041	−.02	4.01	6611	−.108	−.16	4.85
6211	−.045	−.03	3.98	6612	.123	.16	5.01
6212	−.002	−.02	3.96	6701	−.247	−.30	4.71
6301	−.013	−.04	3.92	6702	−.113	−.13	4.58
6302	.035	.05	3.97	6703	.202	.25	4.83
6303	.011	.08	4.05	6704	−.123	−.16	4.67
6304	.017	.01	4.06	6705	.219	.29	4.96
6305	.027	.04	4.10	6706	.054	.02	4.98
6306	−.031	−.02	4.08	6707	.216	.21	5.19
6307	−.005	.00	4.08	6708	.001	.05	5.24
6308	−.041	−.02	4.06	6709	.084	.06	5.30

Table 3.A.3 (continued)

Date	$U\Delta R20$	$\Delta R20$	$R20$	Date	$U\Delta R20$	$\Delta R20$	$R20$
6710	.045	.09	5.39	7111	−.104	−.03	6.12
6711	.249	.23	5.62	7112	−.051	−.02	6.10
6712	.198	.21	5.83	7201	.061	.01	6.11
6801	−.023	.04	5.87	7202	.325	.29	6.40
6802	−.180	−.19	5.68	7203	−.151	−.10	6.30
6803	.060	.05	5.73	7204	−.061	−.02	6.28
6804	.255	.31	6.04	7205	−.032	−.02	6.26
6805	−.182	−.21	5.83	7206	−.096	−.07	6.19
6806	−.011	.04	5.87	7207	.040	.04	6.23
6807	−.130	−.19	5.68	7208	.123	.12	6.35
6808	−.131	−.15	5.53	7209	.057	.07	6.42
6809	−.016	−.02	5.51	7210	.113	.13	6.55
6810	.146	.19	5.70	7211	−.179	−.15	6.40
6811	.180	.21	5.91	7212	−.127	−.05	6.35
6812	.116	.19	6.10	7301	.047	.04	6.39
6901	.430	.43	6.53	7302	.119	.48	6.87
6902	.109	.08	6.61	7303	−.006	−.02	6.85
6903	−.075	−.04	6.57	7304	−.020	−.02	6.83
6904	−.015	−.02	6.55	7305	−.006	.01	6.84
6905	−.148	−.19	6.36	7306	.164	.15	6.99
6906	.344	.38	6.74	7307	.077	.09	7.08
6907	−.162	−.20	6.54	7308	.443	.41	7.49
6908	−.099	−.08	6.46	7309	−.253	−.19	7.30
6909	−.065	−.08	6.38	7310	−.247	−.26	7.04
6910	.329	.35	6.73	7311	.348	.39	7.43
6911	−.065	−.07	6.66	7312	−.203	−.21	7.22
6912	.276	.31	6.97	7401	.132	.12	7.34
7001	.101	.10	7.07	7402	.097	.10	7.44
7002	−.091	−.13	6.94	7403	.098	.10	7.54
7003	−.387	−.39	6.55	7404	.324	.26	7.80
7004	.147	.40	6.95	7405	.297	.29	8.09
7005	.754	.36	7.31	7406	.002	.03	8.12
7006	.077	.52	7.83	7407	−.075	−.08	8.04
7007	−.298	−.33	7.50	7408	.145	.13	8.17
7008	−.081	−.20	7.30	7409	.226	.22	8.39
7009	.034	.12	7.42	7410	−.075	−.02	8.37
7010	−.226	−.17	7.25	7411	−.304	−.29	8.08
7011	−.033	.04	7.29	7412	−.134	−.07	8.01
7012	−.738	−.85	6.44	7501	−.058	−.01	8.00
7101	−.004	.01	6.45	7502	−.168	−.27	7.73
7102	−.388	−.38	6.07	7503	−.054	−.03	7.70
7103	.181	.20	6.27	7504	.452	.60	8.30
7104	−.396	−.38	5.89	7505	.111	.03	8.33
7105	.285	.16	6.05	7506	−.255	−.11	8.22
7106	.316	.36	6.41	7507	−.053	−.10	8.12
7107	.307	.33	6.74	7508	.106	.16	8.28
7108	.118	.16	6.90	7509	.108	.13	8.41
7109	−.616	−.56	6.34	7510	.180	.24	8.65
7110	−.270	−.19	6.15	7511	−.439	−.44	8.21

Table 3.A.3 (continued)

Date	$U\Delta R20$	$\Delta R20$	$R20$	Date	$U\Delta R20$	$\Delta R20$	$R20$
7512	.163	.21	8.42	7807	—	.11	8.67
7601	−.317	−.32	8.10	7808	—	−.07	8.60
7602	−.056	−.03	8.07	7809	—	−.18	8.42
7603	.006	.03	8.10	7810	—	.22	8.64
7604	−.171	−.16	7.94	7811	—	.26	8.90
7605	.012	.05	7.99	7812	—	−.12	8.78
7606	.160	.19	8.18	7901	—	.21	8.99
7607	−.137	−.12	8.06	7902	—	−.11	8.88
7608	−.017	.00	8.06	7903	—	.22	9.10
7609	−.175	−.15	7.91	7904	—	−.04	9.06
7610	−.082	−.07	7.84	7905	—	.19	9.25
7611	−.065	−.04	7.80	7906	—	−.15	9.10
7612	−.324	−.28	7.52	7907	—	−.26	8.84
7701	−.225	−.26	7.26	7908	—	.15	8.99
7702	.369	.43	7.69	7909	—	.13	9.12
7703	.108	.12	7.81	7910	—	.16	9.28
7704	−.101	−.04	7.77	7911	—	1.13	10.41
7705	−.037	−.02	7.75	7912	—	−.23	10.18
7706	−.064	−.03	7.72	8001	—	.03	10.21
7707	—	−.16	7.56	8002	—	.93	11.14
7708	—	.09	7.65	8003	—	1.34	12.48
7709	—	−.06	7.59	8004	—	.03	12.51
7710	—	.08	7.67	8005	—	−1.51	11.00
7711	—	.22	7.89	8006	—	−.47	10.53
7712	—	−.02	7.87	8007	—	−.32	10.21
7801	—	.12	7.99	8008	—	.80	11.01
7802	—	.15	8.14	8009	—	.51	11.52
7803	—	.10	8.24	8010	—	.44	11.96
7804	—	.08	8.32	8011	—	.50	12.46
7805	—	.07	8.39	8012	—	.11	12.57
7806	—	.17	8.56				

Appendix C

Unanticipated Inflation and Growth in
Industrial Production: The Semiannual Database

Livingston collects data in May and November each year on the expected levels of the consumer price index and industrial production in the following December (for the May forecast) or the next June (for the December forecast). The annualized anticipated inflation rate is then computed from the difference between the forecasted price index and the level when the forecast is made. These data have been kindly supplied by Donald Mullineaux of the Philadelphia Federal Reserve Bank and have been calculated following the procedure reported in Carlson (1977).

Unanticipated industrial production growth between May and December, say, is computed as the difference between the actual December level and that forecast for December in the previous May, all divided by the May value. This series is multiplied by 100 to convert it to percentage points. The actual or observed data were collected from issues of the *Business Conditions Digest* and the *Federal Reserve Bulletin*. The first published number was utilized and care was taken to maintain consistency in base years in each calculation.

Unanticipated inflation is the difference between the actual inflation rate between, say, May and December, and that forecasted in May. On the assumption that the April consumer price index was known at the time of the December forecast, the actual inflation rate was computed as the compounded inflation between May and December and then annualized and converted to percentage points. More precisely,

$$\text{ACTINF} = 100 \left\{ \left[\prod_{i=0}^{7} (1 + I_{t-i}) \right]^{1.5} - 1 \right\},$$

where I is the monthly inflation rate. The unanticipated inflation variable employed in the monthly inflation and equity returns equations is obtained as $(1 + \text{UNINFA}/100)^{1/12} - 1$.

The fiscal surprise variable is taken from von Furstenberg (1981, table 9, p. 373) for the 1955–78 period. It is the difference between the actual and normal government surplus divided by net national product and converted to percentage points by multiplication by 100. The difference is the residual from a regression equation in which the percentage GNP gap, the lagged change in the unemployment rate, and the difference between actual and officially forecasted inflation rates are employed as regressors. The second- and fourth- quarter values of the surprise variable are used for the June and December data. For 1979 and 1980, this variable has been arbitrarily set equal to zero.

For the December 1954–December 1976 period, the unanticipated change in the new-issue Treasury coupon rate is taken from McCulloch's data (see our table 3.A.3). In order to center the data at mid-June and mid-December, the change during the second half of the year is defined as one-half of the June 1–July 1 change plus the total change from July 1 to December 1 plus one-half the change from December 1 to January 1. For the half-year periods since 1976, we have extended McCulloch's data in the manner described in Appendix B.

The annualized 6-month inflation forecast (the 551 number refers to the forecast for the second half of 1955 made in May), annualized unanticipated inflation, unanticipated growth in industrial production (not annualized), the fiscal surprise (percentage points of net national product), the unanticipated change in the coupon rate, this change divided by the beginning of period level of the new issue coupon, and the latter are all listed in table 3.A.4. All data are in percentage points.

Table 3.A.4   **Semiannual Data Base**

Date	Expected Inflation	Fiscal Surprise	Unanticipated Inflation	Unanticipated Individual Production	Unanticipated $\Delta R20$	Unanticipated $\%\Delta R20$
512	1.8527	—	.7538	−.06216	−.02	−.00742
521	.3169	—	.0715	−.11514	−.12	−.04404
522	−.1434	—	2.1679	.06453	.09	.03383
531	−.9911	—	−.0441	.05574	.29	.10357
532	−1.3142	—	2.8815	−.03237	−.20	−.06339
541	−.5231	—	1.1283	.00000	−.35	−.11905
542	.1246	—	.1508	.04597	−.04	−.01527
551	.5244	.299	−.6839	.06769	.10	.03724
552	.7433	.440	.4133	.04245	.04	.01399
561	.3436	.957	.0029	−.01528	.01	.00340
562	1.4435	1.269	3.5997	.03830	.41	.13875
571	1.0899	.694	1.8671	−.01973	.06	.01724
572	.0746	.413	2.3509	−.06250	−.16	−.04591
581	.0673	−1.095	2.9441	−.05074	−.42	−.12069
582	.6455	−.965	.6279	.09160	.50	.15576
591	.6118	.073	−.2994	.06972	.23	.06101
592	.9672	.602	1.6456	.07419	.13	.03133
601	.4602	2.223	.4044	.03636	−.36	−.08238
602	.2053	1.688	1.7639	−.07248	−.24	−.05818
611	1.0178	.955	.6405	.04175	−.13	−.03308
612	1.0518	.805	−.0083	.02273	.16	.04113
621	.9932	−.198	−.0489	−.01478	−.11	−.02733
622	.9953	.099	.3388	−.00339	−.05	−.01250
631	1.0212	1.500	−.8308	.03261	.05	.01269
632	.8668	.630	.6263	.01918	.08	.01961
641	1.0960	−.774	.1121	.01572	−.05	−.01192
642	1.2827	.531	.3655	.02883	.01	.00239
651	.9446	.521	.3312	.03577	−.01	−.00235
652	1.5610	−1.473	1.3049	.04003	.24	.05647
661	1.8209	−1.170	1.6202	.05529	.31	.06813
662	2.0501	−2.122	1.6253	.00963	−.04	−.00817
671	2.1049	−2.755	−.0560	−.03907	.22	.04527
672	2.5932	−2.532	1.5570	.01353	.68	.13373
681	3.0848	−2.635	1.4555	.01420	−.14	−.02393
682	2.7118	−1.202	1.7690	.02307	.45	.07792
691	3.1563	.477	2.9057	.04144	.35	.05542
692	3.5959	.714	2.7333	−.00345	.34	.05120
701	3.5504	−.323	2.5353	−.01870	.40	.05698
702	3.5720	−.543	1.7353	−.04152	−1.19	−.15525
711	3.9860	−1.061	.6702	−.01952	.15	.02327
712	3.0325	−.702	−.4596	−.01132	−.74	−.11255
721	3.5777	.038	.0518	.00929	.03	.00491
722	3.2278	−.790	−.0490	.02307	.03	.00483
731	4.0025	−.372	3.1375	.01928	.32	.05024
732	5.1748	−.579	5.1456	−.00646	.19	.02701
741	7.1272	.388	6.0971	−.00711	.85	.11676
742	7.7054	.467	4.8397	−.069323	−.21	−.02599

Table 3.A.4 (continued)

Date	Expected Inflation	Fiscal Surplus	Unanticipated Inflation	Unanticipated Individual Production	Unanticipated $\Delta R20$	Unanticipated $\%\Delta R20$
751	5.6368	−3.284	−.0968	−.085376	.03	.00375
752	5.8424	−.869	1.8686	.038182	−.07	−.00857
761	5.2983	−.489	−.6644	.010127	−.28	−.03390
762	5.2306	−.306	.3962	.030023	−.84	−.10345
771	5.9251	.285	1.8018	.024096	.12	.01624
772	5.9926	−1.039	.1963	−.022367	.16	.02094
781	6.4049	.335	1.6839	−.000716	.62	.07818
782	6.9763	.404	3.3139	.020790	.22	.02554
791	8.3092	.000	4.5474	.009973	1.14	.016
792	10.1440	.000	5.1948	.017173	1.27	.142
801	10.6766	.000	4.6452	−.030223	.32	.031
802	10.5082	.000	−.2392	.070822	1.90	.183

Notes

1. The variability in the real bill rate in the 1952–80 period would likely have been even lower in the absence of deposit rate ceilings. More specifically, the large negative values in 1973 and 1974 are due to bill rates becoming "out of line" relative to private short-term yields due to disintermediation.

2. The premium that equities earned over Treasury bills is similar to the extent that returns on bonds and bills are roughly equal. As is indicated in the last column of table 3.2, government bonds outperformed government bills by nearly 4 percentage points per annum in the 1926–40 period, with the result that the equity premium over bills was significantly greater than that over bonds. The reverse was true, although to a lesser degree, in the 1968–80 perod.

3. Nonetheless, many have attributed the poor performance of equities in the 1969–78 decade to increased inflation and/or uncertainty regarding inflation. Feldstein (1980) has argued that biases in the tax law reduce share values in inflationary periods, while Modigliani and Cohn (1979) have attributed the reduction to an inflation-induced error of investors. Malkiel (1979) has contended that increased uncertainty regarding future price and government regulation changes has lowered share values by increasing the relative risk premium demanded on equity investments. In contrast, one of us has argued that these phenomena explain the relatively modest rise in promised new-issue debt yields (decline in real after-tax yields) but not the sharp decline in share values (Hendershott 1981).

4. Shiller (1979) has suggested that changes in long-term bond coupon rates have been largely unanticipated.

5. Huston McCulloch has constructed the unanticipated changes in long-term Treasury coupon rates in the 1947–77 period. These data are discussed in Appendix B and are employed in the econometric work in secs. 3.2 and 3.4.

6. This comparison is reported in Hendershott (1982).

7. The annualized geometric return over N periods on an asset earning R in period i is $[\Pi_{i=1}^{n}(1 + R_i) - 1]^{N/12}$.

8. Both of these series are described in Appendix B.

9. We value $(1 - \tau_d)R20 - g$ at zero and ρ at 0.06.

10. Because there was also weak evidence that equities earned negative returns relative to bonds around business cycle peaks, a negative turnaround dummy variable was defined analogously to the positive one and tested. The coefficient on this variable was never near a standard error from zero in any bond or equity equation.

11. The Livingston survey data have been questioned by Pearce (1979) on the grounds that they are not "rational" and are less consistent with observed bill rates than are rational inflation expectations. On the other hand, Mishkin (1981) is unsure that the Livingston data are irrational, and Carlson (1981) makes a strong argument that "irrationality" might not be surprising.

12. The precise series used equals $(1. + UNINFA/100)^{1/12} - 1$, where UNINFA is from the semiannual database listed in Appendix C.

13. When Carlson and Kling (1982) specify expected inflation from an ARIMA model and test for lead or lags between unexpected inflation and real activity via bivariate autoregressions, they, too, find price surprises leading real activity negatively.

14. The Durbin-Watson statistics for the equations in table 3.5 vary between 2.25 and 2.45.

15. See Bodie (1976), Jaffee and Mandelker (1976), Nelson (1976), and Fama and Schwert (1977).

16. The Durbin-Watson statistics for the equity equations over the different time periods vary between 1.95 and 2.15.

17. The equation might be interpreted as suggesting a higher tax rate on dividends; with $\Delta R20/(.55\ R20 + .04)$ as the regressor, the coefficients would sum to $-.45$. With $\Delta R20/(R20 + .04)$ as the regressor, the coefficients sum to -0.75.

18. There is an alternative interpretation. Because unanticipated inflation is greatest precisely when oil shocks occurred, this variable may be capturing nothing more than the negative impact on share values of the unexpected increase in energy prices. We will attempt to distinguish between these two interpretations in future work.

19. The "true" constant term which abstracts from political cycle effects is obtained as the sum of the coefficients on the political dummies and four times the estimated constant, all divided by 4. For eqs. (T3) and (T4), the true constants are 0.0063 and 0.0059.

20. The data are from their table 2, p. 17.

21. The spread between private rates and bills could also be affected by changes in risk and in the level of interest rates. The latter could matter because the income from private securities is taxed at the state and local level while that from bills is not.

22. The CD rates are first of month data recorded by Salomon Brothers.

23. A Cochraine-Orcutt semidifference transformation—with a semidifference parameter of 0.15–0.25—lowers the equation standard error for all of the equations in table 3.9 but hardly changes the coefficient estimates.

24. Thus the result is also consistent with Mishkin's findings (1981) for quarterly data from the 1953–79 period. When the lagged inflation rate is added to eq. (6), the procedure followed by Mishkin, the coefficient is 0.3 and the coefficient on the bill rate declines by a similar amount.

25. For the derivation of a nonzero β from a structural model, see Melvin (1982).

26. The Federal Reserve's capacity utilization rate for manufacturing averaged 84.3% during 1953–69 versus 81.4% for 1970–80. With a desired ratio of 90%, this is a 50% increase in the shortfall.

27. The result differs from Mishkin (1981) who does not find a significant implied relationship between real bill rates and either real GNP growth, the GNP gap, or the unemployment rate.

28. When the lagged inflation rate is added to equation (T4), a coefficient of 0.18 is estimated with a standard error of 0.05, and all other coefficients decline by roughly 18%. That is, the result is consistent with a very short lagged response (18% after the first month) to all variables.

29. On the relationship among new-issue coupon rates on alternative long-term debt instruments, see Cook and Hendershott (1978), Hendershott et al. (1982), and Van Horne (1978).

30. Melvin (1983) provides evidence that the liquidity and inflation effects exactly offset 6 months after an increase in monetary growth.

References

Blinder, Alan S. 1980. The consumer price index and the measurement of recent inflation. *Brooking Papers on Economic Activity* 2:539–65.

Blinder, Alan S., and Newton, W. J. 1981. The 1971–74 controls program and the price level. *Journal of Monetary Economics* 8:1–24.

Bodie, Zvi. 1976. Common stocks as a hedge against inflation. *Journal of Finance* 31:459–70.

Carlson, John A. 1977. A study of price forecasts. *Annuals of Economic and Social Measurement* 6:27–56.

———. 1979. Expected inflation and interest rates. *Economic Inquiry* 17:597–608.

———. 1981. Perceptions (or misperceptions) of inflation. In *Inflation: causes, consequence, and control*, ed. W. A. Gale. Cambridge: Oelgeschlager, Gunn & Hain.

Carlson, John A., and Kling, John L. 1982. Do price surprises lead or lag real activity? Krannert Working Paper no. 809. Purdue University.

Cook, Timothy Q. 1981. Determinants of the spread between treasury bill and private sector money market rates. *Journal of Economics and Business* 33:177–87.

Cook, Timothy Q., and Hendershott, Patric H. 1978. The impact of taxes, risk, and relative security supplies on interest rate differentials. *Journal of Finance* 33:1173–86.

Dougherty, Ann, and Van Order, Robert. 1982. Inflation and housing costs. *American Economic Review* 72:154–64.

Fama, Eugene F. 1975. Short term interest rates as predictors of inflation. *American Economic Review* 65:269–82.

———. 1977. Interest rates and inflation: the messages in the entrails. *American Economic Review* 67:487–96.

Fama, Eugene F., and Schwert, G. W. 1977. Asset returns and inflation. *Journal of Financial Economics* 5:115–46.

Fama, Eugene F., and Gibbons, Michael R. 1981. Inflation, real returns, and capital investment. *Journal of Monetary Economics* 7:296–323.

Feldstein, Martin S. 1980. Inflation and the stock market. *American Economic Review* 70:839–62.

Garbade, Kenneth, and Wachtel, Paul. 1978. Time variation in the relationship between inflation and interest rates. *Journal of Monetary Economics* 4:755–65.

Hendershott, Patric H. 1981. The decline in aggregate share values: taxation, valuation errors, risk and profitability. *American Economic Review* 71:909–22.

———. 1982. Inflation, resource utilization, and debt and equity returns. In *The changing roles of debt and equity in financing U.S. capital formation*, ed. B. M. Friedman. Chicago: University of Chicago Press (for NBER).

Hendershott, Patric H., and Hu, Sheng Cheng. 1981. Inflation and extraordinary returns on owner occupied housing: some implications for capital allocation and productivity growth. *Journal of Macroeconomics* 3:177–203.

Hendershott, Patric H., and Shilling, James D. 1982. The impacts on capital allocation of some aspects of the Economic Recovery Tax Act of 1981. *Public Finance Quarterly* 10:242–74.

Hendershott, Patric H., and van Horne, James C. 1973. Expected inflation implied by capital market rates. *Journal of Finance* 28:301–14.

Hendershott, Patric H.; Shilling, James D.; and Villani, Kevin E. 1982. The determination of home mortgage rates: empirical results for the 1975–81 period. Paper presented at a joint session of the American Finance Association and the American Real Estate and Urban Economics Association meetings, December 1982, New York City.

Ibbotson, Roger G., and Sinquefield, Rex A. 1980. *Stocks, bonds, bills, and inflation: Historic returns (1926–1978)*. Charlottesville: Financial Analysts Research Foundation, University of Virginia.

Jaffee, Jeffrey, and Mandelker, Gershon. 1976. The "Fisher effect" for risky assets: an empirical investigation. *Journal of Finance* 31:447–58.

McCulloch, J. Huston. 1975. The tax-adjusted yield curve. *Journal of Finance* 30:811–30.

———. 1977. The cumulative unanticipated change in interest rates: Evidence on the misintermediation hypothesis. NBER Working Paper no. 222.

Malkiel, Burtin G. 1979. The capital formation problem in the United States. *Journal of Finance* 34:291–306.

Melvin, Michael. 1982. Expected inflation, taxation, and interest rates: the delusion of fiscal illusion. *American Economic Review* 72:841–45.

———. 1983. The vanishing liquidity effect of money on interest: analysis and implications for policy. *Economic Inquiry*: in press.

Merton, Robert C. 1980. On estimating the expected return on the market. *Journal of Financial Economics* 8:323–61.

Mishkin, Frederic S. 1978. Efficient markets theory: implications for monetary policy. *Brookings Papers on Economic Activity* 3:707–52.

———. 1981. The real interest rate: an empirical investigation. In *The costs and consequences of inflation*. Carnegie-Rochester Conference Series on Public Policy. Amsterdam: North-Holland.

———. 1981. Monetary policy and long-term interest rates: an efficient markets approach. *Journal of Monetary Economics* 7:29–55.

———. 1981. Are market forecasts rational? *American Economic Review* 71:295–306.

Modigliani, Franco, and Cohn, Richard A. 1979. Inflation, rational valuation and the market. *Financial Analysts Journal* (March–April), pp. 24–44.

Nelson, Charles R. 1976. Inflation and rates of return on common stocks. *Journal of Finance* 31:471–82.

Pearce, Douglas K. 1979. Comparing survey and rational measures of expected inflation. *Journal of Money, Credit, and Banking* 11:447–56.

Shiller, Robert J. 1979. The volatility of long-term interest rates and expectations models of the term structure. *Journal of Political Economy* 87:1190–1219.

Van Horne, James C. 1978. *Financial market rates and flows.* Englewood Cliffs, N.J.: Prentice-Hall.

Von Furstenberg, George M. 1981. Saving. In *How taxes affect economic behavior*, ed. H. J. Aaron and J. A. Pechman. Washington, D.C.: Brookings Institution.

Comment   Jess Barry Yawitz

Patric Hendershott and Roger Huang have indeed undertaken a major research effort in their paper, "Debt and Equity Yields: 1926–1980." One cannot help but be impressed with this investigation of the return performance of the two major sectors of the financial asset market over nearly a half century. The paper has much to recommend it as a useful first step and, not surprisingly, there is also considerable room for refinements and improvements.

I am pleased to see that nearly all of my original criticisms have been incorporated into the current version of Hendershott and Huang's paper. As a result, my comments will be quite brief. Before proceeding, however, it may be useful to make explicit my major criticism of the Hendershott and Huang paper. I have a strong bias which argues for first developing a set of hypotheses to explain asset returns and then recasting these hypotheses into a testable model. While Hendershott and Huang do attempt to motivate the importance of most of the variables used in their empirical work, a single unifying model is not presented. As a result, the Hendershott and Huang approach generally suffers from being

Jess Barry Yawitz is John E. Simon Professor of Finance and director of the Institute of Banking and Financial Markets at Washington University and a research associate of the NBER.

too simplistic; they utilize numerous combinations of variables to explain returns, yields, and yield changes without carefully specifying causal relationships.

I suggest that a useful approach to modeling yield spreads and bond returns is first to develop a pricing model. A bond can be viewed as a set of individual financial assets, some of which benefit the borrower and some of which benefit the lender. If a particular feature benefits the borrower, such as a call option, the price of the bond is reduced. Similarly, if the feature benefits the lender, as with a put or attached warrant, the price is higher. When a specific price is observed on a bond, it is apparent that the net value of all of the bond's characteristics is equal to this price.

In the case of new issues, the coupon plays the role of the balancing feature on the bond. Once all of the other characteristics are determined, the coupon generally is set at the particular value that will allow the bond to be sold at par. Since at issue the coupon rate is identical to the yield to maturity, one cannot hope to explain yields without taking explicit account of the other characteristics of the bond.

Hendershott and Huang begin by presenting summary statistics which document the variability in real and nominal rates of return on stocks and bonds over the last half century. The purpose of their paper "is to increase our understanding of the determinants of these variations." While Hendershott and Huang divide their paper into four broad parts, I prefer to view the paper as (1) an exploratory analysis of bond and equity data for the 1926–80 period and (2) an empirical analysis of those factors which were important in determining rates of return on financial assets after 1952.

Hendershott and Huang provide a useful structure in which to explore the yield data compiled by Ibbotson and Sinquefield (1980). As Hendershott and Huang point out, "It makes good analytical sense to examine the data for any regularities without the imposition of too much structure . . ." By "breaking the data" at various points, Hendershott and Huang are able to (1) document the increased volatility in real and nominal bill rates from 1952–80 compared to 1926–51; (2) demonstrate that the premium earned on equities over bonds has varied widely; and (3) show that equities have offered extraordinary positive returns around business cycle troughs and negative returns around peaks. I would strongly recommend that this section of the Hendershott and Huang paper be read by all those interested in studying the return performance of alternative financial assets.

The only econometric analysis performed in the first part of the paper is a series of Granger causality tests applied to bill, bond, and equity returns. Without going into detail, I would suggest that this question needs to be considered in greater detail in light of the efficient market implications of Hendershott and Huang's findings that in several instances lagged returns are important in explaining current returns.

At several points in their paper, Hendershott and Huang attempt to provide empirical support for their hypothesis that changes in long-term (20-year) bond yields have been unanticipated for the most part. This question is addressed by regressing monthly changes in the 20-year Treasury yield on unanticipated changes in this yield. Hendershott and Huang interpret an R^2 of .88 as indicative of the fact that nearly 90% of the changes in long-term bond yields were unanticipated over the period in question. I would point out that the positive and significant constant should be picking up the general upward drift in rates during the period. Since the yield curve was also generally upward sloping, the constant is capturing in part the *anticipated* increase in rates as evidenced in the patterns of forward rates. I also submit that the conclusion that monthly changes in 20-year yields are largely unanticipated is to be expected. A 20-year yield is simply an appropriate average of 240 one-month rates, the current one-month spot rate and 239 one-month forward rates. The expected 20-year yield one month hence contains all 239 forward rates plus one new forward rate. If the period were even shorter than a month, say a day, the expected change in the 20-year yield must be nearly zero.

My earlier point regarding the need for more formal modeling before undertaking the empirical is evidenced in Hendershott and Huang's analysis of the determinants of monthly realized returns on long-term corporate bonds. Hendershott and Huang estimate several equations using the bill rate, a capital gain variable, a business cycle dummy, and unanticipated inflation. While it is possible to hypothesize how each of the independent variables could affect corporate bond returns, Hendershott and Huang need to be more clear on the way that each might do so. This is an instance in which a formal model of yield spreads would be valuable.

In conclusion, let me restate my earlier opinion that this paper is an important first step in what must be an ongoing line of research. It remains for Hendershott and Huang and those of us conducting research in this area to consider in greater detail the menu of questions raised in this paper.

4   Inflation and the Role of Bonds in Investor Portfolios

Zvi Bodie, Alex Kane, and Robert McDonald

4.1 Introduction

The inflation of the past decade and a half has dispelled the notion that default-free nominal bonds are a riskless investment. Conventional wisdom used to be that the conservative investor invested principally in bonds and the aggressive or speculative investor invested principally in stocks. Short-term bills were considered to be only a temporary "parking place" for funds awaiting investment in either bonds or stocks. Today many academics and practitioners in the field of finance have come to the view that for an investor who is concerned about his real rate of return, long-term nominal bonds are a risky investment even when held to maturity.

The alternative view that a policy of rolling-over short-term bills might be a sound long-term investment strategy for the conservative investor has recently gained credibility. The rationale behind this view is the observation that for the past few decades, bills have yielded the least variable real rate of return of all the major investment instruments traded in U.S. financial markets. Stated a bit differently, the nominal rate of return on bills has tended to mirror changes in the rate of inflation so that their real rate of return has remained relatively stable as compared to stocks or longer-term fixed-interest bonds.

Zvi Bodie is professor of economics and finance at Boston University's School of Management and codirector of the NBER's project on the economics of the U.S. pension system. Alex Kane is associate professor of finance at Boston University's School of Management and a faculty research fellow of the NBER. Robert McDonald is assistant professor of finance at Boston University's School of Management and a faculty research fellow of the NBER. The authors thank Michael Rouse for his able research assistance.

167

This is not a coincidence, of course. All market-determined interest rates contain an "inflation premium," which reflects expectations about the declining purchasing power of the money borrowed over the life of the loan. As the rate of inflation has increased in recent years, so too has the inflation premium built into interest rates. While long-term as well as short-term interest rates contain such a premium, conventional long-term bonds lock the investor into the current interest rate for the life of the bond. If long-term interest rates on new bonds subsequently rise as a result of unexpected inflation, the funds already locked in can be released only by selling the bonds on the secondary market at a price well below their face value. But if an investor buys only short-term bonds with an average maturity of about 30 days, then the interest rate he earns will lag behind changes in the inflation rate by at most one month. For the investor who is concerned about his real rate of return, bills may therefore be less risky than bonds, even in the long run.

The main purpose of this paper is to explore both theoretically and empirically the role of nominal bonds of various maturities in investor portfolios. How important is it for the investor to diversify his bond holdings fully across the range of bond maturities? We provide a way to measure the importance of diversification, and this enables us to determine the value of holding stocks and a variety of bonds, for example, as opposed to following a less cumbersome investment strategy, such as concentrating in stocks and bills alone.

One of our principal goals is to determine whether an investor who is constrained to limit his investment in bonds to a single portfolio of money-fixed debt instruments will suffer a serious welfare loss. In part, our interest in this question stems from the observation that many employer-sponsored tax-deferred savings plans limit a participant's investment choices to two types, a common stock fund and a money-fixed bond fund of a particular maturity.[1]

A second goal is to study the desirability of introducing a market for indexed bonds (i.e., an asset offering a riskless real rate of return). There is a substantial literature on this subject,[2] but to our knowkedge no one has attempted to measure the magnitude of the welfare gain to an individual investor from the introduction of trading in such securities in the U.S. capital market.

In the first part of the paper we develop a mean-variance model for measuring the value to an investor of a particular set of investment instruments as a function of his degree of risk aversion, rate of time preference, and investment time horizon. We then take monthly data on real rates of return on stocks, bills, and U.S. government bonds of eight different durations, their covariance structure, and combine these estimates with reasonable assumptions about net asset supplies and aggregate risk aversion in order to derive a set of equilibrium risk premia. This procedure allows us to circumvent the formidable problems of deriving reliable estimates of these risk premia from the historical means, which are negative during many subperiods. We then employ these parameter values in our model of optimal consumption and portfolio selection in order to address the two empirical issues of principal concern to us. The paper concludes with a section summarizing the main results and pointing out possible implications for private and public policy.

4.2 Theoretical Model

4.2.1 Model Structure and Assumptions

Our basic model of portfolio selection is that of Markowitz (1952) as extended by Merton (1969, 1971). Merton has shown that when asset prices follow a geometric Brownian motion in continuous time and portfolios can be continuously revised, then as in the original Markowitz model, only the means, variances, and covariances of the joint distribution of returns need to be considered in the portfolio selection process.

In more formal terms, we assume that the real return dynamics on all n assets are described by stochastic differential equations of the form:

$$\frac{dQ_i}{Q_i} = R_i dt + \sigma_i dz_i, \qquad i = 1, \ldots, n,$$

where R_i is the mean real rate of return per unit time on asset i and σ_i^2 is the variance per unit of time. For notational convenience we will let R represent the n-vector of means and Ω the $n \times n$ covariance matrix, whose diagonal elements are the variances σ_i^2 and whose off-diagonal elements are the covariances σ_{ij}.

Investors are assumed to have homogeneous expectations about the values of these parameters. Furthermore, we assume that all n assets are continuously and costlessly traded and that there are no taxes.[3]

The change in the individual's real wealth in any instant is given by

(1) $$dW = W \sum_1^n w_i R_i \, dt - C dt + W \sum_1^n w_i \sigma_i \, dz_i,$$

where W is real wealth, C is the rate of consumption, and w_i is the proportion of his real wealth invested in asset i.

The individual's optimal consumption and portfolio rules are derived by finding

(2) $$\max_{\{C, w\}} E_0 \int_0^H e^{-\rho t} U(C_t) dt,$$

where E is the expectation operator, ρ is the rate of time preference, $U(C_t)$ is the utility from consumption at time t, and H is the end of the investor's planning horizon.

The individual's derived utility of wealth function is defined as

(3) $$J(W_t) = \max_t E_t \int_t^H e^{-\rho s} U(C_s) ds.$$

J is interpreted as the discounted expected value of lifetime utility, conditional on the investor's following the rules for optimal consumption and portfolio behavior. This value can be computed as a function of current wealth. The specific utility function with which we have chosen to work is the well-known constant relative risk aversion form,

$$U(C) = \frac{C^\gamma}{\gamma}, \text{ for } \gamma < 1 \text{ and } \gamma \neq 0,$$
$$\log C, \text{ for } \gamma = 0,$$

with $\delta \equiv 1 - \gamma$ representing Pratt's measure of relative risk aversion. This functional form has several desirable properties for our purposes. First, the investor's degree of relative risk aversion is independent of his wealth, which in turn implies that the optimal portfolio proportions are also independent of wealth. Second, actually solving the problem in (2) allows us to find an explicit solution for the derived utility of wealth function (Merton 1971), which takes the relatively simple form

(4) $$J(W) = q \frac{W^\gamma}{\gamma},$$

where $$q \doteq \left[\frac{1 - e^{-H\left(\frac{\rho - \gamma v}{\delta}\right)}}{\frac{\rho - \gamma v}{\delta}} \right]^\delta$$

and v is a number which reflects the parameters of the investor's investment opportunity set and his degree of risk aversion.[4] Specifically, when there is no risk-free asset, v is defined by:

(5) $$v = \frac{A}{G} + \frac{D}{2G\delta} - \frac{\delta}{2G}$$

where $A \equiv i'\Omega^{-1}R$, $B \equiv R'\Omega^{-1}R$, $G \equiv i'\Omega^{-1}i$, $D \equiv BG - A^2$, where i is a vector of dimension n all of whose elements are one.

The degree of relative risk aversion plays an important role in the specific numerical results which follow, so we interpret this parameter by means of a simple example. Suppose an individual faces a situation in which there is a .5 probability of losing a proportion x of his current wealth and a .5 probability of gaining the same proportion. What proportion of current wealth would the individual be willing to pay as an insurance premium in order to eliminate this risk?[5]

Table 4.1 displays the value of this insurance premium for various values of x and δ. The second row, for example, shows that for a risk

Table 4.1   **Proportion of Current Wealth an Investor Would Be Willing to Pay to Avoid a Risky Prospect with a Payoff of $=xW$ (%of Wealth)**

Proportion of Wealth at Risk	Coefficient of Relative Risk Aversion (δ)						
x	1	2	3	4	5	6	10
1%	.005%	.010%	.015%	.020%	.025%	.030%	.050%
10%	.50%	1.00%	1.49%	1.97%	2.43%	2.88%	4.42%
20%	2.02%	4.00%	5.86%	7.56%	9.06%	10.35%	13.84%
50%	13.40%	25.00%	32.92%	37.76%	40.72%	42.61%	46.00%

which involves a gain or loss of 10% of current wealth an investor with a coefficient of relative risk aversion of one would only pay ½ of 1% of his wealth (or 5% of the magnitude of the possible loss) to insure against it, while an investor with a δ of 10 would pay 4.42% of his wealth (which is fully 44.2% of the magnitude of the possible loss). If the investor with a δ of 10 faces a risky prospect involving a possible gain or loss of 50% of his wealth, he would be willing to pay 92% of the possible loss to avoid the risk.

4.2.2 Optimal Portfolio Proportions and Equilibrium Risk Premia

The vector of optimal portfolio weights derived from the optimization model described above is given by

$$(6) \qquad w^* = \frac{1}{\delta}\Omega^{-1}\left(R - \frac{A}{G}i\right) + \frac{\Omega^{-1}i}{G}.$$

Note that these weights are independent of the investor's rate of time preference and his investment horizon. Merton (1972) has shown that A/G is the mean rate of return on the minimum variance portfolio and that $(\Omega^{-1}i)/G$ is the vector of portfolio weights of the n assets in the minimum variance portfolio. Denoting these by $R_{\min}$ and $w_{\min}$, respectively, we can rewrite equation (6) as

$$(6') \qquad w^* = \frac{1}{\delta}\Omega^{-1}(R - R_{\min}i) + w_{\min}.$$

The demand for any individual asset can thus be decomposed into two parts represented by the two terms on the right-hand side of equation (7):

$$(7) \qquad w_i^* = \frac{1}{\delta}\sum_{j=1}^{n} v_{ij}(R_j - R_{\min}) + w_{i,\min},$$

where v_{ij} is the ij_{th} element of Ω^{-1}, the inverse of the covariance matrix. The first of these two parts is a "speculative demand" for asset i, which depends inversely on the investor's degree of risk aversion and directly on a weighted sum of the risk premia on the n assets. The second component is a "hedging demand" for asset i which is that asset's weight in the minimum-variance portfolio.[6]

Under our assumption of homogeneous expectations the equilibrium risk premia on the n assets are found by aggregating the individual demands for each asset (eq. [6']) and setting them equal to the supplies. The resulting equilibrium yield relationships can be expressed in vector form as

$$(8) \qquad R - R_{\min}i = \bar{\delta}(\Omega w_M - \sigma_{\min}^2 i),$$

where $\bar{\delta}$ is a harmonic mean of the individual investors' measures of risk aversion weighted by their shares of total wealth, w_M is the vector of net supplies of the n assets each expressed as a proportion of the total value of all assets, and σ^2_{min} is the variance of the minimum variance portfolio.

The portfolio whose weights are given by w_M has come to be known in the literature on asset pricing as the "market" portfolio, and we will adopt that same terminology here. Equation (8) implies that

(9) $R_i - R_{min} = \bar{\delta}(\sigma_{iM} - \sigma^2_{min}), \qquad i = 1, \ldots, n,$

where σ_{iM} is the covariance between the real rate of return on asset i and the rate of return on the market portfolio.

This relationship holds for any individual asset and for any portfolio of assets. Thus for the market portfolio we get

(10) $R_M - R_{min} = \bar{\delta}(\sigma^2_M - \sigma^2_{min}).$

It is interesting to compare this with the traditional form of the capital asset pricing model which assumes the existence of a riskless asset. In that special case R_{min} is simply the riskless rate and σ^2_{min} is zero.

By substituting the equilibrium values of $R_i - R_{min}$ from equation (8) into equation (6'), we get for investor k

(11) $w^*_k = \dfrac{\bar{\delta}}{\delta_k} w_M + \left(1 - \dfrac{\bar{\delta}}{\delta_k}\right) w_{min}.$

This implies that in equilibrium every investor will hold some combination of the market and the minimum variance portfolios. If the investor is more risk averse than the average he will divide his portfolio into positive positions in both the market portfolio and the minimum variance portfolio, with a higher proportion in the latter the greater his degree of risk aversion. If he is less risk averse than the average he will sell the minimum variance portfolio short in order to invest more than 100% of his funds in the market portfolio.

4.2.3   The Welfare Loss from Incomplete Diversification

Suppose the investor faces an investment opportunity set consisting of less than the full set of n assets. How much additional current wealth would he have to be given in order to make him as well off as he was with the full set of n assets?

Let $J(W|n)$ be the lifetime utility of an investor who chooses from among n assets, and let $J(W|n - m)$ be the lifetime utility of an investor choosing from among a restricted set of assets. Let W represent the investor's actual level of current wealth and $\hat{W}$ the level at which his welfare would be the same under the restricted opportunity set. $\hat{W}$ is defined by $J(W|n) = J(\hat{W}|n - m)$.

Thus $\hat{W} - W$ is the extra wealth necessary to compensate the investor for having a restricted opportunity set and is greater than or equal to zero. From equation (4) we get

$$(12) \qquad \hat{W} = W \left\{ \frac{\left[1 - e^{-H\left(\frac{\rho - \gamma v}{\delta}\right)}\right]}{(\rho - \gamma v)} \cdot \frac{(\rho - \gamma \hat{v})}{\left[1 - e^{-H\left(\frac{\rho - \gamma \hat{v}}{\delta}\right)}\right]} \right\}^{\frac{\delta}{\gamma}},$$

where $\hat{v}$ is calculated according to equation (5) and corresponds to the restricted opportunity set.[7]

Equation (12) implies that the magnitude of the welfare loss will in general depend on the investor's risk aversion, δ, rate of time preference, ρ, and investment horizon, H. Since $\hat{W}$ is proportional to W, a convenient measure of this loss is $\hat{W}/W - 1$, the loss per dollar of current wealth, which is independent of the investor's wealth level. Since $\hat{W} \geq W$, this number is always greater than or equal to zero.

Of course, certain restrictions on the investment opportunity set need not decrease investor welfare. We know from equation (11) that even if the investor had only two mutual funds to choose from, there would be no loss in welfare, provided they were the market portfolio and the minimum variance portfolio. Merton (1972) has shown that any two portfolios along the mean-variance portfolio frontier would serve as well. But, in general, restricting the number of assets in the opportunity set does lead to a loss in investor welfare.

4.2.4   The Shadow Riskless Rate and the Gain from Introducing a Riskless Asset

We define the shadow riskless real rate of interest as that rate at which an investor would have no change in welfare if his opportunity set were expanded to include a riskless asset. When the investment opportunity set includes a riskless asset, Merton (1971) shows that the lifetime utility of wealth function is the same as (4), except that v is replaced by λ, where

$$(13) \qquad \lambda = R_F + \frac{(R - R_F i)' \, \Omega^{-1} (R - R_F i)}{2\delta}.$$

We find the expression for the shadow riskless rate by setting v equal to λ and solving for R_F. This gives

$$(14) \qquad R_F = R_{\min} - \delta \sigma_{\min}^2.$$

This implies that a risk-averse investor will always have a shadow riskless real rate which is less than the mean real return on the minimum variance portfolio. The return differential is equal to his degree of relative risk aversion times the variance of the minimum variance portfolio.

If there is a zero net supply of this riskless asset in the economy, the equilibrium value of R_F will just be $R_{\min} - \bar{\delta}\sigma^2_{\min}$. Therefore, by assumption, an investor with average risk aversion will not gain from the introduction of a market for index bonds. For an investor whose risk aversion is different from the average there will be a welfare gain, ignoring the costs of establishing and operating such a market. We measure this gain analogously to the way we measured the welfare cost of incomplete diversification in the previous section.

As before, let W be the investor's actual level of wealth and $\hat{W}$ the level at which his welfare would be the same under an opportunity set expanded to include a riskless asset offering a real rate of $R_{\min} - \bar{\delta}\sigma^2_{\min}$. Since in this case $\hat{W} \leq W$, we take as our measure of the welfare gain from indexation $1 - (\hat{W}/W)$, or the amount the investor would be willing to give up per dollar of current wealth for the opportunity to trade index bonds.

4.3   The Data and Parameter Estimates

In this section we will describe our data and how we used them to estimate the parameters needed to evaluate the welfare loss from restricting an investor's opportunity set and the gain from introducing a real riskless asset. It must be borne in mind that we were not trying to test the model of capital market equilibrium presented in section 4.2 empirically but rather to derive its implications for the specific questions being addressed in this paper. It was therefore important to maintain consistency between the underlying theoretical model and the parameter estimates derived from the historical data, even if that meant ignoring some of the descriptive statistics yielded by those data.

Our raw data were monthly real rates of return on stocks, one-month U.S. government Treasury bills, and eight different U.S. bond portfolios. We used monthly data in order to best approximate the continuous trading assumption of Merton's model, and because one month is the shortest interval for which information about the rate of inflation is available. The measure of the price level that we used in computing real rates of return was the Bureau of Labor Statistics' Consumer Price Index, excluding the cost-of-shelter component. We excluded the cost-of-shelter component because it gives rise to well-known distortions in the measured rate of inflation.

The bill data are from Ibbotson and Sinquefield (1982), while the bond data are from the U.S. Government Bond File of the Center for Research in Security Prices (CRSP) at the University of Chicago. The stock data are from the CRSP monthly NYSE file. We divided the bonds into eight different portfolios based on duration. We felt that duration was superior to maturity as a criterion for grouping the bonds since it takes into account a bond's coupon as well as its maturity.[8] The durations of the bond portfolios range from 1 to 8 years.

Table 4.2 presents the means, variances, and correlation coefficients of the monthly real rates of return on the 10 asset categories for three subperiods between January 1953 and December 1981. The first is the 12 years from January 1953 to December 1964, a period of relative price stability; the second is the 8 years from 1965 to 1972, a period of moderate inflation; and the third is the 9 years from 1973 to 1981, a period of relatively rapid inflation.

The measure of the real rate of return used in all cases was the natural logarithm of the monthly real wealth relatives $Q_i(t)/Q_i(t - 1)$. On the assumption that these returns follow a geometric Brownian motion in continuous time, $dQ_i | Q_i = R_i dt + \sigma_i dz_i$, the log of the wealth relative over a discrete time interval is normally distributed with mean μ_i and variance σ_i^2, where $\mu_i = R_i - (\sigma_i^2/2)$. The means reported in table 2 were converted to annual rates by multiplying them by 12 and the standard deviations by multiplying them by $\sqrt{12}$. This makes them comparable to the means and standard deviations one would obtain using a 1-year holding period.

A most striking aspect of these descriptive statistics can be seen in part C of the table: all assets have negative mean returns over the last subperiod. This presents a dilemma for anyone requiring estimates of the risk premia called for in models of capital market equilibrium, since their recent historical pattern is grossly inconsistent with the pattern implied by the variance-covariance matrix estimated from the same data.

As Merton (1980) has shown, in order to get a reliable estimate of the mean of a continuous-time stochastic process, it is necessary to observe the process over a long span of time. Variances and covariances, however, can be measured fairly accurately over much shorter observation periods. We therefore chose to ignore the historical means reported in table 4.2, while using the estimated covariance matrix.

The standard deviations of all 10 assets reported in table 4.2 increased significantly over the 3 periods. Since we were interested in computing welfare losses and gains for investors in today's U.S. capital markets, we used in our calculations the variance and correlation coefficients estimated for the most recent period, 1973–81.

The standard deviations for this last subperiod fall into a clear pattern. The lowest is for bills, .0126, which is well below that on 1-year bonds, the next lowest reported in the table. The standard deviation on bonds rises continuously with duration, reaching a maximum of .1095 on duration 8. Stocks have a standard deviation of .1735, which is 1.6 times that of duration 8 bonds and about 14 times that of bills. In the previous two subperiods, while all the standard deviations are lower than in the 1973–

Table 4.2   Distribution of Monthly Real Rates of Return (Annualized)

	Common Stocks	1-Month Bills	Bonds (by Duration in Years)							
			1	2	3	4	5	6	7	8
A. 1953–64:										
Mean	.1202	.0113	.0183	.0213	.0218	.0151	.0188	.0122	.0074	.0243
S.D.	.1179	.0081	.0105	.0170	.0235	.0268	.0311	.0305	.0361	.0155
Observations	144	144	144	144	144	144	138	110	84	42
			Correlation Coefficient							
Stocks		.04	−.02	−.09	−.10	−.06	−.13	−.15	−.12	.15
Bills			.70	.40	.25	.23	.22	.24	.25	.42
Bonds 1				.81	.70	.68	.65	.65	.56	.63
2					.85	.82	.78	.80	.74	.59
3						.90	.83	.82	.80	.60
4							.86	.86	.83	.65
5								.88	.86	.79
6									.91	.75
7										.95

Table 4.2 (continued)

	Common Stocks	1-Month Bills	Bonds (by Duration in Years)							
	Common Stocks	1-Month Bills	1	2	3	4	5	6	7	8
B. 1965–72:										
Mean	.0413	.0122	.0162	.0179	.0101	.0007	.0032	.0078	.0339	.0113
S.D.	.1345	.0064	.0155	.0298	.0370	.0427	.0519	.0427	.0453	.0377
Observations	96	96	96	96	96	96	96	52	30	6
Correlation Coefficients										
Stocks		.11	.25	.33	.38	.33	.33	.08	.03	.23
Bills			.64	.52	.37	.38	.27	.32	.38	0
Bonds 1				.86	.78	.74	.67	.69	.60	.11
2					.83	.80	.73	.76	.77	.98
3						.82	.84	.85	.86	.57
4							.83	.86	.49	.41
5								.94	.77	.61
6									.66	.72
7										.88

	Common Stocks	1-Month Bills	1	2	3	4	5	6	7	8
C. 1973–81:										
Mean	−.0269	−.0050	−.0044	−.0141	−.0186	−.0284	−.0320	−.0549	−.0298	−.0485
S.D.	.1735	.0126	.0316	.0529	.0693	.0812	.0922	.1034	.1049	.1095
Observations	108	108	108	108	108	108	108	95	99	106
					Correlation Coefficients					
Stocks		.20	.32	.32	.27	.31	.22	.22	.30	.33
Bills			.54	.39	.35	.35	.26	.22	.27	.22
Bonds 1				.88	.85	.82	.80	.73	.78	.77
2					.94	.92	.87	.81	.85	.86
3						.95	.93	.85	.88	.88
4							.91	.83	.89	.87
5								.89	.92	.89
6									.91	.88
7										.91

Notes: The measure of the real rate of return used is the natural logarithm of the monthly real wealth relative. The reported means were converted to annual rates by multiplying them by 12 and the standard deviations by multiplying them by $\sqrt{12}$. This makes them comparable to the means and standard deviations of the continuously compounded rates of return one would obtain using a one-year holding period.

81 subperiod, they fall into approximately the same pattern of relative magnitudes.

Turning to the matrix of correlation coefficients, we see that in the last subperiod all of the correlations are positive. Stocks had correlations ranging from .20 (with bills) to .33 (with duration 8 bonds), and they do not rise uniformly with the duration of the bonds. The pattern for bonds and bills is that correlations are highest among bonds of adjacent durations and fall off more or less uniformly as one moves to more distant durations. In the 1965–72 subperiod the pattern of correlations is quite similar to 1973–81 for all assets, but in the noninflationary 1953–64 subperiod the correlations among bills and bonds follow the same pattern, while the real returns on stocks appear to be essentially uncorrelated with the real returns on bills and bonds.

In addition to the variance-covariance matrix, the next input we need for equation (8) in order to generate numerical results is the vector of weights for the market portfolio. Here we face some problems of both a theoretical and an empirical sort.

At the theoretical level, one issue is whether to treat U.S. government bonds as net wealth. There is considerable controversy among monetary theorists on this issue, and a substantial literature on it exists.[9] We decided to treat U.S. government debt as net wealth of the private sector.

We also ignore the default risk premium on corporate bonds by lumping them together with Treasury bonds. This amounts to assuming that they have the same variance-covariance structure.

Another problem is our exclusion of some important categories of assets in our computation of the market portfolio. Most notable among these are residential real estate, consumer durables, human capital, and social security wealth.[10] While we do not include these in the present paper, our plan for future extensions of this research is to seek appropriate data on these other asset classes and redo our calculations to include them.

There remains the empirical problem of determining the relative weights of those assets which we do include in the market portfolio in the present study. The ratio of the market value of corporate equity to the book value of total government debt was approximately 1.5 in 1980. Thus, 60% was the equity weight in the market portfolio. The relative supplies of government debt by duration were approximated from a table in the *Treasury Bulletin* which breaks down the quantities of government debt by maturity: issues maturing in less than 1 year, in 1–5 years, and so forth. We arbitrarily spread the weights evenly among the years within each of these groupings.

This procedure obviously omits corporate debt. However, using flow-of-funds data we computed the percentage of equity by treating both corporate equity and the net worth of unincorporated businesses as equity. Debt then consisted of federal, corporate, and unincorporated business credit market liabilities. This procedure also yielded a 60% equity-to-wealth ratio. By lumping corporate debt together with U.S. government debt we are ignoring any default risk premia.

The foregoing ignores financial intermediaries, in effect supposing that households hold the securities of nonfinancial businesses and the government directly. A different procedure would be to net out securities held by intermediaries, and consider the public's holding of bank liabilities as debt. (Deposits could be treated as Treasury bills, for example.) We plan to experiment with this alternative in future research.

The ultimate set of weights we used for the market portfolio was:

		Bonds by Duration in Years							
Stocks	Bills	1	2	3	4	5	6	7	8
.60	.05	.15	.033	.033	.033	.033	.022	.022	.022

Finally, in order to determine the equilibrium risk premia we need to set a value for $\bar{\delta}$, the economy-wide average degree of relative risk aversion. In a recent paper, Grossman and Shiller (1981) concluded that a value of 4 is most consistent with the observed movements of the value of the stock market over the past 90 years. Friend and Blume (1975) had estimated it to be 2, while Friend and Hasbrouck (1982) found 6 to be more appropriate. As we show below, a value of 4 produces an imputed risk premium on stocks which is in line with direct time-series estimates of this premium obtained by other researchers using a variety of estimation techniques. We therefore choose 4 as our value for $\bar{\delta}$ in the calculation of the equilibrium risk premia which we use in the remainder of the paper. To a large extent the particular value of $\bar{\delta}$ is unimportant, since the deviation of δ_k from $\bar{\delta}$, and not the level, is what matters most for our results.

Table 4.3 presents the full set of imputed real risk premia ($R_i - R_{min}$) which we calculated using the formula embodied in equation (8), the variance-covariance matrix of monthly real returns estimated over the period 1973–81, and the vector of market weights and value of $\bar{\delta}$ presented above. The table also shows the individual asset variances, their covariances with the market portfolio, and their betas on the market portfolio. The last two columns give the values corresponding to the minimum variance and market portfolios, respectively.

The table shows that the real risk premium on the market portfolio is approximately 5% per year, which is almost 4 times its variance of 1.26% per year. Since we have set $\bar{\delta}$ at 4, the risk premium on the market portfolio would be exactly 4 times its variance if the variance of the minimum variance portfolio were zero rather than .0144% per year. The

Table 4.3   Imputed Risk Premia, Variances, and Covariances with the Market Portfolio (Annualized)

| | Stocks | 1-Month Bills | Bonds (by Duration in Years) | | | | | | | | Portfolios | |
			1	2	3	4	5	6	7	8	Minimum Variance	Market
Risk premium	.0760	.0009	.0061	.0108	.0126	.0161	.0151	.0165	.0205	.0227	0	.0497
Variance	.0301	.00016	.0010	.0028	.0048	.0066	.0085	.0107	.0110	.0120	.00014	.0126
Covariance with market	.0191	.0003	.0017	.0028	.0033	.0042	.0039	.0043	.0053	.0058	.00014	.0126
Beta coefficient	1.52	.02	.13	.22	.26	.33	.31	.34	.42	.46	.01	1.00

Notes: 1. The risk premia were computed according to the formula $R_i - R_{min} = \overline{\delta}(\sigma_{iM} - \sigma^2_{min})$, with $\overline{\delta}$ the economy-wide average coefficient of relative risk aversion set equal to 4; the σ_{iM} are the covariances with the market portfolio reported in the third row of the table.

2. The variances and covariances reported above were computed from the distribution of the natural logs of the monthly real wealth relatives over the period 1973–81. They were annualized by multiplying them by 12.

3. The reported beta coefficients are the covariance with the market divided by the variance of the market portfolio.

risk premium on bills is only 9 basis points, and the variance is only slightly higher than the minimum, which is not surprising since as we shall see in the next section the minimum variance portfolio is essentially bills.

With the sole exception of duration 5, the risk premia on bonds rise uniformly with duration reaching a maximum of 2.27% per year. Finally, the risk premium on stocks is 7.60% per year or approximately 1.5 times the risk premium on the market portfolio. Since the beta of stocks is approximately 1.5, this result should not be surprising to readers familiar with the capital asset pricing model.[11] It is also in line with the long-run time-series estimates derived by Ibbotson and Sinquifield (1982) and Merton (1980).

4.4 The Welfare Loss from Incomplete Diversification

In this section we address the question of how much welfare an investor loses by having his choice of assets limited. The main conclusion of the theoretical discussion in section 4.2 was that even if an investor's opportunity set is limited to only two assets, there will be no loss in welfare provided that these two assets are the market portfolio and the minimum variance portfolio (or any other set of two frontier portfolios). But we are interested in the actual menu of asset choices offered in practice by many employer-sponsored tax-sheltered savings plans in the United States. These plans usually offer participants a choice of two or three funds: a stock fund, an intermediate-term fixed interest bond fund, and sometimes as a third option a money market fund.

Table 4.4 presents the risk premia, variances, and asset compositions of the optimal portfolios chosen from the full set of 10 assets for investors with coefficients of relative risk aversion ranging from 2 to 10. Figure 4.1, which is the familiar efficient portfolio frontier, displays graphically the mean-variance combinations tabulated in the second and third columns of table 4.4.

The middle row of table 4.4 corresponds to the market portfolio and the last row to the minimum variance portfolio, which consists essentially of bills, hedged with small offsetting short and long positions in bonds of the various durations. Table 4.4 shows that a very risk-averse investor, with a coefficient of risk aversion of 6, would hold 40% of his portfolio in stocks, 40% in bills, and the remaining 20% in bonds of various durations. He would thereby attain a risk premium of about 3.3% per year with a variance of 0.57% per year. Even an extremely risk-averse investor, one whose δ value is 10, would still invest roughly 24% of his funds in stocks, 67% in bills, and the remainder in bonds of various durations, in order to attain a mean risk premium of 1.95% per year with a variance of only 0.21% per year.

Note that for coefficients of relative risk aversion smaller than the

Table 4.4   Risk Premia, Variances, and Asset Composition of Optimal Portfolios

Coefficient of Relative Risk Aversion	Risk Premium (% per Year)	Variance (% per Year)	Common Stocks	1-Month Bills	Bonds (by Duration in Years)							
					1	2	3	4	5	6	7	8
2	9.94	4.98	120.6	-98.4	37.0	1.2	13.9	12.6	1.3	3.4	8.4	-.1
3	6.62	2.22	80.2	-29.5	22.3	2.6	6.9	6.4	2.7	2.6	4.3	1.4
4 (market portfolio)	4.97	1.26	60.0	5.0	15.0	3.3	3.3	3.3	3.3	2.2	2.2	2.2
5	3.97	.81	47.9	25.7	10.6	3.8	1.2	1.5	3.7	2.0	1.0	2.7
6	3.29	.57	39.8	39.5	7.7	4.0	-.2	.3	4.0	1.8	.2	3.0
10	1.95	.21	23.6	67.0	1.8	4.6	-3.0	-2.2	4.6	1.5	-1.5	3.6
Minimum variance portfolio	0	.014	-.6	108.4	-7.0	5.5	-7.2	-5.9	5.4	1.0	-4.0	4.5

Notes: The covariance matrix used was estimated over the 1973–81 period and reported in table 5.2, part C. The risk premia of stocks, bills, and bonds used are the ones reported in table 5.3.

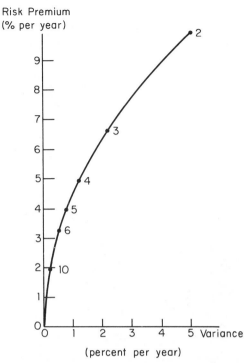

Fig. 4.1   Efficient portfolio frontier. Source: table 4.4. Note: The numbers on the frontier are coefficients of relative risk aversion and indicate the point which would be optimal for an investor having the corresponding degree of risk aversion.

economy-wide average of 4, the investor takes larger short positions in bills and long positions in stocks and bonds of most durations. In the first row, for example, we see that an investor with a risk aversion coefficient of 2 nearly doubles the mean risk premium on his portfolio relative to the average investor but also increases the variance by a factor of 4.

Short-selling Treasury bills is difficult in practice. This difficulty can be overcome in two ways. First, a large investment house or pension fund could allow its less risk-averse investors to sell short to the more risk-averse investors, as a purely internal transaction. Second, and more likely, a less risk-averse investor can simply take a long position in stock market futures as a way to hold a levered position in stocks.

Table 4.5 and figure 4.2 present our estimates of the welfare loss to an investor from having his opportunity set restricted to various subsets of the 10 asset classes. The numbers in this table represent the amount of money the investor would need to be given per $10,000 of his current wealth to make him as well off with the restricted choice set as he would

Table 4.5   Welfare Loss from Incomplete Diversification (Dollars per $10,000 of Wealth)

Coefficient of Relative Risk Aversion	Stocks and Bills	2 Assets: Stocks and bonds of duration:				3 Assets: Stocks, Bills, and Bonds of 2 Years Duration
		1-Year	2-Years	4-Years	8-Years	
2	$325	$442	$551	$671	$756	$40
3	246	174	113	58	39	29
4	202	63	26	119	372	24
5	170	34	137	596	1,445	21
6	146	61	389	1,426	3,301	19

Notes: These estimates correspond to an assumed rate of time preference of 4% per year and an infinite horizon. In setting the mean rates of return we assumed that the mean on bills is zero and calibrated the others accordingly. The risk premia and covariances used were the ones estimated over the 1973–81 period, reported in table 4.2, part C, and table 4.3.

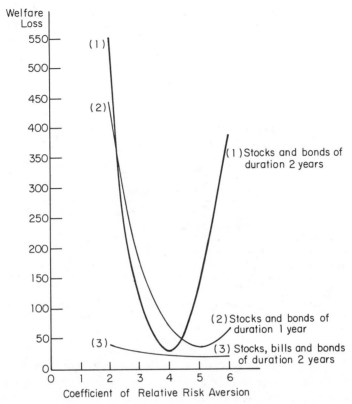

Fig. 4.2   Welfare loss from incomplete diversification. Source: table 4.5.

be with the full set of 10 assets. In order to do these calculations we had to determine the mean rates of return themselves, not just the risk premia. We did this by assuming that the mean on bills is zero and calibrating all other rates accordingly. This assumption was based on the actual mean real return on bills observed over the past 30 years.

We also had to assume a rate of time preference and a specific planning horizon. We arbitrarily set these at 4% per year and infinity, respectively, but did a sensitivity analysis which we report below in table 4.6. It should be noted that the infinite horizon assumption is really meant to represent the case where time of death is uncertain and the parameter ρ in (2) incorporates the rate of mortality as in Merton (1971). Note also that table 4.5 shows the welfare loss from restricting the investor's portfolio choice forever, not just for a limited period.

Table 4.5 and figure 4.2 show that when the investor is restricted to only two assets, the welfare impact of the restriction can be quite sensitive

Table 4.6   Effect of Rate of Time Preference and Time Horizon on the Welfare Loss from Incomplete Diversification (Dollars per $10,000 of Wealth)

A. Rate of Time Preference	2 Assets: Stocks and Bills
0	$394
2% per year	305
4% per year	249

B. Time horizon	2 Assets: Stocks and Bills
1 month	$0.28
5 years	17
Infinite	249

Notes: Part A assumes a coefficient of risk aversion of 4 and an infinite time horizon. The risk premia and covariances used were the ones estimated over the 1973–81 period and reported in table 4.2, part C, and table 4.3.

Part B assumes a rate of time preference of 4% per year. The risk premia and covariances used were the ones estimated over the 1973–81 period and reported in table 4.2, part C, and table 4.3.

to his coefficient of risk aversion. If the two assets are stocks and bonds of 2 years duration (curve 1), we see that the welfare loss is small for an investor with a risk aversion coefficient equal to the average, 4, but increases sharply on either side of this value. If, on the other hand, the two assets are stocks and bonds of 1 year duration (curve 2), then the welfare loss is greatest for the least risk-averse investor but is not extreme for any investor. Investors with coefficients of risk aversion equal to 3 or 4 are better off with stocks and bonds of 2 years duration, whereas investors who are either more or less risk averse than that would prefer stocks and bonds of 1 year duration.

A comparison of the first two columns in table 4.5 reveals that stocks and bonds of duration one year are preferable to stocks and bills for all investors except those with risk aversion of 2. Moving across table 4.5 we see that as the duration of the bond fund increases the welfare loss becomes more sensitive to the coefficient of risk aversion. Thus for bonds of 8 years duration the smallest welfare loss relative to the full 10-asset opportunity set occurs at a coefficient of risk aversion of 3, rising quite sharply on either side of that value and becoming particularly severe for very risk-averse investors.

The last column in table 4.5 shows that when the choice set is expanded from two to three assets, stocks, bills, and bonds of 2 years duration, the magnitude of the welfare loss falls dramatically for all investors, regardless of their degree of risk aversion. Having these three assets to choose from is thus almost as good as having all 10.

The effects of changing our assumptions about the rate of time preference and the horizon are shown in table 4.6. The magnitude of the welfare loss from restricting the choice set to stocks and bills is greater the lower the rate of time preference and the longer the horizon.

These numerical results suggest that if an employer-sponsored savings plan is going to restrict its participants to a choice of only two funds, then since the sponsor does not know the exact degree of risk aversion of the participants, it would make sense to let the two funds be stocks and bonds of 1 or 2 years duration. If, however, the sponsor is willing to expand the number of funds to three, then stocks, bills, and bonds of 2 years duration will eliminate almost all of the welfare loss relative to the full 10-asset opportunity set.

The applicability of our analysis to employer-sponsored tax-deferred savings plans is limited by two factors: assets held outside the plan, and taxes. Without taxes it is trivially obvious that the omission of bills from a savings plan is of no consequence if investors can hold a money market fund on their own account. When there are tax advantages to investing in a savings plan, however, on the margin the investor prefers to hold assets inside the plan. If the plan fails to offer a full menu of assets, the investor will suffer a welfare loss. Our numerical calculations can be viewed as applying to a world in which all assets are invested in a tax-deferred savings plan with a restricted menu of assets. In general, however, our numerical calculations still provide an upper bound on the possible welfare loss, for the following reason: if the investor could in principle invest all wealth in the plan, and *chooses* not to do so in order to diversify, then the welfare loss must be less than for an investor who is (as in our calculations) constrained to hold only those assets offered by the plan.

In practice, of course, additional complications reduce the importance of tax-deferred savings plans. The IRS imposes a limit on the contributions to these plans, and frequently there are penalties or delays associated with the premature withdrawal of funds. These considerations will reduce the percentage of an investor's wealth which is held in such savings plans. Therefore the failure of the plan to offer certain assets is less important, since freely chosen assets held outside the plan will undo the effect of restrictions imposed within the plan. Our numerical estimates again provide an upper bound on the welfare loss.

4.5 Shadow Riskless Rates and the Welfare Gain from Introduction of a Riskless Real Asset

In section 4.2 we defined the shadow riskless rate of interest as that rate at which an investor would have a zero gain in welfare from having his choice set expanded to include an asset which was riskless in real terms. Equation (14) showed that this rate is below the mean real rate of return on the minimum variance portfolio by an amount equal to the investor's degree of relative risk aversion times the variance of the minimum variance portfolio. Given that our estimate of this variance is a mere .0144% per year, it follows that even a very risk averse investor ($\delta = 6$) would be willing to give up less than 9 basis points.

Since the average degree of risk aversion is 4, if a market for riskless real bonds could be established costlessly, the market clearing real interest rate would be about 6 basis points below the mean rate on the minimum variance portfolio. Table 4.7 shows what the welfare gain would be to investors with varying degrees of risk aversion.

The magnitude of the welfare gain to investors does not appear to be large. The numbers in the first column of table 4.7 show the results obtained using the actual covariance matrix estimated for the 1973–81 subperiod. The second column shows the results of an experiment in which we made all nominal debt securities twice as risky by doubling their variances and covariances, leaving the variance of stocks unchanged. While the effect is to approximately double the welfare gain to investors at any degree of risk aversion, the magnitude of the gain still appears small.

These results suggest one possible reason for the nonexistence of index bonds in the U.S. capital market. Since there would probably be some costs associated with creating a new market for such bonds, the benefits would have to exceed those costs. Given the assumptions of our model, in particular the assumption of homogeneous expectations, the benefit from trading in index bonds would have to arise from differences in the degree of risk aversion among investors. If as table 4.7 suggests, the welfare gain does not appear to be large over a fairly broad range of risk aversion coefficients, then one should not be surprised at the failure of a market for index bonds to appear.

Table 4.7   Welfare Gain from Introduction of a Real Riskless Asset (Dollars per $10,000 of Wealth)

		Welfare Gain	
Coefficient Relative Risk Aversion	Actual Covariance Matrix	Double All Variances and Covariances but Stocks
2	$32	$63
3	7	13
4	0	0
5	6	12
6	25	49

Note: Assumptions are the same as for table 5.5.

One should bear in mind that table 4.7 is derived assuming a zero net aggregate supply of index bonds. Thus it does not answer the question of whether the welfare gain from indexing government debt would be significant.

4.6 Summary and Discussion of Findings

We undertook this research with two main policy questions in mind: (1) Is there a significant welfare loss stemming from the practice on the part of many employer-sponsored savings plans of restricting a participant's choice of investments to two or three asset classes? (2) What is the potential welfare gain from the introduction of trading in privately issued index bonds? In this section we summarize and discuss the implications of our findings for each.

With regard to the first of these, we have shown that there is no necessary loss of welfare from restricting an investor's choice set to only two funds, provided these two are properly chosen. If they are the market portfolio and the minimum variance portfolio, then there will be no loss at all. In practice, however, many plans offer a diversified common stock fund and an intermediate-term fixed-interest bond fund as the only two assets, and in such cases there can be a substantial welfare loss to participants whose degree of risk aversion differs appreciably from the average. Most of this loss can be eliminated for risk-averse participants by introducing as a third option a money market fund.

With regard to the second question, our results indicate that the potential welfare gain from the introduction of index bonds in the current U.S. capital market is probably not large. The major reason for the small gain we calculate is the fact that one-month T-bills with their small variance of real returns are an effective substitute for index bonds.

There are some important factors bearing on these two policy questions that we either excluded or ignored in our analysis, and we must consider their potential effect on our conclusions. The first is the fact that we limited ourselves to only a subset of the assets which individuals in the United States hold in their portfolios. Specifically, we excluded residential real estate, consumer durables, and nontradeable assets like human capital and social security wealth.

Undoubtedly the inclusion of these other assets would affect the magnitude of the welfare effects we calculated. Thus the welfare loss to an individual whose employer-sponsored savings plan offers only a stock fund and a bond fund would almost surely be smaller. The loss would appear smaller still were we to take into account the fact that individuals have access to other assets outside of the plan. Nonetheless, it is probably still true that not having a money market option lowers the welfare of investors who are more risk averse than the average. Similarly, the small welfare gain from index bonds, which we calculated, would probably become even smaller, in the context of the broader spectrum of assets, especially when one considers that social security is indexed.

Our agenda for future research starts with a more detailed quantitative analysis of the impact of these additional assets.

Notes

1. An example of particular relevance to academics is the plan managed by the Teachers Insurance and Annuity Association and offered by many private educational institutions in the United States. Under this plan the participant can choose between a common stock fund, the College Retirement Equities Fund (CREF), and a second fund which is essentially a portfolio of intermediate term nominal bonds.

2. See, for example, the paper by Fischer (1975) and the references cited therein.

3. All of these simplifying assumptions are, of course, counterfactual, and there is a considerable literature on the effect of relaxing each of them. The only one we think would materially affect the main results in this paper is the no-taxes assumption. We discuss its likely effects in sect. 4.4.

4. A necessary condition for (4) to be correct is $\rho > \gamma v$. See Merton (1969).

5. Pratt (1964) shows that for small changes in wealth this insurance premium is approximately $1/2\delta x^2$. Note that x^2 is the variance of the proportional change in wealth caused by the risky prospect.

6. See Bodie (1982) for a discussion in terms of nominal rates of return and unanticipated inflation.

7. Note that if $(\rho - \gamma v)/\delta > 0$ then as $H \to \infty$ eq. (12) reduces to

$$(12') \qquad \hat{W} = W\left(\frac{\rho - \gamma\hat{v}}{\rho - \gamma v}\right)^{\frac{\delta}{\gamma}}.$$

8. Duration, as defined by Macaulay (1938), is a weighted average of the years to maturity of each of the cash flows from a security. The weights are the present value of each year's cash flow as a proportion of the total present value of the security. Duration equals final maturity only in the case of pure discount bonds. For coupon bonds and mortgages, duration is always less than maturity. The difference between maturity and duration for ordinary coupon bonds and mortgages is greater the longer the final maturity and the higher the level of interest rates. In our sample of bonds this difference rose steadily over the 1953–81 period due to the rising trend in interest rates. The most pronounced differences were in the 8-year duration category. In 1953 the average maturity of the bonds in our 8-year duration portfolio was just under 9 years, whereas in 1981 the average maturity of the 8-year duration portfolio was 23 years. This variation over the last 30 years calls into question the appropriateness of a bond return series with a constant maturity of 20 years, such as the one tabulated by Ibbotson and Sinquefield (1982).

9. For the arguments on both sides of this debate, see Barro (1974) and Tobin (1980).

10. Including residential real estate would raise another theoretical issue. Individual holdings of residential real estate serve both to diversify the portfolio and to hedge against changes in the relative price of housing services. This hedging demand is ignored in our model, and including it would substantially increase the difficulty of solving for the J function.

11. Equation (9) in our model implies that

$$R_i - R_{\min} = \frac{(\sigma_{iM} - \sigma_{\min}^2)}{(\sigma_M^2 - \sigma_{\min}^2)} (R_M - R_{\min}) .$$

Since $\sigma_{\min}^2$ is very small relative to the covariance of stocks with the market and to the variance of the market, we get $R_{\text{stocks}} - R_{\min} \cong \beta_{\text{stocks}} (R_M - R_{\min})$.

References

Barro, R. 1974. Are government bonds net wealth? *Journal of Political Economy* 82 (Nov.–Dec.):1095–1117.

Bodie, Z. 1982. Inflation risk and capital market equilibrium. *Financial Review* (May).

Fischer, S. 1975. The demand for index bonds. *Journal of Political Economy* 83 (June):509–34.

Friend, I., and Blume, M. 1975. The demand for risky assets. *American Economic Review* 65 (December):900–922.

Friend, I., and Hasbrouck, J. 1982. Effect of inflation on the profitability and valuation of U.S. corporations. In *Proceedings of the Conference on Savings, Investment and Capital Markets in an Inflationary Environment*, ed. Szego and Sarnat. Cambridge, Mass.: Ballinger, 1982.

Grossman, S., and Shiller, R. 1981. The determinants of the variability of stock market prices. *American Economic Review* (May) vol. 71, pp. 222–227.

Ibbotson, R. G., and Sinquefield, R. A. 1982. *Stocks, bonds, bills and inflation: The Past and The Future*. Charlottesville: Financial Analysts Research Foundation.

Macaulay, F. R. 1938. *Some theoretical problems suggested by the movements of interest rates, bond yields, and stock prices in the U.S. since 1856*. New York: NBER.

Markowitz, H. 1952. Portfolio selection. *Journal of Finance* 7 (March):77–91.

Merton, R. C. 1969. Lifetime portfolio selection under uncertainty: the continuous-time case. *Review of Economics and Statistics* 51 (August):247–57.

———. 1971. Optimum consumption and portfolio rules in a continuous-time model. *Journal of Economic Theory* 3 (December):373–413.

———. 1972. An analytic derivation of the efficient portfolio frontier. *Journal of Financial and Quantitative Analysis* 7 (September):1851–72.

———. 1980. On estimating the expected return on the market: an exploratory investigation. *Journal of Financial Economics* 8 (December):323–61.

Pratt, J. W. 1964. Risk aversion in the small and in the large. *Econometrica*. 32 (Jan.–April):122–36.
Tobin, J. 1980. *Asset accumulation and economic activity*. Chicago: University of Chicago Press.

Comment   Martin J. Gruber

The paper by Bodie, Kane, and McDonald, "Inflation and the Role of Bonds in Investor Portfolios," is both interesting and innovative. To the best of my knowledge, it is the first attempt to employ a model of multiperiod equilibrium to examine the welfare loss of restricting the set of assets from which investors can choose. This is a huge undertaking, and the paper shows a great deal of intelligent effort. Like all first papers in an area, there are some things which could be done differently and perhaps improved.

My major concern with this paper is the policy implications which the authors suggest, based on their analysis. The analysis shows that investors can gain most of the advantages of holding the 10 assets classes examined from choosing among three asset classes: a money market fund, stocks, and bonds of 2 years duration. If two funds are offered, they should be a stock fund and a bond fund of 1 or 2 years duration. While these conclusions do describe the investment process facing an investor, one must be very careful in applying these results to the type of investment vehicles which should be offered by private retirement savings plans. This is the stated objective of this paper. The authors' results depend heavily on the investors' ability to sell short as well as to buy any of the portfolios offered. For example, in examining the optimal investment for an individual with a relative risk aversion coefficient of 2 with $10,000 to invest, the authors advocate the following (table 4.4, line 1):

Common stock	Buy	12,060
One-month bill	Sell short	9,840
All other bonds	Buy	7,780

Note that the investment in common stocks is larger than the $10,000 which the investor placed in the pension fund. The authors' results depend on the ability of the investor to short sell any type of portfolio offered by the pension fund and to use the proceeds of this short sale to buy other portfolios. The implications the authors draw for the type of investment portfolios a pension fund should offer individuals is based on

Martin J. Gruber is professor of finance at New York University's Graduate School of Business and co–managing editor of the *Journal of Finance*.

this ability. But in choosing from among the portfolios offered by a pension fund, one cannot short sell one or more portfolios. To draw more meaningful conclusions about the appropriate portfolios for pension funds to offer, the authors must reexamine their problem with short sales restrictions.[1]

Also, in drawing policy implications from this paper, the reader should be aware that the model used assumes that the holder of the pension funds (*a*) owns no other assets; (*b*) has no other sources of income; and (*c*) finances all consumption over his lifetime from the pension fund. While this might be a reasonable description of a subclass of retired individuals, it certainly does not fit the average participant in a pension fund. Care must be taken in drawing policy implications from this paper without a more careful examination of the assets and income stream of pension participants.

I would like briefly to raise a question about the authors' empirical results and then to make a comment about their model. It is always difficult to choose a time frame from which to draw parameters on a model such as that presented by the authors.

Bodie et al. employ an equilibrium model of the form

$$R_i = R_{\min} = \overline{\delta}(\sigma_{im} - \sigma^2_{\min}) \,.$$

They have chosen to use the variance of returns and correlation matrix of returns for the period 1973–81 together with an estimate of $\overline{\delta}$ (the coefficient of relative risk aversion) for the period 1889–1979. They have rejected using the returns for the period 1973–81, but rather generate them from the equation presented above. The authors' results are affected by the fact that the 1973–81 period was a time of rapid and changing inflation. This resulted in a different absolute and relative risk of securities than in earlier periods. For example, long-term bonds have over twice the risk (standard deviation) relative to stocks in this period that they had in earlier periods. One might reasonably ask if this change in absolute and relative risk was accompanied by a change in $\overline{\delta}$. While Bodie et al. accepted the Grossman and Shiller estimate of $\overline{\delta}$ found as 4 over the period 1889–1979, they ignored the comments made by Grossman and Shiller in the same article that the estimates of $\overline{\delta}$ for recent subperiods were much higher.

I would like to discuss briefly an alternate way of viewing the equilibrium model employed in this paper. Solving the authors' equation (10) for $\overline{\delta}$ and substituting into equation (9), we see that

(1) $$R_i - R_{\min} = \frac{(R_m - R_{\min})}{\sigma^2_m - \sigma^2_{\min}}(\sigma_{im} - \sigma^2_{\min}) \,.$$

While this form of the model is correct, there is an alternative way of writing it which, I think, is simpler and will be more familiar to readers.

Since this model must hold for all assets and portfolios, it holds for an asset which has a zero beta with the market portfolio, or

$$R_z - R_{min} = \frac{R_m - R_{min}}{\sigma_m^2 - \sigma_{min}^2} (-\sigma_{min}^2).$$

Solving for R_{min}, substituting into equation (1) above, and simplifying, we find

(2) $R_i = R_z + \beta_i(R_m - R_z).$

The two-factor (Black) CAPM model holds in real terms with the continuous formulation of variables.

In fact, we could have derived this quite simply without resorting to Merton's work. Under a log or power utility function and i.i.d. returns, we know that myopic decisions are optimal.[2] Since investors are maximizing a utility function in terms of means and variances of real returns, equation (2) follows directly from Roll's work.[3]

In summary, I believe the authors have made an interesting start at examining an important and complex problem. They indicate at several points in their paper that this is the first step in a continuing research project. I look forward to following their continuing research.

Notes

1. In the revised version of their paper, the authors advocate the use of futures as the more likely way to alleviate the short sales restriction for the less risk-averse investor. One should be aware that the incorporation of futures into the analysis could significantly modify the authors' conclusions. The expected return, variance, and covariance with other assets of a portfolio of futures is significantly different from a leveraged portfolio of stocks because the purchase of futures involves no cash outflow; dividends are not received by the holder of stock futures; and marking to the market involves intermediate cash flows.

2. See Edwin J. Elton and Martin J. Gruber, "The Multiperiod Consumption Investment Problem and Single Period Analysis," *Oxford Economic Papers* 26 (July, 1974):289–301.

3. See Richard Roll, "A Critique of the Asset Pricing Theory's Tests; Part 1: On Past and Potential Testability of the Theory," *Journal of Financial Economics* 4 (March, 1977):129–76.

5 The Substitutability of Debt and Equity Securities

Benjamin M. Friedman

The substitutability of debt and equity securities in investors' portfolios is an old and important issue both in monetary economics and in the theory of finance. More than two decades ago, Tobin (1961) emphasized that the structure of macroeconomic models of the asset markets depends fundamentally on investors' willingness to substitute debt and equity claims, with consequent strong implications for such familiar questions as the financing of capital formation, the economic impact of government deficits, and the potential efficacy of monetary policy. At the same time, following Modigliani and Miller (1958), the theory of corporate finance has focused heavily on the distinctions between debt and equity claims and on the implications of the fact that corporations issuing these claims confront a competitive market in which investors price these forms of ownership according to their own objectives rather than those of the issuing corporation.

The basic reasons why debt and equity may be either close or distant substitutes are well known. Perhaps the most obvious distinction is that (nonindexed) debt is a claim on a fixed nominal payment stream, while equity is not, so that the two assets' risk properties with respect to changes in the economy's overall price level differ sharply.[1] Similarly, because of the residual nature of equity claims, the two assets also have

Benjamin M. Friedman is professor of economics at Harvard University and program director for financial markets and monetary economics at the NBER. I am grateful to Arturo Estrella and Jeff Fuhrer for research assistance and many helpful discussions; to Zvi Bodie, Stephen Goldfeld, Patric Hendershott, Vance Roley, and other members of the NBER debt-equity project, and especially to Gary Smith, for comments on an earlier draft; to Jeffrey Frankel for correcting an error in some earlier calculations; and to the NBER, the National Science Foundation (grant SES81-12673), and the Alfred P. Sloan Foundation for research support.

different risk properties with respect to changes in relative prices—or equivalently, in a world in which not all markets are perfectly competitive, changes in supply-demand conditions in specific product and factor markets.[2] In comparison with money and other short-term instruments, however, debt and equity claims have much in common with one another. To the extent that both debt and equity represent claims to long-lived payment streams, their shared risk properties with respect to interest rate changes hold them apart from money and other short-term claims. Also, unlike money (and some money substitutes), conventional debt and equity claims are not normally acceptable as a means of payment.[3]

All of these factors affecting investors' willingness to substitute debt and equity securities are familiar enough at the qualitative level, but the actually prevailing debt-equity substitutability and its consequences for important issues of economic behavior remain questions that can only be resolved empirically. It is simply not possible, on the basis of a priori considerations alone, to say which risks or other factors are foremost in investors' minds and hence how investors resolve the tug-of-war that pits the distinctions between debt and equity claims against their similarities. Moreover, because objective circumstances differ from one time and place to another, there is no reason to assume that the relative weights investors place on even the most important of these considerations are universal constants. As changes in the nonfinancial structure of an economy or in the posture of economic policy alter the character of the risks investors face, or as financial market practices and institutions evolve, debt and equity securities may become either closer or more distant substitutes.

The object of this paper is to investigate empirically the degree of substitutability between debt and equity securities in the United States, and to see whether the recent evidence indicates stability or change in this relationship. Section 5.1 applies fundamental relationships connecting portfolio choices to expected asset returns, based on the maximization of expected utility, to infer key asset substitutabilities from the experience of asset returns in the United States during 1960–80. Section 5.2 compares these inferred substitutabilities with the observed portfolio behavior of U.S. households over this period. Section 5.3 performs analogous comparisons for two further alternative systems for grouping financial assets into the broad aggregates (debt, equity, etc.) that are necessary for formal analysis. Section 5.4 focuses on whether there is reason to believe that asset substitutabilities have changed since 1960—to anticipate, the answer is yes—and examines an extended model in light of this finding. Section 5.5 briefly summarizes the paper's principal conclusions and offers some concluding comments.

5.1 Implications of Asset Returns

The substitutability or complementarity of one asset for another is a way of describing how investors' portfolio choices respond to changes in expected asset returns. Because the data available for empirical applications necessarily indicate the composition of investor's portfolios only at specific intervals, it is useful to derive a discrete-time model of this aspect of portfolio behavior.

Following the familiar theory of expected utility maximization,[4] the investor's single-period objective as of time t, given initial wealth W_t, is

(1) $$\max_{\boldsymbol{\alpha}_t} E[U(\widetilde{W}_{t+1})]$$

subject to

(2) $$\boldsymbol{\alpha}_t'1 = 1$$

where $E(\cdot)$ is the expectation operator, $U(W)$ is utility as a function of wealth, $\boldsymbol{\alpha}_t$ is a vector expressing the portfolio allocations in proportional form

(3) $$\boldsymbol{\alpha}_t = \frac{1}{W_t} \cdot A_t$$

for vector A of asset holdings, and wealth W evolves according to

(4) $$\widetilde{W}_{t+1} = W_t \cdot \boldsymbol{\alpha}_t' \, (1 + \tilde{r}_t)$$

for perceived net asset returns r_t between time t and time $t + 1$. As is well known, if $U(W)$ is any power (or logarithmic) function such that the coefficient of relative risk aversion,

(5) $$\rho = - W \cdot \frac{U''(W)}{U'(W)},$$

is constant, and if the investor perceives asset returns $\tilde{r}$ to be distributed as

(6) $$\tilde{r}_t \sim N(r_t^e, \Omega),$$

then the resulting optimal asset demands exhibit the convenient properties of homogeneity in total wealth and linearity in the expected asset returns.[5]

If no asset in vector A bears a risk-free return, so that the variance-covariance matrix Ω is of full rank, then solution of the first-order condition for the maximization of (1) subject to (2) yields

(7) $$\boldsymbol{\alpha}_t^* = B\,(r_t^e + 1) + \pi,$$

where

(8) $B = \left\{ \dfrac{-U'\,[E(\widetilde{W}_{t+1})]}{W_t \cdot U''[E(\widetilde{W}_{t+1})]} \right\} \cdot [\Omega^{-1} - (1'\,\Omega\,1)^{-1}\,\Omega^{-1}\,1\,1'\,\Omega^{-1}]$

(9) $$\pi = (1'\,\Omega^{-1}1)^{-1}\,\Omega^{-1}1.$$

Alternatively, in the presence of a risk-free asset bearing return r^f, it is necessary to partition the asset demand system. The resulting solution, in which $\hat{\alpha}$, $\hat{r}^e$, and $\hat{\Omega}$ refer to the subset of risky assets only, is

(10) $$\hat{\alpha}_t^* = \hat{B}\,(\hat{r}_t^e - r_t^f \cdot 1 + 1),$$

where

(11) $$\hat{B} = \left\{ \dfrac{-U'\,[E(\widetilde{W}_{t+1})]}{W_t \cdot U''[E(\widetilde{W}_{t+1})]} \right\} \cdot \hat{\Omega}^{-1}$$

and the optimum portfolio share for the risk-free asset is just $(1 - \hat{\alpha}^{*\prime}1)$. In either case, if the time unit is sufficiently small to render W_t a good approximation to $E(\widetilde{W}_{t+1})$ for purposes of the underlying expansion, then the scalar term within brackets in either (8) or (11) reduces to the reciprocal of the constant coefficient of relative risk aversion ρ.[6]

Because this system of asset demands provides the basic vehicle for the analysis that follows, it is useful at the outset to note explicitly several of its properties. First, because of the assumptions of constant relative risk aversion and normally distributed return assessments, the respective asset demands are each proportional to the investor's wealth, and they depend linearly on the associated expected returns. Second, as Brainard and Tobin (1968) have emphasized, the effect of the constraint (2) is to render the asset demands linearly dependent, so that matrix B (or $\hat{B}$) and vector π satisfy the "adding up" constraints

(12) $$\beta_j'1 = 0, \text{ all } j,$$

and

(13) $$\pi'1 = 1,$$

where vectors β_j are the columns of B. Third, because Ω is a variance-covariance matrix and therefore symmetrical, B (or $\hat{B}$) indicates symmetrical asset substitutions associated with cross-yield effects.[7] Fourth, B (or $\hat{B}$) is strictly proportional to a straightforward transformation of the variance-covariance matrix, with the factor of proportionality equal to the reciprocal of the coefficient of relative risk aversion. Each of these four properties figures importantly in the analysis presented below.

The primary focus of interest here is the specific off-diagonal elements (or, depending on the asset aggregation scheme employed, element) of B that describe the substitutability or complementarity of debt and equity securities—that is, the response of the demand for debt to changes in the expected return on equity, and vice versa. Following Brainard and Tobin (1968), the standard assumption (at least in the macroeconomic literature) is that all assets are gross substitutes, so that the only question left to be resolved empirically is the absolute magnitude of the presumably negative off-diagonal β_{ij} elements measuring debt-equity substitutability. The β_{ij} in (8) and (11) are marginal responses, so that the associated elasticities of substitution, defined in the usual way as[8]

$$(14) \qquad\qquad \epsilon_{ij} = \frac{dA_i}{dr_j^e} \cdot \frac{r_j^e}{A_i}$$

simply follow from (7) and (3) as

$$(15) \qquad\qquad \epsilon_{ij} = \beta_{ij} \cdot \frac{r_j^e}{\alpha_i}.$$

In general, however, assets may or may not be gross substitutes. From (8) and (11) it is clear that not just the magnitude but also the sign of each asset demand response to variations in expected yields depends on the variance-covariance structure describing perceived asset returns. In the presence of a risk-free asset, Blanchard and Plantes (1977) have shown that a necessary (but not sufficient) condition for gross substitutability of all assets—that is, for all of the off-diagonal $\hat{\beta}_{ij}$ in (11) to be negative—is that the partial correlations among all asset returns be nonnegative.[9] In the absence of a risk-free asset, as is typically assumed here, no such straightforward condition on Ω to guarantee the negativity of all of the off-diagonal β_{ij} is apparent, and the most straightforward way to assess the question of gross substitutability is simply to inspect the elements of B directly.[10]

In financial markets as well developed as those in the United States, most investors confront a rich, and at times bewildering, variety of financial instruments. Different securities represent claims structured in sharply different ways and therefore bear returns subject to different risks. Government securities differ from private securities. Even among private securities, claims against some obligors can differ importantly from identically structured claims against others. For purposes of the questions addressed here, however, it is important to focus on broadly defined asset categories, thereby disregarding much of this variety and implicitly treating as perfect substitutes many distinct claims among which investors are presumably not entirely indifferent.

Some aggregation among assets, therefore, is clearly necessary. Table 5.1 indicates an aggregation of the many forms of financial claims typically held by households in the United States into five broad categories: money, time and saving deposits, short-term debt, long-term debt, and equity. The table also indicates the amount of each asset category in the aggregate portfolio of the U.S. household sector as of year-end 1980.[11]

Table 5.1   Disaggregation of Household Sector Financial Assets

Asset		1980:IV Value
Money (*M*)		$ 268.0
Time and saving deposits (*T*)		624.7
Short-term debt (*S*)		884.3
Money market fund shares	74.4	
Competitive-return time deposits	669.7	
U.S. government securities	102.0	
Open market paper	38.2	
Long-term debt (*L*)		464.3
U.S. government securities	180.2	
State and local obligations	74.2	
Corporate and foreign bonds	86.9	
Mortgages	122.5	
Equity (*E*)		1,215.6
Mutual fund shares	63.7	
Directly held equity shares	1,151.8	
Total		3,456.9

Source: Board of Governors of the Federal Reserve System.
Notes: Values in billions of dollars. Detail may not add to total because of rounding.

The analysis here ignores entirely all nonfinancial assets, both because the available rate-of-return data are weak (nonexistent in many cases) and because a careful treatment of investment in nonfinancial assets lies beyond the scope of this paper.

The object of the aggregation shown in table 5.1 is to preserve the fundamental distinctions among assets while at the same time reducing the number of separate categories to within manageable range for purposes of empirical analysis.[12] "Money," including currency and demand deposits, distinguishes assets that bear zero nominal rates of return and that provide means-of-payment services. "Time and saving deposits" distinguishes assets that bear (nonzero) nominal rates of return subject to fixed legal ceilings. "Short-term debt," including all other deposit instruments and all open market debt instruments maturing in less than one year, distinguishes assets that bear market-determined nominal rates of return but that are subject to little interest rate risk. "Long-term debt," including all other debt instruments, distinguishes assets that bear nominal rates of return and that are subject to substantial interest rate risk. "Equity" distinguishes assets that bear residual ownership risk.

The first column of table 5.2 shows the annualized mean real returns, in percentage form, observed on these five aggregate assets on a quarterly basis during 1960–80. The nominal returns associated with these real

Table 5.2   **Mean Real Returns, 1960–80**

	Before Tax (%)	After Tax (%)
r_M	−5.43	−5.43
r_T	−1.24	−2.53
r_S	.78	−1.16
r_L	−1.60	−3.83
r_E	5.24	3.13

Note: Values in percent per annum.

returns are zero for money; a weighted average yield for time and saving deposits; the 4–6-month prime commercial paper yield for short-term debt; the Moody's Baa corporate bond yield, plus annualized percentage capital gains or losses inferred by applying the consol pricing formula to changes in the Baa yield, for long-term debt; and the dividend price yield, plus annualized percentage capital gains or losses, on the Standard and Poor's 500 index for equity. In each case the real return is just the respective nominal return minus the annualized percentage change in the consumer price index.[13]

The second column of table 5.2 shows the corresponding after-tax returns on these five aggregate assets, computed by applying the marginal tax rates shown in table 5.3 to each quarter's before-tax returns before subtracting the consumer price index change.[14] The marginal tax rates applied to interest and dividends are values estimated by Estrella and Fuhrer (1983), on the basis of Internal Revenue Service data, to reflect the marginal tax bracket of the average recipient of these two respective kinds of income in each year. The marginal tax rate applied to capital gains is an analogous estimate, including allowances for deferral and loss offset features, due to Feldstein et al. (1983).

As is clear in (7)–(11), the substitutability or complementarity among assets in investors' portfolios depends on the variance-covariance structure of the returns that investors associate with those assets. Hence what matters in this context is not necessarily the actual experience of returns but investors' perceptions and expectations, which may or may not closely approximate the corresponding ultimate outcomes. Because expectations are not directly observable, arriving at values to use in their place for purposes of empirical analysis is always problematical. One solution to this problem, which is applicable in some isolated cases in which data are available, is to rely on survey information.[15] The most plausible alternative, which rests on the assumption of at least some form of "rationality" in investors' perceptions, is to infer the distribution of expected returns at least partly on the basis of the observed experience of actual returns.

Table 5.3   Marginal Tax Rates, 1960–79

	Interest	Dividends	Capital Gains
1960	.2955	.4949	.047
1961	.2989	.5022	.047
1962	.2905	.4968	.047
1963	.2893	.5022	.047
1964	.2631	.4597	.046
1965	.2552	.4359	.046
1966	.2599	.4376	.046
1967	.2695	.4476	.045
1968	.2745	.4500	.045
1969	.2803	.4423	.065
1970	.3064	.4536	.064
1971	.3360	.4721	.064
1972	.3128	.4559	.063
1973	.3220	.4614	.063
1974	.3341	.4967	.063
1975	.3341	.4759	.062
1976	.3407	.4834	.062
1977	.3243	.4786	.062
1978	.3353	.4874	.062
1979	.3442	.4744	.044

Table 5.4 shows the variance-covariance matrix of the actual return experience corresponding to the mean after-tax real returns in table 5.2.[16] As is familiar, these data show the large variation (even in real terms) associated with equity and, to a somewhat lesser extent, with long-term debt. As is also familiar, the variation associated with short-term debt is the smallest among any of the five aggregate assets.

What would these variance-covariance properties imply for the substitution properties among the five assets if they did accurately represent investors' assessments? Table 5.5 shows the transformation of Ω from the right-hand side of (8) computed on the basis of the Ω matrix in table 5.4 (and appropriately scaled to allow for the statement of returns in percentage form). To recall, these values indicate, to within a (positive) constant indicating the investor's relative risk aversion, the marginal re-

Table 5.4   Variance-Covariance Structure of After-Tax Real Returns, 1960–80

	r_M	r_T	r_S	r_L	r_E
r_M	15.78				
r_T	14.61	13.61			
r_S	9.99	9.28	7.09		
r_L	34.97	33.18	21.50	209.35	
r_E	32.79	31.43	22.58	161.77	597.96

Table 5.5   Portfolio Responses Implied by Variance-Covariance Structure

	r_M	r_T	r_S	r_L	r_E
M	748				
T	-851	1029			
S	102	-174	69.3		
L	.842	-4.34	2.77	.873	
E	.178	-.80	-.0559	-.154	.213

sponses of optimal asset demands to changes in expected returns. For $\rho = 1$, a plausible and often assumed magnitude, these values are simply identical to the optimal marginal responses.[17]

What immediately stands out in table 5.5 is that the implied system of optimal asset demands does not render all assets gross substitutes. Money is a complement for all assets except time and saving deposits, while short-term and long-term debt are complements for one another. Debt and equity securities are clearly substitutes, however. On the assumption that $\rho = 1$, so that the values in table 5.5 represent the elements β_{ij} in (8), the corresponding elasticities of substitution follow as in (15). Table 5.6 shows the 1960-80 mean asset shares which, together with the mean after-tax asset real returns in table 5.2, facilitate calculating elasticities from the optimal marginal responses in table 5.5 The results of such calculations are likely to be misleading in many cases, however, because four of the five mean net returns are negative. On the basis of the mean values as shown, the marginal response of the demand for short-term debt to the expected return on equity (which has a positive mean) implies an elasticity of substitution $\epsilon_{SE} = -2.54$, while the corresponding elasticity for equity and long-term debt is $\epsilon_{LE} = -3.74$.[18]

It is also useful to examine whether the assumption that no risk-free asset exists, as is implicit in using the values in table 5.5 to imply whether assets are substitutes or complements, importantly affects these conclusions. In brief, the answer is no, although in this case the absolute

Table 5.6   Mean Values of Household Financial Asset Holdings, 1960-80

	Value	Fraction
Money (M)	$ 137.2	.083
Time and saving deposits (T)	471.9	.275
Short-term debt (S)	137.6	.069
Long-term debt (L)	215.4	.129
Equity (E)	681.2	.444
Total	1,643.3	1.000

Source: Board of Governors of the Federal Reserve System.
Note: Values in billions of dollars. Detail may not add to total because of rounding.

magnitude of the elasticity of substitution for equity and short-term debt is implausibly large. The signs of all elements in (11) are identical to the corresponding signs shown in table 5.5, except for that relating money and short-term debt. The respective elasticities of substitution of short-term and long-term debt for equity, calculated as above but using (11) instead of (8), are $\epsilon_{SE} = -27.0$ and $\epsilon_{LE} = -3.45$. Once again, even in the presence of a risk-free asset, not all of the five risky assets would be gross substitutes. As table 5.7 shows, the partial correlations among the risky assets' after-tax real returns include a negative value and hence fail to satisfy the Blanchard-Plantes necessary condition.

Section 5.2 goes on to examine how the observed portfolio behavior of U.S. households has corresponded with the optimal behavior indicated in table 5.5. Even before turning to the observed asset choices, however, it is helpful to focus on one aspect of the historical asset return experience that presents particular challenges for explaining investors' behavior. The optimal portfolio shares of the five asset aggregates, computed from (7) using the historical after-tax return means and variance-covariance matrix, indicate positive holdings of only two assets—time and saving deposits, and equity.[19] These two assets did have the largest shares of households' actual portfolios during this period, as table 5.6 indicates, but holdings of the other three assets were of course positive as well. Hence the actual asset choices made by households clearly differed from the optimal choices implied by the simple model developed above from the basics of expected utility maximization. Either households' perceptions of returns systematically differed from the actual experience during this period, or else households were incorporating other factors into their portfolio decisions. The analysis that follows attempts to consider each of these possibilities.

5.2   Household Sector Portfolio Behavior

The model of portfolio behavior developed in section 5.1 takes the maximization of expected utility as the sole objective guiding investors' asset choices. When one of the assets under consideration is money, however, the need for means-of-payment services constitutes another factor influencing asset selection. Following Tobin (1969), among other

Table 5.7   Partial Correlations among After-Tax Real Returns, 1960–80

	r_M	r_T	r_S	r_L
r_T	.97			
r_S	.12	.11		
r_L	−.13	.21	.12	
r_E	.09	.07	.11	.32

writers, a convenient way to represent the demand for such services in a model with asset demands homogeneous in portfolio wealth is by the flow of transactions relative to wealth. In the linear model (7), the implied generalization is accordingly

$$(16) \qquad \alpha_t^* = B(r_t^e + 1) + \delta\left(\frac{Y_t}{W_t}\right) + \pi,$$

where Y is the investor's transactions, δ is a vector of coefficients, and all other terms are as before.[20] Because money provides means-of-payment services, the usual presumption is that $\delta_M > 0$. Moreover, δ must satisfy an "adding up" constraint analogous to (13), so that this presumption also implies $\delta_i < 0$ for at least some asset $i \neq M$.

Table 5.8 presents results for the estimation of (16) by ordinary least squares, using quarterly U.S. data for 1960–80. Data used for α are seasonally adjusted shares of the U.S. household sector's aggregate portfolio during 1960–80. As Lintner (1969) has explicitly shown, the linearity of asset demand relationships like (7) or (16) readily admits of aggregation across investors with diverse preferences (ρ), endowments (W), and assessments (r^e, Ω). The intended end result here of empirical analysis based on aggregate data is therefore an estimate of the relevant parameters describing the behavior of the collectivity of investors that together play a large role in determining the overall substitutability of debt and equity securities in the United States. Data for the household sector consist for the most part of the portfolio holdings of individual investors, and the household sector is the dominant holder of securities— and the ultimate holder of all wealth—in the U.S. economy.[21]

The data for α are respective shares, and for W the aggregate level, of the household sector's portfolio of financial assets, constructed for each asset by decrementing backward from the reported 1980 year end value using the corresponding seasonally adjusted quarterly flows.[22] In addition, for equities (the only financial asset for which the asset stock data are at market value), quarterly valuation changes are included without seasonal adjustment. As the discussion in section 5.1 explains, the data used here omit holdings of nonfinancial assets, in part to avoid data inadequacies and in part simply to limit the scope of the analysis. The data also omit the household sector's outstanding liabilities, since the great bulk of household borrowings is tied to the ownership of nonfinancial assets.[23] The data for r^e are actual real return data for money, time and saving deposits, and short-term debt. For long-term debt and equity the data are actual real return data for the component of returns excluding capital gains, plus fitted values of the respective percentage capital gains from a simple univariate autoregressive process.[24] The data for Y are quarterly gross national product flows, seasonally adjusted.

Table 5.8 shows the estimated values and t-statistics for the elements of

Table 5.8 Portfolio Responses Estimated from Equilibrium Model

Asset	$\beta_{\cdot M}$	$\beta_{\cdot T}$	$\beta_{\cdot S}$	$\beta_{\cdot L}$	$\beta_{\cdot E}$	$\bar{R}^2$	S.E.	D-W
M	.0155 (17.0)	-.0144 (-14.6)	-.000962 (-2.8)	-.000103 (-2.2)	-.0000173 (-0.6)	.88	.0024	.59
T	-.0559 (-5.4)	.0758 (6.8)	-.0222 (-5.8)	.000248 (0.5)	-.000666 (-2.1)	.77	.0275	.31
S	.00253 (0.2)	-.0239 (-2.0)	.0214 (5.1)	-.0000302 (-0.1)	.000854 (2.4)	.63	.0301	.29
L	.0211 (13.0)	-.0196 (-11.2)	-.000713 (-1.2)	.000127 (1.5)	-.0000173 (-0.3)	.92	.00433	.55
E	.0166 (5.9)	-.0179 (-5.9)	.00255 (2.4)	-.000242 (-1.7)	-.000153 (-1.7)	.99	.0075	.79

matrix B in (16) as well as summary statistics for each equation including the coefficient of determination (adjusted for degrees of freedom), the standard error of estimate, and the Durbin-Watson statistic.[25] A comparison of the estimated marginal response values β_{ij} with the implied optimal responses in table 5.5 shows little congruence. The estimated values are uniformly smaller in absolute value than are the implied optimal values, as would ordinarily be the case in the presence of errors in measuring the unobservable expected returns but here it is by one or more orders of magnitude. Nine of the estimated values differ in sign from the implied optimal values, however, although in only four cases are the differences statistically significant at the .05 level. Among the 10 pairs of off-diagonal coefficients that (8) implies should be identical, four differ in sign; three of the four conflicting pairs are in the row and column corresponding to money and its expected return.

On the key issue of substitutability of debt and equity securities, the estimated values indicate (without contradiction in signs of paired values) that short-term debt and equity are complements and that long-term debt and equity are substitutes—results that are, respectively, inconsistent and consistent with the solution in table 5.5. Once again, it is necessary to base the corresponding elasticities of substitution on the short-term or long-term debt demand and the equity return in order to avoid sign changes due to negative mean net returns. Here, however, there are two separate estimates of each marginal response β_{ij} $(i \neq j)$, because the matrix of estimated coefficients is not symmetric. The respective pairs of implied elasticity estimates are $\epsilon_{SE} = (.039, .116)$ and $\epsilon_{LE} = (-.0004, -.006)$. Although both ϵ_{LE} values are negative, both are small in absolute value in comparison with $\epsilon_{LE} = -3.74$ implied by the solution in table 5.5.

One immediately noticeable aspect of the summary statistics shown in table 5.8 is the uniformly low Durbin-Watson statistics, indicating residuals in all five equations that unambiguously display significant serial correlation at the .01 level. This result is hardly surprising in a quarterly model, in light of the well-known sluggishness of household portfolio behavior in the presence of (broadly defined) transactions costs. Especially in the context of occasional large moves in equity prices, which suddenly shift the relative portfolio shares of all assets, it is implausible to expect full realignment of asset holdings to expected returns within a calendar quarter.[26] Some model of portfolio adjustment out of equilibrium is therefore appropriate.

The most straightforward and familiar model of portfolio adjustment under transactions costs found in the asset demand literature is the multivariate partial adjustment form

$$(17) \qquad\qquad \Delta A_t = \Theta(A_t^* - A_{t-1})$$

where A^* is the vector of equilibrium asset holdings corresponding to α^* in (16) and Θ is a matrix of adjustment coefficients with columns satisfying an "adding up" constraint analogous to (12).[27] Applying (17) to (16) yields

(18) $\Delta A_t = \Phi(r_t^e + 1) \cdot W_t + \xi Y_t + \psi W_t - \Theta A_{t-1},$

where

(19) $\Phi = \Theta B$

(20) $\xi = \Theta \delta$

(21) $\psi = \Theta \pi,$

so that the columns of matrix Φ and vector ξ all satisfy "adding up" constraints analogous to (12) while that for vector ψ is analogous to (13).

The top panel of table 5.9 presents results for the estimation of (18) by ordinary least squares, using the same quarterly data for 1960–80 described above. Because each term in (18) takes the dimension of nominal dollars, however—unlike the homogeneous form (16)—here care is necessary to avoid spurious correlations due to common time trends. Hence for purposes of estimation all nominal magnitudes (ΔA, W, Y, and A) are rendered in real per capital values.[28] In addition, both ΔA_t and W_t exclude the current period's capital gains or losses (although the vector of lagged asset stocks A_{t-1} reflects previous periods' gains and losses), so that the estimated form focuses strictly on the household sector's aggregate net purchases or sales of each asset associated with the sector's net saving. Defining the asset flows in this way is equivalent to assuming that investors do not respond within the quarter to that quarter's changes in their holdings due to changing market valuations but do respond to market valuations as of the beginning of each quarter.

The top panel of table 5.9 reports summary statistics for each equation and estimated values and t-statistics for the matrix Φ of immediate marginal responses of asset demands to expected returns. Not surprisingly, the use of the partial adjustment form sharply improves the overall fit properties of all five equations. Serial correlation remains significant in only two equations, and the standard errors, after conversion from real dollars per capita to portfolio shares as in table 5.8, are uniformly smaller—in some cases by almost an order of magnitude.[29]

Although the immediate marginal portfolio responses ϕ_{ij} may be useful for some purposes, what primarily matters in the context of the questions raised at the outset of this paper is the matrix of equilibrium marginal responses B, solved following (19) as $B = \Theta^{-1}\Phi$. The lower panel of table 5.9 shows the implied matrix B, together with associated t-statistics found by using the full-information maximum likelihood method to reestimate (18) in a nonlinear form representing the elements

Table 5.9 Portfolio Responses Estimated from Partial Adjustment Model

Asset	$\phi_{\cdot M}$	$\phi_{\cdot T}$	$\phi_{\cdot S}$	$\phi_{\cdot L}$	$\phi_{\cdot E}$	$\bar{R}^2$	S.E.	D-W
M	.00122 (0.9)	-.000847 (-0.6)	-.000562 (-2.4)	-.0000530 (-2.2)	.0000406 (2.5)	.33	7.28	2.09
T	-.0110 (-3.0)	.0129 (3.5)	-.00218 (-3.4)	.00000966 (0.1)	.0000735 (1.6)	.76	20.14	1.11
S	.00771 (1.7)	-.00915 (-2.0)	.00153 (1.9)	.0000381 (0.4)	-.0000702 (-1.2)	.73	25.73	1.33
L	.00188 (1.0)	-.00258 (-1.4)	.000921 (2.9)	.0000191 (0.6)	-.0000165 (-0.7)	.22	10.01	1.61
E	.000200 (0.3)	-.000271 (-0.5)	.000297 (2.9)	-.0000139 (-1.3)	-.0000275 (-3.8)	.33	3.24	1.94

Implied Equilibrium Responses

Asset	$\beta_{\cdot M}$	$\beta_{\cdot T}$	$\beta_{\cdot S}$	$\beta_{\cdot L}$	$\beta_{\cdot E}$
M	.0197 (3.4)	-.0210 (-3.5)	.00258 (2.7)	-.000347 (-2.0)	-.0000673 (-0.5)
T	.00771 (0.2)	-.00142 (0.0)	.00377 (0.3)	-.00135 (-0.8)	-.00180 (-2.0)
S	-.106 (-2.1)	.114 (2.1)	-.0339 (-2.0)	.00292 (1.7)	.00340 (3.1)
L	.0314 (2.4)	-.0398 (-3.0)	.0104 (4.1)	.00017 (0.6)	-.00022 (-1.0)
E	.0469 (1.6)	-.0516 (-1.6)	.0171 (3.0)	-.00139 (-2.3)	-.00132 (-2.5)

of matrix Φ in the form (19) so as to derive direct estimates of the underlying β_{ij} values.[30] In addition, so as to derive t-statistics comparable to those shown in table 5.8, in which the equivalent of an identity matrix is imposed a priori in place of the adjustment matrix Θ, for purposes of the maximum likelihood estimation the estimated Θ_{ij} values were taken as given.[31]

These estimated equilibrium asset demand responses again bear little resemblance overall to the implied optimal responses in table 5.5. Once again each response is smaller, in absolute value, by at least one order of magnitude. Of the 25 estimated β_{ij}, 11 differ in sign from the corresponding B elements in table 5.5, including three negative values among the five on-diagonal β_{ii} indicating the "own" response of the demand for an asset to the expected return on that asset. Among the 10 pairs of off-diagonal β_{ij}, all four pairs in the row and column corresponding to money and its expected return uniformly disagree in sign, while the remaining six pairs uniformly agree in sign. In light of the ample (but troubled) literature on the demand for money, it is hardly surprising that the "pure portfolio" approach followed here should meet only limited success in explaining money demand and/or the response of other asset demands to the expected return on money.[32] These estimates for the partial adjustment model correspond to those shown in table 5.8 for the equilibrium model in indicating that long-term debt and equity are substitutes, as in table 5.5, but (unlike in table 5.5) short-term debt and equity are complements. The associated pairs of implied elasticities (calculated, as usual, from the mean return on equity) are $\epsilon_{SE} = (.154, .776)$ and $\epsilon_{LE} = (-.005, -.034)$.

Because the five equations comprising (18) have identical sets of regressors, either ordinary least-squares or (unconstrained) maximum likelihood methods necessarily yield estimates satisfying the "adding up" constraints emphasized by Brainard and Tobin. By contrast, such estimates in general do not satisfy other cross-equation restrictions implied by the theory of portfolio choice outlined in section 5.1. In this context a further potential advantage of the nonlinear maximum likelihood method underlying the β_{ij} estimates in table 5.9 is the facility it provides for imposing such restrictions.

Table 5.10 presents an alternative set of maximum likelihood estimates for (18), subject to the restriction that the matrix of equilibrium marginal responses B be symmetric. (Familiar practice notwithstanding, there is no reason to assume symmetry of the matrix of immediate marginal responses Φ.) The table shows the usual summary statistics for each equation, and estimated values and t-statistics for the symmetric matrix of equilibrium portfolio responses.[33] Here two of the five on-diagonal β_{ii} elements—those indicating the respective "own" responses of long-term debt and equity—have negative estimated values, although neither dif-

Table 5.10   Symmetric Portfolio Responses Estimated from Partial Adjustment Model

Asset	$\beta_{\cdot M}$	$\beta_{\cdot T}$	$\beta_{\cdot S}$	$\beta_{\cdot L}$	$\beta_{\cdot E}$	$\bar{R}^2$	S.E.	D-W
M	.118 (5.7)					.16	8.16	2.28
T	−.165 (−5.8)	.252 (5.1)				.76	20.40	1.15
S	.0480 (4.8)	−.0870 (−3.9)	.0313 (1.9)			.72	25.96	1.32
L	.000755 (0.6)	−.00319 (−1.1)	.00341 (1.1)	−.00000524 (−0.0)		.17	10.32	1.59
E	−.00267 (−1.9)	.00284 (1.2)	.00424 (0.7)	−.000974 (−0.6)	−.00343 (−0.9)	.14	3.67	1.71

fers significantly from zero. Among the 10 off-diagonal β_{ij} elements, seven agree in sign with the implied optimal responses shown in table 5.5 while three—all in the row and column corresponding to equity and its expected return—disagree.

As is the case for the unconstrained estimates shown in tables 5.8 and 5.9, the constrained estimates indicate that short-term debt and equity are complements, while long-term debt and equity are substitutes. The associated implied elasticities (calculated in the usual way) are $\epsilon_{SE} = .192$ and $\epsilon_{LE} = -.024$. As is to be expected, imposition of the symmetry constraint enlarges the standard error of each equation, and the appropriate test of the symmetry constraint itself yields $\chi^2 (10) = 43.8$, warranting rejection of the implied restrictions at any plausible significance level.[34]

In addition to symmetry, the theory summarized in section 5.1 implies that the matrix of equilibrium portfolio responses also be proportional to the transformation of the asset return variance-covariance matrix shown in (8), with the constant of proportionality (approximately) equal to the reciprocal of the coefficient of relative risk aversion. Nevertheless, estimating (18) by the same nonlinear maximum likelihood method, subject to the further constraint that matrix B be proportional to the implied optimal response matrix in table 5.5, yields $\chi^2 (9) = 19.2$, warranting rejection at the .05 level (but not the .01 level) of the further restrictions imposed in addition to the symmetry restrictions.[35]

In sum, neither estimates for equilibrium model (16) nor those for partial adjustment model (18) yield a representation of the U.S. household sector's observed 1960–80 portfolio behavior that is very satisfactory in terms of the theory summarized in section 5.1. Moreover, these models do allow (albeit in a simple, though standard, way) for two potentially important influences on portfolio choice that the straightforward theory of expected utility maximization omits—the demand for means-of-payment services, and the transactions costs associated with portfolio adjustments. Sections 5.3 and 5.4 therefore turn to examine whether it is plausible to assume that the stochastic structure of asset returns represented in tables 5.2 and 5.4 accurately reflects the perceptions that guided investors' asset selection during this period.

5.3 Two Alternative Asset Aggregation Systems

As the discussion in section 5.1 emphasizes, any scheme for reducing to analytically manageable terms the number of assets from which investors choose their portfolios is bound to be highly arbitrary. A possible explanation for the unsatisfactory estimates summarized in tables 5.9 and 5.10, therefore, is that the five-asset aggregation system introduced in table 5.1 either over- or understates the important distinctions on which investors actually focus in making asset choices.

Tables 5.11 and 5.12 show the basic properties of realized asset returns, and the corresponding estimation results for asset demand system (18), under an alternative aggregation system that distinguishes only three separate asset categories: money plus time deposits, including all instruments bearing nominal returns subject to (zero or nonzero) fixed legal ceilings; short-term plus long-term debt, including all instruments bearing market-determined nominal rates of return; and equity, as before. The idea underlying this alternative is simply to group together assets bearing nonmarket nominal returns without distinguishing those that provide means of payment services, and to group together assets bearing market-determined nominal returns without distinguishing those subject to substantial interest rate risk. The returns associated with each composite asset category are just those of its two components, as described in section 5.1, weighted by their respective dollar magnitudes in each quarter.

According to the implied optimal portfolio responses shown in table 5.11, the composite debt asset and equity are clearly substitutes, with elasticity of substitution $\epsilon_{SL,E} = -4.41$. On balance, however, the estimated portfolio responses shown in table 5.12 are no more satisfactory than those shown in tables 5.9 and 5.10 for the five-asset classification. In the absence of the symmetry constraint, the two estimated values corresponding to the substitutability of debt and equity differ in sign and most of the estimated responses are again small (in absolute value) by at least an order of magnitude in comparison with the implied optimal responses. With the symmetry constraint imposed, debt and equity are complements with elasticity $\epsilon_{SL,E} = 3.62$, and the order of magnitude differences partly disappear. The loss of fit associated with the symmetry restriction is clearly large, however, and the test statistic value $\chi^2(3) = 46.3$ warrants rejecting it at any plausible significance level.

Tables 5.13 and 5.14 present analogous asset return properties and estimation results for a second alternative aggregation scheme, again distinguishing only three asset categories: money plus time deposits plus short-term debt; long-term debt; and equity. The idea underlying this alternative is to group together all assets bearing nominal returns that are essentially fixed (and known in advance, at least on a quarterly basis) and hence subject to inflation risk only.[36] In effect, the application of the "pure portfolio" model to this set of aggregates is equivalent to assuming that investors first decide, on the basis of mean-variance utility maximization, how large a portfolio of liquid assets to hold, and secondarily divide their liquid assets among money, time deposits, and short-term debt instruments on the basis of other considerations.[37] The return associated with the composite liquid asset category is a weighted average of the returns associated with its three components.[38]

The implied optimal portfolio responses shown in table 5.13 for this

Table 5.11   Properties of Real Returns under First Alternative Asset
                    Aggregation

A. Mean Returns

	Before Tax (%)	After Tax (%)
Money plus time and saving deposits (MT)	−2.22	−3.21
Short-term plus long-term debt (SL)	−.27	−2.44
Equity (E)	5.24	3.13

B. Variance-Covariance Structure (After Tax)

	r_{MT}	r_{SL}	r_E
r_{MT}	13.83		
r_{SL}	22.16	90.85	
r_E	31.35	115.92	597.96

C. Portfolio Responses Implied by Variance-Covariance Structure

	r_{MT}	r_{SL}	r_E
MT	1.67		
SL	−1.73	2.01	
E	.0581	−2.79	.221

Table 5.12   Estimated Portfolio Responses under First Alternative Asset
                    Aggregation

Asset	$\beta_{.MT}$	$\beta_{.SL}$	$\beta_{.E}$	$\bar{R}^2$	S.E.	D-W
Unconstrained estimates:						
MT	.00850	−.00275	−.00357	.57	27.79	1.62
	(2.3)	(−2.0)	(−3.5)			
SL	−.0220	.00457	.00527	.70	28.43	1.47
	(−4.0)	(2.5)	(3.6)			
E	.0135	−.00182	−.00169	.23	3.47	1.74
	(6.2)	(−1.9)	(−3.4)			
Symmetric estimates:						
MT	−.0477			.41	33.92	1.15
	(−1.6)					
SL	.134	−.364		.55	34.52	1.10
	(1.7)	(−1.7)				
E	−.0867	.229	−.143	.03	3.89	1.56
	(−1.7)	(1.7)	(−1.7)			

Table 5.13   **Properties of Real Returns under Second Alternative Asset Aggregation**

A. Mean Returns

	Before Tax (%)	After Tax (%)
Money plus time and saving deposits plus short-term debt (MTS)	−1.62	−2.80
Long-term debt	−1.60	−3.83
Equity	5.24	3.13

B. Variance-Covariance Structure (After Tax)

	r_{MTS}	r_L	r_E
r_{MTS}	11.18		
r_L	29.91	209.35	
r_E	30.24	161.77	597.96

C. Portfolio Responses Implied by Variance-Covariance Structure

MTS	.641		
L	−.578	.727	
E	−.0635	−.150	.213

Table 5.14   **Estimated Portfolio Responses under Second Alternative Asset Aggregation**

Asset	$\beta_{\cdot MTS}$	$\beta_{\cdot L}$	$\beta_{\cdot E}$	$\bar{R}^2$	S.E.	D-W
Unconstrained estimates:						
MTS	−.0192	.00283	.00575	.78	11.71	1.53
	(−1.7)	(1.3)	(2.7)			
L	.00201	−.000231	−.00117	.16	10.41	1.49
	(0.6)	(−0.3)	(−1.8)			
E	.0172	−.00260	−.00458	.25	3.43	1.81
	(2.2)	(−1.8)	(−3.0)			
Symmetric estimates:						
MTS	−.0135			.78	11.74	1.52
	(−2.5)					
L	.00266	−.000299		.16	10.42	1.48
	(2.0)	(−0.8)				
E	.0108	−.00237	−.00847	.18	3.58	1.73
	(2.6)	(−2.4)	(−2.7)			

aggregation scheme indicate that all three assets are gross substitutes, with elasticities $\epsilon_{MTS,E} = -.465$ between liquid assets and equity, and $\epsilon_{LE} = -3.64$ between long-term debt and equity. The unconstrained estimates shown in table 5.14, however, bear little apparent relation to these optimal responses. Most of the estimated responses are smaller (in absolute value) by at least an order of magnitude, all three estimated on-diagonal "own" responses are negative, and the estimated off-diagonal responses indicate (without any sign contradictions) that liquid assets are a complement for both long-term debt and equity. With the symmetry constraint imposed, the elasticities are $\epsilon_{MTS,E} = .079$ and $\epsilon_{LE} = -.058$. Here the $\epsilon_{MTS,E}$ value again indicates complementarity rather than substitutability, but the ϵ_{LE} value at least agrees in sign with and approaches in magnitude the corresponding optimal ϵ_{LE} implied by the solution in table 5.13. The test statistic value for the symmetry restriction is $\chi^2(3) = 8.0$, which warrants rejecting the restriction at the .05 level but not at the .01 level.

Comparison of these results with those presented in section 5.1 and 5.2 on the basis of a five-asset scheme hardly settles the question of which arbitrary asset aggregation system provides the best representation of how investors perceive the menu of assets confronting them. Nevertheless, it is instructive that the estimates continue to indicate that either long-term debt or the composite debt asset is a substitute for equity. In addition, the estimate of $\epsilon_{SL,E}$ in the first three-asset alternative and ϵ_{LE} in the second are not all that different from some of the ϵ_{LE} estimates reported in sections 5.1 and 5.2. More broadly, however, on the basis of these results there is little ground for attributing the unsatisfactory properties of these models' empirical estimates in other respects to the asset aggregation system per se.

5.4   Changes over Time in the Structure of Asset Returns

The variance-covariance matrix exhibited in table 5.4 reflects the stochastic structure of the after-tax asset returns actually realized during 1960–80. Hence the portfolio responses to expected return variations exhibited in table 5.5, which are implied from that variance-covariance matrix using (8) and $\rho = 1$, adequately describe investors' optimal behavior only to the extent that investors actually knew that the stochastic structure of asset returns was as it turned out to be. The question that immediately arises is how investors would have acquired this information.

The rationale for asserting that economic agents (on average) accurately know the relevant properties of the world in which they live usually rests on some presumption of stationarity: If the properties in question are economically relevant, agents will have an incentive to discover them;

if the properties persist, agents will in fact do so. By contrast, if the relevant properties are changing over time, so that an appeal to economic incentives and (even sometimes quite astonishing) powers of observation is insufficient, how the representative agent comes to know these properties is highly problematical.[39]

The relevant question here, therefore, is how stable were the 1960–80 sample properties of asset returns summarized in section 5.1. Tables 5.15 and 5.16 report mean returns and variance-covariance structures for the two subsamples 1960:I–1970:II and 1970:III–1980:IV.[40] As is well known, investors confronted not only lower mean real returns but also more volatile real returns on all five categories of assets during the 1970s, and the data shown here clearly reflect these differences.

More important, table 5.17 shows that the changes in the variance-covariance structure of asset returns that took place between the 1960s

Table 5.15   **Subsample Mean Real Returns**

	Before Tax (%)	After Tax (%)
1960:I–1970:II:		
r_M	−2.75	−2.75
r_T	.85	−.15
r_S	2.06	.72
r_L	−1.71	−3.07
r_E	5.89	4.16
1970:III–1980:IV:		
r_M	−8.11	−8.11
r_T	−3.34	−4.92
r_S	−.51	−3.04
r_L	−1.48	−4.59
r_E	4.60	2.10

Table 5.16   **Subsample Variance-Covariance Structure of After-Tax Real Returns**

	r_M	r_T	r_S	r_L	r_E
1960:I–1970:II:					
r_M	3.59				
r_T	3.19	2.94			
r_S	1.68	1.56	1.16		
r_L	14.54	12.42	7.29	112.76	
r_E	20.84	18.86	10.30	112.61	444.46
1970:III–1980:IV:					
r_M	13.66				
r_T	13.30	12.97			
r_S	8.24	8.04	5.96		
r_L	52.10	51.05	33.33	309.88	
r_E	39.87	39.74	31.45	213.28	763.87

Table 5.17   Subsample Implied Portfolio Responses

	r_M	r_T	r_S	r_L	r_E
1960:I–1970:II:					
M	963				
T	−1016	1211			
S	69.7	−206	133		
L	−17.6	13.4	2.67	1.81	
E	.763	−2.31	1.48	−.250	.318
1970:III–1980:IV:					
M	5432				
T	−5663	5957			
S	233	−294	58.4		
L	−6.55	3.22	2.75	.711	
E	3.97	−3.83	−.184	−.127	.168

and the 1970s bore strong implications for optimal portfolio behavior, including implications for the substitutability of debt and equity securities. The table shows the implied optimal asset responses corresponding to the respective subsample variance-covariance matrices in table 5.16, based again on (8) and $\rho = 1$. Many of the own- and cross-return responses changed by relatively large magnitudes, and the response indicating the substitutability of short-term debt and equity even changed sign, between the two subsamples. For the 1960s the prevailing stochastic return structure implies that short-term debt and equity were complements, with $\epsilon_{SE} = 128$. The analogous stochastic return structure for the 1970s implies that short-term debt and equity were substitutes, with $\epsilon_{SE} = -4.34$. By contrast, the stochastic return structure in both subsamples implies that long-term debt and equity were substitutes, with $\epsilon_{LE} = -8.67$ and $\epsilon_{LE} = -1.95$, respectively.[41]

In light of these changes in the stochastic structure, and hence in the implied optimal portfolio responses, it is hardly surprising that straightforward estimation of either equilibrium model (16) or partial adjustment model (18) should yield unsatisfactory results, nor that the elasticity of substitution between short-term debt and equity be a particularly unsatisfactory aspect of these results. At a minimum, some allowance for these within-sample changes is necessary. Nevertheless, simply including 15 moving-average variances and covariances in each equation is hardly likely to be an efficient approach.[42]

Some more compact way of summarizing the information contained in the evolving variance-covariance structure of asset returns is therefore necessary. Following Sharpe (1964) and Lintner (1965), a plausible summary measure for this purpose is the ratio of the covariance of each asset's return with that on the "market" portfolio to the variance of the "market" return itself—that is, each asset's "beta." Figure 5.1 shows the 1960–80 quarterly values of these "betas" computed on a trailing eight-quarter basis for the five aggregate assets defined in table 5.1, with the "market" portfolio defined in each quarter simply as the total of the five aggregate assets.[43]

Generalizing equilibrium model (16) to allow for the changing "beta" values over time results in

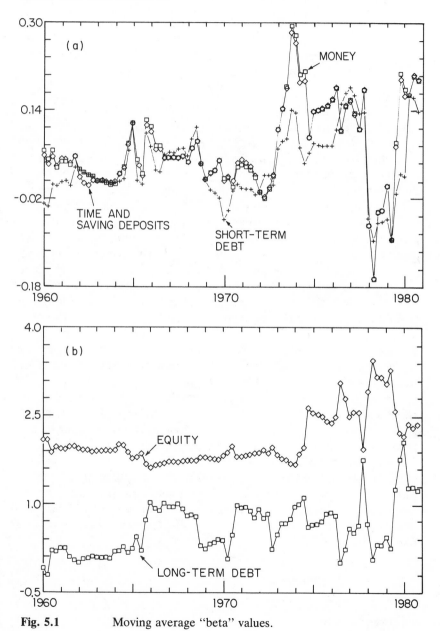

Fig. 5.1   Moving average "beta" values.

(22) $$\alpha_t^* = B(r_t^e + 1) + \Gamma x_t + \delta \left(\frac{Y_t}{W_t}\right) + \pi,$$

where x is a vector of "beta" values and Γ a matrix of coefficients with columns satisfying an "adding up" constraint analogous to (12). Applying partial adjustment process (17) to (22) then yields

(23) $\Delta A_t = \Phi(r_t^e + 1) \cdot W_t + Z x_t \cdot W_t + \xi Y_t + \psi W_t - \Theta A_{t-1}$

where

(24) $$Z = \Theta\Gamma.$$

Table 5.18 summarizes the results of estimating (23), subject to the restriction that B be symmetric, for the full 1960–80 sample. Here the values of x are as shown in figure 5.1, and all other data and estimation procedures are as described in section 5.2. The table presents summary statistics and estimated values and t-statistics for the β_{ij}, corresponding to those in table 5.10, as well as estimated values and t-statistics for the z_{ij}.

In comparison to the results in table 5.10, those in table 5.18 show that including the five moving-average "beta" terms typically does not improve the fit (after correction for degrees of freedom) of the estimated asset demand equations. Among the individual "betas," those for long-term debt and equity are each significant at the .05 level in two estimated equations, although in neither case is one of the two the "own" equation. The other three "betas" are rarely if ever significant. These values are at best difficult to interpret, however, because they represent the matrix of impact effects Z associated with the "betas," rather than the corresponding matrix of equilibrium effects Γ.[44] The usual β_{ij} coefficients on the expected returns appear to indicate that short-term debt and equity are substitutes while long-term debt and equity are complements, but in the presence of the "betas" these coefficients no longer bear the same structural interpretation as in (7) and (8). Moreover, the relevant test statistic value, $\chi^2 (10) = 81.1$, once again warrants rejection of the symmetry restriction at any plausible significance level.

In sum, the inclusion in the analysis of summary information describing the changing stochastic structure of asset returns apparently affects the estimated substitution properties of the asset demand system, but the properties of the expanded system do not necessarily respresent an improvement and hence the associated estimates do not give grounds for much confidence.

5.5 Concluding Comments

Table 5.19 brings together the respective estimates of the elasticity of substitution between debt and equity securities developed throughout

Table 5.18   Symmetric Portfolio Responses Estimated from Extended Model

Asset	β_M	β_T	β_S	β_L	β_E	$\bar{R}^2$	S.E.	D-W
M	.0127 (2.0)					.13	8.32	2.19
T	.0368 (2.1)	.452 (2.2)				.70	22.70	1.08
S	−.0891 (−2.4)	−.972 (−2.2)	−2.09 (2.2)			.68	27.78	1.20
L	.0256 (2.1)	.314 (2.2)	−.673 (−2.2)	.218 (2.2)		.19	10.22	1.87
E	.0140 (2.2)	.165 (2.2)	−.353 (−2.2)	.115 (2.2)	.0590 (2.2)	.02	3.92	1.53

Effects of Moving Average Portfolio Covariances

Asset	z_M	z_T	z_S	z_L	z_E
M	−.0483 (−1.1)	.0526 (1.2)	−.00215 (−.3)	−.000257 (−.4)	−.000317 (−.2)
T	−.00305 (−.0)	−.00134 (−.0)	−.00484 (−.3)	−.00718 (−3.5)	−.0154 (−3.7)
S	.0426 (.3)	−.0528 (−.3)	.0243 (1.1)	.00742 (3.4)	.0140 (3.0)
L	.00341 (.1)	.0113 (.2)	−.0188 (−2.0)	.000507 (.6)	.00279 (1.4)
E	.00542 (.2)	−.00980 (−.4)	.00153 (.6)	−.000491 (−1.3)	−.00102 (−1.4)

Table 5.19   Summary of Estimated Debt-Equity Substitution Elasticities

Table	Description	ϵ_{SE}		ϵ_{LE}	
6.5	Implied optimal	−2.54		−3.74	
6.8	Estimated equilibrium model	$\begin{cases} .039 \\ .116 \end{cases}$	(2.4) (2.4)	$\begin{cases} -.000 \\ -.006 \end{cases}$	(−.3) (−1.7)
6.9	Estimated partial adjustment model	$\begin{cases} .154 \\ .776 \end{cases}$	(3.1) (3.0)	$\begin{cases} -.005 \\ -.034 \end{cases}$	(−1.0) (−2.3)
6.10	Estimated symmetric partial adjustment model	.192	(.7)	−.024	(−.6)
6.11	Implied optimal	−4.41			
6.12	Estimated symmetric partial adjustment model	3.62	(1.7)		
6.13	Implied optimal	−.465		−3.64	
6.14	Estimated symmetric partial adjustment model	.079	(2.6)	−.058	(−2.4)

Notes: Numbers in parentheses are *t*-statistics. Elasticity shown from tables 5.11 and 5.12 is $\epsilon_{SL,E}$. First elasticity shown from tables 5.13 and 5.14 is $\epsilon_{MTS,E}$.

this paper, including values implied on the basis of optimal asset demand behavior in relation to actual asset return properties during 1960–80, as well as values estimated on the basis of the observed portfolio behavior of the U.S. household sector over this period. As is clear from this set of comparisons, there is little ground here for drawing any conclusion at all about even the sign, much less the magnitude, of the substitutability of *short-term* debt and equity. Although the implied optimal behavior indicates that these two assets are substitutes, the observed behavior indicates that households have treated them as complements. By contrast, the values assembled here consistently indicate that *long-term* debt and equity are indeed substitutes although the regression estimates of the associated substitution elasticity are typically very small (in absolute value) in comparison with the optimal elasticity implied by the underlying variance-covariance structure and unit relative risk aversion.[45]

For several reasons, it is difficult to know what (if any) broader economic and financial conclusions to draw from these results. Even for the one fairly consistent result that runs throughout the paper, the substitutability of long-term debt and equity, focusing on the sign leads to different implications than does focusing on the magnitude. At one level, the finding that (long-term) debt and equity are substitutes validates the standard assumption underlying a variety of familiar models in monetary economics and finance. At the same time, many of these models' more important substantive conclusions may or may not follow, depending on this key parameter's magnitude.

In addition , the analysis undertaken here indicates several conclusions at a more detailed level that also warrant caution: First, while the observed variance-covariance structure of real asset returns in the United States during 1960–80 implies that debt and equity securities are substitutes, the variance-covariance structure changed between the 1960s and the 1970s, and the resulting differences imply sharply changed optimal substitution responses of the demand for debt and equity to their respective expected returns. For the relationship between short-term debt and equity, even the implied sign of the relevant optimal response differs between the two subsamples.

Second, the estimated substitution properties of assets other than long-term debt and equity do not bear much systematic resemblance to the optimal responses implied by the observed variance-covariance structure. The system of asset aggregation employed does not appear to affect this conclusion in an important way, nor does taking explicit account of the nonstationary stochastic return structure appear to improve the relevant estimates.

Third, the data consistently warrant rejecting the hypothesis of symmetrical asset demand responses to variations in expected yields on alternative assets. This result does not contradict the theory of portfolio behavior based on expected utility maximization in general, but it does contradict the familiar specific form of that theory relying on joint normal (or lognormal) assessment of asset returns and on constant relative (or absolute) risk aversion.

To be sure, the empirical analysis presented here does not lack limitations to provide potential explanations for the more perplexing aspects of these results. The treatment of the aggregate household sector as if it were one individual's portfolio, the exclusion of nonfinancial assets (and hence of liabilities), the use of actual instead of instrumented returns except for capital gain and loss components, and the simplicity of the approaches taken to allow for means-of-payment services and transactions costs all constitute potential reasons for believing that there may well be substantial discrepancies between the behavioral parameters estimated here and the corresponding actual properties of household portfolio behavior.

Even so, the troubling possibility remains that the most important explanation for the problematical aspects of the results found here is instead that the expected asset returns and the associated variance-covariance structure inferred here do not closely correspond to the perceptions that investors actually held. One potential reason for suspecting discrepancies, of course, is the ever-present need for arbitrary assumptions in order to proxy unobservable expectations.[46] Even more troubling, however, is the possibility that investors systematically misperceived the real asset returns they confronted—in other words, that investors not only lacked perfect foresight about each quarter's capital gains and losses but, even over a substantial period of time, failed to understand the basic properties of the distributions generating real returns. With four of five assets exhibiting negative mean real returns over the entire two decades, and the implied optimal holdings consistent with those mean returns positive for only two of the five assets, it is difficult to reject out of hand the possibility that investors went through much of this period consistently anticipating more favorable returns than in fact materialized. That such behavior presents formidable obstacles to formal analysis, or even that it contradicts currently fashionable ideas about the formation of "rational" expectations, cannot rule it out.

Notes

1. Tobin (1961) relied on this distinction in arguing that, if it were necessary to aggregate debt with either money or equity in a macroeconomic model, the former choice would be superior. Subsequent empirical work emphasizing the same distinction has included Fama and Schwert (1977) and Bodie (1982).

2. This line of reasoning also leads to a distinction, which lies beyond the scope of this paper, between default-free government debt and defaultable private debt.

3. Exceptions arise, however, as in corporate merger or acquisition transactions settled by direct exchanges of securities.

4. See, for example, Arrow (1965) or Cass and Stiglitz (1970).

5. For evidence supporting the assumption of constant relative risk aversion, see Friend and Blume (1975). Although Fama (1965) and others have shown that individual securities returns are not strictly normally (or lognormally) distributed, Lintner (1975) has shown that the approximation involved here is close enough for most purposes, and more recently Fama and MacBeth (1973) have also relied on the normality assumption. See Friedman and Roley (1979b) for the explicit derivation of expressions (7)–(11) below under the assumptions of constant relative risk aversion and joint normally distributed return assessments. (These two assumptions are not strictly compatible, because normality in principle admits negative gross returns for which constant relative risk aversion utility is not defined; but the approximation involved here is hardly troubling.)

6. The rationale for mean-variance analysis provided by Samuelson (1970) and Tsiang (1972), for example, suggests that mean-variance analysis per se is only an approximation that depends on (among other factors) a small time unit. The time unit used in the empirical work presented in this paper is a calendar quarter. Although the observed variation of some asset prices is large over this time unit, it is the expected variation that matters here.

7. More precisely, under constant relative risk aversion symmetry holds only as an approximation that is acceptable as the time unit is small; see again n. 6 above. Symmetry would hold exactly in this model only under the alternative assumption of constant absolute risk aversion. See Roley (1983) for a thorough analysis of the conditions determining symmetry in asset demand systems.

8. These expressions for Σ_{ij} are invariant to whether r_j is expressed in decimal form (as implicitly above) or in percentage form (as in the empirical analysis presented below). Here and throughout this paper, elasticities of substitution ϵ_{ij} are defined in terms of net returns r_j^e as is more typical in the portfolio demand literature, rather than gross returns $(1 + r_j^e)$ as would be analogous to the consumer demand literature because of the reciprocal relationship between expected gross returns and asset prices. Because the marginal responses β_{ij} are invariant to this distinction, the corresponding gross return elasticities just equal the net return elasticities as shown in (15) but with $(1 + r_j^e)$ in place of r_j^e.

9. Uniformly nonnegative partial correlations imply uniformly nonnegative simple correlations, of course, so that the latter is also a necessary (though weaker) condition for gross substitutability of all assets when a risk-free asset exists.

10. Even in the presence of a risk-free asset, it is just as easy to inspect the Ω^{-1} directly as to compute the partial correlations on which Blanchard and Plantes (1977) focus.

11. These data, from the Federal Reserve Board's flow-of-funds accounts, give market values for equity and par values for all other assets. Because interest rates exhibited an upward secular trend during 1960–80, the period analyzed here, par value data presumably overstate holdings of long-term debt. This problem does not arise for money or for time and saving deposits, and it is too small to be of consequence for short-term debt.

12. See Jones (1979) for a careful treatment of the conditions required for asset aggregation. Section 5.3 briefly considers two further alternative asset aggregation schemes.

13. Some preliminary experimentation using the respective price deflators for gross national product and for personal consumption expenditures indicated that the results presented in this paper are not sensitive to the choice of specific inflation measure.

14. Because the Internal Revenue Service data needed to estimate these marginal tax rates for 1980 were unavailable at the time of writing, the 1979 rates were used to calculate 1980 after-tax returns. No major tax changes occurred in 1980.

15. For examples of work based on interest rate surveys, see Friedman (1979b) and Kane (1983).

16. As Smith points out (see his comments below), table 5.4 shows the unconditional variance-covariance structure of returns. Hence it both overstates and understates inves-

tors' knowledge. The overstatement comes from implicitly giving investors, within the sample, knowledge of the full-sample return distribution parameters. The understatement comes from ignoring investors' use of the serial correlation properties of returns. Smith's suggestion of using regressions (perhaps with rolling samples) to derive conditional estimates is sensible, and I have implemented it in subsequent work along these lines; see Friedman (1984). The use of the "beta" values derived in sec. 5.4 is analogous.

17. The results found by Friend and Blume (1975) suggest a value of ρ between 1 and 2. More recent work by Grossman and Shiller (1981), using altogether different evidence, suggests a greater value. Bodie et al. (in this volume) assume $\rho = 4$.

18. The corresponding gross-return elasticities are $\epsilon_{SE} = -83.6$ and $\epsilon_{LE} = -123$. Because the gross return means are positive, it is also possible to calculate the analogous gross return elasticities of substitution referring to the response of the demand for equity to the expected return on either short-term or long-term debt. These elasticities are $\epsilon_{ES} = -12.4$ and $\epsilon_{EL} = -33.4$, respectively.

19. The finding that investors would not have held positive amounts of long-term debt under these assumptions is familiar; see Bodie (1982) and Bodie et al. (in this volume). What is surprising here is that, in the presence of money and time and saving deposits, as well as short-term debt, under these assumptions investors would not have held positive amounts of short-term debt either.

20. Deriving δ directly from the underlying expected utility maximization would require an explicit representation of the transactions process and the associated role of means-of-payment services.

21. The analysis here includes only the assets that households own directly and via personal trusts. An alternative approach would be to include assets in which households have an interest via pension and insurance arrangements. Inferring the risk properties of pension and insurance assets would be highly problematical, however (unless, of course, the pension or insurance intermediary form were treated simply as a shell performing no risk-transformation services at all). In the limit, if all assets in the economy were aggregated together and imputed to the household sector as ultimate owner, there would be no basis for distinguishing the resulting asset demand equations from the corresponding asset supply equations.

22. The purpose of this procedure is to generate series of seasonally adjusted end-of-quarter asset stocks without any gaps or inconsistencies due to splicing of data series. (The Federal Reserve System does not construct such series.)

23. Out of $1,494 billion of household sector liabilities outstanding as of year end 1980, $971 billion consisted of mortgage debt and $385 billion of installment and other consumer credit.

24. The two capital gain equations used are

$$cg_{Lt} = -1.63 + 0.567 \ cg_{L,t-1} - 0.366 \ cg_{L,t-2}$$
$$(-1.2) \quad (5.0) \quad\quad\quad (-2.8)$$

$$+ 0.387 \ cg_{L,t-3} - .000615 \ cg_{L,t-4}$$
$$(2.9) \quad\quad\quad (-0.0)$$

$$\bar{R}^2 = .28 \quad\quad \text{S.E.} = 11.25 \quad\quad \text{D-W} = 1.99$$

$$cg_{Et} = 5.85 + 0.393 \ cg_{E,t-1} - 0.268 \ cg_{E,t-2}$$
$$(2.1) \quad (3.5) \quad\quad\quad (-2.2)$$

$$- 0.00331 \ cg_{E,t-3} + 0.0170 \ cg_{E,t-4}$$
$$(-0.0) \quad\quad\quad (0.1)$$

$$\bar{R}^2 = .12 \quad\quad \text{S.E.} = 23.18 \quad\quad \text{D-W} = 2.00$$

where the standard errors are in percent per annum. In light of the familiar random walk rendering of the efficient market hypothesis, it is interesting to note how much of the variance of observed capital gains (which are just transformations of observed price changes) even relatively simple autoregressive processes achieve—ex post. Multivariate analogs to these equations, including also lagged values of the associated coupon or dividend/price yields as well as short-term yields, produce $\bar{R}^2 = .47$ and S.E. $= 9.66$ for long-term debt capital gains, and $\bar{R}^2 = .36$ and S.E. $= 19.77$ for equity capital gains. These returns are based on monthly average data for the last month in each quarter, so that Working's (1960) point about spurious autocorrelation applies. Even so, the fit of these (ex post) equations is striking.

25. The table excludes the estimated values of δ and π, so as to avoid diverting attention (and allocating space) to results not central to the paper's objectives. Subsequent tables of empirical results presented below reflect the same selectivity. Because the estimation automatically accommodates scale changes, here (unlike in table 5.5) it is unnecessary to rescale the estimated β_{ij} to allow for the statement of returns in percentage form.

26. The expected returns evolve not independently, of course, but by the market-clearing behavior of asset demanders and asset suppliers (including, to a limited extent, households). To the extent that households' behavior is a major element determining market-clearing returns, these returns are not really predetermined in (16), and an instrumental variables procedure is appropriate. Here only the capital gain component of the returns on long-term debt and equity are instrumented.

27. In previous work I have criticized this partial adjustment model for not adequately reflecting the greater sensitivity to expected returns of the allocation of new cash flows in comparison to the reallocation of existing asset holdings under most transactions cost technologies, and have suggested an "optimal marginal adjustment" model as an alternative; see, for example, Friedman (1977). Applying the optimal marginal adjustment model in the context of the analysis presented above is an object left here for future work.

28. The price and population variables used to deflate the nominal magnitudes are the consumer price index (1967 = 1.00) and the total U.S. population (in millions). For purposes of comparison with the magnitudes shown in tables 5.1 and 5.6, their respective 1980:IV and 1960–80 mean values are 2.658 and 1.322 for the price index, and 228.6 and 204.9 for population. Using the current period's price (and population) to deflate the vector of lagged asset stocks in (18) represents a multivariate generalization of the "nominal-adjustment" model suggested by Goldfeld (1976).

29. In terms of shares of the 1960–80 mean portfolio, the five standard errors (in the order used in the tables) are .00136, .00377, .00482, .00187, and .00061.

30. Because the five equations being estimated all share identical sets of regressors, full information maximum likelihood is equivalent to ordinary least squares. As a check, the equations were actually estimated twice, once using each method. The corresponding sets of results were identical.

31. More precisely, each equation was estimated three times: twice as explained in n. 30 (without any constrained values) and then a third time, by maximum likelihood, with the θ_{ij} held fixed at the values estimated (identically) the first two times. Fixing the θ_{ij} in this way does not affect the estimated values of the other coefficients, but does affect the associated t-statistics.

32. The literature associating an implicit nonpecuniary return to holding money balances is potentially instructive here; see, for example, Barro and Santomero (1972) and Klein (1974).

33. As is the case for the β_{ij} coefficients shown in table 5.9, the t-statistics reported in table 5.10 are derived by taking the θ_{ij} values as given. Here the system of equations was first estimated by the nonlinear maximum likelihood method, subject to the symmetry restriction on B but no restriction on Θ. The resulting θ_{ij} values were those imposed on the final estimation. Once again, this procedure does not affect the estimated values of the coefficients, but it does affect the associated t-statistics. The summary statistics shown in Table 10 are comparable to those in table 5.9, in that they refer to the initial joint estimation of the θ_{ij} along with the other coefficients.

34. Roley (1983) also rejected the symmetry restriction. From an inspection of the

pattern of signs among the off-diagonal β_{ij} values shown in table 5.9, it appears as if only the coefficients in the row and column corresponding to money and its expected return are inconsistent with symmetry of matrix B. Nevertheless, an attempt to estimate (18) subject to a symmetry constraint applied only to the remaining four rows and columns of B yielded unsatisfactory results.

35. The implied coefficient of relative risk aversion is -168 (with t-statistic -4.3), which is clearly implausible.

36. This alternative aggregation scheme is the one proposed by Smith; see his comments in this volume.

37. See Ando and Shell (1975) for a theoretical justification for this two-part strategy. Several authors have investigated empirically the allocation of the household sector's liquid asset portfolio; see, for example, Fortune (1972).

38. Using simply the short-term debt return, as suggested by Smith, yields essentially identical results.

39. See Friedman (1979a) for a discussion of the information acquisition process in a parallel context in the macroeconomics literature.

40. A break at mid-1970 not only represents the sample midpoint but also roughly corresponds to several familiar changes in the objective circumstances determining real asset returns, including the Federal Reserve System's adoption of a monetary aggregate target in February 1970 and its suspension of Regulation Q interest ceilings on large time deposits in June 1970. More broadly, but also a good deal more roughly, the 1970s were a decade of slower real growth, more frequent business recessions, faster price inflation, less capital formation, and larger federal government deficits than the 1960s. There is also substantial evidence of another break associated with the Federal Reserve's further change in operating procedures in October 1979—see, for example, Friedman (1982)—but splitting the 1960–1980 sample at that point would serve little purpose here.

41. All implied substitution elasticities shown in table 5.17 have unchanging sign across the two subsamples except that between short-term debt and equity, but the elasticities of substitution between long-term debt and money and between long-term debt and time deposits differ in sign from the corresponding implied elasticities for the full sample shown in table 5.5.

42. Friedman (1980) and Friedman and Roley (1979a) dealt with this problem by selectively including moving average variances (but not covariances) in estimated asset demand equations.

43. Hence the "market" portfolio excludes nonfinancial assets; see again the discussion in sec. 5.1.

44. Programming the nonlinear estimation package to solve directly for the γ_{ij}, analogously to the β_{ij}, would make proper convergence of the nonlinear maximum likelihood estimation problematical.

45. Part of this systematic discrepancy may well be due to a risk-aversion value greater than unity, but the value that would be required to reconcile it altogether is clearly implausible.

46. See again the discussion in sec. 5.1.

References

Ando, Albert, and Shell, Karl. 1975. Demand for money in a general portfolio model in the presence of an asset that dominates money. In *The Brookings model: perspective and recent developments*, ed. Gary Fromm and Lawrence B. Klein. Amsterdam: North-Holland.

Arrow, Kenneth J. 1965. *Aspects of the theory of risk-bearing*. Helsinki: Yrjo Jahnssonin Saatio.

Barro, Robert J., and Santomero, Anthony J. 1972. Household money holdings and the demand deposit rate. *Journal of Money, Credit and Banking* 4:397–413.

Blanchard, Olivier J., and Plantes, Mary Kay. 1977. A note on gross substitutability of financial assets. *Econometrica* 45:769–71.

Bodie, Zvi. 1982. Investment strategy in an inflationary environment. In *The changing roles of debt and equity in financing U.S. capital formation*, ed. Benjamin M. Friedman. Chicago: University of Chicago Press.

Brainard, William C., and Tobin, James. 1968. Pitfalls in financial model-building. *American Economic Review* 58:99–122.

Cass, David, and Stiglitz, Joseph E. 1970. The structure of investor preferences and asset returns, and separability in portfolio allocation: a contribution to the pure theory of mutual funds. *Journal of Economic Theory* 2:122–60.

Estrella, Arturo, and Fuhrer, Jeffrey. 1983. Average effective marginal tax rates on interest and dividend income in the United States, 1960–1979. Mimeographed. National Bureau of Economic Research.

Fama, Eugene F. 1965. The behavior of stock prices. *Journal of Business* 38:34–105.

Fama, Eugene F., and MacBeth, James D. 1973. Risk, return, and equilibrium: empirical tests. *Journal of Political Economy* 81:607–36.

Fama, Eugene F., and Schwert, G. William. 1977. Asset returns and inflation. *Journal of Financial Economics* 5:115–46.

Feldstein, Martin; Poterba, James; and Dicks-Mireaux, Louis. 1983. The effective tax rate and the pretax rate of return. *Journal of Public Economics*, 21:129–158.

Fortune, Peter. 1972. *A constrained econometric analysis of household sector liquid asset allocation*. Boston: Federal Reserve Bank of Boston.

Friedman, Benjamin M. 1977. Financial flow variables and the short-run determination of long-term interest rates. *Journal of Political Economy* 85:661–89.

———. 1979a. Optimal expectations and the extreme information assumptions of "rational expectations" macromodels. *Journal of Monetary Economics* 5:23–41.

———. 1979b. Interest rate expectations versus forward rates: evidence from an expectations survey. *Journal of Finance* 34:965–73.

———. 1980. Price inflation, portfolio choice, and nominal interest rates. *American Economic Review* 70:32–48.

———. 1982. Federal Reserve policy, interest rate volatility, and the U.S. capital raising mechanism. *Journal of Money, Credit and Banking* 14:721–45.

————. 1984. Crowding out or crowding in? Evidence on debt-equity substitutability. Mimeographed: National Bureau of Economic Research.

Friedman, Benjamin M., and Roley, V. Vance. 1979a. Investors' portfolio behavior under alternative models of long-term interest rate expectations: unitary, rational or autoregressive. *Econometrica* 47:1475–97.

————. 1979b. A note on the derivation of linear homogeneous asset demand functions. Mimeographed. National Bureau of Economic Research.

Friend, Irwin, and Blume, Marshall E. 1975. The demand for risky assets. *American Economic Review* 65:900–922.

Goldfeld, Stephen M. 1976. The case of the missing money. *Brookings Papers on Economic Activity*, pp. 683–730.

Grossman, Sanford J., and Shiller, Robert J. 1981. The determinants of the variability of stock prices. American Economic Review 71:222–27.

Jones, David S. 1979. A structural model of the United States equity market. Ph.D. diss., Harvard University.

Kane, Edward J. 1983. Nested tests of alternative term-structure theories. *Review of Economics and Statistics* 65:115–23.

Klein, Benjamin. 1974. Competitive interest payments on bank deposits and the long-run demand for money. *American Economic Review* 64:931–49.

Lintner, John. 1965. The valuation of risk assets and the selection of risky investments in stock portfolios and capital budgets. *Review of Economics and Statistics* 47:13–37.

————. 1969. The aggregation of investors' judgments and preferences in purely competitive security markets. *Journal of Financial and Quantitative Analysis* 4:347–400.

————. 1975. The lognormality of security returns, portfolio selection and market equilibrium. Mimeographed. Harvard University.

Modigliani, Franco, and Miller, Merton H. 1958. The cost of capital, corporation finance, and the theory of investment. *American Economic Review* 48:261–97.

Roley, V. Vance. 1983. Symmetry restrictions in a system of financial asset demands: theoretical and empirical results. *Review of Economics and Statistics* 65:124–30.

Samuelson, Paul A. 1970. The fundamental approximation theorem of portfolio analysis in terms of means, variances, and higher moments. *Review of Economic Studies* 37:537–42.

Sharpe, William F. 1964. Capital asset prices: a theory of market equilibrium under conditions of risk. *Journal of Finance* 19:425-42.

Tobin, James. 1961. Money, capital, and other stores of values. *American Economic Review* 51:26–37.

————. 1969. A general equilibrium approach to monetary theory. *Journal of Money, Credit and Banking* 1:15–29.

Tsiang, S. C. 1972. The rationale for the mean-standard deviation analysis, skewness preference, and the demand for money. *American Economic Review* 62:354–71.

Working, Holbrook. 1960. Note on the correlation of first differences of averages in a random chain. *Econometrica* 28:916–18.

Comment   Gary Smith

This is a nice paper, reflecting some very interesting ideas and a great deal of work. Benjamin Friedman should be proud, but a little tired. Even so, I do want to suggest some ways that he might do things differently. I want to discuss five major points and then, time permitting, several minor points.

The heart of this paper is the use of the powerful implications of mean-variance portfolio theory with constant relative risk aversion. This is a significant and attractive extension of the literature on asset demand equations. Friedman seems disappointed that 9 of his 25 estimated parameters have the wrong signs. But I find it encouraging that 16 of 25 have the right signs. The glass is two-thirds full, not one-third empty.

I would suggest that, instead of using data alone and then comparing the estimates with the theoretical values or imposing the theoretical values exactly, Friedman use a flexible Bayesian combination of the data with the theory. The additional requirement is a proper covariance matrix for the portfolio means and covariances. This price is high but well worth paying.

My second major point is that Friedman's present portfolio variances and covariances are mismeasured. The numbers in table 5.4 assume that God rolls the same dice every quarter to determine the returns from money, bonds, and stocks. The 84 quarterly observations would then accurately gauge the expected values, variances, and covariances for these returns. But if, as Friedman assumes, God alters the odds to change the expected returns each quarter, then the variances across time will overstate the variances each quarter.

Friedman's model is $r_t = r_t^e + \epsilon_t$, where r_t and r_t^e are the actual expected returns in period t; ϵ_t is the stochastic difference between the two. We commonly assume that ϵ_t has a zero expected value and constant variance, and the r_t^e and ϵ_t are independent. Now let's allow r_t^e to vary over time with a mean value r: $r_t^e = \bar{r} + u_t$. We may as well assume that u_t

Gary Smith is professor of economics at Pomona College.

is independent of both $\bar{r}$ and ϵ_t. Now, the variance in the return across time consists of the variance in the expected return over time plus the quarterly variance with respect to each quarter's expected return,

$$E(r_t - \bar{r})^2 = E(u_t^2) + E(\epsilon_t^2)$$
$$= \text{var }(r_t^e) + \text{var }(\epsilon_t).$$

For a single-period portfolio selection, the variance of ϵ_t is the appropriate measure of risk. But Ben instead calculates $E(r_t - \bar{r})^2$, which includes the variance of r_t^e over time. For example, each quarter the nominal return on 3-month Treasury bills is absolutely certain. And yet this known return varies considerably from quarter to quarter. The nominal 3-month Treasury bill rate has a high measured variance over time, even though its portfolio risk each quarter is zero.

Now consider "money" in table 5.4, whose real rate of return is minus the inflation rate. Its measured standard deviation over these 20 years is about 4. The author uses this number as if investors' estimate of the annual inflation rate for the coming quarter is plus-or-minus 8%, a confidence interval 16 percentage points wide. Investors may not be perfect, but they are not that much in the dark.

What we want here is an estimate of the variance of $\epsilon_t = r_t - r_t^e$. If investors always know the inflation rate for the coming quarter, then this variance is zero. The 15.78 variance given in table 5.4 would be entirely variation in the expected rate of inflation over the past 20 years. In practice, I think that inflation forecasts one-quarter ahead, though not perfect, are pretty accurate and that there has been considerable variation in inflation expectations.

For a crude illustration, let's pretend that investors' expected inflation is simply equal to the previous quarter's actual inflation rate, so that $r_t^e = r_{t-1}$. It turns out that average value of $(r_t - r_t^e)^2$ is then just 3.4, implying that only one-fifth of the 15.78 variance in table 6.4 is portfolio risk. The remaining four-fifths is due to changes in inflation expectations during the 1960s and 1970s.

Similarly, short-term debt has the smallest variance in table 5.4 because it has surely had the smallest variance over time in its expected real return,[1] not necessarily because it has the least portfolio risk. I think that the quarterly portfolio risks for money, time and savings deposits, and short-term debt are very similar and much smaller than shown in table 5.4. Their nominal returns for the coming quarter are known with considerable certainty, and so is the inflation rate.

Long-term debt and equity do have considerable quarterly portfolio risk due to the possibility of significant capital gains and losses. But these risks are overstated in table 5.4 to the extent that there were significant variations in anticipated real returns over this 20-year period. I think that quarterly forecasts of interest, dividends, and inflation are pretty accurate. Just about all that we want to put in table 5.4 are uncertainties about quarterly capital gains and losses.

Overall, we want to construct a quarterly series of expected returns for these assets and then calculate the squared deviations between actual and expected returns. Interestingly, Friedman has constructed expected return series much as I have suggested. For money, time and saving deposits, and short-term debt, he uses the actual real returns as the expected real returns, as if these were risk-free assets. For the expected real returns on long-term debt and equity, he uses the actual interest, dividend, and inflation data (as if these were forecast perfectly) and an autoregressive estimate of capital gains. These expected returns are quite plausible. But he now should replace the numbers in table 5.4 with the calculated squared deviations between the actual returns and his expected returns data.

A corollary is that the implausible numbers in table 5.4 are undoubtedly responsible for the implausible numbers in table 5.5. The own coefficients of r_M and r_T, for example, are incredibly large, while the own coefficients of r_L and r_E are unbelievably small.

My third major point is that the returns on the three short-term assets (money, time and saving deposits, and short-term debt) are very highly correlated and have essentially the same (almost zero) variance. I do not think that portfolio theory can explain the division of wealth among these three assets. Instead, we will have to appeal, as Friedman does in his empirical work, to differences in liquidity and transaction costs.

Stated somewhat differently, the differences in the three mean returns on the short-term assets in table 5.2 cannot be explained solely by risk differences. The three corresponding variances in table 5.4 are small and nearly equal. And the correlations between the returns are nearly one: $\rho_{MT} = .997$. $\rho_{MS} = .994$, and $\rho_{TS} = .945$. As I explained above, I think that the true quarterly portfolio variances are even smaller and more equal, and that the true portfolio correlations are even closer to one. Money and time and saving deposits both have fixed nominal returns (barring default) and both are affected equally by inflation. Except for unanticipated ceiling rate changes within a quarter, their real returns should be perfectly correlated and their portfolio risk shall equal the inflation error. Short-term debt differs only in that there may be some small error in forecasting one's nominal return for the coming quarter.

For the portfolio analysis, I would put these three assets together into a single, virtually risk-free asset with an expected return equal to the anticipated real return on short-term debt. The yields on money and on time and saving deposits would be augmented implicitly by nonpecuniary advantages. To estimate separate demands for these three assets, we could then identify the three separate returns and introduce transaction variables.

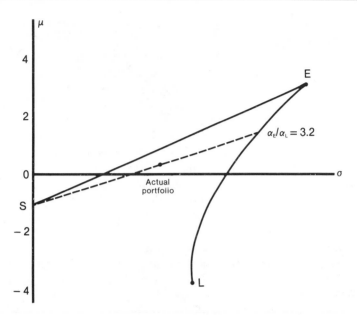

Fig. 5.C.1   Long-term bonds would not be in a rational portfolio.

My fourth major point is that the asset demand estimates are probably being led astray by the apparent unattractiveness of long-term debt. In Friedman's data, long-term debt has a high variance, a high beta, and a low expected return. The model is going to have difficulty explaining why people hold any of this unattractive asset.

In my figure 5.C.1, I have put the three short-term assets together in a single risk-free asset as suggested above. All mean-variance efficient portfolios exclude long-term debt. Similarly, Friedman finds that the optimal unconstrained portfolio for someone with constant relative risk aversion has a negative amount of long-term debt. My figure 5.C.2 shows the relationship between mean returns and asset betas. In theory, the three points should lie on a straight line. In practice, long-term debt has too low a mean return for its beta.

One possibility is that long-term debt is not really as risky as Friedman's data indicate. Its portfolio variance may be substantially reduced if, as suggested earlier, we take out the variation over time in its expected return and look only at the uncertainty regarding each quarter's capital gain or loss. Another possibility is that Friedman's use of a consol pricing formula has significantly exaggerated the size of the capital gains and losses. Another angle is that actual holdings of long-term debt are exaggerated by the use of par values rather than market values. Finally, it may just be that individual investors simply made the same mistake that

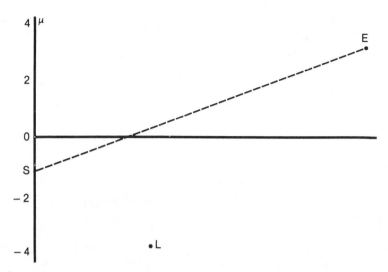

Fig. 5.C.2   The return on long-term bonds is too low for its beta.

savings institutions made, by consistently underestimating future interest rates and repeatedly overestimating the returns from acquiring long-term debt.

My fifth major point is that I am not persuaded that there is a logical reason for splitting the data between the second and third quarters of 1970. The reported differences in return variances between these two periods may be differences in expected-return variances rather than portfolio risks. The question is not whether returns varied more in the 1970s than in the 1960s, but rather whether it was harder to forecast quarterly returns in the 1970s. It may have been so, but we need to look at portfolio risk data before deciding. The one obvious break in the sample is during the fourth quarter of 1979, when the Fed began its experiment in stabilizing monetary aggregates and letting interest rates fluctuate. It was undeniably hard to forecast interest rates in 1980-82. Confirmation of this change can be found in the data on the monthly returns on long-term bonds. The standard deviation of these monthly returns visibly leaps upward at the end of 1979.

Now let's turn to a number of less important points:

1. The portfolio model has a single-period horizon with no transaction costs. Ben then uses transaction costs to motivate a partial adjustment toward the optimal portfolio. But in the presence of transaction costs, the rational investor would not plan a period at a time. Instead, he or she would take into account future saving and future changes in optimal

portfolio. What eludes us here is an integrated model of portfolio behavior in an imperfect capital market.

2. Taxes are levied on nominal rather than real returns. As a consequence, during inflations real rates of return are relatively lower for investors in high tax brackets. And there is thus more incentive during inflations to find ways to reduce one's tax rate. This is why investment in lightly taxed nonfinancial assets was important in the inflationary 1970s. The Fed now has some flow-of-funds data for nonfinancial assets, and a portfolio model incorporating physical assets should be high on someone's agenda.

3. Friedman's distinction between "money" and "time and saving deposits" is based not on liquidity, as it should be, but on whether the nominal yield is zero or not.

4. Friedman's use of the average marginal tax rate is nice. But because of consumer surplus, indivisibilities, and corner solutions, we really want the marginal tax rate for the marginal investor.

5. Friedman uses a single autoregressive equation spanning the entire 20 years to replicate investors' capital gains expectations. It would be more plausible to estimate 84 equations, one each quarter, using only the data that was actually available at each point in time.

6. Friedman finds some serial correlation in the quarterly capital gains data. This finding does not refute the random walk hypothesis, since these data have been averaged over time. This is a subtle argument that apparently was first made by Working (1960).

7. Friedman converts his data to real per capita values. A more common procedure in the asset-demand-equation literature is to divide each variable by wealth or by lagged wealth.

Note

1. The real returns on money and on time and savings deposits have varied over time because their nominal returns have been legally constrained while the inflation rate has varied. The real returns on long-term debt and on equity have varied a great deal due to sizable capital gains and losses.

6 Contingent Claims Valuation of Corporate Liabilities: Theory and Empirical Tests

E. Philip Jones, Scott P. Mason, and Eric Rosenfeld

6.1 Introduction

A fundamental issue in the study of capital structure is how securities issued by firms are valued in the financial markets. Typical corporate capital structures contain many individual securities, which in themselves are complicated by numerous covenants and indenture provisions. In addition, the valuation of any individual security must consider complex interactions among different claims. The corporate liability pricing model derived in Black and Scholes (1973) and Merton (1974) represents a theoretical breakthrough on this problem, with potentially significant practical applications. The critical insight of their model is that every security is a contingent claim on the value of the underlying firm. Hence these securities can be priced via an arbitrage logic which is independent of the equilibrium structure of risk and return. Every security must obey a general equation which depends only on riskless interest rates, the market value of the entire firm, and its volatility. The model distinguishes among securities via boundary conditions which correspond to covenants and indenture provisions. Since all of these data are directly observable or can be readily estimated, the model can be used to predict actual market prices.

Although this model has been the premier theory of how value is allocated among claimants on firms for almost a decade, its empirical validity remains an open question. Ingersoll has tested the model's ability to predict prices for dual purpose funds (1976) and to predict call policies

E. Philip Jones is assistant professor of finance at Harvard University's Graduate School of Business. Scott P. Mason is associate professor of business administration at Harvard University's Graduate School of Business and a faculty research fellow of the NBER. Eric Rosenfeld is assistant professor of finance at Harvard University's Graduate School of Business.

for convertible bonds (1977). But we know of no test of the model in its presumably most important application, namely, the valuation of debt and equity in typical corporate capital structures. In addition to being of academic interest, such a test has significant practical implications. If it can be established that the model predicts actual market prices, then the model can be used to price new and untraded claims, to infer firm values from prices of traded claims like equity, and to price covenants separately.

In this paper evidence is presented on how well a model which makes the usual assumptions in the literature does in predicting market prices for claims in standard capital structures. The goal is to examine the predictive power of this prototypical model. The results suggest that the usual assumption list requires modification before it can serve as a basis for valuing corporate claims.

The usual assumptions made in the contingent claims valuation literature, for example, Ingersoll (1976, 1977), are as follows:

(A.1) Perfect markets: The capital markets are perfect with no transactions costs, no taxes, and equal access to information for all investors.

(A.2) Continuous trading.

(A.3) Itô dynamics: The value of the firm, V, satisfies the stochastic differential equation.

$$dV = (\alpha V - C)dt + \sigma V dz$$

where total cash outflow per unit time C is locally certain. α and σ^2 are the instantaneous expected rate of return and variance of return on the underlying assets.

(A.4) Constant σ^2.

(A.5) Nonstochastic term structure: The instantaneous interest rate $r(t)$ is a known function of time.

(A.6) Shareholder wealth maximization: Management acts to maximize shareholder wealth.

(A.7) Perfect bankruptcy protection: Firms cannot file for protection from creditors except when they are unable to make required cash payments. In this case perfect priority rules govern the distribution of assets to claimants.

(A.8) Perfect antidilution protection: No new securities (other than additional common equity shares) can be issued until all existing nonequity claims are extinguished. Deals between equity and subsets of other claimants are prohibited.

(A.9) Perfect liquidity: Firms can sell assets as necessary to make cash payouts, with no loss in total value.

Translating this set of assumptions into an explicit model for valuing claims in a typical capital structure is considerably more difficult than suggested by previous examples in the literature. A common capital structure consists of equity and multiple issues of callable nonconvertible sinking fund coupon debt. This differs from the standard example of a single issue of nonconvertible debt, due to Merton (1974), because of both the sinking fund and multiple issue features. One effect of sinking funds is to reduce the effective maturity of debt. Another effect, due to the option to retire at market or par (with or without an option to double the sinking fund payment), is to make debt more like equity. Multiple issues of debt introduce interactions among issues of debt, so that maximizing the value of equity need not be equivalent to minimizing the value of a given issue of debt, as in the single debt issue case. One accomplishment of this paper is to translate the usual assumption list into a model for realistic capital structures.

The plan of the paper is as follows. Section 6.2 presents a theoretical analysis of the valuation problem for a firm with equity and multiple issues of callable nonconvertible sinking fund coupon debt, based on the usual assumption list. Section 6.3 describes the empirical methodology, including numerical analysis techniques, sample data, and testing procedure. Section 6.4 presents an analysis of the results, and Section 6.5 gives a conclusion.

6.2 Theory

The theoretical basis of the corporate liability pricing model is developed in Black and Scholes (1973) and Merton (1974). They use an arbitrage argument to show that corporate liabilities which are functions of the value of the firm and time obey a partial differential equation which depends on the known schedule of interest rates $r \equiv r(t)$ and the variance rate of firm value σ^2, as well as on payouts and indentures on claims, but does not depend on expected returns on assets and liabilities of the firm. Nor does it depend on any equilibrium structure of risk and return. Readers are referred to these papers for a derivation of the basic partial differential equation.

A starting point for the analysis of realistic capital structures is the standard example of contingent claims valuation as applied to nonconvertible corporate bonds, namely the formulation in Merton (1974) of a callable coupon bond with no sinking fund. Merton shows that the equity $E(V, t)$ is a firm with one issue of such debt obeys the following partial differential equation and boundary conditions.

(1a) $$0 = \tfrac{1}{2}\sigma^2 V^2 E_{VV} + (rV - cP - d)E_V + E_t - rE + d$$

$$E(0, t) = 0$$

$$E(V, t^*) = \max(0, V - P)$$

$$E(\bar{V}, t) = \bar{V} - k(t)P$$

$$E_V(\bar{V}, t) = 1 ,$$

where $P \equiv P(t)$ is the outstanding bond principal at time t, c is the coupon rate per unit principal, $k(t)$ is the call price schedule per unit principal, $d \equiv d(V, t)$ is the known dividend policy, and t^* is the maturity date of the bond. The upper free boundary, $\overline{V}(t)$, corresponds to the optimal call barrier at or above which the firm will call the bonds. Similarly, Merton shows that the valuation problem for the debt issue $D(V, t)$ can be formulated as follows:

(1b) $0 = \frac{1}{2}\sigma^2 V^2 D_{VV} + (rV - cP - d)D_V + D_t - rD + cP$

$D(0, t) = 0$

$D(V, t^*) = \min(V, P)$

$D(\overline{V}, t) = k(t)P$

$D_V(\overline{V}, t) = 0.$

The plan for section 6.2 is as follows. Section 6.2.1 generalizes the analysis of callable nonconvertible coupon bonds to allow for sinking funds, with and without noncumulative) options to double the sinking fund payment. Sinking funds are important because they dramatically decrease the effective maturity of bonds and because the option to sink at market or par makes bonds more like equity than otherwise. Section 6.2.2 then generalizes the analysis to deal with multiple issues of callable nonconvertible sinking fund coupon bonds. The ultimate contingent claims formulation of this valuation problem will bear only a generic resemblance to equations (1a) and (1b).

6.2.1 Sinking Funds

Most issues of corporate debt specify the mandatory retirement of bonds via periodic sinking fund payments. Typically the firm is required to retire a specified fraction of the initial bonds each period. Generally the firm has the option to redeem these bonds through either of two mechanisms: (1) it can purchase the necessary bonds in the market and deliver them to the trustee or (2) it can choose the necessary bonds by lot and retire them by paying the standard principal amount to their owners. Often the firm also has the option to double the number of bonds retired each period if it wishes. Hence the firm faces the following choices each period: (1) Should the bonds be called? (2) Assuming the bonds are not called, should the mandatory number of bonds be sunk at market or par? (3) Assuming the bonds are not called, should the sinking fund payment be doubled? (If this option exists.)

First, we consider the contingent claims formulation of this problem where the firm has no option to double the sinking fund payment. Next the option to double is introduced.

Sinking Funds with No Option to Double. Suppose that the firm decides not to call its debt and has no option to double. Then it must decide whether to sink bonds at market or par. Since the only difference is in the cash payout involved, and since higher firm value implies higher equity value, management will choose whichever costs less. For any given $r(t)$, if the firm value is relatively low, then debt will trade below par and the firm will choose to sink at market. And, for some $r(t)$, if firm value is relatively high, then debt will trade above par and the firm will choose to sink at par.

Consider the stylized case of a continuous sinking fund. Let s be the rate at which bonds are sunk, and let $P(t) = P(0) - st$ be the remaining principal assuming the bonds have not been called. Then $\gamma(t) \equiv s / P(t)$ is the fractional rate at which bonds are sunk. If debt trades below par, then total sinking fund payments are $\gamma D(V, t)$ where $\gamma \equiv \gamma(t)$. If debt trades above par, then total sinking fund payments are $\gamma P \equiv s$. Hence a general expression for total sinking fund payments is $\gamma \min (D, P)$. Thus the contingent claims formulation of the valuation problem for equity in the presence of a single issue of callable nonconvertible sinking fund coupon debt, with no option to double, is

(2a) $0 = \frac{1}{2}\sigma^2 V^2 E_{VV} + [rV - \gamma \min (D, P) - cP - d]E_V$
$$+ E_t - rE + d$$

$$E(0, t) = 0$$

$$E(V, t^*) = \max(0, V - P)$$

$$E(\overline{V}, t) = \overline{V} - kP$$

$$E_V(\overline{V}, t) = 1.$$

Similarly, from (1b), the contingent claims formulation of the valuation problem for debt in this capital structure is

(2b) $0 = \frac{1}{2}\sigma^2 V^2 D_{VV} + [rV - \gamma \min (D, P) - cP - d]D_V$
$$+ D_t - rD + \gamma \min (D, P) + cP$$

$$D(0, t) = 0$$

$$D(V, t^*) = \min(V, P)$$

$$D(\overline{V}, t) = kP$$

$$D_V(\overline{V}, t) = 0.$$

In summary, the valuation problem for a capital structure with equity and a single issue of callable nonconvertible sinking fund coupon debt, with no option to double, divides into three regions of firm value as a function of time. One region is defined by the fact that debt trades below par. This region corresponds at the maturity of the debt issue to firm values where bankruptcy occurs. A "par barrier" separates this region from the one above. The region above lies between the par barrier sand the call barrier, so that debt trades between par and the call price. Since the call barrier converges to par at the maturity of the debt issue, this region converges to a point. The third region lies above the call barrier. It corresponds at the maturity of the debt issue to firm values where bankruptcy does not occur.

Sinking Funds with an Option to Double. Most sinking funds give the firm an option to double the sinking fund payments. This section deals with noncumulative options to double, where the right to double is unaffected by past doubling decisions. There also exist cumulative options to double, where the right to double is affected by past decisions. Given the option to double the sinking fund payment, the actual principal that will be outstanding at any future date is unknown. Hence the values of equity and debt can no longer be written as functions of firm value and time alone. However, the following theorem says that these values can be written as functions of firm value, current principal, and time:

THEOREM 1: Assume that the optimal retirement rate, $\dot{P}(V, P, t)$, for bonds can be expressed as a deterministic function of firm value, current principal, and time. Then equity and debt and functions $E(V, P, t)$ and $D(V, P, t)$ that obey the following partial differential equations:

(3a) $0 = \frac{1}{2}\sigma^2 V^2 E_{VV} + [rV - \gamma^* \min(D, P) - cP - d]E_V - \gamma^* PE_P$
$+ E_t - rE + d$

(3b) $0 = \frac{1}{2}\sigma^2 V^2 D_{VV} + [rV - \gamma^* \min(D, P) - cP - d]D_V - \gamma^* PD_P$
$+ D_t - rD + \gamma^* \min(D, P) + cP$

where $\gamma^*(V, P, t) \equiv -\dot{P}/P$.

Proof: Apply Itô's lemma to $E(V, P, t)$ and $D(V, P, t)$, noting that P is locally certain. Substitute this into the standard arbitrage proof given in Merton (1974). Q.E.D.

Theorem 1 provides a valuation logic once the optimal policy with respect to doubling the sinking fund payment has been determined. Consider the decision whether to double the current sinking fund payment, assuming that management acts optimally thereafter. Suppose that the sinking fund payment is not doubled, so that the fraction of bonds retired is $\gamma dt = sdt/P$. Let V and P be firm value and current principal before the sinking fund payment. Hence the value of equity after the sinking fund payment is $E[V - \min(D, P)\gamma dt, (1 - \gamma dt)P, t]$. Suppose alternatively that the sinking fund payment is doubled. By analogy the value of equity after the sinking fund payment is $E[V - 2\min(D, P)\gamma dt, (1 - 2\gamma dt)P, t]$. The difference between the two equity values is thus [min. (D, P), $E_V + PE_P]\gamma\, dt$. If the bracketed expression is positive, the firm should not double the sinking fund payment; otherwise it should.

Since min (D, P) is less than the call price kP, doubling the sinking fund payment is a cheap way of calling a fraction of the bonds. Hence there will be a "doubling barrier" $\bar{\bar{V}}(P, t)$ which lies below the call barrier $\bar{V}(P, t)$. The firm will double the sinking fund payment above the doubling barrier but not below it. The firm is indifferent between doubling and not doubling right at the barrier; hence the expression we just derived vanishes at the barrier. Using this logic in (3a), the contingent claims formulation of the valuation problem for equity in the presence of a single issue of callable nonconvertible sinking fund coupon debt, with a noncumulative option to double, is as follows:

(4a) $0 = \tfrac{1}{2}\sigma^2 V^2 E_{VV} + [rV - \gamma\min(D, P) - cP - d]E_V - \gamma PE_P$
$\qquad + E_t - rE + d,\ 0 \le V \le \bar{\bar{V}}(P, t)$

$\qquad 0 = \tfrac{1}{2}\sigma^2 V^2 E_{VV} + [rV - 2\gamma\min(D, P) - cP - d]E_V - 2\gamma PE_P$
$\qquad + E_t - rE + d,\ \bar{\bar{V}}(P, t) \le V \le \bar{V}(p, t)$

$\qquad E(0, P, t) = 0$

$\qquad E(V, 0, t) = V$

$\qquad E(V, P, t^*) = \max(0, V - P)$

$\qquad \min[D(\bar{\bar{V}}, P, t), P]E_V(\bar{\bar{V}}, P, t) + PE_P(\bar{\bar{V}}, P, t) = 0$

$\qquad E(\bar{V}, P, t) = \bar{V} - kP$

$\qquad E_V(\bar{V}, P, t) = 1.$

ontingent claims formulation of the valuation problem for debt in this capital structure is

(4b) $0 = \tfrac{1}{2}\sigma^2 V^2 D_{VV} + [rV - \gamma\min(D, P) - cP - d]D_V - \gamma PD_P$
$\qquad + D_t - rD + \gamma\min(D, P) + cP$
$\qquad\ \ $ for $0 < V < \bar{\bar{V}}(P, t)$

$\qquad 0 = \tfrac{1}{2}\sigma^2 V^2 D_{VV} + [rV - 2\gamma\min(D, P) - cP - d]D_V - 2\gamma PD_P$
$\qquad\quad + D_t - rD + 2\gamma\min(D, P) + cP$
$\qquad\quad\ $ for $\bar{\bar{V}}(P, t) \le V \le \bar{V}(P, t)$

$\qquad D(0, P, t) = 0$

$\qquad D(V, 0, t) = 0$

$\qquad D(V, P, t^*) = \min(V, P)$

$\qquad \min[D(\bar{\bar{V}}, P, t), P][D_V(\bar{\bar{V}}, P, t) - 1] + PD_P(\bar{\bar{V}}, P, t) = 0$

$\qquad D(\bar{V}, P, t) = kP$

$\qquad D_V(\bar{V}, P, t) = 0.$

Actual sinking fund indentures cause claims to be nonhomogeneous functions of firm value and current principal. The reason is that the fractional rate at which bonds are retired (γ or 2γ where $\gamma = s/P$) grows as current principal declines. However, there is a reasonable approximation to actual sinking fund indentures that simplifies the analysis and leads to additional insights. Namely, assume that the fractional rate at which bonds must be sunk is γ, a constant, or 2γ if the sinking fund payment is doubled. In effect this assumes that the current decision whether to double the sinking fund payment does not affect permitted future fractional rates at which bonds are sunk.

This assumption plus the assumption that dividends are proportional to firm value reduce the dimensionality of the equations in (4a) and (4b). Consider standardized values for firm value ($x \equiv V/P$), equity ($f \equiv E/P$), and debt ($g \equiv D/P$); and define the proportional dividend rate as $\delta \equiv d/V$. Substituting these into (4a) and using the new assumptions, the following standardized formulation

(5a)
$$0 = \tfrac{1}{2}\sigma^2 x^2 f_{xx} + [(r + \gamma - \delta)x - \gamma \min(g, 1) - c]f_x$$
$$+ f_t - (r + \gamma)f + \delta x, \ 0 \le x \le \bar{\bar{x}}\,(t)$$

$$0 = \tfrac{1}{2}\sigma^2 x^2 f_{xx} + [(r + 2\gamma - \delta)x - 2\gamma - c]f_x$$
$$+ f_t - (r + 2\gamma)f + \delta x, \ \bar{\bar{x}}\,(t) \le \bar{x} \le x(t)$$

$$f(0, t) = 0$$

$$f(x, t^*) = \max(0, x - 1)$$

$$(1 - \bar{x})f_x(\bar{x}, t) + f(\bar{x}, t) = 0$$

$$f(\bar{x}, t) = \bar{x} - k$$

$$f_x(\bar{x}, t) = 1.$$

Note that this implies a doubling barrier which lies between the par barrier and the call barrier, so that the firm is always sinking at par if it doubles the sinking fund payment. To see that this is so, reconsider the expression derived before, namely, $\min(D, P)E_V + PE_P$. Suppose that the debt is trading below par, so that this expression is $DE_V + PE_P = (V + E)\,E_V - PE_P$. Under the new assumptions, equity is a homogeneous function of firm value and current principal. Hence by Euler's condition $E = VE_V + PE_P$. Substituting this into the expression gives $E(1 - E_V) \ge 0$, which says that the sinking fund payment should not be doubled.

Similarly, using (4b), debt is proportional to a standardized solution, $g(x, t)$, where

(5b)
$$0 = \tfrac{1}{2}\sigma^2 x^2 g_{xx} + [(r + \gamma - \delta)x - \gamma \min(g, 1) - c]g_x$$
$$+ g_t - (r + \gamma)g + \gamma \min(\gamma \min(g, 1) + c, \ 0 \le x \le \bar{\bar{x}}(t)$$
$$0 = \tfrac{1}{2} + \sigma^2 x^g{}_{xx} + [(r + 2\gamma - \delta)x - 2\gamma - c]g_x + g_t$$
$$- (r + 2\gamma)g + 2\gamma + c, \ \bar{\bar{x}}(t) \le x \le \bar{x}(t)$$

$$g(0, t) = 0$$
$$g(x, t^*) = \min(x, 1)$$
$$(1 - \bar{\bar{x}})g_x(\bar{\bar{x}}, t) + g(\bar{\bar{x}}, t) - 1 = 0$$
$$g(\bar{x}, t) = k$$
$$g_x(\bar{x}, t) = 0.$$

In summary, the valuation problem for a capital structure with equity and a single issue of callable nonconvertible sinking fund coupon debt, with a noncumulative option to double, divides into four regions of firm value as a function of time. One region is defined by the fact that debt trades below par. In this region bonds are sunk at market and sinking fund payments are not doubled. This region corresponds at the maturity of the debt issue to firm values where bankruptcy occurs. A second region lies between the par barrier and the doubling barrier. In this region bonds are sunk at par and sinking fund payments are not doubled. A third region lies between the doubling barrier and the call barrier. In this region bonds are sunk at par and sinking fund payments are doubled. Since the call barrier converges to par at the maturity of the debt issue, both the second and third regions coverage to a point. The fourth region lies above the call barrier. It corresponds at the maturity of the debt issue to firm values where bankruptcy does not occur. For some given $r(t)$, $k(t)$, and c, it is possible that debt will always trade below par. Thus bonds are always sunk at market and the sinking fund payment is never doubled. In these cases there is only one region, since the par barrier, doubling barrier and the call barrier do not exist.

Unfortunately, incorporating the option to double the sinking fund payment in a capital structure with numerous debt issues dramatically increases the dimensionality of the valuation problem. Therefore the option to double is ignored in the numerical approximations. The results in this section imply that this leads to underpricing of equity and the overpricing of debt.

6.2.2 Multiple Debt Issues

This section generalizes the analysis to allow for multiple debt issues. This feature of debt is important because it introduces interactions among bonds that are not present in the standard example of one debt issue. For expositional simplicity, this section considers the case of two issues of callable nonconvertible sinking fund coupon debt (with no options to double).

The value of any remaining claims in a capital structure initially composed of equity and two issues of callable nonconvertible sinking fund coupon debt, with no options to double, will depend on whether either debt issue has been redeemed via a call decision, as well as on firm value and time. In effect the capital structure of the firm can be in any one of four states, which is indexed by the variable θ. If there are n debt issues then there are 2^n such states. $\theta = 0$ in the state where both issues of debt have been previously called. The valuation problem in this state is trivial; equity value equals firm value. $\theta = 1$ is the state where bond 1 is alive but bond 2 has been called. $\theta = 2$ is the state where bond 2 is alive but bond 1 has been called. Finally, $\theta = 3$ is the state where neither bond has been called.

With this notation the values of claims can be written as functions of the current capital structure state as well as firm value and time. Letting $E(V, \theta, t)$ $D(V, \theta, t)$, and $D'(V, \theta, t)$ be the values of equity and the two debt issues, they obey the following system of partial differential equations in any relevant capital structure state:

(6a) $0 = \frac{1}{2}\sigma^2 V^2 E_{VV} + (rV - \pi - \pi' - d)E_V + E_t - rE + d;$
        $\theta = 1, 2, 3$

(6b) $0 = \frac{1}{2}\sigma^2 V^2 D_{VV} + (rV - \pi - \pi' - d)D_V + D_t - rD + \pi;$
        $\theta = 1, 3$

(6c) $0 = \frac{1}{2}\sigma^2 V^2 D'_{VV} + (rV - \pi - \pi' - d)D'_V + D'_t - rD' + \pi';$
        $\theta = 2, 3 .$

π and π' are simply total cash payouts to the two debt issues. Taking account of whether bonds have been called and whether it makes sense to sink at market or par,

$$\pi(V, 1, t) = \pi(V, 3, t) \equiv \gamma \min(D, P) + cP$$

$$\pi(V, 2, t) \equiv 0$$

$$\pi'(V, 2, t) = \pi'(V, 3, t) \equiv \gamma' \min(D', P') + c'P'$$

$$\pi'(V, 1, t) = 0 .$$

Note how current values of debt issues enter into valuation equations for other claims. Hence equations (6a)–(6c) must generally be solved simultaneously. It is always possible to eliminate one relevant equation, since the claims sum to firm value.

Boundary conditions are needed to relate the solutions to (6a), (6b), and (6c) for different capital structure states to each other and to complete the contingent claims formulation of the general valuation problem. For each relevant security in each state a lower boundary condition, a terminal boundary condition, and an upper (free) boundary condition must be specified. The lower boundary condition in every case is trivial; limited liability translates zero firm value into zero value for every claim: $E(0, \theta, t) = D(0, \theta, t) = D'(0, \theta, t) = 0$.

Each state has a unique terminal boundary. Let t^* be the maturity of debt issue D and let $t^{*\prime}$ be the maturity of debt issue D'. Without loss of generality $t^* \leq t^{*\prime}$. First suppose that the firm is in capital structure state $\theta = 1$, where the second debt issue has been called. Then the terminal boundary coincides with the maturity of the first debt issue. The terminal boundary condition in this case is standard for a capital structure with a single issue of callable nonconvertible coupon debt:

$$E(V, 1, t^*) = \max[0, V - P(t^*)]$$
$$D(V, 1, t^*) = \min[V, P(t^*)].$$

Next suppose that the firm is in capital structure state $\theta = 2$, where the first debt issue has been called. Then the terminal boundary coincides with the maturity of the second debt issue. Again the terminal boundary condition is standard:

$$E(V, 2, t^*) = \max[0, V - P'(t^{*\prime})]$$
$$D'(V, 2, t^{*\prime}) = \min[V, P'(t^{*\prime})].$$

Finally, suppose that the firm is in capital structure state $\theta = 3$, where neither debt issue has been called. Then the terminal boundary coincides with the earlier maturity date, since the firm must transit to a new capital structure state on this date. In the example the first debt issue matures at t^*. Since the debt is callable, the only relevant region has to do with firm values which are insufficient to cover the remaining principal on the first debt issue, so that the firm is bankrupt. Since firm value is insufficient to meet principal payments on the first debt issue alone, equity is worthless in this region: $E(V, 3, t^*) = 0$. The value of the two debt issues in this region depends on seniority. If the first issue is senior, then

$$D(V, 3, t^*) = V$$
$$D'(V, 3, i^*) = 0.$$

If the second issue is senior, then

$$D(V, 3, t^*) = \max[0, V - P'(t^*)]$$
$$D'(V, 3, t^*) = \min[V, P'(t^*)].$$

Finally, if neither issue is senior, then both get pro rata shares:

$$D(V, 3, t^*) = VP(t^*)/[P(t^*) + P'(t^*)]$$
$$D'(V, 3, t^*) = VP'(t^*)/[P(t^*) + P'(t^*)].$$

It remains to specify upper free boundary conditions corresponding to optimal call decisions in each of the capital structure states. First suppose that the firm is in capital structure states $\theta = 1$, where the second debt issue has been called. The upper free boundary conditions in this case are standard for a capital structure with a single issue of callable nconvertible coupon debt:

$$E[\bar{V}(1, t), 1, t] = \bar{V}(1, t) - k(t)P(t)$$
$$E_V[\bar{V}(1, t), 1, t] = 1.$$

Similarly, if the firm is in capital structure state $\theta = 2$, where the first debt issue has been called, then the conditions are

$$E[\bar{V}(2, t), 2, t] = \bar{V}(2, t) - k'(t)P'(t)$$
$$E_V[\bar{V}(2, t), 2, t] = 1.$$

Finally, suppose that the firm is in capital structure state $\theta = 3$, where both debt issues are alive. The upper free boundary in this state corresponds to the barrier where the firm calls one of the bond issues and thus transits to another state. Since management chooses the bond to call so as to maximize shareholder wealth,

$$E[\bar{V}(3, t), 3, t] = \max\{E[\bar{V}(3, t) - k(t)P(t), 2, t],$$
$$E[\bar{V}(3, t) - k'(t)P'(t), 1, t]\}.$$

Similarly the "high contact" optimization condition is

$$E_V[\bar{V}(3, t), 3, t] = \partial \max E[\bar{V}(3, t) - k(t)P(t), 2, t],$$
$$E[\bar{V}(3, t) - k'(t)P'(t), 1, t]/\partial V$$

Suppose that it is optimal to call the first debt issue at $\bar{V}(3, t)$, then the values of the debt issues on this barrier are

$$D[\bar{V}(3, t), 3, t] = k(t)P(t)$$
$$D'[\bar{V}(3, t), 3, t] = D'[\bar{V}(3, t) - k(t)P(t), 2, t].$$

Conversely suppose that it is optimal to call the second debt issue, then

$$D[V(3, t), 3, t] = D[V(3, t) - k'(t)P'(t), 1, t]$$
$$D'[V(3, t), 3, t] = k'(t)P'(t).$$

In summary, the valuation problem for capital structures containing equity and two issues of callable nonconvertible sinking fund coupon debt corresponds to the simultaneous solution of a system of partial differential equations. Appropriate combinatorial application of these principles leads directly to a formulation of the valuation problem for capital structures containing equity and n issues of callable nonconvertible sinking fund coupon debt. This approach is necessitated by the fundamental problem of determining the optimal call policy governing the n callable bonds. This formulation identifies that policy which maximizes the value of the equity.

It is important to understand the dimensionality of the n issue case. First note that there are 2^n possible capital structure states, including the trivial state of an all-equity firm. Furthermore, there are a number of securities to be value in each state. One way to calculate the number of different solutions to partial differential equations required in the n issue case is as follows. There are $\binom{n}{n} = 1$ capital structure states corresponding to 0 bonds having been called. In this one state there are $n + 1$ securities outstanding for a total of $n + 1$ solutions. There are $\binom{n}{n-1} = n$ capital structure states corresponding to one bond's having been called. In each of these n states there are n securities outstanding. Continuing in this way, we find that there are $\sum_{j=0}^{n-1} \binom{n}{n-j}(n + 1 - j)$ solutions in all. Hence one high priority line of research in terms of applying contingent claims valuation to realistic capital structures is the derivation of rational theorems which rule out various capital structure states (e.g., which show that certain kinds of bonds are always called first).

6.3 Data and Methodology

Data were collected for 15 firms on a monthly basis from January 1975 to January 1981. The firms were chosen based on a number of criteria at the beginning of 1975:

1. Simple capital structures (i.e., one class of stock, no convertible bonds, small number of debt issues, no preferred stock).
2. Small proportion of private debt to total capital.
3. Small proportion of short-term notes payable or capitalized leases to total capital.
4. All publicly traded debt is rated.

Based on these criteria the following firms were selected:

1.	Allied Chemical	9.	Proctor & Gamble
2.	Anheuser Busch	10.	Pullman
3.	Brown Group	11.	Raytheon
4.	Bucyrus Erie	12.	Republic Steel
5.	Champion Spark Plug	13.	Seagram
6.	Cities Service	14.	Sunbeam
7.	CPC	15.	Upjohn
8.	MGM		

The contingent claims valuation model requires three kinds of data in order to solve for prices of individual claims as functions of total firm value: (1) indenture data, (2) variance rate data, and (3) interest rate data. The bond indentures define the boundary conditions which constitute the economic description of various claims. For example, the following data were collected for each bond for each firm: principal, coupon rate, call price schedule, call protection period, sinking fund payments, and options to sink at market or par. The bond convenant data were collected from Moody's *Bond Guide*, except that sinking fund payments were collected from the monthly Standard and Poor's *Bond Guide*. For purposes of testing the model, actual bond prices were also collected from the latter sources.

The following procedure was used to estimate a variance rate for each firm in the sample, as of each January from 1977 through 1981. For each of the trailing 24 months, we calculated the percentage return on the total of all claims, including any payouts, that were outstanding at the beginning of the month. (To estimate the market value of nontraded debt, we assumed that the ratio of market value to book value was the same as for traded debt.) The sample variance of this percentage return gives an estimate of the variance rate for the firm as a whole. Table 6.1 summarizes the estimates.

The standard assumption in contingent claims analysis is that the future course of interest rates, $r(t)$, is known. Specifically, it is often assumed that the instantaneous rate of interest is constant through time (i.e., a flat term structure). The assumption of a flat term structure results in a fundamental problem for the empirical test of the contingent claims

Table 6.1	Estimates of Standard Deviation of Returns to Firm (Annualized) January 1977–January 1981				
	1977	1978	1979	1980	1981
1. Allied Chemical	.193	.204	.184	.196	.185
2. Anheuser Busch	.225	.228	.217	.245	.255
3. Brown Group	.200	.152	.151	.157	.192
4. Bucyrus Erie	.301	.268	.211	.231	.268
5. Champion Spark Plug	.257	.178	.215	.227	.220
6. Cities Service	.160	.149	.129	.169	.327
7. CTC	.191	.176	.143	.131	.173
8. MGM	.190	.155	.258	.303	.420
9. Proctor & Gamble	.150	.146	.165	.149	.156
10. Pullman	.330	.236	.308	.348	N.A.
11. Raytheon	.278	.182	.227	.280	.291
12. Republic Steel	.168	.170	.141	.158	.173
13. Seagram	.268	.234	.171	.216	.380
14. Sunbeam	.258	.204	.240	.287	.288
15. Upjohn	.320	.207	.215	.233	.216

model. If a flat term structure is assumed then the model will misprice riskless bonds. Therefore the test of whether contingent claims analysis can price risky bonds is systematically flawed. This problem is handled by the assumption that the future course of the one-year rate of interest will be consistent with the one-year forward interest rates implied by the current term structure. This procedure will result in the correct pricing of riskless bonds. The following procedure was used to estimate implied one-year forward interest rates for 25 years, as of each January from 1977 through 1982. First, identify all par government bonds as of that date. These data were gathered from the *Wall Street Journal*. There are usually fewer than 25 such bonds. Therefore linear interpolation was used to complete a 25-year yield curve for par government bonds. Then this yield curve was solved for implied one-year forward rates. Hence the implied forward rates pertain to a par term structure.

The method of Markov chains is used to approximate solutions to the problems posed in the previous section. Parkinson (1977), Mason (1978), and Cox et al. (1979) use Markov chains to approximate solutions to valuation problems similar to the ones considered in this paper. The method of finite differences has been used by Brennan and Schwartz (1976a, 1976b) to treat similar contingent claims equations. The methods of Markov chains and finite differences are very similar, as demonstrated in Brennan and Schwartz (1978) and Mason (1978). Readers are referred to these papers for background on numerical analysis techniques.

If all claims are publicly traded, then the value of the firm can be observed and prices for all claims, relative to the observed firm value, can be predicted. However, since all claims on the test firms are not publicly traded, an alternative approach had to be taken. Namely, the equity pricing function was used to estimate firm value. In other words, what firm value is consistent with the actual equity value? Then this estimated firm value was used to predict debt prices. Note that this procedure amplifies systematic errors in pricing the debt. For example, suppose that the model systematically underprices equity and overprices debt, as functions of firm value. Then this procedure will make two compounding errors. First, it will overestimate the value of the firm. Then it will overestimate debt as a function of firm value. Hence it will overestimate debt for both reasons. Counting each year from 1977 through 1981, and counting each bond existing in each year for each of the 15 firms, we solved numerically for prices of 163 bonds, as well as for equity values. The next section describes our results.

6.4 Empirical Results

Table 6.2 summarizes the empirical results for the 163 bonds in the sample. It reveals that the average percentage pricing error—defined as

Table 6.2 Percentage Pricing Error for Various Partitions of Sample

Partition	Number of Bonds	Percent of Sample	Error		Absolute Error		Difference of Means Test*
			Mean	S.D.	Mean	S.D.	
All	163	100.0	.0149	.0714	.0589	.0430	N.A.
High rated	133	81.6	.0023	.0637	.0518	.0373	5.072
Low rated	30	18.4	.0707	.0767	.0906	.0517	
Low variance†	40	24.5	.0096	.0611	.0527	.0323	1.597
High variance	43	26.4	.0339	.0746	.0660	.0485	
Short term	74	45.4	.0077	.0761	.0611	.0460	1.164
Long term	89	54.6	.0208	.0667	.0571	.0403	
Senior	147	90.2	.0083	.0701	.0570	.0417	3.678
Junior	16	9.8	.0751	.0523	.0763	.0506	
Low coupon	64	39.3	−.0228	.0669	.0589	.0391	5.937
High coupon	99	60.7	.0392	.0632	.0589	.0454	
Discount	143	87.7	.0075	.0703	.0569	.0420	3.700
Premium	20	12.3	.0679	.0547	.0731	.0475	
Low current yield	86	52.8	−.0065	.0684	.0557	.0403	4.238
High current yield	77	47.2	.0388	.0670	.0625	.0456	

*(Equal variances). The test assumes independent observations. As might be expected, our sample exhibits positive correlation among errors for the same bond in different years (as well as in other ways). This biases the test toward detecting a significant difference in means.

†Since firm variance rates are remarkably similar, we examined the two extreme quartiles.

predicted price minus actual price, divided by actual price—is less than 1½%. The standard deviation of the percentage pricing error is about 7%. The average absolute value of the percentage pricing error is about 6%. The accompanying histogram in figure 6.1 gives additional information on these errors.

Although there is almost no systematic bias in pricing errors for the sample as a whole, there might be systematic bias among subsets of bonds that simply cancel out in the entire sample. We tested for this by dividing the sample according to conventional classifications. For example, table 6.2 indicates that the model underprices bonds with high ratings ($\geq A$ rating) and overprices bonds with low ratings ($< A$ rating) and that this difference is statistically significant.

Statistical significance is measured by a difference of means test. This test assumes that the two underlying populations are normally distributed with the same variance. In addition it is assumed that the samples are made up of independent draws. To the extent that the samples are not made up of independent draws, the test is biased. It is likely that the samples studied in this section have positively correlated errors; thus the reports of statistical significance are biased upward.

Table 6.2 shows that the model underprices bonds on firms with low variance rates and overprices bonds on firms with high variance rates.

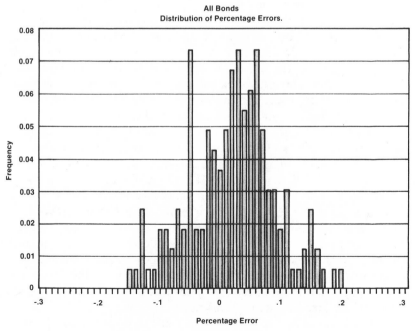

All Bonds
Distribution of Percentage Errors.

Fig. 6.1   All bonds.

The table indicates that the model underprices bonds with stated maturities less than 15 years and overprices bonds with stated maturities greater than 15 years. Of course, total variance equals the variance rate multiplied by time. Hence overpricing high variance and long maturity bonds may be two sides of the same coin. The table shows that the model prices senior bonds correctly on average, but overprices junior bonds. Finally, the table shows that the model underprices low coupon bonds (coupon rate $\leq 7\%$) and overprices high coupon bonds (coupon rate $> 7\%$).

In summary, the model tends to underprice safe bonds and overprice risky bonds in a systematic way. This leads us to conclude that the usual assumptions in the contingent claims valuation literature are violated in some systematic way. Three assumptions are questioned in particular: (1) the assumption of zero personal taxes, (2) the assumption of a constant variance rate, and (3) the assumption of perfect antidilution protection. The plan is as follows. First, there is a discussion of what kinds of pricing errors would ensue from violation of each of these three assumptions. Then empirical evidence is presented from the sample that is designed to discriminate among pricing errors induced by violation of each of these assumptions.

6.4.1   Personal Tax Assumption

According to assumption (A.1), which is standard in the contingent claims valuation literature, there are no personal taxes. This implies that investors capitalize ordinary income and capital gains in the same way. However, conventional wisdom says that investors prefer capital gains to ordinary income for tax reasons. Furthermore, Ingersoll (1976) finds that inclusion of differential taxes on ordinary income and capital gains improves the ability of the contingent claims valuation model to predict prices for the income and capital shares of dual funds.

If differential taxes cause investors to capitalize ordinary income differently from capital gains, then failure to include this in the model could lead to overpricing bonds with higher current yields relative to bonds with lower current yields. (See Ingersoll [1976, p. 110] for a careful discussion of this issue.) First consider highly rated bonds. Recall that the interest rates in the model are derived from a term structure for par government bonds. Given the tax treatment of bonds trading in the secondary market, high-quality discount bonds should be underpriced relative to high-quality premium bonds. This is due to the fact that the IRS allows investors to amortize secondary market premiums against interest income while also allowing realized gains due to secondary market discounts to be taxed at capital gains rates.

Another dimension of any tax effect has to do with risk. Consider low-quality par bonds versus high-quality par bonds (e.g., new issue bonds on high-variance vs. low-variance firms). The expected capital loss on the low-quality bonds is larger in absolute terms than the expected capital loss on the high-quality bonds. Hence the low-quality bonds will have a higher coupon rate than the high-quality bonds. Since the higher taxes on the low-quality bond are ignored, any tax effect will cause low-quality to be overpriced relative to high-quality bonds. In particular, since government par bonds are perfectly safe, any tax effect will cause corporate par bonds to be overpriced in general. Similar considerations say that any tax effect will cause junior par bonds to be overpriced relative to senior par bonds. And similar considerations also suggest that any tax effect will cause longer maturity par bonds to be overpriced relative to shorter maturity par bonds.

6.4.2   Variance Rate Assumption

According to assumption (A.4), which is standard in the contingent claims valuation literature, the variance rate of firm value σ^2 is a constant. Empirical evidence for common equity suggests that its variance rate goes up as its level goes down. Of course, this is consistent with a constant variance rate for firm value—because of the possibility of leverage effects. However, it is also consistent with a nonconstant firm value variance rate.

Suppose that the variance rate of firm value is not a constant, but rather increases as firm value decreases. For example, the stochastic process for firm value might belong to the constant elasticity of variance class. And suppose that a constant variance rate is falsely assumed in estimating σ^2. What kinds of pricing errors would this include? These errors would be similar in type to those induced by an underestimate of a variance rate that is in fact constant. In other words, in either case the probability of financial distress is significantly underestimated.

Underestimating the variance will not matter much for high-quality bonds. But it will cause low-quality bonds to be overpriced by a significant amount. Hence underestimating the variance will cause corporate bonds to be overpriced in general and will cause low-quality bonds to be overpriced relative to high-quality bonds. Similar considerations suggest that underestimating the variance will cause junior bonds to be overpriced relative to senior bonds and longer maturity bonds to be overpriced relative to shorter maturity bonds.

6.4.3   Dilution Assumption

According to the perfect antidilution assumption in (A.8), which is standard in the contingent claims valuation literature, no new bonds can be issued until all old bonds have been extinguished. Furthermore, according to the perfect liquidity assumption in (A.9), firms can simply sell assets in order to make cash payouts. Hence in the model equity maximizes its value by funding all cash payouts through asset sales.

However, firms which call bonds normally have the option to fund the call by issuing new bonds with the same priority. Holding firm value constant, this allows management to dilute any remaining bonds, as compared to the model which allows for no dilution. On the other hand, the model causes firm value to go down when bonds are called, as compared to refunding with new bonds that keeps firm value constant. Now suppose equity can choose between refunding and asset liquidation to finance a call decision. The option to refund can have value to equity. Failure to include the option to refund in our model will cause equity to be underpriced and debt to be overpriced in general. Since the option to refund has value because of the possibility of diluting existing debt, junior debt will be overpriced relative to senior debt and longer maturity debt will be overpriced relative to shorter maturity debt. In other words, debt can be economically junior either because it is explicitly junior or because it has a relatively longer maturity than other debt.

6.4.4 Empirical Evidence on Violation of These Assumptions

The empirical evidence tends to confirm the existence of a tax effect, a variance effect, and a dilution effect. Table 6.2 gives evidence of a tax effect. It shows that the model underprices discount bonds relative to premium bonds. These results continue to obtain when examining only high-quality bonds, where variance rate effects and dilution effects are minimal. Table 6.2 gives further evidence of a tax effect. It shows that the model overprices bonds with above-average coupon yields relative to bonds with below-average coupon yields. (The median coupon yield in the sample is approximately 9%.) Again, the results continue to obtain when examining only high-quality bonds. Hence there is unambiguous evidence for the existence of a tax effect.

There is also empirical evidence for a variance effect. A naive test for the existence of a variance effect in whether bonds of firms with high estimated variance rates are overpriced relative to bonds of firms with low estimated variance rates, since risky bonds are more sensitive to underestimating variance than safe bonds. Table 6.2 showed that this is the case. However, this is a naive test, because a tax effect alone would cause risky bonds to be overpriced relative to safe bonds. This is because, everything else equal, risky bonds have higher expected capital losses than safe bonds, which is compensated for by higher current yield. To test for a variance effect independent of any tax effect, the sample is first split according to high versus low current yield. This is done to control for the tax effect. Then pricing errors are compared for bonds of high- versus low-variance firms within each subsample. Table 6.3 reports these re-

Table 6.3   **Percentage Pricing Errors for Various Subpartitions of Sample**

Subpartition	Number of Bonds	Percent of Sample	Error		Absolute Error		Difference of Means Test
			Mean	S.D.	Mean	S.D.	
Low current yield:							
Low variance	22	13.5	−.0058	.0592	.0480	.0352	.656
High variance	16	9.8	.0080	.0666	.0536	.0903	
High current yield:							
Low variance	18	11.0	.0284	.0580	.0585	.0272	.976
High variance	27	16.6	.0492	.0748	.0734	.0514	
High current yield and variance:							
Senior	20	12.3	.0297	.0691	.0623	.0422	2.459
Junior	7	4.3	.1050	.0612	.1050	.0612	

sults. It shows that bonds of high-variance firms continue to be overpriced relative to low-variance firms within each subsample, although the effect is more pronounced for bonds with high current yield. Furthermore, almost identical results hold when junior bonds are excluded from the sample, to check against the possibility that variance only proxies for a dilution effect. These results are interpreted as evidence for a variance effect in addition to a tax effect.

Lastly, the question remains, Is there evidence for a dilution effect in addition to a tax effect and a variance effect? A naive test for the existence of a dilution effect is whether economically junior bonds are overpriced—that is, either bonds which are explicitly junior or bonds that are effectively junior because of their longer maturity—relative to economically senior bonds. Table 6.2 showed that this is the case; junior bonds are overpriced relative to senior bonds.

As before, this is a naive test, because either a tax effect or a variance effect alone would cause junior bonds to be overpriced relative to senior bonds. To get a more sophisticated test, the sample is first restricted to bonds with high current coupon yield issued by corporations with high variance rates, which tends to control for tax and variance effects. Table 6.3 shows the results. Although junior bonds continue to be overpriced relative to economically senior bonds, the effect is not strong. Hence there appears to be a dilution effect, but it is not as strong as the tax and variance effects.

6.5 Conclusion

In this paper a theoretical model is derived for valuing claims in realistic capital structures containing equity and multiple issues of callable nonconvertible sinking fund coupon debt, based on the usual assumptions in the contingent claims valuation literature. This model is tested on a number of bonds for 15 firms yearly from 1977 through 1982. The predicted prices are not systematically different from actual prices for the sample as a whole. However, predicted prices are systematically different from actual prices for various types of bonds in the sample. Evidence exists for a systematic tax effect and a systematic variance effect in the results. There is also evidence for a less significant dilution effect associated with the option to refund.

Establishing the empirical validity of contingent claims analysis as a corporate liability pricing model is a large and complex task. A number of theoretical and methodological problems must be addressed. For example, as demonstrated in this paper, sinking funds and optimal call policies for multiple bond capital structures warrant further theoretical study. It has also been demonstrated that the detailed consideration of the interaction of multiple bond convenants can significantly increase the dimensionality of the overall valuation problem. This underscores the need for research into more efficient numerical analysis methods.

We view this paper as an important first step in establishing the empirical validity of contingent claims analysis. Given the results of the paper, current research is under way, using an expanded database, where the problem formulation takes explicit account of personal taxes, the option to refund, the cost of financial distress, and changing variance rates. Once the results of this current research are known, a portfolio test will be conducted to determine if market inefficiencies can explain any of the discrepancies between the model prices and market prices.

References

Black, F., and Scholes, M. 1973. The pricing of options and corporate liabilities. *Journal of Political Economy* 81:637–59.

Brennan, M., and Schwartz, E. 1976. Convertible bonds: valuation and optimal strategies for call and conversion. *Journal of Finance* 32:1699–1716.

———. 1977. The valuation of American put options. *Journal of Finance* 32:449–62.

———. 1978. Finite difference methods and jump processes arising in the pricing of contingent claims: a synthesis. *Journal of Financial and Quantitative Analysis* 13:461–74.

Cox, J.; Ross, S.; and Rubenstein, M. 1979. Option pricing: a simplified approach. *Journal of Financial Economics* 7:229–63.

Ingersoll, J. 1976. A theoretical and empirical investigation of the dual purpose funds. *Journal of Financial Economics* 3:83–123.

———. 1977. A contingent claims valuation of convertible securities. *Journal of Financial Economics* 4:269–322.

Mason, S. 1978. The numerical analysis of certain free boundary problems arising in financial economics. Ph.D. diss. Harvard Business School, Boston, MA.

Merton, R. C. 1973. Theory of rational option pricing. *Bell Journal of Economics and Management Science* 4:141–83.

———. 1974. On the pricing of corporate debt: the risk structure of interest rates. *Journal of Finance* 29:449–70.

Parkinson, M. 1977. Option pricing: the American put. *Journal of Business* 5:21–36.

Comment   Fischer Black

This is a costly model. It uses a lot of computer time. At the end of it all, the average error in pricing bonds is 6%. I am surprised that Jones et al. are able to create a model with such a large error. Surely an investment banker can price a new bond more accurately than that. I am disappointed, because I think that the best application of option theory is to risky bonds. I hope that the best models will be more accurate.

Part of the problem is that the authors handicap themselves. They don't allow themselves to use some of the information that an investment banker is able to use. For example, they don't use information about the current prices of comparable bonds.

Overall, I like the paper very much. I find it very stimulating. I think it is the most thought-provoking paper on the valuation of corporate bonds that I've seen. It is well written, too. There is math in it, but the math is sufficiently hidden that it doesn't get in the way of understanding what the paper is saying.

In trying to figure out how Jones et al. can be so far off in pricing the bonds, I began to think about the assumptions they make. They are very careful about certain assumptions, such as looking at the exact indenture provisions on the bonds. There are other assumptions, though, that one might take differently than they did. These assumptions might make a difference in the values they get.

For example, they assume that a firm goes along, makes the sinking fund and other payments on its outstanding bonds, and eventually pays off its bonds. The firm ends up with no debt. In fact, firms don't seem to do that. They go along for a while, paying off some of their existing debt. But then they decide to make some new investments, so they issue more debt. That affects the value of the debt that is already outstanding. Putting this feature into their model could make a significant difference in the values they get.

Another assumption that can be handled in different ways is the assumption that firms behave in the way the model thinks is optimal. In Ingersoll's study of convertible bonds, using methods like those in this paper, it appears that firms call their bonds too late. They don't call them at what seems to be the optimal time. Maybe the same thing applies to the firms in this paper. Maybe they are not behaving in a way that the model says is optimal. That may explain some of the differences here between value and price.

I think that if you ask corporate treasurers how they decide what to do, they will often give relatively unsophisticated answers. They will give you rules of thumb that incorporate factors we think ought to be incorpo-

Fischer Black is vice-president of Goldman, Sachs and Co., and a research affiliate of the NBER.

rated, but usually not in an elegant way. It's conceivable to me that if we are able to incorporate these rules of thumb in the model, we might get better values.

Another important issue is the way one estimates the volatility of the firm. With stock options, the volatility is perhaps the most important input to the option valuation model. With corporate bonds, the volatility may be less important, but it is important enough to make the difference between a correct valuation and an incorrect valuation in most cases. I believe that the procedure that is followed in this paper is essentially equivalent to taking the actual historical volatility of the firm as the estimated future volatility. That's going to give you incorrect volatility estimates.

Moreover, the errors in estimating volatility will be correlated across firms. There will be times when the volatility estimates are too low for most firms, and other times when they're too high for most firms. In the period covered by this paper I think the volatility estimates are too low, since volatilities increased over that period.

Errors in estimating volatility are especially important when the authors look at the pattern of errors across high- and low-volatility firms. Firms that seem to have high volatility will often be firms for which we have overestimated volatility, and firms that seem to have low volatility will often be firms for which we have underestimated volatility. I think it might be better if the authors used implied volatilities in place of historical volatilities. A firm's implied volatility is the volatility that gives the right equity value when used in the model.

There's another point I can't resist making, because it's related to a discovery Scott Mason reported in his dissertation. He found that there is some uncertainty about how bonds will be handled in case of bankruptcy. Suppose we are in a period where interest rates have risen. A firm with low coupon bonds outstanding gets into bankruptcy. For one reason or another, it has enough assets so that it could buy back at least one issue of its bonds. The bonds are not due for several years. Does the firm have to buy back the bonds at par, or can it buy them back at the present value of a riskless bond with that coupon and other provisions? In this paper, the authors assume that the bonds will be bought back at par, even when the present value of a riskless bond with similar terms is below par. This assumption is probably realistic, and probably won't make much difference in most cases anyway, but it will make some differences in the values. The authors mention allowing for changes in the firm's volatility as its value changes, and taking into account the fact that interest rates are stochastic. These assumptions will make a difference, too, but I don't think they will make as much of a difference as using implied volatilities instead of historical volatilities and taking account of future debt issues by the firm.

7   Capital Structure Change and Decreases in Stockholders' Wealth: A Cross-sectional Study of Convertible Security Calls

Wayne H. Mikkelson

7.1   Introduction

Several studies document a statistically significant decrease in the price of firms' common stock at the earliest public announcement of certain types of capital structure changes. For example, Masulis (1978) reports statistically significant negative average common stock returns at the announcement of intrafirm exchange offers that involve the issuance of common stock for debt, common stock for preferred stock, or preferred stock for debt. Mikkelson (1981) reports a significant negative average common stock return at the announcement of convertible debt calls that force conversion of debt to common stock. Dann and Mikkelson (1984) and Korwar (1982) also report a negative average return at the announcement of the issuance of convertible debt and common stock, respectively. None of these studies of capital structure changes, however, resolves the issue of what factors determine the negative average stock price response. Nor do they completely explain the motivation for these capital structure changes.

This study attempts to shed light on these unresolved issues by investigating potential determinants of negative stock price reactions to the announcements of convertible debt and convertible preferred stock calls that force conversion. The empirical analysis extends Mikkelson's (1981) study of convertible security calls by estimating the cross-sectional relationship between abnormal common stock price responses to call

Wayne H. Mikkelson is associate professor of finance at the University of Oregon's College of Business Administration. The author would like to thank Jerry Bowman, Larry Dann, Ben Friedman, Mike Hopewell, Michael Jensen, Ron Masulis, Megan Partch, and the participants of the UCLA and University of Oregon finance workships for their helpful comments. The author would also like to thank Mike Ahearn and François Chaballier for valuable research assistance.

announcements and variables that represent possible determinants of stock price reactions. The variables are measures of the following effects of calls: (1) the change in interest expense tax shields, (2) the potential redistribution of wealth from common stockholders to preferred stockholders and debtholders, (3) the decrease in the value of conversion privileges held by convertible securityholders, (4) the relative increase in shares outstanding, and (5) the change in earnings per share.

The empirical results indicate that wealth redistribution from common stockholders to debtholders has no measurable effect on stockholders' wealth. Some evidence, however, suggests that the conversion of debt to common stock alters the relative priority of outstanding preferred stock claims sufficiently to affect share price. There is no evidence of an association between common stock returns and decreases in the value of called convertible securities at the announcements of calls. The potential wealth transfers from convertible securityholders are typically quite small relative to the market value of common stock. In addition, there is no support for the notion particularly popular among practitioners that the negative stock price response to call announcements is attributable to a decrease in earnings per share or an increase in the supply of outstanding shares.

The results reveal a positive association between the reduction in interest expense tax shields and the announcement period common stock returns. One interpretation is that the association between stock returns and the corporate tax variable solely reflects the wealth impact of a decrease in interest expense tax shields. This interpretation implies that on average the market does not anticipate complete replacement of the tax shields with a subsequent issuance of new debt, even though refinancing the called debt may be in stockholders' interests.

A second interpretation of this evidence recognizes that the negative stock price response may reflect informaion about the calling firm's value. This interpretation presumes that the decision to call and to reduce financial leverage is in the interests of stockholders but is based on information not reflected in the calling firm's security prices. For example, a call decision may convey management's lowered assessment of the firm's optimal level of interest payments or preferred dividends and thereby convey management's reduced expectations about future earnings. A convertible security call and the associated decrease in financial leverage, therefore, can be viewed as a value-maximizing response to a decrease in the firm's earnings prospects, even though the share price reaction to a call announcement is negative.

Under the second interpretation, the evidence of a relationship between stock returns at the time of call announcements and changes in interest expense tax shields may in part, or even entirely, reflect information about the firm's value or earnings prospects. The results presented in this study, however, do not resolve the extent to which the stock price responses to call announcements reflect a tax effect versus an information effect.[1]

The paper is organized as follows: section 7.2 discusses possible determinants of stock returns at the announcements of convertible security calls. A specification of a cross-sectional relationship between common stock returns and the possible determinants is also developed in this section. Section 7.3 describes the sample of convertible security calls and the empirical proxies for the possible determinants of stock returns. Estimates of the cross-sectional relationship are presented in section 7.4. Section 7.5 interprets the findings. The final section presents a summary and the conclusions of the study.

7.2 Potential Determinants of Changes in Stockholders' Wealth at Announcement of Convertible Security Calls

This section discusses potential determinants of changes in stockholders' wealth in response to call announcements and develops a simple model of the determination of the stock price response to call announcements. A specification of the potential impact on common stockholders' wealth, expressed as a return, is presented for the following effects of convertible security calls: (1) a reduction in interest expense tax shields, (2) an increase in the relative priority of a subset of claims senior to common stock, (3) a reduction in the conversion premium of called securities, (4) an increase in shares outstanding, and (5) a change in earnings per share.

Several assumptions are made in developing a simple model of the share price effects of a convertible security call. First, the calling firm has three classes of securities outstanding: (1) callable convertible debt (CD), (2) nonconvertible debt (D), and (3) common stock (CS). Second, the value of the convertible debt (V_{CD}) exceeds its call price and the optimal response of the convertible bondholders is conversion. Third, the call is unanticipated by the market.[2]

In expression (1), the market value of common stock (V_{CS}) immediately prior to the call announcement equals the total value of the firm (V_F) less the market values of the callable convertible debt (V_{CD}) and the remaining outstanding debt securities (V_D):

$$(1) \qquad V_{CS} = V_F - V_{CD} - V_D.$$

Temporarily, it is assumed that the market value of convertible debt equals its conversion value, which equals the product of the fraction of outstanding shares issued on conversion (α) and the market value of outstanding common stock. In (2), the market value of common stock is expressed in terms of the number of shares outstanding (n) and share price (P).

$$(2) \qquad nP = V_F - \alpha(nP) - V_D$$

The pre-announcement share price, as given by (3), equals the difference between the value of firm and the value of senior securities divided by the total number shares outstanding after conversion of outstanding convertible securities:

$$(3) \qquad P = (V_F - V_D)/[(1 + \alpha)n].$$

The post-announcement share price (P') can be expressed as the difference between the post-announcement value of the firm (V_F') and the value of outstanding senior securities (V_D') divided by $[(1 + \alpha)n]$,

$$(4) \qquad P' = (V_F' - V_D')/[1 + \alpha)n].$$

Thus, the announcement period per share return (expression [5]) implied by the pre-announcement and post-announcement share prices equals the change in the difference between firm value and the value of senior securities $[\Delta(V_F - V_D)]$ divided by the market value of shares, including shares issued on conversion, prior to the call announcement $[(1 + \alpha)nP]$,

$$(5) \qquad (P' - P)/P = \Delta(V_F - V_D)/[(1 + \alpha)nP].$$

The remainder of this section discusses several possible effects of a convertible security call on stockholders' wealth and presents specifications of the potential effects on share price based on expression (5).

7.2.1   Reduction in Interest Expense Tax Deductions

If the calling firm has sufficient earnings to fully utilize the interest expense tax deductions provided by convertible debt, ceteris paribus a call reduces cash flows available to securityholders. However, the net tax effect of a reduction in debt outstanding on stockholders' wealth is ambiguous. The net effect depends on whether the decrease in leverage is expected to be temporary and on the extent to which the loss of corporate tax benefits is offset by other types of tax shields or by the elimination of costs, such as default-related costs and personal tax disadvantages associated with the called debt.

Various models of optimal capital structure that include corporate taxes imply different valuation effects of a reduction in the amount of debt outstanding. For example, Miller's (1977) analysis implies that for any level of financial leverage of a firm, the loss in interest expense tax deductions due to the conversion of debt is offset exactly by the gain of eliminating interest payments that have been "grossed up" to provide taxable debtholders with their required return net of personal taxes. As a result, the conversion of debt to common stock and the reduction in interest expense tax deductions have no effect on the wealth of common stockholders.

DeAngelo and Masulis (1980) present an analysis of optimal capital structure that incorporates uncertainty about a firm's ability to fully utilize interest expense tax deductions. In their model, firms issue debt up to the point where the marginal benefits of uncertain interest expense deductions equal the marginal costs of debt. Consequently, a reduction in financial leverage generally affects stockholders' wealth.

Assuming a call is completely unanticipated, a corporate tax effect of a call announcement decreases firm value by an amount equal to the present value of the change in interest expense tax shields (ΔT). Substituting ΔT into the numerator of the right-hand side of equation (5) gives equation (6), the corporate tax effect expressed as a relative change in share price:

$$(6) \qquad (P' - P)/P = \Delta T/[(1 + \alpha)nP].$$

Miller's model implies that ΔT is exactly offset by the elimination of personal tax disadvantages of debt, while DeAngelo and Masulis's model implies that ΔT may be only partially offset by the reduction in debt related costs. In equation (7), which incorporates the different predictions of these models, the value of γ is between zero and one, depending on the marginal effect of a reduction in interest expense tax deductions on firm value,

$$(7) \qquad (P' - P)/P = \gamma(\Delta T)/[(1 + \alpha)nP].$$

Thus, the tax effect as measured by a return per share of common stock equals the net marginal effect of a reduction in interest expense tax deductions on firm value $[\gamma(\Delta T)]$ divided by the sum of the preannouncement value of common stock and the conversion value of the called securities $[(1 + \alpha)nP]$.

7.2.2   Change in the Value of Senior Securities

An unanticipated announcement of a convertible debt call that forces conversion may cause a wealth transfer from common stockholders to preferred stockholders and debtholders. Any claims on the firm's assets with a priority higher than common stock, but not higher than the called debt, increase in priority relative to the debt claims converted to common stock. Even if the firm's expected cash flows and asset structure are unchanged by the call announcement, the value of a subset of claims senior to common stock may increase due to the elimination of competing debt claims. A corresponding decrease in the value of common stock reflects a wealth transfer from common stockholders.[3]

Holding the value of the firm constant in expression (5), the impact of a change in the value of senior securities (ΔV_D) on the value of common stock is expressed as a return per share in (8):

$$(8) \qquad (P' - P)/P = -\Delta V_D/[(1 + \alpha)nP].$$

The relative price change equals the change in the value of senior securities divided by the product of the total number of shares outstanding following conversion and the pre-announcement share price.

7.2.3 Transfer of Conversion Premium from Convertible Securityholders

If prior to a call announcement the market does not fully anticipate the timing of a call, the market value of convertible debt (V_{CD}) in general exceeds its conversion value (αV_{CS}).[4] An effect of a call announcement is to eliminate any conversion premium ($V_{CD} - \alpha V_{CS}$), so that following the call announcement the market value of convertible debt equals its conversion value. The decrease in the market value of the called securities is a wealth transfer from the called securityholders to the remaining securityholders of the firm.

Holding aside all other effects of a call announcement on the value of the firm or on the value of senior securities, and assuming that the transfer of the conversion premium is captured entirely by common stockholders, the impact of a decrease in conversion premium on the price of a share of common stock is given by (9):

$$(9) \qquad (P' - P)/P = (V_{CD} - \alpha V_{CS})/[(1 + \alpha)nP].$$

The total wealth of the convertible securityholders decreases by the amount of the pre-announcement conversion premium ($V_{CD} - \alpha V_{CS}$) less the portion of conversion premium regained on conversion $\{[\alpha/(1 + \alpha)](V_{CD} - \alpha V_{CS})\}$. The quantity $(1 + \alpha)$ in the denominator of expression (9) reflects the fact that only the fraction $[1/(1 + \alpha)]$ of the conversion premium is captured by the holders of common stock claims outstanding prior to the call.

7.2.4 Increase in Shares Outstanding

Some corporate officers and investment bankers attribute the negative stock price reactions to call announcements to the eventual increase in the number of shares outstanding. One price impact often cited is in effect a movement along a downward-sloping demand curve for the calling firm's shares. Also mentioned is a price effect due to a decrease in earnings per share caused by conversion of the called securities. Both effects lack rigorous support in theory. On the other hand, neither notion has been tested thoroughly. For this reason, both potential effects are examined in this study.

Supply Effect. If the demand for a firm's common stock is not perfectly elastic, the increase in the number of shares outstanding due to conversion of debt may explain some part of the decrease in share price at call announcements. That is, if the common stock claims of the calling firm do not have close substitutes, ceteris paribus an unanticipated increase in the number of shares outstanding is associated with a detectable price decrease. On the other hand, if shares of common stock have perfect or very close substitutes in the form of another security or a portfolio of securities, no significant price change is caused solely by an increase in the number of shares outstanding.

Existing evidence does not support the notion of a supply effect on share prices. Neither Scholes's (1972) examination of secondary distributions of common stock nor Marsh's (1979) study of U.K. rights offerings of common stock uncovers evidence of price changes that depend on the size of the offering. A study of convertible security calls differs from Scholes's study in that calls result in an increase in the number of shares outstanding, and also differs from Marsh's study in that a call does not produce a direct change in the firm's asset structure. Estimation of the relationship between abnormal common stock returns at the call announcements and the ensuing increase in the number of shares outstanding provides new evidence on the importance of a supply effect.

This study tests the hypothesis that the size of the relative increase in the number of shares outstanding due to conversion (α) is unrelated to the relative stock price change $[(P' - P)/P]$ in response to call announcements, adjusting for the possible price effects of corporate taxes and wealth redistribution. However, no theory of price pressure or supply effects exists that implies a particular specification of the relationship between stock price and the quantity of shares outstanding. For this study, therefore, only a general form relationship is specified. That is, $(P' - P)/P = f(\alpha)$ and $f'(\alpha) < 0$.

Failure to reject the null hypothesis is consistent with a perfectly elastic demand for shares, that is, no supply effects. But since the test is based on estimation of a cross-sectional relationship, there is an assumption of a homogeneous relationship between common stock returns and the relative changes in shares outstanding for the sample of calling firms. If the assumption of a homogeneous relationship is incorrect, the finding of no relationship between the stock price responses and the relative increases in shares outstanding may simply reflect an incorrect specification of the test.

Earnings Dilution Effect. Financial economists generally argue that there are no valuation effects attributable solely to changes in earnings per share. Prevailing theory of capital structure in a setting of no taxes, as first presented by Modigliani and Miller (1958), implies that to the extent a reduction in earnings per share of common stock reflects a decrease in expected cash flows per share due to a change in capital structure, there is compensating decrease in the required return for common stock. That is, changes in capital structure per se, even if they bring about a decrease in earnings per share, do not necessarily affect shareholders' wealth.

The issuance of new shares due to conversion of convertible debt or preferred stock reduces earnings per share, while the reduction in interest expenses or preferred dividends increases earnings per share. Typically, the net effect of a call and conversion is to reduce earnings per share. After adjusting for the possible effects of corporate taxes and wealth redistribution, the Modigliani-Miller theory predicts no price effect of a change in earnings per share. Therefore, estimation of the cross-sectional relationship between the stock price responses to call announcements and the associated relative changes in earnings per share ($\Delta EPS/EPS$), taking account of the effects of corporate taxes and wealth redistribution, provides an opportunity to test directly for a price effect due to dilution of earnings per share.[5]

7.2.5 Specification of the Cross-sectional Relationship

On the assumption that the possible determinants examined in this section are additive, expression (10) is the cross-sectional relationship to be estimated:

$$(10) \qquad (P' - P)/P = \beta_0 + \beta_1 \left[\gamma(\Delta T)/(1 + \alpha)nP\right]$$
$$+ \beta_2 \left[-\Delta V_D/(1 + \alpha)nP\right]$$
$$+ \beta_3 \left[(V_{CD} - \alpha V_{CS})/(1 + \alpha)nP\right]$$
$$+ \beta_4 \left[f(\alpha)\right] + \beta_5 \left([\Delta EPS/EPS]\right).$$

A positive value of β_1 is consistent with a corporate tax effect on share price. An increase in the value of senior securities implies a positive value for β_2. Loss of a conversion premium by convertible securityholders implies a positive value for β_3. A supply effect is consistent with a negative value for β_4, while a positive value for β_5 is implied by an earnings dilution effect. The sample of calls and the empirical proxies for the variables in (10) are described in the next section.

7.3 Data

7.3.1 Sample of Calls

The sample consists of 107 convertible debt calls and 57 convertible preferred stock calls from the period 1962–78.[6] Each call announcement is reported in the *Wall Street Journal*, and no other firm-specific news, related or unrelated to the call announcement, is revealed by the *Wall*

Street Journal Index or the cited call announcement article. In every case, the conversion value exceeded the call price at the time of the call announcement. In addition, all of the firms were listed on the New York or American Stock Exchange at the time of the announcement. Summary statistics of the convertible security calls are discussed in the following section.

7.3.2   Empirical Proxies for the Possible Determinants of Changes in Stockholders' Wealth

The Relative Price Change at Announcement. An estimate of a 2-day announcement period risk-adjusted common stock return is the empirical measure of the stock price impact of a call announcement. Risk-adjusted returns (AR_{jt}) for firm j equal the difference between the unadjusted stock returns (R_{jt}) and expected returns derived from firm j's market model. That is, on day t

(11) $$AR_{jt} = R_{jt} - (\hat{b}_0 + \hat{b}_1 R_{Mt}),$$

where $\hat{b}_0$ and $\hat{b}_1$ are coefficient estimates of the linear relationship between firm j's daily stock returns taken from the Daily Returns File gathered by the Center for Research in Security Prices of the University of Chicago (CRSP) and the daily returns of the CRSP Value-weighted Index (R_{Mt}).[7] The period used to estimate the parameters b_0 and b_1 begins 61 trading days following the date of the call announcement and ends 200 trading days following the announcement date.[8]

Table 7.1 presents average adjusted common stock returns for 21 trading days centered on the date of the initial published report of the call announcement (day 0). Column 1 presents the trading day relative to day 0. For the sample of convertible debt calls, the average adjusted daily returns are presented in column 2 and the percentage of positive adjusted returns is presented in column 3. For the sample of convertible preferred stock calls, the average adjusted returns and the percentage of positive adjusted returns are presented in columns 4 and 5, respectively.

The stock price response to the announcements of convertible debt calls appears to be confined primarily to trading days -1 and 0. For the sample of convertible debt calls, the average adjusted returns on days -1 and 0 are large in absolute value relative to any of the surrounding trading days. In addition, the relatively low percentage of positive adjusted returns on days -1 and 0 also implies an impact confined to these days. Furthermore, over trading days $+11$ through $+60$ no statistically significant average adjusted returns are observed.

For the convertible preferred stock calls, no dramatic stock price impact is observed on any day around day 0. However, on day -1 only 18 of 57 adjusted returns are positive, which suggests a possible stock price impact on day -1. The percentages of positive returns in column 5

Table 7.1   **Adjusted Daily Common Stock Returns**[a] **for 21 Trading Days around the Date of the Earliest Published Report (Trading Day 0) of Convertible Debt Calls (107 Events) and Convertible Preferred Stock Calls (57 Events)**

Trading Day (1)	Convertible Debt Calls		Convertible Preferred Stock Calls	
	Average Adjusted Return (%) (2)	Proportion of Positive Returns (3)	Average Adjusted Return (%) (4)	Proportion of Positive Returns (5)
−10	.15	.47	.59	.63
−9	.10	.44	−.27	.42
−8	.13	.48	.23	.65
−7	−.19	.43	−.43	.44
−6	−.15	.46	−.15	.47
−5	.08	.48	−.08	.44
−4	.29	.56	.01	.51
−3	.02	.46	.20	.51
−2	.03	.51	.30	.56
−1	−.92	.35	−.22	.32
0[b]	−1.23	.30	−.21	.44
1	−.05	.47	.00	.60
2	−.20	.43	−.04	.53
3	−.04	.47	−.02	.51
4	−.27	.43	.60	.47
5	−.15	.48	−.08	.44
6	.10	.50	.45	.61
7	.16	.46	−.23	.40
8	.36	.52	−.08	.51
9	−.13	.40	−.04	.47
10	−.29	.41	−.12	.44

[a]Adjustment is the difference between raw daily stock returns and returns predicted by the firm's market model. The estimate of the market model is based on the firm's raw daily returns and the CRSP Value Weighted Index returns from trading days +61 through +200.
[b]Date of the earliest published report of the call announcement in the *Wall Street Journal*.

provide no evidence of a price impact on any other day nearby trading day 0. Based primarily on the returns data for convertible debt calls, the announcement period adjusted return for preferred stock calls is also measured over trading days −1 and 0.[9]

The first row of panels A and B of table 7.2 presents summary statistics of the 2-day announcement period adjusted returns (AR_{2a}) for the samples of convertible calls. The mean 2-day adjusted return is −2.21% for the convertible debt calls (row 1, panel A) and is −.44% for the convertible preferred stock calls (row 1, panel B). The standard deviation and range of AR_{2a} are not markedly different between the two samples of calls, but the hypothesis that the mean 2-day announcement period returns of the samples are equal is rejected at the .01 level. For the convertible debt calls, the hypothesis that the mean 2-day announcement period return equals zero is rejected at the .01 level, but this hypothesis is not rejected at .10 level for the convertible preferred stock calls. These data imply a differential average impact of convertible debt and convertible preferred stock calls on common stockholders' wealth. In the course of data collection, however, no potentially relevant differences were observed between the timing or content of convertible debt and convertible preferred stock call announcements that might explain the different average announcement period returns.

Change in Interest Expense Tax Deductions. Three estimates of the reduction in interest expense tax shields are computed. The estimates are based on different assumptions about the market's view of the permanence or duration of the reduction in interest expense tax shields. The assumptions range from the expectation of a 1-year decrease to a permanent decrease in interest expense tax shields. No attempt has been made to estimate the calling firm's effective marginal tax rates at the time of the call announcements. For all three measures of the reduction in interest expense tax shields, the calling firm's effective marginal tax rate is assumed to equal .48.

The first estimate of the reduction in tax shields (TD) is the product of the tax rate and the total face value of the called debt. This measure presumes that removal of the debt portion of the called debt claims is a permanent reduction in the amount of debt outstanding. Thus, TD estimates the present value of a perpetual stream of interest expense tax shields.

The second measure is the amount of annual interest expense tax deductions (TI) provided by the called debt. This estimate equals the product of the tax rate and the amount of annual interest payments of the called debt issue. The assumption underlying this measure is that the call of debt is viewed as only temporarily reducing the amount of available interest expense tax deductions. That is, the expected reduction in the firm's cash flows equals the value of one year's interest expense deductions.

The third measure is the product of the corporate tax rate and an estimate of the present value of the remaining interest expenses of the called debt ($TPVI$). The remaining interest payments are discounted by the yield to maturity for corporate debt with a comparable *Moody's* quality rating at the time of the call announcement. An implicit assumption of this measure is that the expected duration of the reduction in interest expense tax shields equals the time remaining to maturity at the time of call announcement. Thus, the expected duration of the decrease in interest expense deductions implied by this measure is less than for the estimate *TD* but greater than for the estimate *TPVI*.

Summary statistics for the three measures of the change in interest expense tax deductions are presented in rows 2, 3, and 4 of panel A of table 7.2. Each of the tax variables shown in table 7.2 is measured relative to the market value of common stock (V_{CS}) prior to the call announcement. Data on the terms of the called debt issue and the number of shares outstanding are obtained from *Moody's* manuals and the *Wall Street Journal*. The common stock prices are taken from the *Commercial and Financial Chronicle* or the *Wall Street Journal*. The mean value of the estimate of the reduction in interest expense tax shields divided by the market value of common stock is $-.035$ for TD/V_{CS}, $-.016$ for $TPVI/V_{CS}$, and $-.002$ for TI/V_{CS}.

Change in the Value of Senior Securities. In general, a substantial portion of a firm's senior securities, that is, debt and preferred stock, are either privately held or publicly held and traded infrequently.[10] Unlike common stock, therefore, it is not possible to obtain a direct measure of the impact of a call announcement on the total value of senior securities. Instead, a proxy for the impact of wealth redistribution among classes of securityholders is used.

For a call of convertible debt, the change in the value of debt securities that remain outstanding following the call (ΔV_D) is assumed to depend on the amount of debt called (ΔD) and the amount of debt relative to common stock outstanding after the call (D/V_{CS}). A general form specification is

$$(12) \qquad \Delta V_D = h(\Delta D, D/V_{CS}),$$

where $h_1 > 0$ and $h_2 > 0$. That is, the change in the value of outstanding debt is greater, the larger the amount of debt called and the greater the ratio of debt to common stock outstanding after the call. Similarly, the impact on the value of outstanding preferred stock (ΔV_{PS}) is assumed to be a function of the amount of debt called (ΔD) and the amount of preferred stock relative to common stock (PS/V_{CS}) outstanding following the call. That is,

$$(13) \qquad \Delta V_{PS} = k(\Delta D, PS/V_{CS}),$$

where $k_1 > 0$ and $k_2 > 0$.

The intuition for the hypothesized signs of h_1 and k_1 is that for a given amount of outstanding debt or preferred stock, the greater the amount of debt claims retired, the greater is the increase in the relative priority of the remaining debt and preferred stock claims. Thus, the greater is the impact on the values of outstanding debt and preferred stock. The positive signs predicted for h_2 and k_2 reflect that for a given amount of debt claims retired, the total dollar wealth redistribution from common stockholders is expected to be larger, the greater is the relative amount of debt or preferred stock claims that remain outstanding after the call.

For a call of convertible preferred stock, it is assumed that only the relative priority of outstanding preferred stock claims is affected. The general form expression for the impact on the value of preferred stock (ΔV_{PS}) is

$$(14) \qquad \Delta V_{PS} = \ell\,(\Delta PS,\ PS/V_{CS})\,,$$

where ΔPS is the amount of preferred stock called and PS/V_{CS} is the relative amounts of preferred stock and common stock outstanding following the call. Based on the same intuition presented for expressions (12) and (13), ℓ_1 and ℓ_2 are hypothesized to be positive.

Various specifications of $h(\cdot)$, $k\,(\cdot)$, and $\ell(\cdot)$ are employed in the estimation of the cross-sectional relationship given by (10). For all of the specifications, the amount of debt called (ΔD) equals the total face value of the called debt and the amount of preferred stock called (ΔPS) equals the total liquidation value of the called preferred stock. The amounts of preferred stock (PS) and long-term debt (D) that remain outstanding after the call are also measured by the total liquidation value and total face value, respectively. All of these data are obtained from *Moody's* manuals.

For the sample of convertible debt calls, row 5 of panel A in table 7.2 presents summary statistics for the change in the amount of debt outstanding as measured by the ratio of the total face value of the called debt to the market value of common stock (FV_{CD}/V_{CS}). The mean ratio is $-.073$. Rows 6 and 7 present summary statistics for the total face value and total liquidation value of remaining long-term debt and preferred stock, respectively, divided by the market value of common stock. The mean value of D/V_{CS} is .400 and the mean value of PS/V_{CS} is .067. Row 2 of panel B gives summary data on the change in the amount of preferred stock outstanding as measured by the ratio of the liquidation value of called preferred stock relative to the market value of common stock. The mean value of LV_{PS}/V_{CS} is $-.081$. Data on the liquidation value of preferred stock outstanding following the call relative to the market value of common stock is presented in row 3 of panel B. The mean ratio of PS/V_{CS} for preferred stock calls is .049.

Reduction in Conversion Premium. For only 77 of 107 convertible debt calls and 46 of 57 convertible preferred stock calls, a market value of the called securities can be measured within the 2 weeks immediately preceding the call announcement. Rows 8, 9, and 10 of panel A of table 7.2 present the following summary statistics for these 77 convertible debt calls: (1) the ratio of the total value of the called debt (adjusted for

Table 7.2 Summary Statistics of Empirical Proxies for the Abnormal Common Stock Price Change and the Possible Determinants of the Change in Stockholders' Wealth Associated with Convertible Debt and Convertible Preferred Stock Call Announcements

Empirical Measure* (1)	Mean (2)	Median (3)	Standard Deviation (4)	Maximum Value (5)	Minimum Value (6)	Number of Calls (7)
A. Convertible Debt Calls						
(1) AR_{2a}	−.022	−.022	.037	.133	−.107	107
(2) TD/V_{CS}†	−.035	−.029	.028	−.000	−.100	107
(3) TI/V_{CS}†	−.002	−.001	.002	−.000	−.011	107
(4) $TPVI/V_{CS}$†	−.016	−.012	.017	−.000	−.139	107
(5) FV_{CD}/V_{CS}	−.073	−.060	.058	−.001	−.289	107
(6) D/V_{CS}	.400	.209	.726	6.514	.000	107
(7) PS/V_{CS}	.067	.000	.182	1.163	.000	107
(8) $V_{CD}/\alpha V_{CS}$	1.018	1.005	.044	1.217	.953	77
(9) V_{CD}/FV_{CD}	1.628	1.439	.546	3.883	1.094	77
(10) $(V_{CD} - \alpha V_{CS})/V_{CS}$	.002	.001	.005	.017	−.011	77
(11) α	.138	.092	.136	.747	.001	107
(12) $\Delta EPS/EPS$	−.082	−.064	.144	.191	−1.243	107
B. Convertible Preferred Stock Calls						
(1) AR_{2a}	−.004	−.006	.042	.189	−.091	57
(2) LV_{PS}/V_{CS}†	−.081	−.062	.085	−.000	−.425	57
(3) PS/V_{CS}	.049	.000	.103	.531	.000	57
(4) $V_{PS}/\alpha V_{CS}$	1.007	1.008	.028	1.082	.959	46
(5) V_{PS}/C_{PS}	1.597	1.344	.910	6.300	1.042	46
(6) $(V_{PS} - \sigma V_{CS})/V_{CS}$	.000	.000	.004	.014	−.013	46
(7) α	.136	.100	.134	.669	.014	57
(8) $\Delta EPS/EPS$	−.053	−.060	.082	.369	−.230	57

accrued interest) to the total conversion value of the called debt ($V_{CD}/\alpha V_{CS}$),[11] where both value estimates come from the same trading day, (2) the ratio of the total market value of the called debt to its aggregate face value (V_{CD}/FV_{CD}), and (3) the total dollar conversion premium, derived from V_{CD} and αV_{CS}, divided by the market value of common stock $[(V_{CD} - \alpha V_{CS})/V_{CS}]$.

Corresponding measures for the calls of convertible preferred stock are presented in rows 4, 5, and 6 of panel B of table 7.2. Summary data on the total market value of the called preferred stock divided by the aggregate conversion value of the preferred stock ($V_{PS}/\alpha V_{CS}$), measured from the same trading day, is reported in row 4. The ratio of the value of the called securities to the aggregate call value (V_{PS}/C_{PS}) is summarized in row 5. Data on the total dollar conversion premium divided by the market value of common stock $[(V_{PS} - \alpha V_{CS})/V_{CS}]$ is reported in row 6.

For each firm, the values of the common stock and the callable convertible security are based on price quotations reported in the *Commercial and Financial Chronicle* or the *Wall Street Journal* for the same day of trading. The terms of the conversion privileges and the call provisions are identified in *Moody's* manuals and the *Wall Street Journal*.

The mean ratio of market value to conversion value of the called securities equals 1.018 for the convertible debt calls and equals 1.007 for the convertible preferred stock calls.[12] These mean ratios are each significantly different from 1.0 at the .05 level. Measured within the 2 weeks

---

Notes to Table 7.2

*Variable definitions are presented below.

†These variables have negative values since they measure a decrease in tax shields or a reduction in claims outstanding.

Variables:

AR_{2a}	= 2-day announcement period adjusted common stock return.
V_{CS}	= market value of common stock prior to the call announcement.
TD	= tax rate (.48) multiplied by the face value of the called debt.
TI	= tax rate (.48) multiplied by annual interest payments of the called debt.
$TPVI$	= tax rate (.48) multiplied by estimate of the present value of remaining interest payments of the called debt.
FV_{CD}	= face value of the called debt.
D	= face value of long-term debt outstanding after the call.
PS	= liquidation value of preferred stock outstanding after the call.
V_{CD}	= market value of called debt plus accrued interest prior to the call announcement.
αV_{CS}	= conversion value of called securities prior to the call announcement.
α	= relative increase in shares outstanding due to conversion of the called debt.
$\Delta EPS/EPS$	= relative change in earnings per share due solely to the call and conversion of convertible securities.
LV_{PS}	= liquidation value of called preferred stock.
V_{PS}	= market value of called preferred stock prior to the call announcement.
C_{PS}	= aggregate call value of called preferred stock.

just prior to call announcement, the average ratio of conversion value to face value of the called debt securities equals 1.628. The mean ratio of conversion value to call payment value equals 1.597 for the convertible preferred stock sample. As a proportion of the market value of common stock, the average conversion premium is .0019 for convertible debt calls and is .0001 for convertible preferred stock calls.

Based on these sample means, convertible debt and preferred stock call policies appear to occur at similar times, as measured by the ratio of market value to face value or call payment value of the called securities. In addition, just prior to call announcements, both types of securities are priced at similar premiums relative to conversion value.[13]

Increase in Shares Outstanding. The measure of the relative increase in the number of common shares outstanding (α) equals the number of shares issued on conversion divided by the number of shares outstanding prior to the call announcement. Data on shares outstanding and the conversion terms of the called securities were collected from *Moody's* manuals and the *Wall Street Journal.*[14]

The mean relative increase in shares outstanding is .138 for the convertible debt sample (row 11, panel A) and .136 for the convertible preferred stock sample (row 7, panel B). The summary statistics indicate that the distributions of α for the two samples are quite similar.

Change in Earnings per Share. The variable $\Delta EPS/EPS$ measures the relative change in earnings per share due to conversion of the called securities. That is, holding total earnings before interest and taxes constant, $\Delta EPS/EPS$ measures only the effects of (1) an increase in the number of shares outstanding and (2) a reduction in after-tax interest expenses or preferred dividends.[15] Thus, ΔEPS does not measure any change in earnings observed over time. The mean values of $\Delta EPS/EPS$ are $-.082$ and $-.053$ for the convertible debt (row 12, panel A) and convertible preferred stock (row 8, panel B) samples, respectively. The earnings, interest payment, and preferred dividend data used to calculate $\Delta EPS/EPS$ are obtained from *Moody's* manuals.

Based on the summary statistics presented in table 7.2, the samples of convertible debt and convertible preferred stock calls are quite similar. The most apparent differences are associated with the average 2-day stock return (AR_{2a}) and the corporate tax variables. Since no other potentially important differences have been uncovered, a preliminary conclusion is that the decrease in interest expense tax deductions, or an associated factor, explains the larger negative average stock return at the announcements of convertible debt calls.

7.3.3   Specification of the Estimated Cross-sectional Relationship

Various specifications of the following linear regression model are estimated for the sample of convertible security calls:

(15) $A\tilde{R}_{2a} = b_0 + b_1 \left[TD / (1 + \alpha) V_{CS} \right]$
$+ b_2 \left[h(\Delta D, D / V_{CS}) / (1 + \alpha) V_{CS} \right]$
$+ b_3 \left[k(\Delta D, PS / V_{CS}) / (1 + \alpha) V_{CS} \right]$
$+ b_4 \left[\ell(\Delta PS, PS / V_{CS}) / (1 + \alpha) V_{CS} \right]$
$+ b_5 \left[V_{CD} - \alpha V_{CS} \right] / (1 + \alpha) V_{CS}]$
$+ b_6 \left[f(\alpha) \right] + b_7 \left[\Delta EPS / EPS \right] + \tilde{u} .$

In (15), the empirical proxies discussed in this section are substituted for the variables in the cross-sectional relationship specified by (10), and u represents a random error term that has a zero mean. The measures TI and $TPVI$ are substitute measures for TD, the change in interest expense tax shields. For four terms in (15), a general form is given for the relationship between $A R_{2a}$ and the proxy for a potential determinant of the announcement period stock return. As reported in the next section, several specifications of these terms are examined in estimating the cross-sectional relationship.

For each of the potential effects, the null hypothesis tested is that the coefficient of the corresponding independent variable in (15) equals zero. A positive value of $\hat{b}_1$ is consistent with a valuation effect associated with the corporate tax variable. Defining $h(\cdot)$, $k(\cdot)$, and $\ell(\cdot)$ to have non-negative values, negative values of $\hat{b}_2$, $\hat{b}_3$, and $\hat{b}_4$ are consistent with wealth redistribution from common stockholders to more senior security-holders. Negative values for $\hat{b}_2$ and $\hat{b}_3$ are consistent with wealth transfers to debtholders and preferred stockholders, respectively, for calls of convertible debt. A negative value of $\hat{b}_4$ is consistent with a wealth transfer to preferred stockholders for calls of convertible preferred stock. A positive value of $\hat{b}_5$ is consistent with a wealth transfer from the called convertible securityholders to common stockholders. A negative value of $\hat{b}_6$ is consistent with a supply effect, and a positive value of $\hat{b}_7$ is consistent with an earnings per share dilution effect.

7.4   Estimates of the Cross-sectional Relationship

Estimates of the relationship given by (15) are presented in this section. The cross-sectional relationship is estimated using different measures of the change in interest expense tax deductions and using different specifications of the variables expressed in a general form in (15). The cross-sectional relationship is also estimated for several subsets of the calls.

7.4.1   Total Sample of Convertible Debt and Convertible Preferred Stock Calls

Initially, ordinary least squares (OLS) estimates of the cross-sectional relationship given by (16) are analyzed:

$$
(16) \qquad A\tilde{R}_{2a} = b_0 + b_1 \{TD/(1 + \alpha)V_{CS}\}
$$
$$
+ b_2 \{[\Delta D(D/V_{CS})]/(1 + \alpha)V_{CS}\}
$$
$$
+ b_3 \{[\Delta D(PS/V_{CS})]/(1 + \alpha)V_{CS}\}
$$
$$
+ b_4 \{[\Delta P(PS/V_{CS})]/(1 + \alpha)V_{CS}\}
$$
$$
+ b_5 \{\alpha\} + b_6 \{\Delta EPS/EPS\} + \tilde{u} .
$$

The joint hypothesis that the coefficients of (16) equal zero is rejected at the .05 level. However, only the t-value for the coefficient of the interest expense tax deductions variable (b_1) is significant at the .05 level.

Given that the variance of common stock returns is not constant across firms, there is reason to suspect that the error term of the regression model is not homoscedastic. Tests on the residuals of the OLS estimates of (16) indicate that the variance of the error term is positively related to the standard deviation of the 2-day adjusted stock returns.[16] Thus, statistical inferences based on the OLS results are possibly incorrect and the OLS estimates are not presented in detail.

No evidence is found that suggests a relationship between the values of any independent variable in (16) and the variance of the error term. Therefore, in order to correct for heteroscedasticity, each 2-day adjusted announcement period stock return (AR_{2a}) is divided by an estimate of the standard deviation $(\hat{\sigma})$ of the calling firm's 2-day adjusted stock returns. That is, standardized risk-adjusted announcement period returns $(AR_{2a}/\hat{\sigma})$ are regressed on the independent variables of (16).[17] Tests of the residuals of the OLS estimates of the model with standardized adjusted returns uncover no evidence of heteroscedasticity in the error term. Therefore, all of the regression estimates presented in this section are based on a dependent variable that is a standardized two-day return.

Table 7.3 presents OLS estimates of the cross-sectional relationship where the dependent variable is a standardized common stock return. The first three rows contain coefficient estimates of specifications that differ only in terms of the measure of the change in interest expense tax shields. In all three cases, however, the joint hypothesis that the coefficients equal zero cannot be rejected at the .10 level.

The remaining results presented in table 7.3 are estimates for the relationship between the standardized returns and the variable(s) that

Table 7.3 Ordinary Least Squares Estimates of the Linear Relationship between the Standardized 2-Day Adjusted Common Stock Returns and Possible Determinants of Changes in Stockholders' Wealth at the Announcements of Convertible Debt and Convertible Preferred Stock Calls (164 Observations, t-statistics in Parentheses)

	Constant	$\dfrac{TD}{(1+\alpha)V_{cs}}$	$\dfrac{TI}{(1+\alpha)V_{cs}}$	$\dfrac{TPVI}{(1+\alpha)V_{cs}}$	$\dfrac{\Delta D(D/V_{cs})}{(1+\alpha)V_{cs}}$	$\dfrac{\Delta D(PS/V_{cs})}{(1+\alpha)V_{cs}}$	$\dfrac{\Delta PS(PS/V_{cs})}{(1+\alpha)V_{cs}}$	α	$\Delta EPS/EPS$	Adjusted R^2	F-Value
				Independent Variables							
(1)	−.380* (−2.30)	14.756* (2.25)			−2.211 (−.88)	−.290 (−.03)	−10.040 (−.64)	.283 (.28)	−.964 (−.64)	.057	1.57
(2)	−.437** (−2.69)		182.184 (1.62)		−1.775 (−.67)	−.616 (−.07)	−7.034 (−.45)	.177 (.17)	−.637 (−.42)	.042	1.16
(3)	−.488** (−2.78)			21.021 (1.56)	−1.885 (−.70)	−.710 (−.08)	−6.533 (−.42)	.237 (.22)	−.453 (−.29)	.041	1.12
(4)	−.340** (−2.40)	14.544** (2.90)								.050	8.43**
(5)	−.401** (−2.96)		199.037** (2.55)							.039	6.48**
(6)	−.414** (−3.09)			23.563** (2.45)						.036	6.01**
(7)	−.583** (−5.28)				−.312 (−1.20)	−9.501 (−1.16)	.583 (.02)			.019	1.05
(8)	−.488** (−3.17)							−.927 (−1.16)		.008	1.34
(9)	−.538** (−4.34)								1.081 (1.26)	.010	1.60

*Significant at the .05 level (one-tailed test).   **Significant at the .01 level (one-tailed test).

represents a particular potential determinant of the stock price response. Rows 4, 5, and 6 present the estimates for the simple regression of the standardized return on a measure of the change in interest expense tax shields. In each case, the t-value of the estimated coefficient is significant at the .01 level, and the sign of the estimated coefficient is consistent with a corporate tax effect. Row 7 presents the estimates of the relationship between the standardized 2-day common stock return and the variables that measure the possible effects of wealth redistribution. The F-statistic for the regression is not significant at .10 level. The last two rows present the estimates of simple regressions where the independent variable is the measure of the relative increase in shares outstanding (row 8) or the measure of the change in earnings per share (row 9). The t-statistic of the estimated coefficient is not significant at the .10 level for both regressions. The estimated coefficient of $\Delta EPS / EPS$ also is not statistically significant for the subset of 142 calls that were associated with a decrease in earnings per share, that is, $\Delta EPS < 0$.

The results presented in table 7.3 only provide support for a price effect associated with the measure of the change in interest expense tax deductions. For all three measures of interest expense tax shields, the estimates of the simple regression suggest that larger decreases in interest expense tax deductions are associated with larger negative announcement period stock returns. The results do not reveal valuation effects on common stock that are attributable to wealth redistribution from common stockholders to preferred stockholders or debtholders. In addition, the evidence does not support a supply effect or an earnings per share dilution effect on share price.

Estimation of several alternative specifications of the cross-sectional relationship confirms the results reported in table 8.3. For example, no significant nonlinear relationship is found between the standardized common stock returns and the values of α or $\Delta EPS / EPS$. Four specifications of each of the variables that measure the impact of calls on the value of debt and preferred stock are also examined.[18]. In only one instance, for the variable that measures the impact of convertible debt calls on outstanding preferred stock, is the t-value of an estimated coefficient significant at the .05 level. The results presented in table 7.3, therefore, are generally supported by the estimates of alternative specifications of the model.

7.4.2   Subsets of the Calls Sample

Calls Associated with a Negative Stock Price Reaction. Each of the independent variables in the cross-sectional relationships reported in table 7.3 is a potential determinant of a negative share price response to a call announcement. None of the coefficients implies a positive price change. Therefore, a relevant determinant of the stock price response may be missing from the model, especially for the calls associated with a positive stock price response. In addition, a positive stock price response may reflect a prior release of news of the call or it may reflect an accurate prediction of the timing of the call by the market. If either of these problems exists, the tests on the full sample of calls are likely biased against rejecting the hypothesis of no price impact for each of the possible determinants. Furthermore, a test of the residuals of the OLS estimates rejects the hypothesis that the subsample of calls with positive stock price responses and the subsample with negative stock price responses are described by the same cross-sectional model.[19] For these reasons, the cross-sectional relationship is estimated for the sample of calls with a negative announcement period adjusted stock return.

Estimated coefficients for the subset of calls with a negative announcement price response are reported in (17).

$$(17) \qquad [AR_{2a}/\hat{\sigma}_{AR}] = -1.043 + 8.76\{TD/(1+\alpha)V_{CS}\}$$
$$(-8.03) \quad (1.69)$$
$$-1.265\{[\Delta D(D/V_{CS})]/(1+\alpha)V_{CS}\}$$
$$(-.67)$$
$$-11.578\{[\Delta D(PS/V_{CS})]/(1+\alpha)V_{CS}\}$$
$$(-1.78)$$
$$+3.602\{[\Delta P(PS/V_{CS})]/(1+\alpha)V_{CS}\}$$
$$(.35)$$
$$-.243\{\alpha\} - .729\{\Delta EPS/EPS\}$$
$$(-.29) \quad (-.58)$$
$$R^2(\text{adj.}) = .121, \ F = 2.45.$$

For this subsample of 114 calls, the results are generally consistent with the results for the full sample of calls. That is, the coefficient for the variable that measures the change in interest expense tax deductions is significant at the .05 level for a one-tailed test. In addition, no significant t-values (presented in parentheses) are associated with the estimated coefficients of variables that measure the relative increase in the number of shares outstanding or the change in earnings per share. Thus, even when only calls with negative stock price responses are examined, which induces a bias against the null hypothesis of no significant relationship, no support is found for a supply effect or an earnings dilution effect.[20] However, the coefficient of the variable that represents wealth redistribution from common stockholders to preferred stockholders due to calls of convertible debt is significant at the .05 level. The coefficients of the other two wealth redistribution variables are not significant at the .10 level.

Calls with Conversion Premium Data. Within 2 weeks preceding the call announcement, a published price quotation for the called security is found for 123 of the 164 calls. These price data are useful for two reasons. First, an estimate of the difference between the market value and the conversion value of the called security, that is, a conversion premium, can be derived from the prices of the convertible security and the common stock. The total conversion premium of the called security, measured before the call announcement, represents a potential wealth transfer from convertible securityholders to common stockholders. Second, to some extent the size of a conversion premium reflects the market's expectations about the timing of a call announcement. Estimates of conversion premiums, therefore, may be helpful in identifying call announcements that were a greater surprise to the market. Analysis of calls associated with larger pre-announcement conversion premiums can provide a stronger test of the potential determinants of stock price responses to call announcements.

For the sample of 123 calls with conversion premium data, the regressions reported in rows 1, 2, and 3 of table 7.3 are augumented to include a variable that measures the total conversion premium of the called securities $[(V_{CD} - \alpha V_{CS})/(1 + \alpha) \ V_{CS}]$. However, the *F*-statistics of these regressions are not significant at the .10 level.

Expressions (18) and (19) present the estimates of simpler versions of the cross-sectional relationship that include a variable for the conversion premium. In (18), the independent variables are measures of the effects due to a permanent change in interest expense tax shields $[TD/1 + \alpha)V_{CS}]$ and the potential wealth transfer from convertible securityholders $[(V_{CD} - \alpha V_{CS})/(1 + \alpha)V_{CS}]$. The *t*-statistics are in parentheses.

$$(18) \qquad [AR_{2a}/\hat{\sigma}_{AR}] = -.431 + 11.086[TD/(1 + \alpha)V_{CS}]$$
$$(-2.48) \quad (1.80)$$
$$-28.479[V_{CD} - \alpha V_{CS})/(1 + \alpha)V_{CS}],$$
$$(-.78)$$
$$R^2(\text{adj.}) = .041, \ F = 2.57.$$

The negative estimated coefficient for the variable that represents the conversion premium is not consistent with a wealth transfer from the called securityholders to stockholders. For the simple regression reported in (19), the coefficient of the conversion premium variable is again negative.

$$(19) \quad [AR_{2a}/\hat{\sigma}_{AR}] = -.636 - 47.849[(V_{CD} - \alpha V_{CS})/(1 + \alpha)V_{CS}]$$
$$(-4.78) \ (-1.36)$$
$$R^2(\text{adj.}) = .015, \ F = 1.85.$$

The failure to find evidence of a wealth transfer from convertible securityholders is not surprising, however, given the small estimated mean value of the conversion premiums and the apparent measurement error in the estimates of the conversion premiums, as indicated by the fact that 51 of the 123 estimates of the conversion premiums are negative.

The estimated coefficients of the cross-sectional relationship may depend on the accuracy of the market's expectation of the timing of call announcements. If calls with lower estimates of the pre-announcement conversion premiums represent calls that were more accurately anticipated, ceterius paribus the 2-day announcement period returns are closer to zero for these calls. As a result, more accurate anticipation of the timing of call announcements tends to induce a downward bias in the estimates of the coefficients of the variables that measure tax effects, wealth redistribution effects, supply effects, or earnings per share dilution effects.[21]

The possible effect of varying degrees of anticipation of call announcements is examined by estimating the cross-sectional relationship on subsamples of calls grouped by the sign of the estimated conversion premium. Table 7.4 presents estimates of cross-sectional regressions for two subsamples of calls. Panel A represents three sets of coefficient estimates for the 72 calls with positive conversion premiums and Panel B presents estimates for the 51 calls with negative conversion premiums.

The results presented in table 7.4 suggest that the estimates of the coefficients depend on the sign of the conversion premium. For example, the estimated coefficient of the tax variable $[TD/(1 + \alpha)V_{CS}]$ is greater for the sample of calls with positive conversion premiums (row 3) than for the sample of calls with negative conversion premiums (row 6). In addition, the coefficients for the wealth redistribution variables are all negative and one t-value is significant at .10 level for the sample calls with positive conversion premiums. This is consistent with a valuation effect of wealth redistribution. No significant t-values are found among the estimated coefficients for the sample of calls with negative estimated conversion premiums. It should also be noted that the unexplained variance of common stock returns, as indicated by R^2, is noticeably higher for the subsample of calls with negative conversion premiums.

But even though the regression results appear to depend on the degree of anticipation of calls, as measured by conversion premiums, the inferences drawn from the regressions presented in rows 1, 2, and 3 of table 7.4 are not markedly different from the inferences drawn from the results for the full sample of calls. The t-values for the estimated coefficients of variables that represent the possible effect of wealth redistribution are not significant at the .05 level. In addition, there is no evidence in table 7.4 that supports either a supply effect or an earnings dilution effect. And

Table 7.4 Ordinary Least Squares Estimates of the Cross-sectional Relationship between Standardized 2-Day Announcement Period Adjusted Common Stock Returns and Possible Determinants of the Returns for Subsamples of Convertible Security Calls Grouped by the Sign of the Estimated Pre-Announcement Conversion Premium (t-statistics in Parentheses)

	Constant	$\dfrac{TD}{(1+\alpha)V_{cs}}$	$\dfrac{\Delta D(D/V_{cs})}{(1+\alpha)V_{cs}}$	$\dfrac{\Delta D(PS/V_{cs})}{(1+\alpha)V_{cs}}$	$\dfrac{\Delta PS(PS/V_{cs})}{(1+\alpha)V_{cs}}$	α	ΔEPS	Adjusted R^2	F-Value
			Independent Variables						
			A. 72 Calls with Positive Estimated Conversion Premiums						
(1)	−.590* (−2.23)	3.428 (.34)	−5.484 (−1.49)	−16.761 (−1.50)	−6.340 (−.28)	−1.514 (−.93)	−3.338 (−1.31)	.115	1.43
(2)	−.741** (−4.04)		−1.972 (−1.14)	−17.374 (−1.60)	−1.726 (−.08)			.078	1.92
(3)	−.567* (−2.33)	13.022* (1.81)						.045	3.28*
			B. 51 Calls with Negative Estimated Conversion Premiums						
(4)	−.239 (−.67)	12.616 (.76)	6.493 (.61)	28.885 (.60)	−7.695 (−.31)	−.481 (−.27)	.669 (.29)	.060	.22
(5)	−.422* (−1.99)		.129 (.02)	23.536 (.52)	−6.431 (−.28)			.009	.15
(6)	−.350 (−1.40)	3.910 (.35)						.003	.12

*Significant at the .05 level (one-tailed test).
**Significant at the .01 level (one-tailed test).

like the results for the full sample, the results for the sample of calls with positive conversion premiums imply an impact on share price that is associated with the decrease in interest expense tax shields.

7.5   Interpretation of the Results

The principal finding of the cross-sectional analysis is a positive and statistically significant relationship between the announcement period adjusted stock returns and measures of the change in interest expense tax shields. One interpretation of this effect is that the negative stock price response reflects the expected reduction in the firm's after-tax cash flows due to a decrease in interest expense tax deductions. This interpretation is consistent with the finding of a significant negative average stock price reaction to convertible debt call announcements, but not to convertible preferred stock call announcements. This interpretation is troublesome, however, because it does not identify a benefit to securityholders of calling convertible securities, and it raises questions about whether managers' call decisions are in stockholders' interests.

A second interpretation attributes some part of the apparent tax effect to information about the calling firm's value that is implicitly conveyed by the call decision. This interpretation presumes that the capital market correctly believes that managers' call decisions are in the interests of stockholders and are in part based on information that is not reflected in security prices. Therefore, if the managers' assessment is that the net benefits of a call and conversion are positive and the decision to call is based on earnings prospects that are less favorable than those held by the capital market, a call decision may convey unfavorable information about the value of the firm. That is, a call announcement is associated with a negative stock price reaction, even though the call decision is a positive net present value decision based on managers' more complete information.

According to the second interpretation, the variable that measures the change in interest expense tax deductions may reflect both (1) a reduction in tax shields and (2) a reduction in firm value due to information conveyed by the call. For example, if the decision to call is motivated by a lowered assessment of the amount of interest expenses that can be supported by the firm's cash earnings and the capital market infers that motivation from the decision to call, the decrease in share price reflects both the reduction in interest expense tax shields and the expected decrease in cash earnings. In that case a relationship between the price response to call announcements and a measure of the reduction in interest expense tax deductions is consistent with theories that imply the optimal level of financial leverage depends on earnings coverage of interest payments and utilization of available interest expense tax deductions.

This study does not resolve to what extent the results reflect a corporate tax effect or an effect due to information conveyed about firm value. However, one piece of evidence supports an information effect. For the sample of 57 calls of convertible preferred stock, further investigation uncovers a significant relationship (at the .10 level) between the common stock returns at the announcements of preferred stock calls and the amount of preferred stock called, as measured by liquidation value.[22] That is, even for convertible securities that provide no corporate tax deductions, there is evidence that the stock price response to a call announcement depends on the size of the issue called. This finding also suggests that the larger negative stock price response to calls of convertible debt than to calls of convertible preferred stock may reflect the effect of a reduction in expected earnings that is reinforced by the effect of a reduction in interest expense tax deductions. But in the final analysis, whether the announcement period stock price responses reflect a downward revision in expected earnings is left as an open issue.[23]

The high frequency of estimates of negative conversion premiums just prior to the call announcement suggests that many calls are anticipated quite accurately. Therefore, the measured stock price responses in some cases appear to reflect only a small revision in the expected timing of a call. Furthermore, examination of the subset of calls with estimates of positive conversion premiums (table 7.4) indicates that the magnitude of the coefficient of the tax variable depends on the anticipation of the call announcement. Consequently, the entire valuation effect associated with the interest expense tax shields variable, that is, the price response that would be observed if the call announcement were a complete surprise, is probably larger than is suggested by the results presented in section 7.4.

Estimates of the conversion premium prior to the call announcement also indicate that on average the potential wealth transfer from convertible securityholders is small relative to the market value of common stock. Within 2 weeks preceding the call announcement, the average total dollar conversion premium equals $591,000, or 0.1% of the market value of common stock. In addition, a wealth transfer from the called securityholders is not found to be a significant explanatory variable for the stock price responses to convertible security calls. Thus, the potential wealth transfer from convertible securityholders does not appear to be an important motivation for call decisions.

The results also do not provide strong support for a stock price impact attributable to changes in the relative priority of debt and preferred stock that remain outstanding following a call. Since convertible debt typically is a subordinated debt claim, the shifts in the relative priority of debt claims are probably minor. Therefore, it is not surprising that wealth transfers to debtholders are not detected. For outstanding preferred stock, conversion of debt to common stock replaces a higher priority claim with a lower priority claim. Thus, the impact on the relative priority of preferred stock is clearer. Some evidence reported in section 7.4 (see notes 20 and 22) is consistent with a positive effect on the value of preferred stock. The results for the sample of calls with negative stock price responses (expression [17]) and for the sample of calls with positive conversion premiums (panel A, table 7.4) also provide some support a valuation effect on common stock due to a wealth transfer to preferred stockholders. However, direct measurement of preferred stock price responses for a subsample of announcements of convertible debt calls does not uncover any price changes that are consistent with a wealth transfer to preferred stockholders.[24] Thus, the results provide some support, but not strong support, for a valuation effect attributable to wealth redistribution to preferred stockholders.

Finally, there is no evidence of price responses to convertible security call announcements that are attributable to an increase in the number of shares outstanding. The announcement period adjusted stock returns are not related cross-sectionally to the relative increases in number of shares outstanding that result from the call of convertible securities. This does not support the notion of a supply effect on share prices. In addition, the relationship between the common stock returns and the effect of the convertible security calls on earnings per share is not statistically significant. Contrary to arguments commonly presented by practioners, the evidence does not support a price effect due to a change in earnings per share.

7.6 Summary and Conclusions

This study investigates possible determinants of stock price reactions to announcements of capital structure changes. Specifically, the study presents estimates of the cross-sectional relationship between risk-adjusted common stock returns at the announcements of convertible security calls that force conversion and variables that represent potential determinants of the valuation effects of call announcements. The variables include proxies for (1) the change in interest expense tax shields, (2) the change in the relative priority of outstanding securities, (3) the wealth transfer from the holders of called convertible securities, and (4) the increase in the number of shares outstanding.

Estimation of a cross-sectional regression model provides evidence that the stock price responses to convertible security call announcements are related to measures of the decrease in interest expense tax deductions. The results, however, do not resolve to what extent this finding reflects a valuation effect due to corporate taxes per se versus a valuation effect due to information conveyed by call announcements. Weak evidence consistent with a price effect due to wealth redistribution from common stockholders to preferred stockholders is also found. The potential stock price effects of an increase in the number of shares outstanding are not supported by the results.

Evidence of price effects related to a measure of the change in interest expense tax deductions is consistent with the results of a similar study. Masulis's (1983) cross-sectional study of both leverage-increasing and leverage-decreasing intrafirm exchange offers also reports a positive statistically significant relationship between announcement period common stock returns and a measure of the change in interest expense tax shields. And he also interprets his results as being consistent with an information effect. In view of Masulis's findings, the results presented in this study of convertible security calls appear to reflect a general pattern in stock price responses to capital structure changes. However, a complete explanation of the motivation for capital structure changes requires a better understanding of managers' incentives to make capital structure decisions that convey unfavorable information about the value of the firm.

Notes

1. This study does not address the interesting question of why the calling firms issued convertible securities. The only rationale for the issuance of convertible securities that is accepted generally among financial economists is that debt or preferred stock with conversion privileges reduces costs associated with conflicts of interest between common stockholders and more senior securityholders (e.g., see Smith and Warner 1979). At this time, however, there is no strong empirical support for this rationale. The results of this study of convertible security calls, therefore, must be interpreted subject to not fully understanding the motivation for the issuance of convertible securities.

2. Call announcements are not likely completely unanticipated, since calls of convertible securities are not uncommon events. Prior to a call announcement, a firm's stock price reflects both the probability of a call and the expected timing of a call. Thus, the stock price response to a call announcement reflects only the revisions in the probability and expected timing of a call. The importance of anticipation of call announcements is examined in sec. 7.4.2.

3. Smith and Warner (1979) discuss the notion that the issuance of debt with conversion privileges mitigates the asset substitution incentive engendered by the issuance of debt claims. Consequently, the call and conversion of convertible debt may be expected to exacerbate this incentive and reduce the value of outstanding debt. However, Mikkelson (1981) reports a positive, but statistically insignificant, return for straight debt during the week of a call announcement. If there is any price impact on the value of outstanding debt, a shift in the relative priority of outstanding claims appears to be the dominant effect on the value of senior securities.

4. A nonzero probability of the conversion value being less than the face value of the convertible debt prior to the expected expiration date of the conversion privileges implies $V_{CD} > \alpha V_{CS}$.

5. The notion of an earnings per share dilution effect on share price is not rigorously developed in theory. Several corporate finance testbooks, however, present an alternative to the Modigliani and Miller (1958) theory that implies a valuation effect of changes in capital structure per se. Weston and Brigham (1978), for example, present the "net income approach" to valuation of a levered firm that assumes the required return on common stock is independent of financial leverage and implies reductions in leverage decrease shareholders' wealth. In the spirit of this valuation approach, an earnings dilution effect is specified under the assumption that the firm P/E ratio is unaffected by a call of convertible securities and a reduction in leverage. That is, before the call and conversion share price is $P = (c)(EPS)$ and after the conversion share price is $P' = (c)(EPS')$, where c is a constant. Earnings per share before and after the conversion are represented by EPS and EPS', respectively. Thus, the potential earnings per share dilution effect is specified as

$$(P' - P)/P = (EPS' - EPS)/EPS = \Delta EPS/EPS.$$

6. The sample of calls is derived from the sample formed for the time-series study of security returns reported in Mikkelson (1981). Six calls are excluded from this study because of the unavailability of financial data or stock return data following the call announcement.

7. In order to mitigate the bias in the OLS estimates of the market model due to nonsynchronous trading of securities (see Scholes and Williams 1977), the estimate of b_1 is derived from OLS estimates of the coefficients of R_{jt} regressed on R_{mt-1}, R_{mt}, and R_{mt+1}.

8. There are two reasons for using returns following the call announcement to estimate each firm's market model. First, calls typically are announced following a period of generally positive risk-adjusted returns. These returns impart an upward bias to the estimation of the parameters of the market model. Second, to some degree, if not completely, the decrease in systematic risk of common stock due to conversion and a reduction in financial leverage occurs on the call announcement date. Post-announcement returns should provide estimates of the market model coefficients that more accurately reflect the reduction in systematic risk at the announcement date.

9. Several recent investigations of security returns around announcements of capital structure changes have also found a price impact that is concentrated on days -1 and 0. For example, see Dann (1981), Masulis (1980), Dann and Mikkelson (1984), and Korwar (1982).

10. Among the 107 convertible debt calls, in only 19 cases did the calling firm have publicly traded nonconvertible debt outstanding that traded actively enough to compute an announcement week return. Publicly traded nonconvertible preferred stock was outstanding in only 7 cases.

11. The purchaser of a bond pays interest accrued since the preceding coupon payment date but receives no interest payments from the firm on conversion of the debt. Therefore, a zero arbitrage profits condition implies that the sum of the convertible bond price plus accrued interest is not less than the conversion value of the bond. The adjusted bond prices are calculated under the assumption that the holder is entitled to 3 months of accrued interest.

12. Several estimates of conversion premiums are negative. This need not reflect an arbitrage profit opportunity. It may reflect either (1) nonsynchronous price quotes for the firm's common stock and convertible debt or (2) the assumption of 3 months worth of accrued interest (see n. 10). Investigation of a number of estimates of negative premiums and precise measurement of accrued interest indicates that nonsynchronous prices are likely the more important reason for the negative estimates of conversion premiums.

13. The hypothesis that the mean ratios of market value to conversion value are equal for the two samples is not rejected at the .10 level.

14. The actual number of called securities converted to common stock is not easily determined. Instead, it is assumed for the sample of calls that a large, constant proportion of

called securities are converted rather than redeemed at the call price. Table 7.3 indicates that for calls of convertible debt, on average the price per called bond is more than $60 greater than its face value. This suggests that on average the conversion value exceeds the call price by approximately $50 per bond. Thus, the incentive of a bondholder to convert is substantial.

15. Earnings per share (EPS_{-1}) at the fiscal year end preceding the call announcement equals net income (E_{-1}) less preferred dividends (PD_{-1}) divided by the number of outstanding shares of common stock (PD_{-1}), i.e., $EPS = (E_{-1} - PD_{-1}) / S_{-1}$. This measure of earnings per share is the denominator of $(\Delta EPS / EPS)$. Following a convertible debt call announcement, earnings available to common stockholders equal net income for the preceding fiscal year (E_{-1}) less preferred dividends (PD_{-1}) plus the annual after-tax interest payments on the called debt $[(1 - t)I_c]$. Earnings per share equals this quantity divided by the total shares outstanding following the call and conversion $(S_{-1} + \Delta S)$. Thus, the change in earnings per share (ΔEPS) due to the call and conversion of debt equals

$$\Delta EPS = [(E_{-1} - PD_{-1} + (1 - t)I_c) / (S_{-1} + \Delta S)] - [(E_{-1} - PD_{-1}) / S_{-1}].$$

For a call of convertible preferred stock, earnings available to common stockholders increases by the annual preferred dividends (PD_c) of the called issue. The change in earnings per share due to a call of convertible preferred stock equals

$$\Delta EPS = [E_{-1} - PD_{-1} + PD_c) / (S_{-1} + \Delta S)] - [(E_{-1} - PD_{-1}) / S_{-1}].$$

16. The estimate of the standard deviation of the 2-day announcement period adjusted return $(\hat{\sigma}_{AR})$ equals the standard deviation of the 25 2-day risk-adjusted returns from trading days $+ 11$ through $+ 60$. Using this estimate, two tests of homoscedasticity are computed.

The first, proposed by Goldfield and Quandt (1965), involves ranking the observations by the estimate of the standard deviation of 2-day adjusted returns and estimating the cross-sectional relationship separately on the 60 observations with the smallest values of $\hat{\sigma}_{AR}$ and the 60 observations with the largest values of $\hat{\sigma}_{AR}$. The ratio of the sum of squared residuals of the two regressions has the F-distribution. For two sets of estimates of the specification given by (16), the F-value of the ratio of the sum of squared residuals equals 3.47. The hypothesis of a homoscedastic error term is rejected at the .01 level.

The second test, presented by Glejser (1969), regresses the absolute value of the regression residuals $(|e|)$ on the estimate of the standard deviation of the 2-day adjusted common stock return $(\hat{\sigma}_{AR})$. The estimated relationship is $|e| = .006 + .703(\hat{\sigma}_{AR})$ and the t-value of the slope coefficient is 4.16. Again, the hypothesis of homoscedasticity is rejected at the .01 level.

17. An alternative procedure to correct for heteroscedasticity is to divide each of the terms of the regression by $\hat{\sigma}_{AR}$. For reasons that are not clear, this weighted least squares procedure induces another source of heteroscedasticity in the error term. The residuals of a weighted least squares regression are related significantly to the independent variable that measures the change in interest expense tax deductions. This problem is not found when only the dependent variable is divided by $\hat{\sigma}_{AR}$.

18. For the measure of the impact of a convertible debt call on outstanding preferred stock, the following specifications of $k(\cdot)$ are examined: (1) $[\Delta D^2(PS/V_{CS})]$, (2) $[\Delta D^{.5}(PD/V_{CS})]$, (3) $[\Delta D(PS/V_{CS})^2]$, and (4) $[\Delta D(PS/V_{CS})^{.5}]$. Corresponding specifications were also examined for the other two variables that represent the potential wealth redistribution from common stockholders to debtholders or preferred stockholders.

19. For the 114 observations where $AR_{2a} < 0$, the sum of the squared residuals of the regression model given by (16) equals 78.7. The sum of squared residuals equals 293.6 for the full sample of calls. An F-statistic is computed to test the hypothesis that the two samples of calls grouped by the sign of AR_{2a} are explained by the same cross-sectional relationship. The F-statistic equals 5.84, which is significant at the .01 level.

20. Regressions that correspond to the specifications presented in rows 4–9 in table 7.3 are estimated for the subset of 114 calls with $AR_{2a} < 0$. The results show a significant coefficient for each of the three corporate tax variables and insignificant coefficients for the variables that measure the relative increase in shares outstanding and the change in earnings per share. The only departure from the results for the full sample is the finding of a significant negative coefficient for the variable that measures the impact of a convertible debt call on the value of outstanding preferred stock. This result is consistent with a wealth redistribution effect.

21. No patterns were uncovered in the magnitudes of the estimated conversions premiums. For example, the correlation between the estimates of the conversion premium and the ratios of conversion value to face value, or call value (a measure of how much the conversion privileges are in the money), is found to be insignificant. Also, no relationship is found between the conversion premiums and the corporate tax variables.

22. For the sample of 57 calls of convertible preferred stock, the standardized 2-day announcement period stock returns were regressed on the liquidation value of the preferred stock divided by the market value of common shares $[LV/(1 + \alpha)V_{CS}]$. The following estimates were obtained

$$[AR_{2a}/\hat{\alpha}_{AR}] = -.038 + 4.133\ [LV/(1 + \alpha)V_{CS}],$$
$$(-.16)\quad (1.60)$$
$$R^2\ (\text{adj.}) = .044,\ F = 2.55\ .$$

23. If managers act to maximize stockholders' wealth, a conjecture is that calls motivated by unfavorable inside information about the firm's value are more likely to occur when the conversion value is closer to the call price. That is, the value of the downside protection offered by the debt component of a convertible bond is greater, the lower is the conversion value. Thus, the expected valuation impact of a call that conveys unfavorable information is possibly greater at lower conversion values. However, investigation of the calls indicates that the stock price response to call announcements does not depend on the level of conversion value relative to call price.

24. For 19 calls of convertible debt, the calling firm had a publicly traded preferred stock issue outstanding at the time of the call announcement. A total sample of 30 preferred stock issues was formed that consists of 8 nonconvertible issues and 22 convertible issues. Average daily preferred stock returns for these two samples of preferred stock issues are examined over 21 trading days centered on the call announcement date. For neither sample is a significant average preferred stock return found on or nearby the date of the call announcement.

References

Dann, L. Y. 1981. Common stock repurchases: An analysis of returns to bondholders and stockholders. *Journal of Financial Economics* 9:113–38.

Dann, L. Y., and Mikkelson, W. H. 1984. Convertible debt issuance, capital structure change and financing-related information: Some new evidence. *Journal of Financial Economics* 13:157–86.

DeAngelo, H., and Masulis, R. W. 1980. Optimal capital structure under corporate and personal taxation. *Journal of Financial Economics* 8:3–30.

Goldfield, S. M., and Quandt, R. 1965. Some tests for homoscedasticity. *Journal of the American Statistical Association* 60:539–47.

Glejser, H. 1969. A new test for heteroscedasticity. *Journal of the American Statistical Association* 64:316–23.

Korwar, A. N. 1982. The effect of new issues of equity: An empirical investigation. Unpublished manuscript, University of Iowa.

Marsh, P. 1979. Equity rights issues and the efficiency of the UK stock market. *Journal of Finance* 34:839–62.

Masulis, R. W. 1978. The ffect of capital structure change on security prices. Ph.D. dissertation, University of Chicago.

———. 1980. The effects of capital structure change on security prices: A study of exchange offers. *Journal of Financial Economics* 8:139–77.

———. 1983. The impact of capital structure change on firm value, some estimates. *Journal of Finance* 38:107–26.

Mikkelson, W. H. 1981. Convertible calls and security returns. *Journal of Financial Economics* 9:237–64.

Miller, M. H. 1977. Debt and taxes. *Journal of Finance* 32:261–75.

Modigliani, F., and Miller, M. H. 1958. The cost of capital, corporation finance, and the theory of investment. *American Economic Review* 48:261–97.

Scholes, M. 1972. The market of securities: Substitution versus price pressure and the effects of information on share prices. *Journal of Business* 45:179–211.

Scholes, M., and Williams, J. 1977. Estimating betas from nonsynchronous data. *Journal of Financial Economics* 5:309–28.

Smith, C. W., and Warner, J. B. 1979. On financial contracting: An analysis of bond covenants. *Journal of Financial Economics* 7:117–61.

Weston, J. F., and Brigham, E. F. 1978. *Managerial finance*. Hinsdale, IL: Dryden Press.

Comment   Michael C. Jensen

Professor Mikkelson's paper is a valuable documentation of an interesting empirical phenomenon, and I have no serious criticisms of his work. Unfortunately, in the time available I also have had great difficulty in finding insights to add to his analysis. His evidence, along with the evidence of others that continues to emerge, presents a fascinating puzzle that is a nontrivial task to sort out.

Mikkelson's evidence provides some support for the existence of tax

Michael C. Jensen is La Clare Professor of Finance Business Administration and director of the Managerial Economics Research Center at the University of Rochester's Graduate School of Management.

effects. In particular, the significantly negative common stock returns associated with calls of convertible debt are consistent with the hypothesis that increased taxes resulting from the reduction in the debt interest tax shield lowers the value of the firm. The insignificant stock returns for calls of preferred stock strengthen the results because in this case there is, of course, no reduction in tax shields. Furthermore, the significant cross-sectional relation between the size of the reduction in the interest tax shield and the size of the reduction in stock value is also consistent with the tax hypothesis. On the other hand, the fact that there is also a significant relation between stock returns and the amount of preferred stock called is inconsistent with a tax effect.

Mikkelson points out that the evidence is also consistent with an "information effect," which would occur if the call conveys information to the market that implies the firm's value is lower. At the current time, if forced to choose, I would opt for the tax hypothesis, but the answer is far from clear.

I have some doubts about the information effect hypothesis. It has become fashionable recently to give the label "information effect" to those things we do not understand. In the past "transactions cost effect" was a popular label for many ill-understood phenomena. I hasten to add that I believe real information effects exist. However, as a logical matter, there will always be an "information hypothesis" that is consistent with any evidence on the presence of tax effects. In the absence of more structure to the information hypothesis, I remain skeptical.

In addition, as Mikkelson points out, his evidence is consistent with other evidence that generally indicates a negative value effect for various capital structure changes—evidence that makes the puzzle even more complicated and interesting. Masulis (1980a) finds negative stock returns associated with exchanges of stock for debt, stock for preferred and preferred for debt. There is also evidence of negative returns associated with the issuance of convertible debt (Dann and Mikkelson 1982) and with the issuance of common stock (Korwar 1981). On the other hand, Masulis (1980b), Dann (1981), and Rosenfeld (1982), find that stock repurchases are associated with price increases. These positive stock returns are inconsistent with a simple information hypothesis that presumes that the repurchase signals the lack of profitable investment projects. I also doubt that the tax hypothesis can explain all these phenomena. Even if tax effects were found to "explain" the value declines, it is difficult to understand why these capital structure changes occur. Simple theories based on conflict of interest between managers and stockholders are difficult to believe for several reasons—not the least of which is the difficulty in understanding how managers benefit from each of these changes. There is, however, at least one situation where the manager-stockholder conflict of interest view does seem to make sense.

Contrary to the situation for unconditional stock repurchases studied by Dann, Rosenfeld and Masulis, stock prices fall in the cases studied by Dann and DeAngelo (1983) and Bradley and Wakeman (1983) where repurchases are targeted to particular large block holders. These targeted repurchases are commonly associated with the cancellation of a takeover attempt, and the value decline appears to result from the premium paid to the large block holder and from the lost merger benefits to the prospective target shareholders.

Mikkelson's work highlights our ignorance about why firms call convertible securities—especially if such calls are associated with a negative effect on firm value. It is useful to keep in mind that his estimated 2% stock price decline is not large in economic terms even if it is statistically significant. However, as Mikkelson points out, there is reason to believe this is a downward-biased estimate of the size of the effects. There is no evidence that managers benefit from calling convertible securities, and if they do, we have no coherent ideas about how those benefits arise. In considering these issues, it is useful to take a broad view of the problem. There is other evidence on potential management exploitation of stockholders that gives little or no indication that stockholders are hurt by management actions that appear on the surface to present conflicts of interest. It is alleged that stockholders are harmed when firms change their state of incorporation to Delaware—the state which provides the fewest constraints on corporate charter provisions. The study by Dodd and Leftwich (1980) indicates, however, that stock price increases, not decreases, are associated with changes of state of incorporation to Delaware. In addition, the studies by DeAngelo and Rice (1983) and Linn and McConnell (1983) provide little or no evidence of harm to stockholders when antitakeover charter amendments are adopted. In addition, DeAngelo et al. (1984) find, contrary to popular allegations, that outside stockholders experience substantial wealth gains in "going private" or "minority freezeout" transactions. In such transactions the public stock interest in a firm is replaced with full equity ownership by an incumbent management group.

I believe that, as Jensen and Meckling (1976) argue, the firm is best viewed as a legal fiction that serves as a nexus for a complex set of contracts among disparate individuals. Its behavior is best thought of as the equilibrium behavior of a complex system and not as that of a simple choosing entity with preferences. We are only now beginning to understand some of the complex forces at work inside the modern corporation, and it is an understatement to say we have far to go. In Jensen (1983) I discuss the fundamental building blocks of the emerging theory of organizations and some related methodological issues. Until we have a better developed theory of the corporation, it will remain dangerous to draw firm conclusions about such issues as tax effects or information effects from results like those presented by Mikkelson. It is not hard to construct scenarios in which such evidence reflects an entirely different set of causal factors. For example, the evidence might reflect nothing more than the decision rule used by managers to decide when to call convertible issues. Suppose managers act to maximize firm value and call convertibles when forecasts of future cash flow prospects are unfavorable. Suppose also that the decision to call the convertible provides no new information to the market regarding such cash flow prospects because the market receives the unfavorable information at the same time as the issue is called. In such a situation the price decline is due to neither tax or information effects. I do not believe this scenario is correct, but it illustrates the problem.

There is little doubt that we have come a long way since the early breakthroughs in finance starting with capital budgeting in the 1940s and early 1950s and moving on with efficient markets, portfolio theory, capital structure theory, asset pricing theory, contingent claims pricing theory, and agency theory. However, even though our theory and evidence is vastly richer than the earlier models that primarily told us "nothing matters," it is clear we are a long way from understanding how and why things work in the world of corporate finance. This conference and others like it that contribute to our stock of empirical knowledge give us new insights into the fascinating world around us. They also give us new puzzles in the from of evidence that is inconsistent with established beliefs and facts that we simply do not understand. Corporate finance is clearly a growth area, and I expect to see much progress in the future.

References

Bradley, Michael, and Wakeman, L. MacDonald. 1983. The wealth effects of targeted share repurchases, *Journal of Financial Economics*, 11:301–28.

Dann, Larry Y., 1981. Common stock repurchases: An analysis of returns to bondholders and stockholders. *Journal of Financial Economics* 9:113–38.

Dann, Larry Y., and DeAngelo, Harry. 1983. Standstill agreements, privately negotiated stock repurchases, and the market for corporate control. *Journal of Financial Economics* 11:275–300.

Dann, Larry Y., and Mikkelson, Wayne H. 1982. Convertible debt issuance, capital structure change and leverage-related information: Some new evidence. Unpublished manuscript, Dartmouth College.

DeAngelo, Harry, DeAngelo, Linda, and Rice, Edward M. 1984. Going private: Minority freezeouts and stockholder wealth. *Journal of Law and Economics*, forthcoming.

DeAngelo, Harry, and Rice, Edward M. 1983. Antitakeover charter amendments and stockholder wealth. *Journal of Financial Economics* 11:329–60.

Dodd, Peter, and Leftwich, Richard. 1980. The market for corporate charters: "Unhealthy competition" versus federal regulation. *Journal of Business* 53:259–83.

Jensen, Michael C. 1983. Organization theory and methodology. *The Accounting Review* 58:319–39.

Jensen, Michael C., and Meckling, William H. 1976. Theory of the firm: Managerial behavior, agency costs and ownership structure. *Journal of Financial Economics* 3:305–60.

Korwar, A. N. 1981. The effect of new issues of equity: An empirical investigation. Unpublished manuscript, University of California, Los Angeles, California.

Linn, Scott C., and McConnell, John J. 1983. An empirical investigation of the impact of "antitakeover" amendments on common stock prices. *Journal of Financial Economics* 11:361–99.

Masulis, Ronald W. 1980a. The effects of capital structure change on security prices: A study of exchange offers. *Journal of Financial Economics* 8:139–77.

———. 1980b. Stock repurchases by tender offer: An analysis of the causes of common stock price changes. *Journal of Finance* 35:305–19.

Rosenfeld, Ahron. 1982. Repurchase offers: Information adjusted premiums and shareholders' response. Managerial Economics Research Center Monograph and Theses Paper no. MERC MT–82–01, Graduate School of Management, University of Rochester.

8   Real Determinants of Corporate Leverage

Alan J. Auerbach

8.1 Introduction

This study presents empirical estimates of the importance of different characteristics of corporations in influencing the propensity of such corporations to finance their investments by borrowing. It also considers the determinants of the type of borrowing firms do, by estimating jointly the determinants of short-term and long-term borrowing. Such analysis is important because it is difficult to chose among the competing hypotheses about the determinants of corporate borrowing on the basis of economic theory alone.

My task is facilitated by a rich data panel based on information on nearly 200 corporations gathered from several sources, including information on the composition of the capital stocks of individual firms. The large number of variables representing firm characteristics facilitates the evaluation of different models of leverage, while the availability of at least 9 years of data on each firm allows me to distinguish between short-run and long-run determinants of borrowing.

The tax law plays a central role in most models of corporate leverage, and it is recent changes in the tax law that motivate some of the current interest in the question of what determines corporate borrowing. One important issue to which much recent attention has been devoted is the apparently large bias built into the Accelerated Cost Recovery System (ACRS) for depreciable assets introduced by the Economic Recovery Tax Act of 1981. According to most calculations, the combination of the

Alan J. Auerbach is associate professor of economics at the University of Pennsylvania and a research associate of the NBER. The author is grateful to Roger Gordon for helpful discussion, Benjamin Friedman and other conference participants for useful comments, Gregory Clark for assistance with the research, and the NBER for financial support.

investment tax credit and either three-year or five-year write-off gave investments in business equipment deductions and credits that exceeded in present value the benefits conveyed by immediate expensing. As is well known, a corporate tax with expensing (and without interest deductibility) is "neutral" in the sense that it does not distort corporate investment decisions. Put another way, the effective corporate marginal tax rate on investment is zero. The presence of tax benefits in excess of expensing therefore implies the existence of a marginal subsidy, that is, a negative tax rate. Indeed, the ACRS benefits are so generous that the aggregate effective tax rate on equipment investment is now essentially zero, after the introduction in the 1982 tax act of a 50% basis adjustment for investment credits received (see Hulten and Robertson 1982).

Under the current law, structures do not receive this effective tax exemption offered to equipment. Though the tax lifetime for most business structures (15 years) is now much shorter than before, structures typically receive no investment tax credits. As a result, estimates suggest that the effective tax rates on structures now lie below the statutory rate of 46% (i.e., depreciation allowances are more generous than economic depreciation) but much closer to this rate than zero (see, e.g., Economic Report of the President 1982; Hulten and Robertson 1982). Further, nondepreciable assets, such as land, do not qualify for any investment incentives comparable to accelerated depreciation or the investment tax credit.

This suggests that there exists a potentially serious distortion facing the choice of investment mix by corporations.[1] However, such a conclusion is necessarily valid only if a separation prevails between real and financial corporate decisions. Under some models of debt-equity choice, there may be a tax advantage to the use of debt finance which is dissipated by other costs to the firm as leverage increases. If these costs relate systematically to the firm's investment mix, one would expect debt-to-equity ratios to differ for this reason. For example, one could imagine a case in which leverage costs are lower for structures, with the additional leverage this would make possible acting to offset the tax disadvantage structures face on the "real" side.

This is an example of the type of issue I seek to resolve in the analysis that follows. I begin, in section 8.2, with a brief review of the literature on optimal financial structure in the presence of taxation, with particular emphasis on the choice of debt-to-equity ratio. Section 8.3 develops the different variants of the model of corporate borrowing that will be estimated. The model shares with its predecessors the weakness of being an ad hoc model rather than one derived rigorously from a firm's dynamic optimization problem. However, this seems unavoidable in the current context, and the model contains enough flexibility to be compatible with different underlying behavioral hypotheses. Section 8.4 presents a description of the construction of the dataset and the definitions of the variables used in the regressions, and section 8.5 presents the regression results.

8.2 Theories of Corporate Leverage

Most theories of corporate leverage begin with the twin observations that corporate taxation appears to bias the choice of financial policy completely toward debt and that corporations typically finance perhaps only one-quarter of their accumulations of capital by actually issuing debt.[2] The challenge is to explain why the simple Modigliani-Miller (1963) "all debt" result does not hold.

One suggested answer was provided by Miller (1977), who argued that the presence of a progressive personal income tax with favorable treatment of equity income (because of the partial exclusion and deferral advantage associated with capital gains taxation) would lead to an equilibrium with firms facing the same cost of capital for debt and equity. In this equalibrium, the tax advantage to debt would just be offset by a lower before-tax return to equity holders. This model implies that in equilibrium, taxation does not alter the original finding of Modigliani and Miller (1958) that financial policy is irrelevant. Moreover, it offers no reason why financial policy would relate to real investment decisions or other characteristics of firms.

Certain fundamental problems with the Miller result have been pointed out by a number of authors. For example, the implicit tax rate on municipal debt does not appear to be anywhere near the corporate rate suggested by the model.[3] Moreover, the portfolios of individual investors contain both equity and taxable debt rather than exhibiting the segmentation that Miller's hypothesis would predict. Thus, it seems that certain additions must be made to Miller's model to explain observed behavior.

Several of the models I consider have in common the property of there being certain costs faced by firms that increase with leverage, making interior debt-to-equity ratios optimal in spite of the presence of a partial *tax* advantage to debt finance. I consider these models next, discussing their empirically testable implications.

8.2.1   Bankruptcy/Agency Cost Models

The most basic explanation for interior debt-to-equity ratios is costly bankruptcy (see, e.g., Scott 1976). It is important to emphasize that the bankruptcy event must not simply be costly to some security holders in the sense of causing a redistribution of resources among different classes. The possibility of such redistributions could be allowed for adequately by an adjustment of the normal coupon rate on debt. For potential bankruptcy to discourage the issuance of debt, there must be costs to the firm as a whole, such as legal fees, court costs, or the loss on disposition of fixed assets (under liquidation). Moreover, these costs must be sufficiently large to be important relative to debt's tax advantage when bankruptcy is a likely outcome. Empirical evidence tends to refute this (see, e.g., Miller 1977), if we take the observed frequency of bankruptcy as a rough probability measure.

In models of imperfect information, or dynamic models in which financial and investment decisions occur at different times, additional costs associated with bankruptcy can arise because of the inability of bondholders to constrain the behavior of corporate managers. In a static model, it may be difficult for creditors to monitor the behavior of firms (Ross 1977). In dynamic models, managers may have the incentive to choose socially inefficient investment plans, because they do not internalize the effects of such plans on the value of outstanding long-term debt (Jensen and Meckling 1976). For example, firms with high levels of outstanding long-term debt can choose to undertake very risky projects that increase the probability of bankruptcy. Under limited corporate liability, this transfers resources from debtholders to equityholders, and may do so to a sufficient extent that risky projects with low total payoffs will dominate (from the equityholders' viewpoint) safer projects with higher total present value. The inefficiency induced by this moral hazard is a social cost that, presumably, must be borne by the firm and its owners ex ante in the form of higher coupon payments to holders of long-term debt. It would clearly be in the stockholders' interest to constrain the firm's behavior in order to avoid such costs. While mechanisms to achieve this do exist (e.g., bond covenants restricting future borrowing), it would be costly if not impossible to use them to replicate the desired outcome.

If such costs to leverage remain, it may be possible to identify differences across firms in the level of such costs. For example, Myers (1977) suggests that the moral hazard problem is more acute for firms whose value derives from the anticipated rents from future investment opportunities rather than from existing assets or assets which the firm is committed to purchase. Presumably, there would also be less of a problem for firms with a narrow range of investment opportunities from which to choose. A second determinant of the level of agency costs should be the firm's bankruptcy risk, holding debt level constant. One can model this using an option-pricing framework by assuming that bankruptcy will occur if the value of the firm as a whole drops below the level of claims against the firm. The cost of such a "bankruptcy option" depends, following the standard option-pricing results (Black and Scholes 1973; Merton 1973), on the firm's value as well as the variance of its value over time.

Myers also suggests that the agency problem may give rise to maturity matching of financial claims and real assets, although he also points out that the problem could be alleviated if firms engaged only in short-term borrowing, since debt would always be fully redeemed before the making of decisions about future projects. One could imagine the occurrence of either of these practices, but it is more difficult to derive a model that produces them. One purpose of our empirical analysis is to determine whether such behavior can actually be detected in practice.

8.2.2 Limited Tax Shield Models

The U.S. corporate income tax treats gains and losses asymmetrically. Losses may be carried back up to three years to obtain a refund of past taxes, but the excess of any remaining losses must be carried forward, without interest, and subject to expiration after 15 years (7 years during this paper's sample period). Firms without taxable income need not be in financial distress or on the verge of bankruptcy. However, the prospect of not being able to use the future tax deductions provided by interest payments makes debt less attractive, and may cause firms to limit their leverage. This is the essence of the explanation offered by DeAngelo and Masulis (1980). It is attractive as an explanation of debt policy because, unlike bankruptcy or agency costs, tax costs are easily measured.

The hypothesis also has a number of testable implications. First, firms with substantial loss carry-forwards should, ceteris paribus, choose to issue less debt. Second, firms investing in assets with a greater fraction of their total after-tax returns generated by investment tax credits and depreciation deductions should also use less debt finance. This is seen most simply if we imagine a project which costs one dollar and lasts for one period, yielding a gross return f subject to taxation at rate τ, after a depreciation deduction equal to a fraction d of gross rents. If r is the required after-tax rate of return required by the firm (in addition to the return of the initial one dollar investment), then the after-tax return satisfies

$$(1) \qquad\qquad (1 - \tau)f + \tau df = (1 + r).$$

This implies that the firm's taxable income is

$$(2) \qquad\qquad f(1 - d) + \frac{(1 + r)(1 - d)}{(1 - \tau) + \tau d},$$

which decreases with d. This result carries over directly to a multiperiod model if capital decays geometrically and depreciation deductions exceed actual depreciation by a given fraction of income, say α. In this case, taxable income as a fraction of capital is a function only of α and not of the asset's depreciation characteristics.[4] More realistically, effective tax rates on assets differ not through variations in α but through differences in the timing of depreciation deductions and qualification for investment tax credits. Thus, the magnitude of a firm's taxable income will depend not only on the effective tax rate on the assets it owns but also on their age structure. For example, a unit of equipment under the original 1981 version of ACRS would receive tax benefits in the first year of service sufficient to shelter income equal to 37% of the asset's purchase price.[5] On the other hand, this same asset would receive no deductions at all after five years. Because acceleration of this sort (though not as extreme) has been present for many years, the fraction of a firm's income sheltered by deductions and credits will generally increase with the rate at which the firm accumulates capital, given the firm's capital stock composition.

A final implication of this model of leverage determination is that the firm's riskiness, this time as measured by the fluctuations of earnings before interest but after taxes,[6] should also discourage borrowing because the asymmetric tax treatment of gains and losses will lower the expected tax savings from any given level of debt.

8.2.3   Tax Clientele Models

If the Miller equilibrium holds, each firm will be completely indifferent in its choice of debt-to-equity ratio. The foregoing models suggest that asymmetries in the legal treatment of gains and losses, either through limited corporate liability under bankruptcy or the lack of a loss offset in the tax law, may cause the Miller result to break down. An additional reason why this may happen concerns the issue of whether investors can obtain the same patterns of returns holding either only debt or only equity. If they cannot, then a firm's financial policy will generally matter and will affect the welfare of different individuals differently (Auerbach and King 1983). In this case, the choice of financial policy by a firm acting "in the interests of its shareholders" depends on who these shareholders are. Tax clienteles may develop for different firms, with investors in higher personal tax brackets having a greater relative preference for the firms they own to finance through retentions rather than borrowing (Auerbach 1984). Put another way, such investors would rather borrow on their own account than have firms do it for them, if their personal tax rate is sufficiently high. Since most equity finance comes through retained earnings, this suggests that a corporation facing increasing costs to leverage will use less debt finance, the higher is the tax rate of its clientele.

8.2.4   Summary

There are several empirical implications of the foregoing models about overall debt-to-equity ratios. Risky firms should borrow less, whether risk is measured by fluctuations in valuation or in earnings. Fast-growing firms should borrow less because of their higher ratio of growth opportunities to existing capital and because of their greater tax shield from depreciation deductions and investment tax credits. Firms investing in assets receiving generous tax treatment, such as equipment, generally, relative to structures and land, should use less debt for the same reason. Firms with high-tax clienteles should use less debt than others.

I have more limited predictions about the maturity structure of debt that firms will choose. If firms engage in maturity matching, one would expect to see a smaller fraction of long-term debt used to finance equipment, which typically depreciates more rapidly. One might also expect that firms eschewing long-term debt for agency reasons would shift to short-term debt rather than equity finance. Particularly with respect to the question of maturity structure, it is important that the model I estimate has the capacity to separate long-term determinants of leverage from those that may dominate borrowing decisions in the short run.

8.3   A Model of Corporate Borrowing

My approach differs from that taken in much of the literature on financial decisions in two major respects. I model the borrowing by individual firms as a continuous process. That is, my model attempts to explain changes in levels of debt rather than discrete new issues. This seems appropriate for firms as large as those in the sample. I also express all variables in real terms, corrected for inflation. The process by which such variables were obtained from book value data is described in the next section. My model is similar in some respects to that estimated by Taggart (1977) using quarterly aggregate time-series data. However, there are several important differences and allowances for the ability to distinguish effects across firms as well as over time. I estimate both a single-equation model for all debt and a two-equation model to explain short-term and long-term debt.

The basic model is intended to capture three characterizations of firms' borrowing behavior: (1) a long-run target debt-equity ratio based on the factors outlined in section 8.2; (2) a lag in adjustment to changes in this desired ratio; and (3) the short-run importance of cash flow constraints. To illustrate the interaction of these points, consider a firm with a major tax loss carry-forward that wishes to undertake an investment project. This firm may wish to use only retained earnings, but sufficient earnings may not be available, particularly as the loss carry-forward probably indicates low cash flow as well as low taxable income. Hence, we might observe this firm borrowing more in the short run than would be predicted by the underlying attractiveness of debt finance. It is important that the model allow such borrowing to be distinguished from borrowing based on longer-term considerations. A simple cross-section regression would not be capable of separating such factors.

I outline first the model of aggregate firm borrowing. The long-run desired debt-to-assets ratio b^* is taken to be a linear function of severai variables. These variables vary over time, over firms, or over both time and firms. I assume that firms borrow to close part of the gap between the current ratio of debt to assets and the desired one,[7] but also are influenced by current cash flow needs. I define this cash flow deficit as the change in the firm's debt-to-assets ratio that would be required for the firm to finance its new investment out of internal funds and borrowing, while at the same time maintaining dividends at their trend level and avoiding the issuance of new shares. The motivation for this variable is that both new share issues and dividend cuts are activities generally taken to be costly to the firm: the former because of tax considerations, the latter because of the undesirable signal it may convey.[8]

The cash flow deficit variable is constructed by subtracting from the sum of gross investment and trend dividends[9] (uses) the sum of after-tax cash flow (after-tax earnings plus depreciation) and the product of the current debt-to-assets ratio and gross investment (sources), and dividing the difference by assets. This variable equals zero when investment and trend dividends can be exactly covered by internal funds plus borrowing at the current debt-to-assets ratio. If it is positive, an increase in the debt-to-assets ratio will be needed if dividend cuts and new share issues are to be avoided.

This variable differs from the standard "external deficit" variable in its inclusion of trend rather than actual dividends. Moreover, it includes borrowing at the current debt-to-asset ratio on the sources side because the partial adjustment model is expressed in debt-to-asset ratios rather than in levels of debt. Formulating the model in this way allows us to distinguish between increases in the level of debt as the firm grows and fluctuations around this trend that result in changes in the incentives to use debt finance.[10]

The basic model, then, is of the form

$$(3) \qquad \Delta b_{it} = \lambda_0 (b_{it}^* - b_{it-1}) + \gamma_0 f_{it},$$

where f_{it} is the firm's deficit as just defined, b_{it} is the firm's ratio of debt to assets (the latter equal to its fixed capital stock plus working capital), and

$$(4) \qquad b_{it}^* = \alpha_0 \cdot x_{it}$$

is the firm's long-run target debt-assets ratio based on the determinants x_{it}.

The model that distinguishes between the ratio of long-term debt to assets (ℓ) and that of short-term debt to assets (s) has two equations of a form similar to (3):

$$(5a) \qquad \Delta \ell_{it} = \lambda_1 (\ell_{it}^* - \ell_{it-1}) + \phi_1 (s_{it}^* - s_{it-1}) + \gamma_1 f_{it}$$

$$(5b) \qquad \Delta s_{it} = \lambda_2 (\ell_{it}^* - \ell_{it-1}) + \phi_2 (s_{it}^* - s_{it-1}) + \gamma_2 f_{it},$$

where each equation includes not only its own gap between desired and actual levels but that from the other equation. Similarly, I define ℓ^* and s^* by

(6a) $$\ell_{it}^* = \alpha_1 \cdot x_{it}$$

(6b) $$s_{it}^* = \alpha_2 \cdot x_{it}$$

Because I make no prior distinction between the variables determining ℓ^* and those determining s^*, the vectors α_1 and α_2 can not be identified using equations (5a) or (5b) alone (unless the cross-effects ϕ_1 and λ_2 are zero). However, they are exactly identified by the equations together. Further, since the two equations have the same set of explanatory variables, maximum likelihood estimation of the system is accomplished by performing ordinary least squares on the equations separately.

The vector x_{it} includes dummy variables for each firm and for each year (save the last). The former are included to account for interfirm differences in the desired ratio of debt to assets, while the latter are intended to pick up year-to-year differences in the incentive to borrow that are common across firms, as might be caused by macroeconomic fluctuations (e.g., changes in the inflation rate or the term structure). Indeed, an interesting side result of the estimation procedure is the pattern of these dummy variables over time.

Also available are many other measures of firm attributes, but most of these either are constant or change slowly over the sample period, making it impossible to include them in regressions along with the individual firm effects. Only the firm's tax loss carry-forward has sufficient year-to-year variance to be included in the initial estimation procedure. The remainder, however, may be used in a second estimation stage to explain the variation in the individual firm constants in a cross-section regression. The need for this two-stage procedure would be obviated if the firm dummies were omitted from the first estimation stage and the various firm characteristics were included in the vector x directly. However, such a procedure would introduce a large, firm-specific error (equal to the unexplained part of the firm's own fixed effect) that would likely be correlated with other explanatory variables, leading to inconsistent estimation.[11]

8.4 Data

The data used in this paper come from three sources. The basic data on firms come from a copy of the COMPUSTAT tape covering the years 1958–77. From this tape, I selected those firms for which all observations of a subset of key variables were available. Long-term debt corresponds to the COMPUSTAT category of all debt maturing in more than one year. Short-term debt also includes long-term debt maturing within one year. Total assets equals fixed capital, plus inventories, plus other current assets net of nondebt current liabilities. (An alternative approach to the measurement of total assets is to use the total market value of equity plus debt. This is discussed below in section 8.5.) Balance sheet and income statement data on long-term debt, capital, inventories, and earnings were corrected from book value through a series of steps described in detail in Auerbach (1984). I review these steps briefly below.

Long-term debt was converted to market value using assumptions about the initial age structure of such debt in 1958, the maturity of new issues, and the coupon rate on such issues. From this corrected data series, I calculated the change in the market value of outstanding long-term debt due to interest fluctuations, adding this plus the inflation gain on net financial liabilities (long-term debt plus short-term debt less financial assets) to book earnings.

Inventories were corrected according to information on the primary method of inventory accounting used by each firm. The inventory valuation adjustment so obtained was subtracted from book earnings to correct for their inclusion of excess inventory profits.

Depreciation was estimated by assuming that book depreciation is correct except for the fact that it is based on initial asset prices. The method used calculates that rate of declining balance (exponential) depreciation, δ, that, when applied to a perpetual inventory calculation for updating capital stocks beginning with the 1958 book value for net fixed capital, yields the stated 1977 book value. (If all assets actually were written off, and did depreciate, at a single rate, this calculation would yield the correct rate.) Using this estimate of δ, I generated a corrected series for capital stocks and depreciation using the perpetual inventory method, starting in 1958. As with debt and inventories, the difference between corrected and book depreciation was subtracted from book earnings. The measure of corrected cash flow entering into the computation of the cash flow deficit f is simply the sum of corrected after-tax profits plus corrected depreciation.

After such corrections, all variables were deflated to be expressed in constant dollars rather than current dollars. Each firm's earnings growth rate was estimated by fitting a quadratic trend over the period 1963–77 for the firm's corrected earnings, before interest but after taxes, and taking the growth rate along this trend at the sample midpoint, 1970. The variance of firm earnings was approximated by the sample variance around this trend, normalized by the squared trend value in 1970.

A second source of data is the actual 10K reports filed by the individual firms. These reports contain more detailed information than is provided by COMPUSTAT. In particular, many firms list separate capital stocks, depreciation, and investment for several classes of capital. The most detailed common breakdown is transportation equipment, other equipment, structures, and land, with some firms aggregating the first two and last two of these categories. Firms that did not provide uninterrupted data between 1969 and 1977, or that did not follow this general asset classification, were omitted from the sample. For the remainder, disaggregated, corrected capital stocks were created following the perpetual inventory method described above, using 1968 and 1977 net capital stocks and investment and depreciation reported for the intervening years. Such capital stocks were not used directly but were divided by their annual sum to generate capital stock fractions. These fractions were averaged over time for each firm and used in the second estimation stage as explanatory variables.

Of the 189 firms for which capital stocks by asset category were computed, 149 have separate categories for land and structures, while 40 combine the two into a single category. Forty firms report separate statistics for transportation equipment, while the remaining firms lump all equipment together. The average capital stock depreciation rates derived for each category appear realistic, though there is substantial variance in these rates across firms. The summary statistics for these depreciation rates are reported in table 8.1. (It should be remembered that the equipment category includes all equipment for 149 firms and that the structures category includes land as well for 40 firms.) The category means are quite consistent with estimates of economic depreciation found in the literature (see, e.g. Hulten and Wykoff 1981).

In the regression reported in this paper, I omit the firms for which no structure/land breakdown is available and add together the equipment categories for those firms reporting transportation equipment separately. This leaves 143 firms in the final sample.[12]

The final source of data is the CRSP tape, which provided daily return and dividend data. In an earlier paper (Auerbach 1983), I performed a series of regressions on daily data for each of the firms in our sample, using observations for every tenth trading day between 1963 and 1977

Table 8.1   **Depreciation Rates**

Category	Number Observed	Mean	Variance
Structures	189	.072	.006
Land	149	.025	.010
Equipment	189	.138	.010
Transportation equipment	40	.225	.010

plus all days on which the firm's common stock went ex dividend. The regressions were of the form

(7) $$g_t = \theta_0 + \theta_1 d_t + \theta_2 m_t + \theta_3 r_t,$$

where g_t and d_t are the stock's capital gains per dollar of stock and dividend per dollar, respectively, and m_t and r_t are the rate of change in the Standard and Poor's Index and the Treasury bill rate. This equation derives from a version of the capital asset pricing model with progressive personal taxes, with θ_2 a measure of the firm's "beta." The term θ_1 ought to be -1 in the absence of taxes. Over the sample of firms for which (7) was estimated, θ_1 has an average of $-.787$. Under certain assumptions, this divergence may be attributed to the differential taxation of dividends and capital gains, and the variation in θ_1 across firms may be traced to differences in tax clienteles.[13] The estimated values of $(\theta_1 + 1)$ and θ_2 are used in the present paper as estimates of the clientele tax rate and beta of each firm. To estimate the variance in value for each firm, I take the variance over this same sample (excluding ex dividend days) of each firm's proportional capital gains, g_t, which yields a normalized measure of the variance of the firm's equity value, and multiply it by the sample ratio of equity to debt plus equity for the firm, yielding an overall volatility measure analogous to the "unlevered" beta.

8.5 Estimation Results

For convenience, I rewrite the one-equation and two-equation models here:

One equation:

$$\Delta b_{it} = \lambda_0 (b_{it}^* - b_{it-1}) + \gamma_0 f_{it}$$
$$b_{it}^* = \alpha_0 \cdot x_{it}$$

Two equations:

$$\Delta \ell_{it} = \lambda_1 (\ell^*_{it} - \ell_{it-1}) + \phi_1 (s_{it}^* - s_{it-1}) + \gamma_1 f_{it}$$
$$\Delta s_{it} = \lambda_2 (\ell^*_{it} - \ell_{it-1}) + \phi_2 (s_{it}^* - s_{it-1}) + \gamma_2 f_{it}$$
$$\ell_{it}^* = \alpha_1 \cdot x_{it}; \; s_{it}^* = \alpha_2 \cdot x_{it}.$$

The measure of total assets by which I divide measures of debt to form ratios includes corrected book values of both fixed capital and working capital, as described in section 8.4. However, one could argue that an alternative, market-value-based measure is preferable, one that simply adds up the value of all claims against the firm, including common and preferred stock, long-term debt, and short-term debt. The benefit of using the second method is that it may more accurately reflect the value of a firm's debt than any measure based on book values, even "corrected" ones. For example, a firm with energy-intensive plant and equipment would suffer a loss in value if energy prices rose unexpectedly, because the discounted value of the quasi rents anticipated to flow from its assets would fall. If measured properly, this would appear as capital stock depreciation, but such a measure is difficult to obtain except indirectly through market valuation. Similarly, a firm with large amounts of income from intangibles (goodwill, patents, monopoly rents, etc.) may have a comprehensive stock of income-generating assets much larger than the measured capital stock. Arguing against the use of the value-based method is the uncertainty about the equilibrium ratio of market value to the *correctly* measured value of assets. This amounts to a question about the long-run value of Tobin's q. For example, under a Miller-type equilibrium with retained earnings serving as the marginal source of finance, firms would be indifferent in their choice of debt-to-equity ratio but the *value* of debt plus equity would increase with leverage (Auerbach 1979).[14] In addition, it is unclear how much firms react to volatile year-to-year fluctuations in value in determining desired levels of debt.

Since each of these methods of defining assets has arguments in its favor, I estimated regressions for both the book-based (method 1) and market-based (method 2) asset measures. The results for the first estimation were relatively similar, so only those for method 1 are discussed in the text. These are shown in table 8.2. (An analogue to table 8.2 for method II is presented and discussed in the appendix.)

The attribute vector, x, includes firm dummies, time dummies, and the previous year's tax loss carry-forward.[15] The estimates are for the period 1969–77, for which data on all variables described above were available.

The first column of table 8.2 shows the estimates for the single-equation model, while the second and third present the reduced-form estimates for the two-equation model. An interesting feature of all three regressions is the relatively large size of the coefficient on the own lagged variable—the annual adjustment speed. These speeds, 27.4% per year for all debt, 30.4% for long-term debt, and 73.8% for short-term debt are particularly large given that they relate not to levels of debt but ratios of debt to assets. A second point is that the cross-effects between long-term and short-term debt are both positive and significant, indicating a substitutability of the two forms of finance. The cash flow deficit is insignificant in all three equations, a somewhat surprising result. It suggests, for example, that a drop in cash flow, holding investment constant, will not affect borrowing independently of other factors. This is rather implausible, and suggests that a more elaborate specification would be useful. The tax loss carry-forward is negative in all three regressions, as predicted, and significant in the first two.

From the estimates in table 8.2, I can solve for the annual desired debt-to-asset ratios for any firm. As a representative example, I consider a firm with no cash flow deficit and no tax loss carry-forward, and with a firm effect equal to the mean of such effects over firms (shown in table 8.2).

Table 8.2   **Models of Borrowing**

Dependent Variable	All Borrowing (Δb) (2.1)	Long-Term Borrowing ($\Delta \ell$) (2.2)	Short-Term Borrowing (Δs) (2.3)
Independent variable:			
Lagged debt (b)	−.274 (.021)	—	—
Lagged long-term debt (ℓ)	—	−.304 (.021)	.040 (.005)
Lagged short-term debt (s)	—	.201 (.108)	−.738 (.026)
Cash flow deficit (f)	−.015 (.029)	.005 (.028)	−.012 (.067)
Tax loss Carry-forward ($\times 10^3$)	−.356 (.139)	−.296 (.136)	−.031 (.032)
Firm dummies (mean)	.070	.070	.002
Year dummies:			
1969	−.010 (.005)	−.017 (.003)	.004 (.001)
1970	−.027 (.005)	−.031 (.005)	.004 (.001)
1971	−.015 (.005)	−.017 (.005)	.004 (.001)
1972	−.008 (.005)	−.007 (.005)	.001 (.001)
1973	−.009 (.005)	−.009 (.005)	.001 (.001)
1974	−.018 (.005)	−.018 (.005)	−.001 (.001)
1975	−.048 (.005)	−.049 (.005)	.001 (.001)
1976	−.020 (.005)	−.020 (.005)	.001 (.001)
SSR	2.53	2.37	.136
$\bar{R}^2$	.208	.239	.467

Note: Standard errors in parentheses.

Table 8.3   **Estimated Desired Debt-to-Assets Ratios**

Year	All Borrowing (b^*) (3.1)	Long-Term Borrowing (ℓ^*) (3.2)	Short-Term Borrowing (s^*) (3.3)	($\ell^* + s^*$) (3.4)
1969	.281	.185	.017	.202
1970	.157	.136	.016	.152
1971	.202	.184	.017	.201
1972	.227	.214	.014	.228
1973	.225	.208	.015	.223
1974	.189	.178	.011	.189
1975	.080	.083	.007	.080
1976	.184	.171	.013	.184
1977	.256	.239	.015	.254

Note: Calculated for a firm with mean fixed effect and no cash flow deficit or tax loss carry-forward.

The estimated targets, b^*, ℓ^*, and s^* for debt in each sample year are shown in table 8.3.[16] The numbers are reasonable in magnitude compared to observed aggregate debt-to-asset ratios. None of the three series shows any noticeable trend over the period, and the estimates tend to move together. An indication that the aggregate equation fits reasonably well relative to the two-equation system comes from the fact that the sum of the estimated values of s^* and ℓ^* is generally very close to b^*. The year-to-year movements reflect those actually observed in the aggregate (see, e.g., the statistics in Robert Taggart's paper in this volume), such as the decline in leverage from 1973 to 1975 and increase thereafter to 1977. However, the movements from year to year in table 8.3 are larger in magnitude, since they reflect changes in long-run targets rather than actually attained values.

I turn next to the second stage of my estimation, that of explaining differences in the desired debt-to-assets ratios of different firms using firm characteristics. I perform cross-section regressions for long-term debt, short-term debt, and all debt, with the dependent variables in the regression being the estimated structural coefficient of the firm's dummy variable in the expressions for ℓ^*, s^*, and b^*, respectively. Because the two methods of defining total assets (corrected book vs. market value) provide somewhat different results, I present both sets, in tables 8.4 and 8.5, respectively. The explanatory variables in each table, all described above, are "unlevered" variances of firm value and earnings, the firm's "clientele tax rate" estimated from ex dividend day regressions, the estimated rate of depreciation of the firm's capital stock, and variables reflecting the composition of the firm's assets. For the first definition of assets (corrected book value) I include the fraction of fixed capital accounted for by structures, equipment, and land (which sum to one), multiplied by the ratio of fixed capital to total assets. This yields the

Table 8.4   **Firm Characteristics and Borrowing**

Dependent Variable (Firm Effect)	All Borrowing (b^*) (4.1)	Long-Term Borrowing (ℓ^*) (4.2)	Short-Term Borrowing (s^*) (4.3)
Constant ($\times A$)	.177 (.053)	.186 (.048)	−.007 (.007)
Variance of Value ($\times 10^{-3}$)	−.117 (.096)	−.119 (.087)	.009 (.012)
Clientele tax rate	−.017 (.024)	−.020 (.022)	.022 (.003)
Variance of earnings	.290 (.131)	.239 (.119)	.044 (.017)
Growth rate of earnings	.409 (.175)	.416 (.159)	.012 (.022)
Rate of capital depreciation	.243 (.229)	.164 (.207)	.057 (.029)
Fraction structures	.271 (.303)	.278 (.274)	.012 (.039)
Fraction land	−.205 (.325)	−.260 (.295)	.027 (.041)
Fraction equipment	.166 (.061)	.136 (.055)	.024 (.007)
SSR	1.34	1.10	.022
$\bar{R}^2$	.147	.145	.157

Note: Standard errors in parentheses.

fraction that each component of fixed capital accounts for of the firm's total assets, fixed and current. The coefficients of these fractions may be interpreted as the optimal debt-to-assets ratio for the particular type of asset, relative to that for current assets. When the market-value-based measure of assets is used, I must adopt some convention for allocating the difference between market value and the value of assets carried over from the first measure. I choose to allocate the entire difference to intangible assets previously unaccounted for, and include in the regression the fraction of the new capital stock measure represented by goodwill. (The remaining three fractions, for structures, land, and equipment, are scaled up or down accordingly.) This fraction has a highly significant and negative coefficient in all three regressions reported in table 8.5. The absolute value of the coefficient on goodwill is nearly as large as that of the constant in the aggregate regression, indicating that very little debt is used to finance goodwill, as I have measured it. This may be interpreted

Table 8.5   **Firm Characteristics and Borrowing (Alternative Assets Definition)**

Dependent Variable (Firm Effect)	All Borrowing (b^*) (5.1)	Long-Term Borrowing (ℓ^*) (5.2)	Short-Term Borrowing (s^*) (5.3)
Independent variable:			
Constant ($\times A$)	.187	.191	.002
	(.040)	(.038)	(.006)
Variance of Value ($\times 10^{-3}$)	−.080	−.086	.006
	(.075)	(.070)	(.011)
Clientele tax rate	−.007	−.010	.003
	(.019)	(.017)	(.003)
Variance of earnings	.189	.148	.037
	(.116)	(.110)	(.017)
Growth rate	.640	.591	.044
	(.166)	(.156)	(.024)
Rate of capital depreciation	.224	.175	.042
	(.180)	(.170)	(.026)
Fraction structures	−.548	−.480	−.056
	(.227)	(.214)	(.033)
Fraction land	.652	.563	.079
	(.206)	(.195)	(.030)
Fraction equipment	.012	−.006	−.004
	(.042)	(.040)	(.006)
Fraction goodwill	−.159	−.142	−.015
	(.033)	(.032)	(.005)
SSR	.786	.697	.017
$\bar{R}^2$	.511	.484	.371

Note: Standard errors in parentheses.

in at least two ways. One may take it as an indication that firms finance intangible assets with less debt, in accordance with the theory of agency (at least to the extent that the intangibles indicate more discretion on the part of the firm's managers). On the other hand, this finding may also reflect the possibility that managers base their borrowing decisions on book asset measures (perhaps corrected for inflation) but not on stock market values.

Except for the asset composition variables, the explanatory variables have very similar coefficients in the two tables, although they are not necessarily consistent with the predictions of the various theories discussed in section 8.2. The clientele tax rate variable is always insignificant, which may reflect on its quality as a tax rate proxy. The growth rate and variance of earnings always have positive coefficients, usually significant. Neither of these results has an obvious explanation. The rate of capital depreciation always exerts a positive effect, which also was not predicted. However, this effect is only significant for short-term borrowing, consistent with the notion of maturity matching. The variance of value does perform as predicted, but never significantly so. All in all, these results provide rather negative evidence with respect to all of the theories of leverage presented above.

The coefficients of the capital stock fractions differ considerably between tables 8.4 and 8.5, presumably because of the inclusion in the latter table of the goodwill fraction. When the first, corrected book measure of assets is used, only equipment has a significant coefficient, which is positive. When goodwill is added both to the measure of assets and to the regression as a fraction of the new asset measure, the coefficient of structures becomes significantly negative and that of land significantly positive. While there is no indication that structures are financed with greater leverage than equipment, the instability of these results is quite disturbing. Given that the allocation of the entire difference between market and corrected book values to goodwill is arbitrary and not necessarily appropriate, it is quite difficult to draw conclusions here.

8.6   Conclusion

Our partial adjustment models of borrowing suggest rapid speeds of adjustment, particularly for short-term debt, and desired ratios of debt, and its long-term and short-term components, to assets during the period 1969–77 that, while not constant, exhibit no obvious trend. Some firm characteristics are insignificant in explaining cross-sectional differences in leverage, while others appear to contradict the prediction of various theories in their effects. The effects of firm growth rates on the level of borrowing is inconsistent with the predictions of "agency" models of leverage. The positive effects of earnings variance on borrowing appear to contradict the "tax shield" borrowing model, but the tax loss carryforward has the negative effect that this model would predict.

The results do not indicate that firms borrow more to invest in structures than in equipment, but the results here vary substantially according to the measure of assets used. Richer models of firm behavior appear to be required before more definitive conclusions can be reached.

Appendix

This Appendix presents in table 8A.1 the first-stage estimation results for the alternative definition of firm assets, based on market value rather

Table 8.A.1   **Models of Borrowing: Alternative Assets Definition**

Dependent Variable	All Borrowing (Δb) (2.A1)	Long-Term Borrowing ($\Delta \ell$) (2.A2)	Short-Term Borrowing (Δs) (2.A3)
Independent variable:			
Lagged debt (b)	−.441 (.021)	—	—
Lagged long-term debt (ℓ)	—	−.437 (.022)	−.032 (.005)
Lagged short-term debt (s)	—	−.171 (.112)	−.794 (.026)
Cash flow deficit (f)	.346 (.019)	.318 (.019)	.025 (.004)
Tax loss Carry-forward ($\times 10^3$)	.051 (.157)	.063 (.153)	.042 (.036)
Firm dummies (mean)	.101	.099	.003
Year dummies:			
1969	−.032 (.006)	−.039 (.006)	.003 (.001)
1970	−.038 (.006)	−.043 (.006)	.005 (.001)
1971	−.043 (.006)	−.044 (.006)	.003 (.001)
1972	−.035 (.006)	−.034 (.006)	.0004 (.001)
1973	.009 (.006)	.005 (.006)	.004 (.001)
1974	.025 (.006)	.022 (.006)	.003 (.001)
1975	−.046 (.006)	−.050 (.006)	.002 (.001)
1976	−.024 (.006)	−.025 (.006)	.002 (.001)
SSR	3.17	2.97	.161
$\bar{R}^2$	.542	.532	.470

Note: Standard errors in parentheses.

than corrected book value. The only important difference is in the significant coefficients in all three equations of the cash flow deficit, which had insignificant coefficients in all three equations in table 8.2. One suspects that this result is attributable to firm's ignoring short-run fluctuations in value. For example, a large decline in the value of the firm would increase the cash flow gap, since "normal" debt increases (the current debt to assets ratio multiplied by the change in assets) would be negative. At the same time, the observed change in the debt-to-assets ratio would be positive, even if there were no change in the level of debt, because of the decline in the value of assets. It is difficult in this model to distinguish between the hypothesis that firms simply ignore changes in value and the hypothesis that the reduction in desired debt is just offset by the increase in the cash flow deficit. To sort out this problem, one would need a model that disaggregates different sources of the cash flow deficit.

Notes

1. A justification for the use of effective tax rates in welfare analysis is given by Auerbach (1982).

2. Such a fraction is typical of the time-series debt-to-capital ratios calculated by Gordon and Malkiel (1981).

3. Gordon and Malkiel (1981) present results suggesting a value between .2 and .3, vs. a corporate tax rate (historically) of at least .46.

4. This follows from the fact that the user cost of capital to which the marginal product of capital will be set equals

$$c = q(r + \delta)\left(1 - \frac{\tau(\delta + \alpha r)}{r + \delta}\right)/(1 - \tau),$$

where q is the relative capital goods price. Therefore, taxable income as a fraction of assets, $(cK - \delta qK)/qK$, equals $[\tau/(1 - \tau)]r(1 - \alpha)$.

5. This results from a 15% deduction and a 10% investment tax credit, which shields income of 22%.

6. One would subtract not taxes actually paid but those that would be paid by the firm were it entirely financed by equity.

7. This partial adjustment specification imposes a common, geometric lag structure on the different determinants of the desired ratio of debt to assets. Further research on this topic might consider more general lag specifications to determine whether these restrictions are justified.

8. These points are quite common in literature. See, e.g., Auerbach (1984).

9. Trend dividends are calculated by regressing the firm's annual dividends on a constant, time and time squared over the period 1963–77.

10. An alternative approach, used in an earlier version of this paper, would be to detrend levels of debt.

11. Additional problems of inconsistency could arise if the remaining errors for each firm were correlated over time, even after being purged of fixed effects. An attempt to control for this using two-stage least squares, with the lagged debt-to-assets ratios and cash flow deficit variables regressed in the first stage on several lagged values of the firm's sales proved unsuccessful, in that the sales variables proved to be very poor instruments. No

other obvious candidates came to mind. Given the rapid adjustment speeds found in the basic model (table 8.2) and the usual tendency of positive autocorrelation to bias such speeds downward, one may hope that the potential problem is not a serious one here.

12. There are 149 firms with complete capital stock data (see table 8.1) but six had missing values for one of the other explanatory variables, the tax loss carry-forward.

13. These interpretations are not universally accepted. See the criticisms of Miller and Scholes (1982), for example.

14. This occurs because a firm's equity is valued at $q_D (A - B)$, where A is the value of a firm's assets, B the value of its debt, and q_D is a constant less than one, based on the relative tax rates on dividends and capital gains.

15. In a few cases in which this value was missing, I used the one from two years before.

16. Note that to obtain ℓ^* and s^*, one must solve for the structural parameters in α_1 and α_2 in (6) from the reduced-form estimates of the two-equation system for ℓ and s.

References

Auerbach, Alan J. 1979. Wealth maximization and the cost of capital. *Quarterly Journal of Economics* 93:433–46.

————. 1982. Tax neutrality and the social discount rate, *Journal of Public Economics* 17:355–72.

————. 1983. Stockholder tax rates and firm attributes. *Journal of Public Economics* 21:107–27.

————. 1984. Taxes, firm financial policy and the cost of capital: an empirical analysis, *Journal of Public Economics* 23:27–57.

Auerbach, Alan J. and King, Mervyn A. 1983. Taxation, portfolio choice and debt equity ratios: a general equilibrium model. *Quarterly Journal of Economics* 98:587–609.

Black, Fischer, and Scholes, Myron. 1973. The pricing of options and corporate liabilities. *Journal of Political Economy* 81:637–54.

DeAngelo, Harry, and Masulis, Ronald. 1980. Optimal capital structure under corporate and personal taxation. *Journal of Financial Economics* 8:3–81.

Economic Report of the President, 1982.

Gordon, Roger, and Malkiel, Burton G. 1981. Corporation finance. In *How Taxes Affect Economic Behavior*, ed. H. J. Aaron and J. A. Pechman. Washington, D.C.: Brookings Institution.

Hulten, Charles R. and Robertson, James W. 1982. Corporate tax policy and economic growth: an analysis of the 1981 and 1982 tax acts. Urban Institute Discussion Paper.

Hulten, C. R., and Wykoff, Frank L. 1981. The measurement of economic depreciation. In *Depreciation, inflation and the taxation of income from capital*, ed. C. R. Hulten. Washington: Urban Institute.

Jensen, Michael, and Meckling, William. 1976. Theory of the firm: managerial behavior, agency costs and ownership structure. *Journal of Financial Economics* 3:305–60.

Merton, Robert. 1973. Theory of rational option pricing. *Bell Journal of Economics* 4:141–83.

Miller, Merton H. 1977. Debt and taxes. *Journal of Finance* 32:261–75.

Miller, Merton H., and Scholes, Myron S. 1982. Dividends and taxes: some empirical evidence. *Journal of Political Economy* 90:1118–41.

Modigliani, Franco, and Miller, Merton H. 1958. The cost of capital, corporation finance, and the theory of investment. *American Economic Review* 48:261–97.

———. 1963. Corporate income taxes and the cost of capital: a correction. *American Economic Review* 53:433–43.

Myers, Stewart. 1977. Determinants of corporate borrowing. *Journal of Financial Economics* 5:147–75.

Ross, Stephen A. 1977. The determination of financial structure: the incentive-signalling approach. *Bell Journal of Economics* 8:23–40.

Scott, James H. 1976. A theory of optimal capital structure, *Bell Journal of Economics* 7:33–54.

Taggart, Robert A. 1977. A model of corporate financing decisions. *Journal of Finance* 32:1467–84.

Comment   Roger H. Gordon

The various existing theories which attempt to explain the determinants of corporate financial policy all have implications for how debt-to-value ratios ought to vary across firms. Yet surprisingly little work has been done to examine the consistency of the data with these forecasts and to estimate how responsive actual behavior is to various factors. In this paper, Auerbach, attempts to fill this gap, discussing theoretically what the various theories imply and then testing empirically how useful the theoretically implied factors are in forecasting a firm's financial policy.

While much work remains to be done, the paper makes a valuable contribution. Its value, though, is more in laying out the questions and describing associations in the data than in estimating the real determinants of corporate leverage. Most of the variables used to forecast financial policy are statistically endogenous, making interpretation of the estimates difficult. (Auerbach does in fact find the coefficient estimates very difficult to interpret.) Unfortunately, it is virtually impossible to avoid these problems. Auerbach used instruments for dividend policy and attempted unsuccessfully to do so for the lagged dependent variable and the cash flow measure. However, the problems are pervasive, as the

Roger H. Gordon is associate professor of economics at the University of Michigan and a research associate of the NBER.

actual level of debt affects many of the observed characteristics of the firm.

To give a sense of the magnitude of the problem, I will discuss a number of the variables in turn:[1]

1. *Lagged debt.* To the degree that the true residuals are autocorrelated, this coefficient is biased upward. As sizable autocorrelation is to be expected in such time series, the coefficient estimate can only serve to give a lower bound on the adjustment speed.

2. *Cash flow deficit.* This variable equals gross investment, times one minus the current debt-to-assets ratio, plus dividends minus after-tax earnings and depreciation. The debt-to-assets ratio is the dependent variable, so endogenous. Taxes are endogenous, as taxes depend on interest deductions. Profits are measured net of interest costs then adjusted to reflect the revaluation of existing debt, so are made endogenous. Investment and the debt-to-assets ratio can be correlated for a variety of reasons beyond those motivating the use of the cash flow deficit. Auerbach does use trend dividends rather than current dividends, but makes no attempt to handle the other problems.

3. *Tax loss carry-forward.* A substantial tax loss carry-forward indicates the presence of too much debt—with a large tax loss carry-forward, debt is dominated by equity for tax as well as agency cost reasons. This positive association with the existing debt-to-assets ratio, contrary to the negative association expected by Auerbach, may be controlled for, though, by also including the lagged dependent variable.

4. *Variance of value.* This variable equals the variance in the rate of return to equity multiplied by (the square of?) one minus the existing debt-to-value ratio. This use of the dependent variable creates endogeneity.

5. *Variance of earnings.* Earnings are measured net of real payments to debtholders. The larger the existing debt is, presumably the larger is the variability of earnings.

Auerbach's estimated coefficients are also biased due to measurement error in several of the variables. One potentially serious source of problems in the Compustat data is the handling of mergers and acquisitions. The tape flags only major changes, though Auerbach does not mention excluding even these cases. When mergers occur, variables such as the earnings growth rate, the variance in earnings, and depreciation rates, as measured based on growth in the capital stock, will all be badly biased. The large standard deviations of the depreciation rates in table 8.1, for example, a standard deviation of 0.1 for the depreciation rate of land when the mean rate is only 0.025, suggest such problems. Since mergers are frequently financed by large amounts of borrowing, spurious correlations in the data are also created.

Another major problem is the measurement of the firm's assets. Auerbach tries two different measures, but unfortunately the resulting sets of coefficient estimates differ substantially. Few inferences remain unchanged between the two versions. Auerbach does not always point out the sharp differences, as in the time pattern of the debt-to-assets ratio. My own feeling is that market value provides a much better measure of K_{it} than does the replacement cost of physical capital. The former measure captures the effects of such events as changes in interest rates, in relative factor prices, in relative output prices, in technology, and so on. It also includes the value of such assets as brand name, patents, and future growth opportunities, assets omitted in any replacement cost measure.

Both measures, though, have substantial measurement error. For example, Auerbach estimates the market value of long-term bonds by assuming that all new long-term bonds are 20-year bonds, not subject to being called, and always as risky as the representative Baa bond. While these assumptions may seem at least as good as any of the simple alternatives, each assumption could be substantially in error, and the estimate of market value could differ substantially from actual market value. Also, by necessity, the measure of debt excludes such obligations as unfunded pension liabilities and noncapitalized leases, yet these obligations are very similar to traditional debentures and potentially quite large. In measuring the value of fixed assets, Auerbach assumes that the replacement cost of capital in 1958 equals the reported book value of capital. This underestimate of capital in 1958 will bias downward the trend in debt-to-assets ratios.

Finally, let me comment on the measurement of the growth rate and the variability in earnings. The growth rate variable is intended to capture the idea of Myers that firms whose value derives more from future growth opportunities ought to use less debt. The natural way to measure this growth rate would seem to be the growth rate in the replacement value of the firm's capital stock, for which data are already available. The estimated growth rate in earnings contains a lot of noise and should be heavily affected by the timing of recessions in the sample period and by when large deductions were taken.

Taken together, there are enough sources of bias that we should not be surprised that the coefficient estimates differ from those suggested by the theories. Much difficult work remains in refining the empirical tests before we can begin to judge the correspondence between the theories and actual behavior.

Note

1. Unless the remaining right-hand-side variables are independent of these variables, all the coefficients will be biased.

9 Investment Patterns and Financial Leverage

Michael S. Long and Ileen B. Malitz

9.1 Introduction

The effect of capital structure on firm value has been a subject of controversy over the years. Most early work, such as Modigliani and Miller (1958), showed that when capital markets are perfect and investment policy is fixed, capital structure is irrelevant to firm value. Later studies (Modigliani and Miller 1963; Baxter 1967) introduced corporate taxes and/or bankruptcy costs in an effort to explain capital structure. The tax/bankruptcy arguments have been extended by Miller (1977), who showed that with personal taxes there is no corporate advantage to leverage, and DeAngelo and Masulis (1980), who hypothesized that the extent of nondebt tax shields determines a firm's optimal capital structure. Recently there has been a movement away from the traditional tax-bankruptcy cost argument toward a consideration of agency costs as the major determinant of financial leverage. Jensen and Meckling (1976) showed that with risky debt outstanding, a firm's investment policy is not fixed. Myers (1977) first recognized the underinvestment problem by noting that shareholders of firms with risky debt will invest only when (or up to the point at which) the expected return on investment is at least as great as the promised payment to bondholders. When the expected return is less than the promised payment, shareholders fail to exercise the investment option (or invest less than the optimal amount), which re-

Michael S. Long is associate professor of finance at the University of Illinois at Chicago. Ileen B. Malitz is assistant professor of finance at the University of Illinois at Chicago.

duces firm value. It is this decline in firm value which limits the amount of debt a given firm can issue.

Myers(1977) correctly identifies investment opportunities, including, for example, the maintenance of equipment, as leading to potential underinvestment. He notes that owners, by devising complex debt contracts, can reduce the effect of potential underinvestment and induce bondholders to pay a higher price for debt. But debt contracts can be effective only when the firm's investment opportunity set is observable.

In this study we show that because intangible, firm-specific, and therefore unobservable growth opportunities reduce the effectiveness of bond covenants, the only way in which owners of firms with a high proportion of intangible investment opportunities can control the agency costs of debt is by limiting the amount of risky debt outstanding. Conversely, this implies that if a firm's investment opportunities consist primarily of tangible assets, such as capital equipment, they can always support a greater level of debt.

The same arguments apply to the asset substitution problem (Black and Scholes 1973; Smith and Warner 1979). While riskier (more capital-intensive) equipment can always be purchased, such investments are observable. With intangible investments, it is a relatively easy matter for owners to increase firm risk without bondholders' being aware of the shift for many years. For example, a firm can concentrate its research and development (R&D) on projects with a low probability of extremely high returns. Since most firms closely guard information concerning R&D projects, this type of risk shifting is difficult for outsiders to detect.

Thus our major conclusion is that it is the type of investment opportunities facing the firm which determines financial leverage. The empirical evidence supports this conclusion.

Our analysis of the effect on investment type on corporate leverage proceeds as follows. In section 9.2 we develop a model showing the cause and effect of underinvestment and asset substitution. We then analyze the differing effects which investments in tangible or intangible assets have on firm value and present our hypothesis. Section 9.3 describes our sample and the variables used to characterize investment alternatives, and presents our empirical results. Included are tests incorporating additional variables suggested by other researchers. Finally, we present and discuss the implications of our findings in section 9.4.

9.2   Investment Choice and Financial Leverage: Theory

In this section we analyze the underinvestment and asset substitution problems as they relate to the type of investment opportunities facing a firm. We show that because investments in tangible assets, such as capital equipment, can be observed, firms with a high proportion of tangible investment opportunities can always support more debt than firms facing intangible, or firm-specific, opportunities. It is these difficult to observe firm-specific investments which provide true economic growth and at the same time reduce financial leverage.

We examine investment-related agency problems by considering a firm which operates for three periods, $t = 0, 1, 2$, in an economy characterized by state-contingent claims which promise to pay \$1.00 in period t, if and only if state S_t occurs. Capital markets are perfect so that there are no taxes or transactions costs. However, there are agency costs related to risky debt. It is assumed that some debt is advantageous because of offsetting agency costs of equity and that these costs have been minimized so that managers act on behalf of owners. The firm starts out at $t = 0$ with initial equity capitalization, an initial asset base, and a set of investment opportunities which can be exercised at $t = 1$. The investments which are accepted will provide earnings at $t = 2$ which depend both on the state of nature and the level of investment. At the end of $t = 2$, the value of the investments is zero, that is, they are fully depreciated. The following notations are used throughout the paper.

C_1	= Amount invested in period 1.
$q_0(S_t)$	= Value at $t = 0$ of a claim for \$1.00 to be delivered in period t, if and only if state S_t occurs, $t = 1, 2; S = 0, \ldots, \ldots, .$
$q_1(S_2)$	= Expected (or implied) value at $t = 1$ of a claim for \$1.00 to be delivered in period 2, if and only if state S_2 occurs and $q_1(S_2) = q_0(S_2) / q_0(S_1)$.
Z	= The unlevered firm's investment problem at $t = 1$.
Z'	= The levered firm's investment problem at $t = 1$.
V	= Value of the unlevered firm.
V'	= Value of the levered firm.
Ve	= Value of equity when there is no risky debt.
Ve'	= Value of equity when there is risky debt.
P	= Promised payment to bondholders at $t = 2$.
Vd	= Value of the firm's debt at $t = 0$.
B	= Price paid for the firm's debt at $t = 0$.
S_{d2}	= State below which operating default occurs at $t = 2$.
S_{b2}	= State below which financial default occurs at $t = 2$.
$R(C_1, S_2)$	= Dollar return on investment at $t = 2$, where $\partial R(C_1, S_2) / \partial C_1 > 0$, $\partial^2 R(C_1, S_2) / \partial C_1^2 < 0$.

It is assumed that the firm derives some level of expected earnings at $t = 1$ from the initial asset base. However, for simplicity, we assume that there is no probability of operating default at $t = 1$ so that these expected earnings, which are the same for an unlevered or levered firm, are ignored in the analyses which follow.

9.2.1 The Underinvestment Problem

Consider first the choice of the level of investment for the unlevered firm. At $t = 1$, owners will maximize their wealth.

$$(1) \qquad \max_{C_1} Z = - C_1 + \int_{S_{d2}}^{\infty} R(C_1, S_2) \, q_1(S_2) dS_2 .$$

This of course equals the net present value (NPV) of the investment to the firm at $t = 1$. The first-order condition for equation (1) leads to the classic microeconomic result: Invest to the point, C_1^*, where the expected marginal return on investment equals its marginal cost.

$$(2) \qquad \partial Z / \partial C_1 = - 1 + \int_{S_{d2}}^{\infty} [\partial R(C_1^*, S_2)/\partial C_1]$$
$$q_1 (S_2) \, dS_2 = 0 .$$

This is equivalent to investing in all projects with a NPV ≥ 0. The value of the firm equals the owners wealth in the firm, and is optimal at this point.

$$(3) \qquad V = Ve = - C_1^* \int_0^{\infty} q_0(S_1) ds_1$$
$$+ \int_0^{\infty} \int_{S_{d2}}^{\infty} R(C_1^*, S_2) q_0 (S_2) dS_2 .$$

Now assume that instead of remaining all equity funded at $t = 0$, owners issue debt which promises to pay an amount P at $t = 2$. The debt is pure discount so that the amount paid, B, reflects anticipated payment at $t = 2$. Owners use these proceeds to repurchase equity at $t = 0$, and fund C_1 by issuing new equity at $t = 1$. At $t = 2$, owners default on debt if the return is less than the promised payment, $R(C_1, S_2) < P$, which occurs in all states $S_2 < S_{b2}$. Thus at $t = 1$, when maximizing their wealth, owners recognize that they receive a return if and only if $S_2 \geq S_{b2}$.

$$(4) \qquad \max_{C_1} Z' = - C_1 + \int_{S_{b2}}^{\infty} [R(C_1, S_2) - P] \, q_1(S_2) dS_2 .$$

Equation (4) leads to a first-order condition, and thus a level of investment C_1', which does *not* maximize firm value.

$$(5) \qquad \partial Z' / \partial C_1 = - 1 + \int_{S_{b2}}^{\infty} [\partial R(C'_1, S_2)/\partial C_1]$$
$$q_1 (S_2) \, dS_2 .$$

The second term in equation (5) is less than the corresponding term in equation (2) because $S_{b2} > S_{d2}$. Because owners only receive payoffs after they have paid bondholders, they invest less than the optimal amount, $C' < C^*$. The value of equity is then the present value of the shareholders' portion of firm value.

$$(6) \qquad Ve' = - C_1' \int_0^{\infty} q_0(S_1) dS_1$$
$$+ \int_0^{\infty} \int_{S_{b2}}^{\infty} [R(C_1', S_2) - P] \, q_0(S_2) dS_2 .$$

Since the proceeds from the sale of debt are distributed to owners, their wealth depends on the price paid for debt. This in turn depends on the ability of potential bondholders to accurately assess owners' investment decisions, which requires knowledge of the firm's investment opportunity set.

Suppose first that potential bondholders do not anticipate underinvestment; that is, they assume $C_1' = C_1^*$. Then the price they are willing to pay reflects the investments they assume the firm will undertake.

(7)
$$B = P \int_0^\infty \int_{S_{b2}}^\infty {}^* q_0(S_2)\,dS_2$$
$$+ \int_0^\infty \int_{S_{d2}}^{S_{b2}*} R(C_1^*, S_2) q_0(S_2)\,dS_2 .$$

Because they assume C_1^* is invested, they also assume that the default state, S_{b2*} is lower than its actual state, S_{b2}. This results in a wealth loss equal to the price paid for the bonds less the true value of debt $(B - Vd)$.

This loss is shown graphically on figure 9.1. Bondholders priced debt as if they would receive the present value of area $OABCS_N$. However, debt is actually worth the present value of area $OA'B'CS_N$. The bondholders overpaid (and transferred to owners) an amount equal to the present value of the shaded area, $AA'BB'$. The effect on owners' wealth depends on whether the gain from bondholders exceeds the decline in the value of

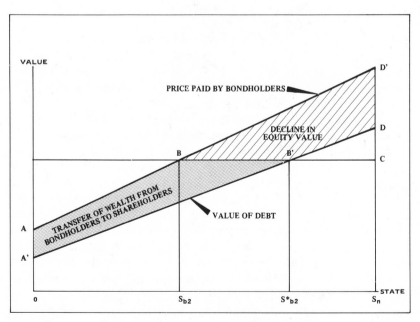

Fig. 9.1   The effect of unanticipated underinvestment on bondholder wealth.

equity (area $BB'DD'$). If owners could underinvest without bondholders anticipating their actions, they would increase their wealth.

But in a rational capital market, bondholders will attempt to anticipate underinvestment. If the firm's investment opportunities are tangible in nature, potential bondholders are able to estimate the investment opportunity set and thus fully anticipate the lower level of investment. They will then pay the true value of debt so that $B = Vd$.

$$(8) \qquad Vd = P \int_0^\infty \int_{S_{b2}}^\infty q_0(S_2)\, dS_2$$
$$+ \int_0^\infty \int_{S_{d2}}^{S_{b2}} R(C_1',\, S_2) q_0(S_2)\, dS_2.$$

The value of debt is equal to the present value of the promised payment in states of no default plus the present value of the firm in states of default on debt. In this case, when B is distributed to owners, the value of the levered firm is less than that of the unlevered firm.

$$(9) \qquad V' = - C_1' \int_0^\infty q_0(S_1)\, dS_1$$
$$+ \int_0^\infty \int_{S_{d2}}^\infty R(C_1',\, S_2) q_0(S_2)\, dS_2.$$

As long as bondholders accurately anticipate underinvestment, owners bear a loss in firm value which increases with the amount promised to bondholders. Then it is to the owner's advantage to provide monitoring of investment decisions. Whether monitoring of investment decisions is provided by bondholders (through debt covenants) or by the capital market itself (implicit monitoring), much of the negative effect of risky debt can be eliminated. Low-growth firms with tangible, generalized investment opportunities, such as plant and equipment, can support more debt because of the ability of potential bondholders to estimate underinvestment and to observe and monitor investment decisions.

But suppose that the firm's investment opportunities are intangible and/or firm specific in nature so that potential bondholders are unable to estimate either the firm's investment opportunities or the extent of underinvestment. Then normally they will assume the worst possible case, which in the limit is zero investment. While owners could promise higher payments to bondholders in order to induce them to purchase debt, Myers has shown that increasing P is not effective. Because firm value declines as the promised payment increases, beyond some point, called the firm's debt capacity, increasing P reduces rather than increases the value of debt. Further, if bondholders are unable to estimate underinvestment, they are also unable to observe or monitor the firm's investment policy. Thus the effectiveness of either bond convenants or implicit capital market monitoring is reduced. Since the market cannot effectively monitor investment decisions, it instead limits the amount of debt. Because high-growth firms cannot be effectively monitored, they will have lower financial leverage.

9.2.2   Asset Substitution

Consider the investment decision as it concerns the risk of the assets purchased. It is well known that increasing firm risk may decrease bond-holder wealth while increasing owners wealth. We examine this problem by assuming that the firm faces a second set of investments at $t = 1$, C_1'' with a return function at $t = 2$ of $R''(C_1'', S_2)$. To highlight the asset substitution problem, we assume that $C_1'' = C_1'$ so that owners maximize their wealth at the same level of investment. The new set of investments is riskier, implying that $S_{b2} < S_{b2}''$, $Sd_2 < Sd_2''$, and

$$\int_{S_{d2}}^{S_{b2}} R(C_1', S_2) q_1(S_2) dS_2 > \int_{S_{d2}}^{S_{b2}''} R''(C_1', S_2) q_1(S_2) dS_2$$

$$\int_{S_{b2}}^{\infty} R(C_1', S_2) q_1(S_2) dS_2 = \int_{S_{b2}''}^{\infty} R''(C_1', S_2) q_1(S_2) dS_2.$$

These patterns of return are shown graphically on figure 9.2. The second set of investments results in a higher probability of operating default as well as a higher probability of financial default. Figure 9.2 shows that the expected marginal return on the original investment over states $S_2 \geq S_{b2}$ (area $S_{b2} A' CS_N$) is equal to the expected marginal return on the riskier investment over states $S_2 \geq S_{b2''}$ (area $S_{b2''} B' C' S_N$). This leads to identical first-order conditions for owners' wealth maximization and thus to the same level of investment. Figure 9.2 also shows that the expected marginal return on the original investment over states $S_2 \geq S_{d2}$ (area $S_{d2} ACS_N$)

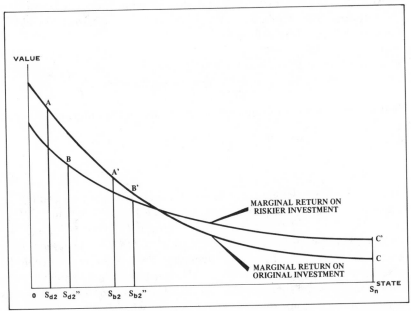

Fig. 9.2   Expected marginal returns on investment with asset substitution.

exceeds the expected marginal return on the riskier investment over states $S_2 \geq S_{d2''}$ (area $S_{d2}''BC'S_N$). Thus, given the above assumptions, the first-order conditions to maximize firm value shows that the less risky investment is preferable.[1]

The value of equity with the original investment is given by equation (6). The value of equity, Ve'', with the riskier investment depends on the returns to owners in states $S_2 \geq Sb_2''$.

(10) $Ve = - C_1' \int_0^\infty q_0(S_1)dS_1$

$+ \int_0^\infty \int_{S_{b2''}}^\infty [R''(C_1', S_2) - P] \, q_0(S_2)dS_2$.

If the riskier investment is chosen, the value of equity changes as follows:

(11) $Ve'' - Ve' = \int_0^\infty \int_{S_{b2''}}^\infty [R''(C'_1, S_2) - R'(C'_1, S_2)]$

$q_0(S_2)dS_2$

$- \int_0^\infty \int_{S_{b2}}^\infty [R'(C'_1, S_2) - P]q_0(S_2)dS_2$.

The first term in (11) is the difference in value of the two investments in states of no default on debt and is positive by assumption. The second term is negative, since owners do not default on debt in states $S_2 \geq Sb_2$ if they choose the original investment. The value of equity may increase if the riskier investment is chosen. Whether or not it does depends on the promised payment to bondholders.

As with underinvestment, if bondholders did not anticipate investment substitution, they would assume that the original investment would be chosen and would be willing to pay

(12) $B = P\int_0^\infty \int_{S_{b2}}^\infty q_0(S_2)dS_2$

$+ \int_0^\infty {}_{S_{d2}}^{S_{b2}} R(C'_1, S_2)q_0(S_2)dS_2$.

But the actual value of debt, given the riskier investment, is

(13) $Vd = P \int_0^\infty \int_{S_{b2''}}^\infty q_0(S_2)dS_2$

$+ \int_0^\infty {}_{S_{d2''}}^{S_{b2''}} R''(C_1', S_2)q_0(S_2)dS_2$.

The price paid for debt exceeds its actual value. This is shown graphically on figure 9.3. The price paid by bondholders is the present value (PV) of area $OABCS_N$. The true value of debt is the PV of area $OB'CS_N$. The overpayment (wealth loss) is the PV of area $OABB'$. This amount is transferred to owners. In addition owners gain the difference between the PVs of area DEF and area $BB'D$. Finally, firm value declines by the difference between shareholders' gain and bondholders' loss (PV of areas $DEF - OAD$). Thus owners may gain even when firm value declines.

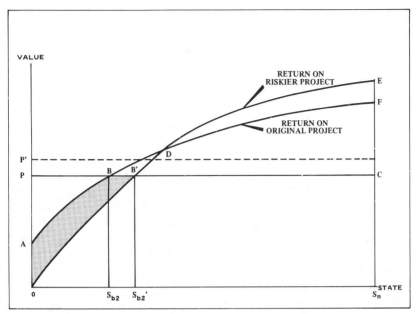

Fig. 9.3   The effect of unanticipated asset substitution on bondholder wealth.

But again, in a rational market the amount paid for debt equals its true expected value; $B = Vd$, so that *any* potential loss in firm value is borne by owners. If bondholders have reason to suspect that owners will move toward riskier investments, the price of debt will be discounted in the capital market. In the extreme, investors may anticipate losses so great that additional debt will not be purchased at *any* promised payment.

Again, it is intangible investment which leads to the problem. When a firm invests in capital equipment, it is relatively simple to estimate the owner's incentives to substitute riskier investments and to observe their contribution to firm risk. This means that it is more likely that bondholders can accurately anticipate asset substitution.[2] But when a firm faces many firm-specific investment opportunities, it is a relatively simple matter for owners to increase firm risk over time. Because of the intangible nature of these investments, market participants often have difficulty estimating their risk and return. Further, since the ultimate effect of increasing the risk of intangible investments may not be known for several years, it is almost impossible for bondholders or the capital market to monitor such investments. For these reasons, we hypothesize that firms with a high proportion of value due to intangible investment opportunities can support less debt than those whose value depends on tangible assets.

9.3 Empirical Results

We test our hypothesis that a firm's choice of capital depends on the type of investment opportunities it faces by examining the cross-sectional behavior of firms during the period 1978–80.

Our primary source of data is the COMPUSTAT Annual Industrial File. All manufacturing firms (SIC four-digit classification 2000–3999) which contained a full set of data for 1978–80 were considered as our initial sample.[3] Additional data were obtained from the CRSP Daily Return Tape. This limited our sample to firms listed on either the New York (NYSE) or American Stock Exchange (AMEX). Our final sample consists of 545 firms of which 139 are in the Standard and Poor 500, 216 are non-Standard and Poor 500 NYSE firms, and 190 are listed on the AMEX. We require two sets of variables: those measuring financial leverage and those measuring the type of investment opportunities.

Measuring financial leverage is relatively straightforward. Our previous analysis suggests that firms will choose a capital structure which reflects the type of investment opportunities they face. However, it is well known that firms do not instantaneously adjust their financing mix to reflect changes in underlying characteristics. Rather, the issue or retirement of debt occurs at fixed points in time as the firm adjusts to its target debt ratio. Thus, the average stock of debt outstanding during any period of time should provide a better indication of a firm's target capital structure than changes in the level of debt. In addition, since our hypothesis centers on the effect of long-term investments on the firm's financing decisions, we wish to consider only long-term, funded debt.[4] We thus measure financial leverage as the book value of all long-term, funded debt.[5]

When considering the effect of investment type on financial leverage, we must devise measures which capture the realization that firms raise capital prior to funding investments. This implies that our investment measures should be current flows rather than stocks.[6] In addition, we must recognize that, as Myers (1977) pointed out, all investments are discretionary in nature and thus may lead to agency problems. But we hypothesize that it is only firm-specific, intangible investment opportunities that reduce the firm's debt capacity and thus their financial leverage. Because all investments provide some growth in the firm's assets, we need variables which distinguish between growth due merely to expansion (NPV = 0) and true economic growth (NPV > 0). True economic growth results from a firm's ability to select investments which create a unique product or process. Two such investments for which there are readily available data are R&D and advertising. To capture the flow of funds into alternative investments, we use the firm's reported R&D and advertising expenditures as our proxies for firm-specific, intangible investments and the firm's reported capital expenditures to measure expansionary or tangible investments.

All of the above variables, financial leverage, R&D, advertising, and capital expenditures, are measured using accounting data. Because there is a large variation in the size of firms, a direct comparison of these variables is impossible. To standardize our measures, we use a size-related denominator and compute ratios. Since we are primarily interested in how firms have raised capital to fund their mix of investments, we seek a standardizing variable which reflects invested capital. We define invested capital as the book values of long-term debt and equity. We then modify this measure by recognizing that there are several categories of capital, such as R&D and advertising, which, because of the difficulty in measuring future benefits, are currently required by GAAP to be expensed. The expensing, rather than the capitalization, of these items is in contrast to the treatment of tangible assets, which are capitalized initially and then depreciated. Because the items which are expensed are precisely those which we hypothesize can support little debt, we adjust our denominator by adding capitalized advertising and R&D. We assume a five-year life for R&D, a three-year life for advertising, and straight-line amortization. Because the use of capitalized R&D and advertising reduces the financial leverage variable for firms with higher such expenditures, there is a potential bias in our results. For this reason, we examine alternative standardizing variables: total assets and invested capital (without capitalized R&D and advertising). To control for any unusual conditions which might affect a variable at any point in time, we average our ratios over a three-year period from 1978 through 1980.

We also wish to consider the effect of the firm's asset (operating) risk on capital structure decisions. The traditional finance literature assumes that operating and financial risk are offsetting decisions, so that firms with greater operating risk will have lower financial leverage. By including a measure of operating risk, we are better able to isolate the effects of investment choice on financial leverage. We are interested in the firm's systematic risk, or beta, which is assumed to capture all of its business or asset risk. We first compute the firm's equity beta, using the geometric average of 20 daily returns to approximate one month.[7] We then unlever the beta as suggested by Hamada (1972) and Rubenstein (1973) using the market value of equity and the book value of debt as a percentage of total value to weight equity and debt, respectively. Because we assume debt is riskless, our measure underestimates systematic risk for high-leverage firms.[8] We include the unlevered beta as an independent variable in all tests using individual firm data.

In addition, to completely neutralize a firm's underlying business risk, we also form equal beta portfolios by first determining the median unlevered beta. We then list all firms in decreasing order of financial leverage and place them into one of two groups: those with unlevered betas above the median and those with unlevered betas below the median. Next we place the first four firms in each group into a 8-firm portfolio. We weight the portfolio so that its unlevered beta is equal to the median beta. We continue the process until all firms are assigned to a portfolio. This process, which creates 68 equal beta portfolios, each with a different degree of financial leverage, greatly reduces the random variation in our predictor variables. This reduction in variation can be seen on table 9.1.

Table 9.1 shows that for each variable, the standard deviation is lower when portfolio data are used. However, because the use of portfolios results in a loss of data, all results are reported for both individual firms and portfolios of firms. Our basic models of the predictors of financial leverage are presented below.

(14)   Leverage = $B_0 + B_1$ (advertising) + B_2 (R&D)
         + B_3 (capital expenditures)

(15)   Leverage = $C_0 + C_1$ (advertising) + C_2 (R&D)
         + C_3 (capital expenditures)
         + C_4 (unlevered beta)

Equation (14) is the model used to test data for the 68 portfolios, while equation (15) is used to test data for the 545 firms. Both models are tested using ordinary least squares regression. Table 9.2 presents the results of tests of equation (14) using the three alternative denominators discussed above, while table 9.3 presents the results using firm data.

Table 9.2 shows that, depending on the denominator used, between 35% and 41% of the variation in debt is explained by investment type. In each case, the signs are as predicted. The results using invested capital plus capitalized R&D and advertising and those using totals assets are quite similar. The results using only invested capital also are similar,

Table 9.1   Summary Statistics

	545 Firms		68 Portfolios	
Variable	Mean	Standard Deviation	Mean	Standard Deviation
Advertising	.0253	.0382	.0402	.0303
Capital expenditure	.0964	.0523	.1240	.0260
R&D	.0241	.0269	.0366	.0217
Unlevered beta	.9229	.4649	N.A.	N.A.
Long-term debt	.2506	.1470	.2560	.1339

Table 9.2   **Advertising, Research and Development and Capital Expenditure as Determinants of Financial Leverage for 68 Portfolios**

Variable	Denominator		
	Invested Capital	Invested Capital, Capitalized R&D and Advertising	Total Assets
Constant	.107	.107	.064
Advertising	−1.211	−1.314	−1.416
	(1.88)	(2.80)	(2.20)
R&D	−2.497	−2.182	−2.370
	(2.36)	(3.22)	(2.23)
Capital expenditure	2.647	2.269	2.820
	(4.33)	(4.39)	(4.60)
Adjusted R^2	.35	.41	.39

Note: Absolute value of t-ratios in parentheses.

Table 9.3   **Advertising, R&D, Capital Expenditures, and Unlevered Beta as Determinants of Financial Leverage for 545 Firms**

Variable	Coefficient	t-Statistic (Absolute Value)
Constant (C_0)	.325	
Advertising (C_1)	−.522	3.43
R&D (C_2)	−.867	3.87
Capital expenditure (C_3)	.520	4.68
Unlevered beta (C_4)	−.098	7.54

Note: Adjusted R^2 = .21.

except that the significance of the advertising variable declines. Because the results are similar, and because we feel that it is appropriate to capitalize rather than expense R&D and advertising, all future tests will use variables standardized by invested capital plus capitalized R&D and advertising.

Table 9.3 shows that, for individual firms, systematic risk and investment type explain 21% of the variation in debt. Not surprisingly, the most significant variable is systematic asset risk, with riskier firms having lower financial leverage.[9] All variables measuring investment type have the predicted sign and are statistically significant. Firms with discretionary investment opportunities have lower financial leverage than those facing tangible investments.[10]

We now wish to determine whether or not the above results indicate a true moral hazard problem. It is possible that our results reflect spurious correlation of our proxies for investment type with other, more important determinants of financial leverage. We investigate this possibility by examining the effect of variables suggested by other researchers on the power of the model. These determinants include non-interest-related tax shields, firm specific (unsystematic) risk, and the availability of internal funds.[11] In addition, we examine whether or not agency problems affect short-term borrowing decisions. Because several of our variables exhibit multicollinearity, we examine the correlation matrices for both firms and portfolios before presenting our results.

Tables 9.4 and 9.5 show that there is a high degree of multicollinearity between capital expenditures and investment-related tax shields, which might affect either the sign or interpretation of the tax variable. However, it is interesting to note that the tax shield is positively related to long-term debt.

In addition, a comparison of tables 9.4 and 9.5 shows that when we neutralize risk, advertising and R&D are positively correlated with operating cash flows. These correlations are not present in individual firm data. Thus when we consider the effect of operating cash flow on the power of the moral hazard model, we might expect different results for the two sets of data. Table 9.4 also shows that while systematic and unsystematic risk are positively correlated, their effect on debt is opposite. With these relationships in mind, we now examine each variable separately and determine its effect on the moral hazard model.

We first examine the effect of investment-related tax shields on the power of our model. Expanding on Miller (1977), DeAngelo and Masulis (1980) first suggested that a firm's financial leverage depends on the availability of investment-related tax shields, such as depreciation and investment tax credits. They show that when such tax shields are available, corporate capital structure is relevant to individual firms. They argue that the presence of nondebt tax shields affects the extent to which corporations can gain from the substitution of debt for equity. Since higher financial leverage increases the probability that nondebt tax shields will be lost, they hypothesize that firms with lower tax shields will employ more debt in their capital structure. This implies that firms investing heavily in capital equipment, which generates large tax shields, should have less debt. We have already observed that the relationship between capital expenditures and financial leverage is positive. However, we wish to test the effect of tax shields directly. We compute the depreciation tax shield as depreciation expense times the corporate marginal tax rate plus the change in deferred taxes. The total investment-related tax shield is the sum of the depreciation tax shield and the investment tax credit.[12]

Table 9.4   **Correlation Matrix, 545 Firms**

	Adver-tising	Capital Expen-ditures	R&D	Unlevered Beta	Operating Cash Flow	Unsystem-atic Risk	Tax Shield	Short-term Debt	Long-term Debt
Advertising	1.000	−.254	−.018	−.011	−.172	.034	−.239	.052	−.176
Capital expenditures		1.000	.004	.068	.368	−.116	.671	.039	.198
R&D			1.000	.368	−.091	.023	−.022	−.115	−.270
Unlevered beta				1.000	.211	.238	−.007	−.253	−.355
Operating cash flow					1.000	−.096	.242	−.082	−.244
Unsystematic risk						1.000	−.105	.141	.133
Tax shield							1.000	−.013	.123
Short-term debt								1.000	.280
Long-term debt									1.000

Note: Standard error of correlation coefficients = .043.

Table 9.5 Correlation Matrix, 68 Portfolios

	Adver-tising	Capital Expen-ditures	R&D	Operating Cash Flow	Unsystem-atic Risk	Tax Shield	Short-term Debt	Long-term Debt
Advertising	1.000	−.096	.416	.501	−.215	−.417	.081	−.487
Capital expenditures		1.000	.270	.158	.040	.562	.166	.373
R&D			1.000	.505	−.121	−.165	.089	−.359
Operating cash flow				1.000	−.268	−.176	−.125	−.642
Unsystematic risk					1.000	−.005	.239	.345
Tax shield						1.000	.033	.378
Short-term debt							1.000	.319
Long-term debt								1.000

Note: Standard error of correlation coefficients = .121.

Table 9.6   **The Effect of Investment-related Tax Shields on Financial Leverage**

	Firms	Portfolios
Constant	.332	.137
Advertising	−.542 (3.55)	−1.436 (2.89)
R&D	−.870 (3.88)	−2.316 (3.30)
Capital expenditure	.654 (4.46)	2.580 (3.94)
Tax shield	−.571 (1.40)	−1.858 (.78)
Unlevered beta	−.099 (7.62)	N.A.
Adjusted R^2	.21	.41

Note: Absolute value of t-statistic in parentheses.

Table 9.6 presents the results of including the investment-related tax shield in our model. We see that because of multicollinearity, the coefficients are negative but insignificant. The coefficients of our moral hazard variables remain as predicted, and all are significant. Thus while we cannot exclude the possibility of tax effect, we can conclude that the moral hazard problem remains and is important in determining financial leverage.

We next turn to the question of whether or not a firm's total risk influences its financial leverage. Agency theory contends that the higher the variance of the firm's returns, the less the underinvestment problem. Because investments which reduce firm risk provide a capital gain to bondholders at the expense of shareholders, owners are likely to forgo such investments. Conversely, because they hold claim to the upper portion of a firm's distribution of return, shareholders are more likely invest in high-variance projects. Thus, all other factors equal, high-variance firms will lower agency costs of debt due to underinvestment and thus higher financial leverage.[13] If, however, we consider the possibility that bankruptcy costs matter, higher-variance firms would have less debt.[14] Thus, if total risk has a positive effect on leverage, we assume that the moral hazard problem outweighs the increased probability of bankruptcy, and vice versa if the effect is negative. If both problems are important, then they should offset each other and the effect of total risk on financial leverage should be neutralized.

We measure total risk as the unsystematic, firm-specific, residual variance of the firm's stock returns, standardized by the market variance.[15]

Table 9.7   The Effect of Firm-specific Risk on Financial Leverage

	Firms	Portfolios
Constant	.299	.034
Advertising	−.523	−1.119
	(3.58)	(2.44)
R&D	−.756	−2.110
	(3.50)	(3.24)
Capital expenditures	.617	2.227
	(5.72)	(4.48)
Firm-specific risk	.005	.010
	(6.72)	(2.50)
Unlevered beta	−.121	N.A.
	(9.32)	
Adjusted R^2	.27	.46

Note: Absolute value of t-statistics in parentheses.

Table 9.7 shows that when using data for individual firms or portfolios, unsystematic risk has a significantly positive effect on financial leverage. We note that with firm data, the effect of unlevered beta on financial leverage is negative. To attempt to determine the overall affect of risk, we also used the firm's total variance of stock returns, unlevered to remove the effect of debt. Our results showed that total risk also is significantly positively correlated with financial leverage. This indicates that control of underinvestment exerts a greater influence on debt capacity than does the increased probability of bankruptcy. While we cannot conclude that bankruptcy costs are irrelevant, we can state that inclusion of risk measures does not affect the ability of the moral hazard variables to explain financial leverage.

We next examine the possibility that the size of a firm's operating cash flows determines financial leverage. There are two possible explanations why cash flows might influence corporate borrowing.

First, as Donaldson (1961) noted, managers may prefer to minimize their costs and constraints by using internally generated funds. This is consistent with Miller's (1977) argument that with personal taxes and no transactions costs firms are indifferent to capital structure. If we then introduce transactions costs, we would expect that firms will choose the form of financing which is least expensive. Therefore, firms with adequate internal funds will provide most of their capital requirements internally, while less liquid firms will be forced to resort to outside funding.

However, it is also possible that a firm's cash flows are a proxy for the type of investment opportunities they face. In the absence of positive net present valued investments, we would expect that if risk were held constant, all firms would have the same before tax operating cash flows. Any observed variation in cash flows can be attributed to variation in economic growth. True economic growth results from a firm's ability to select investments which create unique products or processes. When investment opportunities are firm specific or intangible, they are more likely to generate positive net present values and thus higher cash flows. Thus it is possible that the size of a firm's cash flows is a proxy for firm-specific investment opportunities instead of growth opportunities.

We measure operating cash flows as earnings before interest, depreciation and taxes. If either explanation is correct, we expect cash flow to have a negative relationship with financial leverage.

Table 9.8 indicates that operating cash flow is indeed negatively related to financial leverage. In the model using firm data, inclusion of cash flow does not affect the explanatory power of the moral hazard variables. However, since firms with higher systematic risk should have higher profitability, we consider these results inconclusive. When we examine the effect of cash flow when risk is neutralized, we see that the importance of both advertising and R&D is reduced below statistical significance. This is due to the previously noted high positive correlation among the variables. There are three possible explanations for this phenomenon. First, because our portfolios are ordered by financial leverage, it is

Table 9.8   **The Effect of Operating Cash Flow on Financial Leverage**

	Firms	Portfolios
Constant	.418	.471
Advertising	−.644	−.297
	(4.52)	(.76)
Capital expenditures	.851	2.608
	(7.72)	(6.49)
R&D	−1.235	−.991
	(5.79)	(1.79)
Operating cash flow	−.629	−1.733
	(8.94)	(6.67)
Unlevered beta	−.069	N.A.
	(5.49)	
Adjusted R^2	.31	.65

Note: Absolute value of t-statistics in parentheses.

possible that low leverage firms have high cash flows and independently have high advertising and R&D expenditures. In this case, because cash flows exert a stronger influence on leverage, the importance of advertising and R&D is reduced, but the variables do not proxy for each other. A second possibility is that advertising and R&D create high cash flows and therefore proxy for the availability of internal funds. Finally, it is possible that cash flows are a proxy for all firm-specific investment opportunities, including advertising and R&D.

While we cannot empirically distinguish among the alternative explanations, it appears likely that the first is correct and the variables are independent determinants of leverage. Because capital expenditures is not strongly correlated with cash flows, it is still statistically significant. Capital expenditures also measures the extent of moral hazard problems and its inclusion in the model (after the influence of cash flows has been considered) increases the explained variation in financial leverage by 25%. Thus, while we cannot explain the relationship between advertising, R&D, and cash flows, we can conclude that the moral hazard problem is important.

Finally, we look at whether or not our basic model can explain a firm's use of short-term sources of funds. If short-term borrowing is used in order to resolve agency problems, advertising and R&D should exert a positive effect. But if firms turn to short-term borrowing solely to finance cyclical, short-term requirements, while choosing to finance longer-term requirements by issuing long-term, funded debt, the effect of our variables on the level of short-term debt should be negligible. Table 9.9 shows the results of our basic model using short-term debt as our dependent variable.

Table 9.9 shows that when we use firm data, advertising and capital expenditures have a positive effect on short-term borrowing while R&D has a negative effect. Our results with portfolio data are similar, except that R&D does not enter the equation. In both cases, our explained variation is extremely small. It appears as if firms make short-term borrowing decisions independent of long-term investment requirements and do not attempt to resolve agency problems by the substitution of short-term for long-term debt.

9.4   Conclusions and Implications

We have shown that moral hazard problem, which affects a firm's investment decisions, is a major determinant of corporate leverage. Specifically, we developed a model in which a firm's financial leverage depends on whether it invests in tangible, capital assets or in intangible, firm-specific assets. We tested our model using both a large sample of

Table 9.9   The Effect of Moral Hazard of Short-Term Borrowing

	Firms	Portfolios
Constant	.118	.040
Advertising	.205	.218
	(1.56)	(.80)
Capital expenditures	.163	.457
	(1.69)	(1.43)
R&D	−.099	Did not enter
	(.51)	(.00)
Unlevered beta	−.063	N.A.
	(5.57)	
Adjusted R^2	.06	.01

Note: Absolute value of t-statistics in parentheses.

individual firms and 68 eight-firm portfolios formed to neutralize systematic operating risk. We were able to explain 21% of the variation for individual firms and 41% of the variation when risk was held constant.

We then examined the robustness of our model by including various variables which other researchers have suggested may influence financial leverage. Our intent was not to prove or disprove alternative theories but rather to determine the power of the moral hazard model. We found that including investment-related tax shields or firm-specific risk did not affect our results. When we included a variable measuring before-tax operating cash flow, we found that two of our variables, advertising and R&D, did lose power. While we were unable to determine precisely the relationship among the variables, we did find evidence that they are independent measures. It appears that while the availability of internal funds may be the most important determinant of whether or not a firm seeks external sources of funds, the moral hazard problem can still explain the choice of debt or equity.

We conclude that a major factor which influences corporate leverage decisions is the type of investments a firm undertakes. Given that a firm must seek an outside source of funds, its choice between debt or equity will depend in part on the magnitude of potential agency costs of debt. Because of these costs, corporations which invest heavily in intangibles, such as R&D and advertising, have a tighter capital market imposed debt capacity than those investing in tangible assets. Our findings provide direct empirical evidence that the moral hazard problem is important and that investment and financing decisions are not independent.

Notes

1. The first-order conditions for the two investments are as follows:

(i) $\qquad\qquad -1 + \int_{S_{d2}}^{\infty} [\partial R(C_1', S_2)/\partial C_1'] \, q_1(S_2) \, dS_2 = 0$,

(ii) $\qquad\qquad -1 + \int_{S_{d2''}}^{\infty} [\partial R''(C_1', S_2)/\partial C_1'] \, q_1(S_2) \, dS_2 = 0$.

Since the second term in eq. (i) exceeds that of eq. (ii), when the level of investment is constant the less risky investment is optimal for the firm. It can be shown (see Myers 1977) that when the level of investment varies, the less risky investment may lead to greater underinvestment, that is, area $S_{d2} \, AA' \, S_{b2}$ may be greater than $S_{d2}'' \, BB' \, S_{b2}''$ on fig. 9.2.

2. For example, if alternative capital equipment with different contributions to operating risk is available, this is likely to be known and the effect of the riskier investment on debt values can be anticipated. Or, if the shift in risk is accomplished by replacing existing equipment, it is likely that the price paid for the equipment will approximate its true value. Then all bondholders need be concerned about is that the expected NPV of the new equipment is nonnegative.

3. When there were missing data, the values were collected from *Moody's Industrial Manual*.

4. Myers (1977) has shown that because short-term debt is retired prior to investment choice it does not affect owner's investment decisions. We examine this proposition later in this paper.

5. We investigate the possibility that since agency problems can be circumvented either by issuing convertible debt (Jensen and Meckling 1976) or by leasing the inclusion of these items in our measure of debt may bias our results. However, when we remove convertible debt and leases from our measure of financial leverage, we achieve identical results for both the portfolios and individual firms.

6. The use of investment stocks would seriously bias our results. The stock of debt reflects the current level of debt. The stock of investments reflects all previous investment decisions, many of which were made prior to issuing any of the long-term debt which is currently outstanding. The flow of funds into alternative investments adequately reflects the use to which the funds raised from the sale of debt were put.

7. Betas are determined using 60 "months" of data where possible. Where 60 months are not available less are used except that at least 36 "months" are required.

8. If debt is not riskless, our estimate underestimates the asset beta by a factor equal to the firm's leverage ratio times its true debt beta. If we assume that debt of higher-leverage firms has greater systematic risk, this underestimation is magnified.

9. This relationship is due in part to the negative bias in our computation of unlevered beta for high-leverage firms.

10. It is suggested that our results might be due to a few firms which have extremely high advertising or R&D expenditures. To test this, we eliminated firms in the pharmaceutical industry, which have high R&D expenses, and those in the cosmetics industry, which have above-average advertising outlays. Our results did not significantly change.

11. We also examined the possibility, suggested by Dasgupta and Stiglitz (1980), that a firm's competitive environment determines both whether or not intangible investments are undertaken, and its financial leverage. According to their model, one would expect that firms in medium concentration industries would have greater expenditures in R&D and advertising. Since these firms also face greater demand uncertainty, they can support less debt. We tested the proposition that financial leverage is determined by a firm's competitive environment by considering a model which incorporates industry concentration. We define industry concentration in two ways. First, we compute the percentage of industry output

produced by the four largest firms in each four-digit SIC. We also compute a second measure, designed to reach a maximum at 50% concentration (100% concentration − concentration^2). We found that neither measure is correlated with either the type of investment or with financial leverage and thus had no effect on the power of our model.

12. There are two methods used in accounting for investment tax credits. The flow-through method reports the entire tax benefit in the year of purchase, so that our measure is taken directly from each firm's income statement. The deferral method capitalizes the benefit and amortizes it over five years. For these firms we use the income statement value plus balance sheet changes in investment tax credit accounts.

13. We recognize the potential agency costs involved in the substitution of the same quantity of risky projects for those with less risk and greater value. However, if more positive valued projects are undertaken, then firm value will show a net increase. In most cases, the underinvestment problem dominates the asset substitution problem.

14. Studies of actual bankruptcy costs find that they are quite small and increase less than proportionally with the size of the firm. For example, see Warner (1977) and Ang, Chua, and McConnell (1982).

15. There is a slight negative bias in our measure. We compute unsystematic risk as the total variance of stock returns, standardized by the market variance less the square of the stock beta. It can be shown that, all other things equal, the change in unsystematic risk with respect to the debt-to-equity ratio is slightly negative.

References

Ang, J.; Chua, J.; and McConnell, J. 1982. The administrative costs of bankruptcy. *Journal of Finance* 37:219–26.

Baxter, N. 1967. Leverage, risk or ruin and the cost of capital. *Journal of Finance* 22:395–403.

Black, F., and Scholes, M. 1973. Pricing of options and corporate liabilities. *Journal of Political Economy* 81:637–59.

Dasgupta, P., and Stiglitz, J. 1980. Uncertainty, industrial structure, and the speed of R&D. *Bell Journal of Economics* 11:1–28.

DeAngelo, H., and Masulis, R. 1980. Optimal capital structure under corporate and personal taxation. *Journal of Financial Economics* 8:3–28.

Donaldson, G. 1961. *Corporate debt capacity*. Boston: Graduate School of Business Research, Harvard University.

Hamada, R. 1972. The effects of the firm's capital structure on the systematic risk of common stocks. *Journal of Finance* 27:435–52.

Hite, G., and Jiviland, A. 1977. Some evidence on the determinants of capital structure. Unpublished paper, Ohio State University.

Jensen, M., and Meckling, W. 1976. Theory of the firm: managerial behavior, agency costs, and ownership structure. *Journal of Financial Economics* 3:305–60.

Long, M. 1981. Discretionary investments as a predictior of leverage. Working paper, University of British Columbia.

Malitz, I. 1982*a*. Determining the optimal set of bond covenants. Working paper, Georgetown University.

———. 1982*b*. The optimal set of bond covenants: a theoretical and empirical investigation. Ph.D. diss., University of Maryland.

Miller, M. 1977. Debt and taxes. *Journal of Finance* 32:261–75.

Modigliani, F., and Miller, M. 1958. The cost of capital, corporate finance, and the theory of investment. *American Economic Review* 48:261–97.

———. 1963. Corporate income tax and the cost of capital: a correction. *American Economic Review* 53:433–43.

Myers, S. 1977. Determinants of corporate borrowing. *Journal of Financial Economics* 5:147–75.

Rubenstein, M. 1973. A mean-variance synthesis of corporate financial theory. *Journal of Finance* 28:167–81.

Smith, C., and Warner, J. 1979. On financial contracting: an analysis of bond covenants. *Journal of Financial Economics* 7:117–61.

U.S. Bureau of the Census. 1977. *Census of Manufacturers 1977.* Washington: Government Printing Office.

Warner, J. 1977. Bankruptcy costs: some evidence. *Journal of Finance* 32:337–47.

Williamson, S. 1981. The moral hazard theory of corporate financial structure: an empirical test. Ph.D. diss., Massachusetts Institute of Technology.

Comment   Stewart C. Myers

A firm's optimal debt ratio is usually viewed as determined by a trade off of the costs and benefits of borrowing, holding the firm's assets and investment plans constant. The firm is portrayed as balancing the value of interest tax shields against various costs of financial embarrassment. Of course, there is controversy about how valuable the tax shields are and whether the costs of financial embarrassment are material, but these give only variations on a theme. The firm is supposed to substitute debt for equity, or equity for debt, until the value of the firm is maximized.

Contrast this *static trade-off* theory with a competing popular theory, which dates back at least to Gordon Donaldson's 1961 book, *Corporate Debt Capacity*. This *pecking order* theory goes as follows: (1) Firms prefer internal finance. (2) They adapt their target dividend payout ratios to their investment requirements, although dividends are sticky and target payout ratios are only gradually adjusted to shifts in investment

Stewart C. Myers is professor of finance at the Massachusetts Institute of Technology's Alfred P. Sloan School of Management and a research associate of the NBER.

opportunities. (3) If external finance is required, firms issue the safest security first. That is, they start with debt, then possibly hybrid securities such as convertible bonds, then equity. (However, firms are reluctant to issue stock if they fall into financial distress.)

I used to ignore the pecking order theory because I could think of no theoretical foundation for it. However, recent work based on asymmetrical information, problems of adverse selection, moral hazard, and signaling gives predictions roughly in line with the pecking order theory (see, e.g., Myers and Majluf 1983).

I mention these two theories only to make my own a priori view explicit. I believe both are operating at once. Firms are adjusting toward a target debt ratio, reflecting the benefits and costs that the static trade-off theory emphasizes. However, the sequence of security issues firms make cannot be described as a smooth, gradual adjustment toward a target ratio.

If I am right, it will be extremely difficult to take a cross-section of firms in a particular year and obtain an accurate test of the impact of variables which come from the static trade-off theory. Even if the tested variables truly determine the target ratio, they may not explain the actual ratio, because firms may take extended and erratic excursions away from the target.

Let me now turn to the Long-Malitz paper. They started with the hypothesis that firms borrow more against assets in place than intangibles and growth opportunities. This hypothesis has a good theoretical foundation within the static trade-off framework. They had the excellent idea of using advertising and research and development (R&D) expenditures as a proxy for the value of intangibles and growth opportunities.

These are likely to be robust proxies. There are relatively few problems in measuring R&D and advertising. Moreover, tests of their effects should be relatively insensitive to problems in measuring other things. For example, the authors would have liked to use the replacement instead of the book value of assets as a scaling variable for their regressions. I agree, but I do not think that use of book assets undermined their tests of the impact of advertising and R&D.

Long and Malitz conclude that asset *type* matters for debt policy, holding asset risk constant. The more intangibles and growth opportunities the firm has, the lower its target debt ratio. This is an important positive result.[1]

Long and Malitz's other results are harder to interpret. Consider, for example, the relationship between operating cash flow and capital structure. The problem is to choose a hypothesis. Long and Malitz view high cash flow as a proxy for high profitability and the existence of valuable growth opportunities. However, if the pecking order theory is correct, cash flow also indicates ample internal sources of funds. Either argument implies a negative relationship between cash flow and debt ratios. It is therefore not clear which theory is being tested.

Long and Malitz's tax variables do not perform well, which is disturbing: we would expect to find a strong tax effect in any cross-sectional capital structure test, regardless of whose theory of "debt and taxes" you believe in.

Figure 9.C.1 plots the net tax gain from corporate borrowing against the firm's effective marginal tax rate. In the original Modigliani-Miller theory, which ignores personal taxes, any tax-paying corporation gains by borrowing; the greater the marginal tax rate, the greater the gain. This gives the top line in the figure. In Miller's (1977) paper, the personal income taxes on interest receipts would exactly offset the corporate interest tax shield, providing the firm paid the full 46% statutory tax rate. However, any firm paying less than 46% would see a net tax loss to corporate borrowing. This gives the bottom line.

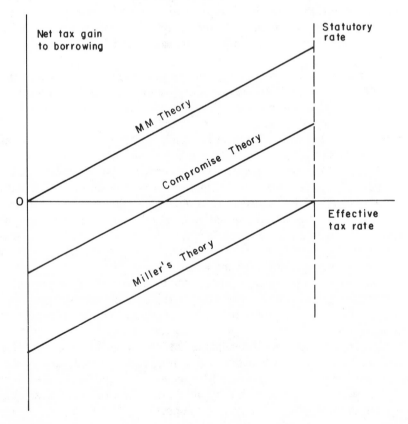

Fig. 9.C.1

Of course, we now have compromise theories, indicated by the dashed line in the figure (DeAngelo and Masulis 1980). But regardless of which theory holds, the slope of the line is always positive. Therefore it is puzzling that Long and Malitz find no cross-sectional relationship between the firm's tax status and financial leverage.

Perhaps the difficulty is finding a good proxy for "tax status." I disagree with Long and Malitz's use of depreciation tax shields and investment tax credits, for two reasons. First, there are many other noninterest tax shields, for example, R&D expenditures, which can be written off immediately. One could argue that investments in intangible assets are given better treatment under our tax law than investment in tangible assets. Second, noninterest tax shields are at best indirect measures of unshielded income, that is, income after all deductions except interest. This, however, can be measured directly.

However, looking at unshielded income takes us right back to looking at operating cash flow, which consequently must play three parts: high cash flow may indicate (1) valuable intangible assets and growth opportunities, (2) ample internal sources of funds, or (3) a high demand for interest tax shields. You cannot test three hypotheses with one variable.

Note

1. Scott H. Williamson (1981) reached the same conclusion after extensive empirical tests. Williamson's proxy for a firm's intangibles and growth opportunities was the difference between the market value of its debt and equity securities and the replacement cost of its tangible assets.

References

DeAngelo, H. and Masulis, R. 1980. Optimal capital structure under corporate and personal taxation. *Journal of Financial Economics* 8:3–29.

Donaldson, G. 1961. *Corporate debt capacity*. Division of Research, Harvard Graduate School of Business Administration, Harvard University.

Miller, M. 1977. Debt and taxes. *Journal of Finance* 32:261–75.

Myers, S., and Majluf, N. S. 1983. Corporate financing and investment policy when firms have information investors do not have. Working paper, MIT and National Bureau of Economic Research.

Williamson, S. H. 1981. The moral hazard theory of corporate financial structure: Empirical tests. Unpublished Ph.D. dissertation, MIT.

10 Capital Structure and the Corporation's Product Market Environment

A. Michael Spence

10.1 Introduction

This paper is a report on my attempts to explore the relationship between the capital structure choices firms make and the characteristics of the product market environments in which they operate. The hypothesis with which I began and which will serve to structure the initial exposition was quite simple. If optimizing a corporation's capital structure is a way of reducing total costs (or equivalently of raising the total market value of the firm), then firms under competitive pressure in the product markets might "optimize" their capital structures more carefully than firms that occupy positions in the product market sheltered to some extent from competition.

I was led to hypotheses of this type by observing, in a number of instances, that firms with strong product market positions appeared to have widely divergent approaches to capital structure policy. Some, like IBM, had little debt for extensive periods of time. Others, like Tandy Corporation, were highly leveraged and readjusted their capital structures periodically by issuing debt and buying in stock. Other corporations, operating in highly competitive environments, seemed to me to exhibit less variability in the amounts of debt they issued (in relation to total assets). Cases of this type, of course, are not necessarily selected randomly. Nor do they establish that capital structure has a significant effect on total costs or firm value. This research is therefore an attempt to explore these hypotheses with a larger and less potentially biased sample of firms.

I should say at the outset that I agree with scholars who argue that

A. Michael Spence is dean of the Faculty of Arts and Sciences at Harvard University and a research associate of the NBER.

corporations are subject to pressure from both product and capital market sources. External product market pressures operate directly on profitability and on returns to investment. Capital markets, through withholding investment funds by bidding down the price of the equity or through takeovers, may intervene when the operations, investment decisions, or financing decisions of the corporation are mismanaged.

By focusing on the product market side, I do not mean to imply that capital market influences are unimportant. On the other hand, to pursue this line of research, as a matter of logic I do have to maintain as a hypothesis that the capital market pressure is not always sufficient to remove all but short-run deviations from optimal financial policies. If this were not true, there would be no deviations to explain. I shall say more about this later in the context of the statistical results.

The capital and product markets are not mutually exclusive constraining forces. A takeover could be the mechanism by which a failure to minimize costs is removed. The hypothesis here is that capital markets do not remove all deviations, and that management, with or without capital market intervention, react to pressure on profits from a competitive environment by trying to reduce costs further. Therefore, if capital structure affects costs, then intensely competitive product market environments will, on average, reduce deviations from optimal capital structure for corporations operating in that kind of environment.

The paper in outline is as follows. Section 10.2 sets out the formal statement of the hypotheses just discussed. Section 10.3 describes the variables used to characterize the product market environment of the firm. Section 10.4 presents the preliminary results of testing the hypothesis. In sections 10.5 and 10.6, I explore two related questions using the same database. One concerns the relationship between a corporation's product market position and its profitability. The other deals with the extent to which the product market variables and certain financial variables are capable of explaining the corporation's *actual* capital structure. I emphasize "actual" here to distinguish these results from those reported in section 10.4, where the issue is the divergence between actual and a calculated optimal capital structure. Section 10.7 summarizes the results and draws some conclusions. An appendix details the sources of the data.

It may be useful to provide a brief statement of the results in advance. I can find very little evidence that deviations of actual from calculated optimal capital structures are influenced at all by the product market environment. These results are consistent with the view that there are no optimal capital structures. I do find that the product market environment explains a substantial amount of the variance across firms in returns on total investment. Thus the product market variables cannot be dismissed as poor descriptions of the product market environment. In addition, I find that the product market variables and measures of profitability are correlated with actual capital structures, and in regressions "explain" a substantial amount of the variance in the ratio of debt to assets.

These results do not establish that the corporation's capital structure influences its costs or its total market value. It is possible that either management or investors have preferences with respect to capitalization that are reflected in what we see in the data, but which are not exclusively preferences for higher as opposed to lower value. On the other hand, the fact that variables describing the product market environment and the firm's profitability "explain" variations in capital structure is certainly not strong evidence that would lead one to accept the hypothesis that capital structure and value are unrelated.

It is difficult to know exactly where these preferences arise. Corporations like IBM and Polaroid with profitable market positions and high levels of investment in research and product development appear to shy away from debt except when financial resource constraints require it. Even then, equity financing has often been preferred. There are numerous examples of firms that avoid debt because they have had what they regard as bad experiences with banks. Historically, Crown Cork and Seal is an example. On the other hand, some corporations like Tandy Corporation persistently readjust their capital structures to keep leverage up. In Tandy's case, those decisions are described by management in annual reports as optimizing the capital structure. Tandy's original growth was financed in part by substantial loans from a few banks. It is likely that there was a somewhat unusual partnership between the corporation and the banks in this case.

Diverse capital structures within an industry could result from tax clienteles.[1] Moreover, investors probably do have industry preferences as part of their strategies for diversification. That would produce capital market pressure for heterogeneity in capital structure at the industry level. If that were the only force operating on capital structure, then one would expect to see deviations of actual from average capital structures that are random with respect to industry characteristics and competitive pressure. That is to say, there would be a nonzero variance in capital structure, but it would not be systematically related to the industry's characteristics. The statistical model below does not require that the variance in the deviation of actual from average capital structure be zero if competitive pressure has no effect.

10.2 The Statistical Model of Deviations of Actual from Optimal Capital Structures

The underlying hypothesis is that firms have optimal capital structures which depend on the industries in which they compete. For the moment, let us assume that each industry i has an optimal capital structure u_i. Let

s_{ji} be the share of the jth firm's assets in industry i. I assume that the optimal capital structure for firm j is

$$(1) \qquad f_j = \sum_i s_{ji} u_i .$$

The actual capital structure of firm j is d_j. Capital structure here is measured by the ratio of debt, both current and long term, to total assets. Let x_j be a vector of attributes of firm j, describing the industries in which it operates and its competitive position in those industries. (I describe what are useful measures of these attributes in the next section.)

The main hypothesis is that the actual capital structure, d, is a random variable with a mean of f and a variance of v^2. The variance is a function of x:

$$(2) \qquad v^2 = H(x) .$$

The hypothesis is that as product market pressure declines, the variance v^2 increases.

There is an assumption implicit in this formulation of the hypothesis. It is that the degree to which the optimal capital structure is indeed optimal is constant across industries. Or, to put it another way, the cost of being away from the optimal capital structure does not vary from one industry to the next. This assumption is unlikely to be strictly true. But to circumvent it, one would need to reinsert an explicit model of the determinants of optimal capital structure, a problem that, as the reader can see, I was trying to avoid. It is perhaps worth noting that similar problems confront most empirical work on industry structure and profitability due to incomplete data on the behavior of the cost functions. In the model tested here, to the extent that industry and firm characteristics are correlated with the costs of being away from optimal capital structure, these variables will pick up that effect. But it will not be identified distinctly from the effects of competitive pressure.

It would be preferable to generalize this model to allow the optimal capital structure to depend on the firm's position in the industries in which it competes, and also on the mix of businesses that it is in. That is to say, it is arguable that optimal capital structure as well as deviations from it depend on x. For reasons that will be apparent shortly, that approach is not computationally feasible at the present time. In fact, the present approach strains resources as it is.

If we assume that d or its log is normally distributed, the probability of observing the sample, conditional on the parameters, is

$$(3) \qquad L = \pi_j (2\pi)^{(-1/2)} \sigma_j^{-1} \exp[(-1/2\sigma^2)(d_j - \sum_i s_{ji} u_i)^2] .$$

The log of the likelihood function, the minimum of which yields the maximum likelihood estimates of the parameters, is

(4)
$$S = (n/2) \log (2\pi) + \sum_j \log (\sigma_j)$$
$$+ \sum_j (\tfrac{1}{2}\sigma_j^2)(d_j - \sum_i s_{ji}u_i)^2.$$

The dependence of the variance on the firm's characteristics is parameterized as follows:

(5)
$$v = \exp (- b \cdot x).$$

This ensures that the likelihood function is convex in b and that v is positive.

The conditions for an optimum are in two groups. First the optimal capital structures for industries. Given $v_j^2, j = 1, \ldots, n$, the maximum likelihood estimate of $u = (u_1, \ldots, u_m)$ is the weighted regression coefficients

(6)
$$u = (S^T D^{-1} S)^{-1} S^T D^{-1} d,$$

where $d = (d_1, \ldots, d_n)$, D is a diagonal matrix with $D_{jj} = v_j^2$, and S is the $n \times m$ matrix whose elements are the s_{ji}. There are practical problems with performing this regression because the number of four-digit industries is 450. We have data on 403 of those. A regression with 403 variables is a nontrivial problem in straight calculation. Nevertheless, the problem is conceptually simple.

The second set of conditions are essentially conditions for the optimal estimates of the determinants of the variances across firms, given the deviations of optimal from actual capital structure. Let

(7)
$$e_j = d_j - \sum_i s_{ji}u_i.$$

Given u, the maximum likelihood estimates of b satisfy

(8)
$$\sum_j [\exp(2bx_j)e_j^2 - 1]x_j = 0.$$

Solutions to these equations in b give the effects of firm and industry characteristics on the variance, that is, the tendency to deviate from the optimal capital structure.

At several points in what follows, I refer to the optimal capital structure for the firm and/or industry. These terms always refer to the calculated optimal structure (6) for the industry and (7) for the firm. Both can be thought of as "suitable" averages of actual capital structures, where the weights in the averages are developed from the shares of each firm's sales (and by calculation assets) in each industry.

We note in passing that

(9)
$$d^2 S / db^2 = 2\sum_j \exp(2bx_j)e_j^2 x_j x_j^T.$$

This second derivative is positive semidefinite. As a result, an extremum in the b's will be a minimum of the objective function.

The second set of conditions entails a nonlinear estimation problem, although a relatively easy one. To find the global maximum, one can solve these two sets of conditions sequentially for u and b. If the process converges, it converges to the maximum likelihood estimates. As I noted above, there are some practical computational problems in implementing this. Nevertheless, this is the conception of the problem with which I began the statistical work.

In section 11.4, I have used somewhat simpler preliminary regressions that retain the content of the model described above. Since the results do not suggest large deviations of actual from optimal capital structures explainable by product market and profitability variables, I have not felt the effort of the nonlinear estimation in step 2 of the maximum likelihood procedure had a sufficiently high payoff to justify the effort and cost.

10.3   The Product Market Environment

The hypothesis outlined above is that firms that are relatively free of competitive pressure will use that freedom in part to maintain capital structures that they prefer. These preferences may or may not be for optimal capital structures. In general, we expect the deviation of actual from optimal to be larger when the competition is less. All of this is of course conditional on there being an optimal capital structure.

There are two ways to measure "competitiveness" in the environment. One is to use various measures of return on investment or assets, perhaps with adjustments for risk. (In this first pass, I have not used security market data to adjust returns for risk, though I plan to do so in future work, particularly in the ROA equations.) Returns measure the *effect* of insulation from competition in the market environment. The second method is to employ product market characteristics, specifically, variables that directly and indirectly measure entry barriers, potential oligopolistic consensus, or both. Further, one can combine certain entry barrier variables that are based on scale advantages with share of market data to obtain measures of the firm's competitive position in the various markets in which it operates. I have used both approaches together on the ground that the entry barrier measures are imperfect, and hence that the return data contain additional information not available in the product market data.

Attaching to each firm are two kinds of variables. One group consists of financial variables, the other of industry variables. For diversified firms, each variable in the latter group is a weighted average across the industries in which the firm operates, with the weights being the share of the firm's sales in each of the relevant industries. For example, if $CI4_i$ is the four-firm concentration ratio for industry i, and $C4_j$ is the four-firm concentration variable for firm j, then

(10) $$C4_j = \sum_i s_{ji} \, CI4_i,$$

where, as before, s_{ji} is the fraction of firm j's sales (or assets) in industry i. Thus the product market environment of each firm is measured by a collection of variables each of which is a weighted average of the attributes of the industries in which the firm participates.

Table 10.1 summarizes the variables that have been used thus far to describe the firm. Product market data are for 1972. Financial data are 5-year averages for 1970–74, the period bracketing 1972. The variables in table 10.1 are the variables I labeled x in the preceding section. They are the hypothesized determinants of the variance.

The definition of capital structure, DEBT/A, includes short-term debt. I included short-term debt because (*a*) some of it is maturing longer-term debt and (*b*) some of the rest (principally bank debt), while formally short term, is often short term only in name. The bank does have options with respect to constraining corporate decisions that are not available to bondholders. So there are important differences. But I felt it would be misleading to label all short-term bank debt "short-term financing," when it is often part of the longer-term capitalization of the corporation.

The financial variables here are all based on book value. In the case of rates of return on assets and equity, there is a good reason for this. We need measures of above- and below-average profitability. Stock market returns reflect risk but not market power except in the period when the market becomes aware of the firm's market power and capitalizes it in the stock price. This is not to say that the book rates of return data are ideal. In fact, there are numerous sources of noise which produce a disconcerting increase in the unexplained variance.

For capital structure, the use of market values would be preferable. But it is costly and difficult to assemble accurate market value data for debt. This study is a cross-section study, so the problems of inflation and interest rate changes that contaminate intertemporal comparisons of leverage using book values do not arise in a severe form here.

I will not review the entire contents of the literature in industrial organization to develop the argument that these variables are pertinent product market characteristics from the standpoint of determining profitability. However, some brief comment is in order. The industry variables are largely industry's characteristics that affect barriers to new competition. That would apply to MES, CDR, A/S, and P/VA as a measure of labor intensity (or absence of capital intensity). Capital intensity is associated with sunk costs and irreversibility that to some extent deters entry. The share of market variable is correlated with relative costs in industries with substantial scale economies. I have interacted market share with several of the entry barrier variables because the latter capture industry attributes that cause there to be scale-related advantages at the firm level.

The firm-specific variables measure capital structure (DEBT/A) and profitability (ROA and ROE). Because ROE is influenced by capital structure, I have used the return before tax and interest on total assets as the main measure of profitability, that is, the one that is most likely to be

Table 10.1

Symbol	Variable	Type
ROE	Return on book value of equity	f
CA/CL	Ratio of current assets to current liabilities	f
ROA	Return on book value of assets (ebit divided by assets)	f
MXR-MO	The max of ROA minus the mean (M) of ROA and zero	f
MXR-SO	The max of ROA minus $(M+S)$ where S is the standard deviation of ROA, and zero	f
MXM-RO	The max of M minus ROA and zero	f
MXS-RO	The max of $(M-S)$ minus ROA and zero	f
DEBT/A	Current plus long-term debt divided by assets	f
PPE/A	Property plant and equipment divided by total assets	f
HERF	The sum of the squared shares of the firm across all industries	f
A	Total assets of the firm	f
OPTIM	The calculated optimal capital structure	f
C4	4-firm concentration ratio	I
C8	8-firm concentration ratio	I
C20	20-firm concentration ratio	I
MES	Minimum efficient scale of plant	I
CDR	Cost disadvantage ratio for small est's	I
A/S	Advertising to sales ratio	I
P/VA	Payroll divided by value added: a measure of labor intensity	I
VA/A	Value added divided by assets	I
SOM	Share of industry sales	I
SOM*A/S	Market share times advertising to sales ration	I
SOM*MES	Market share times minimum efficient scale plant	I
SOM/CDR	Market share divided by cost disadvantage ratio	I
SOM/C4	Market share divided by share of top four firms	I

determined directly by the firm's competitive position in the various industries in which it operates. The ratio CA/CL is a measure of the resources the firm has for investment. The data and tests below strongly suggest that firms with substantial resources use them and tend not to use debt. The variable PPE/A is included in order to test the hypothesis that debt is used more readily if there are durable assets to collateralize the debt. Finally, I have calculated the Herfindahl index of diversification across product markets for each firm. This was done for two reasons. One is that it may directly affect capital structure decisions. The other is that I have used this index to segregate relatively undiversified firms from the full sample of 1,183 firms and have run several of the statistical tests on the more limited sample. In terms of the preceding notation, the Herfindahl index is

(11) $$H_j = \sum_i s_{ji}^2.$$

A firm with a Herfindahl index of .625 must have at least 75% of its sales in a single industry.[2] This is the cutoff I have used in the subsequent analysis to identify relatively undiversified firms.

Finally, an explanation of the variables derived from ROA is required. These are an attempt to separate profitability into four categories: high, very high, low, and very low. The easiest way to explain the variables is to draw a picture of them. Figure 10.1 shows each variable as a function of ROA itself.

10.4   The Results for Deviations of Actual from Optimal Capital Structures

Because of the cost of some of the computations, I ran some preliminary regressions to obtain an indication of the explanatory power of the product market variables. These preliminary results are described below.

One step in the maximum likelihood estimation procedure is the calculation of the weighted regression coefficients,

(12) $$\hat{u} = (S^T D^{-1} S)^{-1} S^T D^{-1} d.$$

This regression has to be repeated (with 403 variables on the right-hand side) each time new estimates of the firm-specific variances are derived. Instead, I estimated the unweighted coefficients

(13) $$\bar{u} = (S^T S)^{-1} S^T d.$$

These are unbiased but not minimum variance estimates of industry optimal capital structures.[3] It is also the first step in the maximum likelihood sequence. Given the estimates $\bar{u}$, I calculate

(14) $$e_j = \sum_i s_{ji} \bar{u}_i - d_j.$$

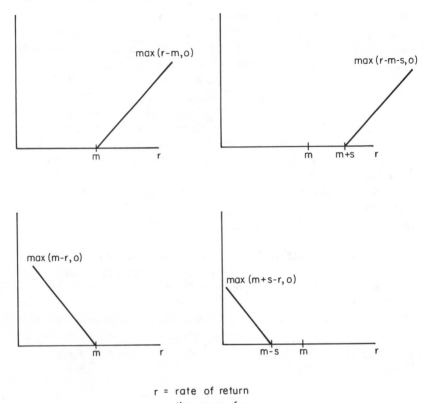

r = rate of return
m = the mean of r
Fig. 10.1   s = the standard deviation of r

for each firm $j = 1, \ldots, n$. These are the deviations of the actual from the estimated optimal capital structures for each firm.

The second step in the maximum likelihood algorithm is a nonlinear estimation problem. I replaced it for exploratory purposes with a simple regression. The dependent variable is the absolute value of e_j, or e_j^2, or the natural log of the absolute value of e_j. The regression is

(15) $$v_j = bx_j + r_j,$$

where the r_j are independently identically distributed normal random variables (we hope). I eliminated observations with missing data and in addition excluded observations for which any of the following were satisfied:

1) The deviation from optimal capital structure was outside the range $[-1, 1]$.

2) The value of ROA was outside the range $[-.5, .5]$.

3) In most cases, I eliminated firms with DEBT/A outside the range $[0, .7]$. The reason for this was that I discovered that in the regressions

explaining deviations of optimal from actual capital structure, the variable DEBT/A explained most of the variance and that was because of a few very high values of DEBT/A. It is worth noting that those outliers are there, but I felt that they made the regression results misleading. Collectively these restrictions reduced the sample of firms by about 200 firms.

The regressions that follow are run with each variable normalized so that its standard deviation is one. Therefore the regression coefficient is the change in the dependent variable measured as a fraction of the standard deviation of that variable that results from a 1 S.D. change in the associated independent variable. The tables reporting the results give the coefficient estimate and the standard error. I will generally refer to a variable as significant if the probability that it is zero is below 10%.

Table 10.2, column 1, contains the estimates for the log of the absolute value of the deviations. The collective explanatory power of these variables is not great. The R^2 is .054. Focusing on the significant coefficients would lead one to the following conclusions. High-return firms have lower than average deviations, while very high-return firms have higher than average differences between actual and optimal capital structure. I did not find this surprising since the motivation for the hypothesis originally was that very high-return firms, protected in the product markets, were subject to less pressure, and hence were more likely to pursue independent capital structure policies.

Table 10.2, column 2, is the same regression with the absolute value of the deviation as the dependent variable. The results are qualitatively similar, and the fit is somewhat better. Here one can see that in addition to the effects mentioned above, low-return firms have above average deviations while very low-return firms are closer to the optimal levels. Corporations with resources in the form of a high CA/CL tend to have larger deviations though the relationship is not statistically strong in this regression. The concentration numbers are best interpreted as coming from a specification of the form

(16) $$\hat{a}c_4 + \hat{b}(c_8 - c_4).$$

In these terms $\hat{a}$ would be $-.119$ and $\hat{b}$ would be $-.313$. Thus both high four-firm concentration and high incremental concentration between four and eight firms lower the deviations. This is counter to the hypothesis that freedom from product market pressure increases the deviation. Labor-intensive firms are nearer to the optimal levels. Generally such firms are less protected by entry barriers. And firms with high absolute levels of DEBT/A have higher deviations, even though the upper tail of the distribution of DEBT/A was removed from the sample.

Table 10.2, column 3, is once again the same regression with the square of the deviation as the dependent variable. The results here are quite close to those for the absolute value of the deviation.

Table 10.2   Determinants of Deviations of Actual from Calculated Optimal Capital Structures

Number of Dependent Variables	Logdev (1)	Abs. Dev. (2)	Dev² (3)	Abs. Dev. (4)	Abs. Dev. (5)
SOM	-.038(.032)	-.026(.031)	-.012(.068)		-.063(.07)
CA/CA	-.001(.038)	.037(.037)	.084(.037)		.042(.037)
C4	.094(.126)	.194(.124)	.301(.125)		.19 (.125)
C8	-.232(.135)	-.313(.134)	-.408(.134)		-.305(.134)
AIS	-.004(.05)	-.007(.049)	-.008(.049)		.002(.048)
P/VA	-.061(.049)	-.061(.048)	-.059(.048)		-.051(.048)
VA/A	.032(.042)	.012(.04)	-.002(.042)		.013(.041)
CDR	.017(.035)	.003(.035)	-.014(.035)		.023(.036)
MES	.010(.061)	-.005(.06)	.065(.06)		-.003(.060)
DEBT/A	.093(.041)	-.204(.04)	.236(.04)		.213(.04)
SOM*A/S	-.08 (.05)	-.081(.05)	-.071(.05)		-.067(.049)
SOM*MES	-.078(.061)	-.037(.061)	-.062(.061)		-.021(.061)
SOM*CDR	.175(.111)	.178(.11)	.18 (.11)		.149(.111)
SOM/C4	-.117(.075)	-.149(.074)	-.148(.074)		-.129(.074)
HERF	-.009(.035)	.037(.035)	.067(.035)	-.016(.033)	.055(.035)
PPE/A	-.020(.039)	.024(.039)	.039(.039)	.017(.032)	.016(.039)
MXR-MO	-.176(.107)	-.124(.105)	-.09 (.105)	-.216(.103)	-.127(.101)
MXR-SO	.269(.097)	.277(.096)	.223(.096)	.292(.096)	.278(.092)
MXM-RO	.083(.071)	.132(.070)	.157(.071)	.157(.071)	.130(.07)
MXS-RO	-.034(.063)	-.089(.063)	-.128(.063)	-.088(.063)	-.09 (.063)
OPTIM					
A					
R^2	.054	.0258	.0744	.0286	.0819
df	939	939	939	953	935
F	2.68	3.85	3.77	4.67	3.97

	(6)	(7)	(8)	(9)
SOM	-.03 (.223)	-.046(.225)	-.079(.229)	
CA/CL	.019(.074)	.100(.075)	.136(.076)	.119(.073)
C4	-.065(.268)	.310(.271)	.619(.276)	
C8	-.153(.277)	-.501(.280)	-.763(.285)	
AIS	-.062(.097)	-.122(.098)	-.105(.100)	
P.VA	-.121(.10)	-.144(.101)	-.117(.103)	
VA/A	.179(.09)	.161(.091)	.071(.093)	
CDR	.048(.075)	.003(.076)	-.026(.077)	
MES	.073(.149)	.094(.151)	.234(.153)	
DEBT/A	.055(.077)	.119(.077)	.125(.079)	
SOM*A/S	-.139(.115)	-.074(.116)	-.057(.118)	
SOM*MES	-.204(.167)	-.119(.169)	-.198(.172)	
SOM*CDR	.164(.255)	.154(.257)	.182(.261)	
SOM/C4	-.147(.137)	-.16 (.139)	-.121(.141)	
HERF	.034(.068)	.048(.069)	.064(.070)	.035(.067)
PPE/A	-.007(.084)	.036(.085)	.069(.086)	-.037(.068)
MXR-MO	-.258(.238)	-.278(.240)	-.142(.244)	-.151(.234)
MXR-SO	.288(.215)	.378(.217)	.239(.221)	.269(.213)
MXM-RO	.117(.145)	.189(.147)	.204(.149)	.203(.146)
MXS-RO	-.086(.125)	-.159(.126)	-.175(.128)	-.145(.125)
OPTIM				
A				
R^2	.1503	.1314	.1036	.0575
df	213	213	213	225
F	1.88	1.61	1.23	1.72

I ran the regression for ABSDEV with the product market variables removed in order to determine whether the financial variables explained most of the variance in the deviations. The results are in table 10.2, column 4. The R^2 falls significantly and the influences of the remaining financial variables remains the same. It is perhaps worth noting that in the squared deviation regression (col. 3) the Herfindahl index has a positive and significant influence on the deviation. The interpretation is that large deviations are more likely if the firm is undiversified. Recall that diversification declines as the Herfindahl index increases.

Column 5 in table 10.2 includes total assets as a right-hand side variable, as a measure of firm size.[4] It is positive in its effect on deviations of actual from optimal capital structure and significant. A related result reported later (table 10.4, col. 26) is that firm size has a negative and significant effect on actual capital structure. As I had expected size to increase the attractiveness of leverage, I do not, at the moment, have an explanation for this result. Note, however, that the Herfindahl measure of diversification is in both equations. It is negative in inference, i.e., high diversification does increase leverage.

The principal point that needs to be made is that the differences between actual and weighted average optimal capital structures are related to certain financial and product market variables but the latter do not explain much of the variation in the deviations. These results are consistent with two different views of capital structure. One is that capital structure does not strongly influence costs or total value for reasons that recent general equilibrium theories predict. The other is that firms do not deviate much from optimal capital structures in ways that are systematically related to their profitability, their diversification and their product market environments. But these results could not be taken as strong disconfirmation of the modern forms of the Modigliani-Miller propositions. Later I will argue that actual capital structures are quite strongly related to financial and product market characteristics of the firm and to the optimal levels of DEBT/A. I will return to this general question when we get to those results.

10.4.1   Undiversified Firms

It would seem desirable to confirm these results by conducting the analysis on a subsample of undiversified firms.[5] There are two aspects to this problem. One involves estimating the optimal industry capital structures using undiversified firms. That would certainly reduce the complexity of the first part of the estimation process. But with this sample of 1,183 firms, it is not possible to do this. There are only 112 single-industry firms, not sufficient with 403 industries. If we take only firms with Herfindahl indices in excess of .625 so that they must have at least 75% of sales in some industries, the number of firms with that set of characteristics is 384 and they only cover 326 industries. The completely undiversified firms cover only 85 industries, and there are not enough observations on each industry to be confident of the results.

On the other hand, I did test all hypotheses including those above using the restricted sample of firms with HERF in excess of .625. For these regressions, the deviations are calculated using the estimated industry optimal capital structures, which in turn were calculated using the full sample of firms, including the diversified ones.

Table 10.2, columns 6, 7, 8, and 9 duplicate columns 1, 2, 3, and 4, but the regressions were run on the restricted sample. The results are similar, the most interesting difference being that the explained variance is roughly doubled in each case. It seems fairly clear that the diversified firm sample contains more noise in the relation between optimal and actual capital structure.

10.5   The Determinants of Rate of Return

The product market variables have a reasonable amount of explanatory power with respect to the rate of return on assets for the corporation. Table 10.3, column 10 is the regression of ROA on the product market variables and certain firm-specific variables. Table 10.3, column 10 contains only the product market variables: specifically, CA/CL and DEBT/A have been excluded. The product market variables themselves explain about 10% of the variance, with labor intensity being the most powerful influence (in the downward direction) on profitability. When the financial variables are added the R^2 jumps to 35%. Clearly there is a very high correlation between high returns, on the one hand, and high liquidity and low debt, on the other. Similar results hold if one substitutes MXR-MO (the high returns) as a dependent variable. The numbers are in table 10.3, columns 11 and 18. Column 11 contains the full set of explanatory variables, and column 18 is confined to the product market variables.

Column 12 shows the explanatory variables for low-return firms. These are broadly similar to the ROA regression, with signs reversed since the variable is mean of ROA—ROA id ROA is less than the mean. Column 13 contains the firm-size variable (total assets). It is not significant as a determinant of ROA.

The financial variables should not be construed as *causes* of high returns on investment except perhaps as a second-order effect. Therefore the coefficients on CA/CL and DEBT/A should be regarded as interesting partial correlations, but the variables are not determinants of ROA. The product market variables do not explain as much of the variance in ROA as they should. One possible reason is that the market share data contain substantial measurement errors. I reran ROA equations for undiversified firms with Herfindahl indices in excess of .625. As noted before, this ensures that there is at least one market in which the firm has

Table 10.3   Determinants of Rates of Return

Number of Dependent Variables	ROA (10)	MXR-MO (11)	MXM-RO (12)	ROA (13)	ROA (14)
SOM	.072(.056)	.072(.057)	.038(.064)	.08 (.058)	.003(.198)
CA/CL	.174(.03)	.155(.031)	-.13 (.035)	.173(.031)	.166(.065)
C4	.073(.103)	.036(.104)	-.144(.118)	.078(.105)	.174(.237)
C8	-.106(.111)	-.058(.112)	.154(.127)	-.111(.112)	-.214(.245)
AIS	.016(.041)	.023(.041)	.006(.047)	-.013(.04)	.115(.085)
P/VA	-.216(.039)	-.18 (.04)	.185(.045)	-.221(.04)	-.215(.086)
VA/A	-.011(.034)	.052(.034)	.134(.039)	-.014(.034)	.069(.078)
CDR	-.007(.029)	-.019(.029)	-.019(.033)	-.012(.03)	.017(.066)
MES	-.037(.05)	-.041(.050)	.012(.057)	-.039(.05)	-.086(.132)
DEBT/A	-.436(.03)	-.432(.031)	.235(.035)	-.442(.031)	-.342(.064)
SOM*A/S	.052(.041)	.092(.042)	.056(.047)	.03 (.041)	-.137(.101)
SOM*MES	.028(.051)	.027(.051)	-.016(.058)	.023(.051)	.001(.149)
SOM/CDR	-.114(.091)	-.181(.092)	-.076(.104)	-.082(.095)	-.185(.225)
SOM/C4	.077(.061)	.084(.062)	-.028(.070)	.065(.062)	.032(.122)
HERF	-.061(.028)	.009(.028)	.174(.032)	-.072(.029)	-.034(.059)
PPE/A	.032(.032)	.038(.032)	-.003(.036)	.035(.033)	.107(.073)
MXR-MO					
MXR-SO					
MXM-RO					
MXS-RO					
OPTIM					
A				-.026(.031)	
R^2	.3558	.3471	.1637	.3447	.3118
df	943	943	943	939	217
F	32.6	31.3	11.5	29.1	6.15

	MXR-MO (15)	MXM-RO (16)	ROA (17)	MXR-MO (18)	ROA (19)
SOM	.004(.198)	.001(.216)	−.047(.066)	−.046(.066)	−.157(.216)
CA/CL	.174(.065)	−.07 (.071)	.198(.122)	.160(.121)	.305(.263)
C4	.150(.237)	−.148(.258)	.271(.131)	−.220(.130)	−.442(.270)
C8	−.142(.245)	.277(.267)	.089(.048)	.094(.048)	.129(.094)
AIS	.157(.085)	.031(.093)	−.24 (.047)	−.205(.046)	−.277(.095)
P/VA	−.122(.086)	.324(.094)	−.062(.04)	.003(.04)	.051(.087)
VA/A	.131(.078)	.101(.085)	.003(.034)	−.01 (.034)	.034(.073)
CDR	−.025(.066)	−.103(.072)	−.025(.059)	−.03 (.059)	−.047(.147)
MES	−.104(.132)	.008(.144)			
DEBT/A	−.349(.064)	.168(.07)			
SOM*A/S	−.092(.101)	.176(.11)	.01 (.049)	.052(.049)	−.172(.113)
SOM*MES	.015(.149)	.031(.162)	.026(.06)	.026(.06)	.011(.165)
SOM*CDR	.089(.225)	−.315(.245)	.053(.107)	−.015(.107)	.355(.248)
SOM/C4	.054	.032(.133)	.08 (.072)	.087(.072)	.042(.136)
HERF	.024(.059)	.149(.064)	.029(.033)	.097(.033)	−.019(.065)
PPE/A	.098(.073)	−.079(.08)	−.041(.037)	−.029(.036)	.058(.078)
MXR-MO					
MXR-SO					
MXM-RO					
MXS-RO					
OPTIM					
A					
R^2	.3130	.1827	.0972	.1034	.1403
df	217	217	945	945	219
F	6.18	3.03	7.27	7.78	2.55

Table 10.3 (continued)

Number of Dependent Variables	MXR-MO (20)
SOM	−.158(.217)
CA/CL	.8
C4	.285(.265)
C8	−.377(.272)
AIS	.170(.095)
P.VA	−.187(.096)
VA.A	.111(.087)
CDR	−.007(.074)
MES	−.063(.147)
DEBT/A	
SOM*A/A	−.128(.113)
SOM*MES	.025(.166)
SOM*CDR	.263(.249)
SOM/C4	.064(.136)
HERF	.039(.066)
PPE/A	.046(.079)
MXR-MO	
MXR-SO	
MXM-RO	
MXS-RO	
OPTIM	
A	
R^2	.1309
df	219
F	2.36

at least 75% of its sales. The results are contained in in table 10.3, columns 14, 15, 16, and 19. Column 19 was only product market variables. Finally, column 20 is like column 19 but the dependent variable is the return for high-return firms. Generally the explained variance is higher, suggesting that the purely product market determinants of ROA are more precise variables for undiversified firms and that the modest showing of the product market variables in the full sample is due in part to noise in the share data or in the rate-of-return figures themselves.

10.6   Actual Capital Structure

Let me now turn to the capital structure. In the case of return on assets, one would expect the product markets to be the principal determinants of ROA. The explanatory power of the financial variables, while interesting, is not causal. For capital structure, it is more likely that an abundance of financial resources would cause the firm to limit its use of debt. I have explored the determinants of capital structure using these data and a sequence of regressions which are reported below. Table 10.4, column 21, is a regression of capital structure on the full complement of product and financial variables, with one exception which I shall come to shortly. The regression explains 40% of the variance. There is a lengthy list of significant variables. Liquidity as measured by CA/CL has a strong negative effect on debt. Apparently, on average corporations use debt as a low-cost source of capital when they need it. High returns reduce debt, and low returns increase it. However, very low returns reduce debt. The Herfindahl index reduces debt. Remember that a high Herfindahl index is associated with the absence of diversification. Thus diversified firms have a pronounced tendency to hold more debt.

Column 22 removes the product market variables and column 23 takes out CA/CL in addition. The explained variance is not reduced dramatically. The capital structure decision appears to be strongly influenced by profitability, financial resources, and diversification.

In preceding sections I calculated an optimal capital structure for each firm, based on the estimated optimal capital structures at the industry level. I put the calculated optimal capital structure for the firm on the right-hand side in the equation explaining actual capital structure. Table 10.4, columns 25 and 26, contain the results: in 26, the product market variables are missing, while in 25 the full complement of variables is included. In both cases the optimum capital structure has a strong positive influence on the actual capital structure, and it increases the explained variance by about 10 percentage points. The explained variance is in the neighborhood of 50%. Thus it appears that the calculated optimal capital structures capture features of the industry environment that influence capital structure decisions.

Table 10.4   Determinants of Actual Capital Structure

Number of Dependent Variables	Debt/A (21)	Debt/A (22)	Debt/A (23)	Debt/A (24)	Debt/A (25)
SOM	.254(.034)			.281(.056)	.168(.05)
CA/CL	−.276(.029)	−.264(.028)		−.277(.029)	−.194(.077)
C4	−.207(.100)			−.202(.101)	−.176(.091)
C8	.199(.108)			.192(.108)	.181(.098)
AIS	−.078(.04)			−.085(.039)	−.039(.036)
P.VA	−.041(.039)			−.049(.039)	−.059(.035)
VA/A	.043(.033)			.043(.033)	.041(.030)
CDR	.032(.028)			.017(.029)	.026(.025)
MES	.007(.048)			.006(.049)	.033(.044)
DEBT/A					
SOM*AIS	.075(.04)			.065(.040)	.065(.036)
SOM*MES	−.022(.049)			−.034(.049)	−.022(.045)
SOM*CDR	−.345(.088)			−.323(.089)	−.260(.080)
SOM/C4	.004(.06)			−.010(.060)	.008(.054)
HERF	−.143(.028)	−.143(.026)	−.148(.027)	−.156(.028)	−.109(.025)
PPE/A	−.047(.031)	−.038(.027)	.034(.027)	−.04(.031)	.011(.028)
MXR/MO	−.457(.084)	−.508(.084)	−.59 (.087)	−.416(.081)	−.396(.076)
MXR/SO	.087(.077)	.128(.078)	.139(.081)	.045(.074)	.090(.070)
MXM-RO	.107(.057)	.119(.057)	.143(.06)	.109(.057)	.065(.052)
MXS-RO	−.027(.051)	−.029(.051)	−.024(.053)	−.027(.051)	−.009(.046)
OPTIM					
A				−.071(.030)	.370(.026)
R^2	.3962	.3699	.3129	.3971	.5041
df	940	952	953	936	939
F	32.5	79.8	72.3	30.8	47.7

	(26)	OPTIM (27)	(28)	(29)	(30)
SOM	−.189(.026)	.272(.066)	.543(.196)		
CA/CL			−.287(.063)	−.274(.061)	
C4		−.016(.120)	.115(.24)		
C8		−.001(.127)	.186(.247)		
AIS		−.152(.048)	.02 (.087)		
P/VA		.117(.047)	.042(.089)		
VA/A		.061(.036)	.025(.081)		
CDR		.003(.034)	−.016(.067)		
MES		−.038(.059)	−.011(.133)		
DEBT/A					
SOM*AIS		.044(.049)	.029(.102)		
SOM*MES		−.013(.06)	−.138(.149)		
SOM*CDR		−.261(.108)	−.437(.275)		
SOM/C4		−.007(.073)	−.081(.123)		
HERF	−.099(.024)		−.047(.060)	−.024(.058)	−.018(.06)
PPE/A	.013(.025)		−.081(.075)	−.041(.059)	.032(.06)
MXR-MO	−.431(.076)		−.366(.211)	−.425(.202)	−.501(.210)
MXR-SO	.133(.07)		.029(.192)	.062(.186)	.071(.193)
MXM-RO	.069(.052)		.013(.13)	.038(.127)	.062(.132)
MXS-RO	−.010(.046)		.030(.112)	.016(.109)	−.002(.113)
OPTIM	.377(.025)				
A					
R^2	.4882	.0786	.3184	.2813	.2175
df	952	947	214	226	277
F	113	6.74	5.26	12.6	10.5

Table 10.4 (continued)

Number of Dependent Variables	Debt/A (31)	Debt/A (32)
SOM	.338(.287)	−.178(.095)
CA/CL	−.199(.103)	
C4	−.455(.358)	
C8	.465(.369)	
AIS	−.101(.124)	
P.VA	−.048(.139)	
VA/A	.129(.128)	
CDR	−.121(.102)	
MES	.081(.236)	
DEBT/A		
SOM*AIS	−.178(.122)	
SOM*MES	−.214(.293)	
SOM*CDR	.195(.378)	
SOM/C4	−.282(.256)	
HERF	−.037(.095)	.052(.086)
PPE/A	.126(.119)	.127(.092)
MXR-MO	−.134(.386)	−.193(.355)
MXR-SO	−.149(.355)	−.101(.327)
MXM-RO	.100(.200)	.051(.186)
MXS-RO	−.005(.166)	.035(.151)
OPTIM	.249(.100)	.338(.089)
A		
R^2	.5058	.4161
df	76	88
F	3.89	7.84

Column 27 is a regression of the calculated optimal capital structure for the firm on variables describing its product market environment. The R_2 is .079, which is modest. The significant variables are market share, advertising intensity, and value added as a fraction of assets.

Columns 28, 29, and 30 are similar regressions run on the sample with HERF > .625. These results accord with the full sample results.

For reasons suggested earlier, I limited the sample to firms with Herfindahl indices in excess of .85. This is the largest value of HERF which leaves the sample size at a hundred firms. If this sample were used to estimate industry capital structures for the industries which have at least one firm, the industry optimal capital structures would be very close to the firm's actual capital structures. With HERT = .85, a firm would have to have at least 92% of its sales in a single industry. Table 10.4, columns 31 and 32, contains the results. In column 32 the product market variables are left out, the effect being to lower the R^2 by 10 from 50 to 40. The results are similar to those for the full sample. Of course the explanatory power of HERF is reduced. The principal difference is that in the small sample, the rate of return variables have lost their statistical significance.

It seems reasonable to ask whether the product market variables explain any of the variance in the calculated optimal capital structure variable. The answer is yes, about 8%. The results are in table 10.4, column 27. Here the right-hand-side variables are confined entirely to product market variables.

10.7   Conclusions

Several conclusions are suggested by these data analyzed in this way. The product market and financial variables explain a significant amount of the interfirm variability in capital structure (i.e., the use of debt). Particularly striking is the propensity of firms with financial resources, high profitability, or both to substitute those resources for debt. Diversified firms use more debt and large firms (as measured by assets) use less, other things equal. Labor intensive firms use less debt. The capital structure therefore appears to be systematically related to the characteristics of the product market environment and to the financial condition of the firm.

The tests for determinants of deviations of actual from calculated optimal capital structures lead to negative results. The deviations were not systematically related to the product market, the competitive conditions, or the financial condition of the firm. There are two possible explanations for these results. One is that there is no optimal capital structure for the firm. The other is that there is an optimal capital structure but that deviations from it are either small or unsystematic. Is there any basis for choosing between these views? It is useful to remember that actual capital is systematically related to the product market environment and the financial condition of the firm. That suggests, but does not prove, that there are optimal capital structures. But it is also consistent with the view that managers have preferences, and that these preferences are to some extent shared. To the extent that they are shared, they will tend to show up systematically in the actual capital structures and then get built into the calculations of the optimal capital structure by the techniques described above. I mention this because it would explain why competitive pressure has so little explanatory power with respect to deviations of the actual from the average capital structure. I have been referring to the average as the optimum. But if the argument just outlined is true, the optimal and the average would not be the same. And one would not expect that product market pressure would be systematically related to differences between actual and average levels of leverage.

The rates of return figures are only moderately well explained by the product market data. This is somewhat disappointing. The data provide a reasonably complete characterization of the product market environment, but it is still not complete enough. It lacks the capacity to explain a large fraction of the variability in rates of return. On the other hand, both product market and financial data seem to explain a substantial portion of the variation in capital structure.

This leads me to conjecture that there is a substantial amount of "noise" not only in the market share data but also in the rate of return data themselves. By noise I mean elements of variation that are related to measurement differences across firms but that are extrinsic to the fundamental relationship between competitive position and profitability. Future research will focus on the determinants of relative profitability across firms and on the related measurement problems.

My overall reaction is as follows. There seems little doubt that the financial condition of a firm (the return on its assets, and liquid assets for investment purposes) influences its capital structure decisions. The product market exhibits a strong influence as well. The question is whether these influences are reflections of differences in optimal leverage or not. The alternative is that they reflect preferences that are shared and hence systematic. Note that if the preferences were random around an optimum, as I conjectured originally, then the product market and financial variables would "explain" actual capital structures because they affect optimal capital structures.

If the deviations of actual from hypothesized optimal capital structures had been well explained by competitive pressure, then one would have been inclined to accept the view that there are optimal capital structures. But they were *not* well explained by competitive pressure or financial condition. Hence one is left with two possibilities: (1) that there are not capital structures, and (2) that there are no systematic deviations from them. If one opts for the latter, then the fact that actual capital structures vary with product market and financial conditions comes as no surprise. If one opts for the former, then some alternative explanation of the actual leverage regressions seems needed. One such alternative is shared or partially shared preferences. One example, which is consistent with the data, would be "Don't use debt if the earnings flow is generous enough to make it unnecessary."

In either case, these data do not permit us to differentiate between these two views. In order to distinguish them, one would need an accurate empirical model of the determinants of market value for firms. If one had that, then the test would be whether the leverage was an influence by seeing whether its coefficient in such a model was significant.

The product market data are moderately successful in accounting for interfirm differences in return on assets, particularly for undiversified firms. For diversified firms, their explanatory power is reduced. I believe that is in part because of noise in market share data. Market shares are notoriously difficult to assess accurately.

Notes

1. This research was supported by the National Bureau of Economic Research. Extensive support in the form of data and computer services was provided by the Project in Industry and Competitive Analysis at the Harvard Business School. I am grateful to both organizations for this support. Benjamin M. Friedman gave me numerous useful ideas and some very helpful critical comments on earlier drafts. I should like to thank him for his help.

1. Robert Taggart made this useful point, for which I am grateful.

2. To see this, suppose that s is the largest share for the firm. Its Herfindahl index is largest if all the rest of its sales are in a single other industry, in which case its share in the second industry is $(1 - s)$. Its index is therefore $2s^2 - 2s + 1$. This function is monotonic on the interval $[.5, 1]$, and has the value .625 when $s = .75$. Thus if $H > .625$, then s must be greater than .75. This is how the index is used to pick off firms with sales concentrated in a single industry.

Performing regressions with 403 right-hand-side variables is not a trivial task, and cannot be undertaken with standard programs. It is not possible simply to invert a 403 × 403-square matrix with standard algorithms. These estimates are derived by directly minimizing the sum of squared residuals using a gradient descent method.

4. This variable was included as a result of a suggestion and comment by Stephen Ross.

5. Checking the results by restricting the sample was suggested by several members present at the first conference.

References

Donaldson, Gordon. 1983. *Decision Making at the Top: The Shaping of Strategic Direction.* New York: Basic Books.

Miller, Merton. 1977. Debt and Taxes. *Journal of Finance* 32:261–75.

Comment   John T. Scott

A difficulty in using data to determine if capital structures are optimal in an economically meaningful sense is that firms conceivably choose capital structures for noneconomic reasons. A structure might be chosen because it is, let us say, "fashionable" rather than because it is a value-maximizing one. One way around this is to build and test models to see if observed capital structures are responsive to factors which various theories of capital structure imply are important. The work of Taggart, Auerbach, and others at this conference is in that spirit. An attractive aspect of Michael Spence's approach to the capital structure question is that, by looking not only at average chosen capital structures but also at the dispersion of such structures, an alternative interesting way to get at the question of whether there is anything economically meaningful in observed capital structures is provided as long as there is a sufficiently strong direct relation between value-maximizing behavior and the competitiveness of product markets. The hypothesis about value-maximizing and competitive conditions is an important one, and its statistical conceptualization is stimulating and of broader usefulness than the issue of capital structure. I do, however, have concerns about the *present* application of the innovative part of the methodology.

I am concerned that the optimal capital structures calculated by Spence's approach will be wrong, even though fairly highly correlated with actual structures, because I do not believe the model that fits them is consistent with capital theory. A premise of the paper is that optimal capital structure for a firm is its assets-weighted average of the optimal capital structures for the industries in which it produces. I think various theories of capital structure offer reasons to question the premise that the value-maximizing capital structure for assets deployed in an industry is unique regardless of the firm controlling the assets. For examples, tax shields would to a large extent be firm specific and imply different optimal leverage for two firms financing assets in the same industry category given different losses in other categories, and tax clienteles could conceivably be different for firms operating in some of the same industry categories. I would like to focus briefly on well-known implications of "bankruptcy costs" for capital structure, to provide a clear explanation of why I am uncertain of the appropriateness of the underlying premise of industry-specific optimal capital structures.

The Modigliani-Miller theorem teaches that, if financial markets work reasonably well, a firm's capital structure will matter only if aspects, about which investors care, of the probability distributions over operating earnings are not invariant to capital structure. A priori, the variance

John T. Scott is associate professor of economics at Dartmouth College.

in the effect of leverage on the probability of incurring costs of getting into trouble with debt might be a cause of significant variance across firms in optimal capital structure. Such costs of trouble have probability zero if there is no debt in the capital structure. They are incurred when realized earnings available for both stockholders and creditors are insufficient to service the contractual interest obligations of debt and when downward capital market revaluations wipe out the value of equity.

If we decompose the randomness of the periodic earnings available for the stockholders and creditors of the firm into a short-run component for a given state and a long-run component measuring the likelihood of the transition to a less desirable state, the probability of "getting into trouble" with a given amount of debt in the capital structure should vary directly with those sources of randomness. Thus, I believe the theory of capital structure teaches us that if there *were* an optimal capital structure for a firm, an important determinant of the variance in the optimal structure across firms would be the variance across firms in the characteristics of the randomness of operating earnings. In short, on the simple issue of bankruptcy costs, I would expect differences in business risk across firms to correlate with the amount of leverage they can achieve before exposing themselves to "too much financial risk," since ceteris paribus more business risk increases the probability of getting into trouble with debt. The relevant risk here is a total risk of the firm which depends on the correlation of returns across the firm's various activities even in the absence of any synergies in production across the firm's lines of business. In other words, pure financial diversification affects the probability of incurring bankruptcy costs. For a simple heuristic example, consider two industries with operating earnings having expected values O_1 and O_2, standard deviations σ_1 and σ_2, and simple correlation coefficient $\rho_{12} = -1$. A firm that deploys a share α_1 of the assets in industry 1 and α_2 in industry 2 has earnings with standard deviation $\alpha_1\sigma_1 - \alpha_2\sigma_2$, which would be zero if $\alpha_1/\alpha_2 = \sigma_2/\sigma_1$. Such a firm could promise all of its expected earnings of $\alpha_1 O_1 + \alpha_2 O_2$ as interest on debt yet have no probability of incurring bankruptcy costs. In general its optimal leverage would not be its assets-weighted average of optimal leverages for single-product firms in industries 1 and 2. Once we relax the assumption of no industry-specific production effects from diversification, it is possible that we would find single-product firms alongside multiple-product firms with the former avoiding real diseconomies of multiproduct operations but incurring some penalty in the form of greater concern with bankruptcy costs while the latter offset diseconomies of multi-industry production with lower expected bankruptcy costs.

One way to test the inappropriateness of the underlying specification would be to take the residuals from the industry-specific effect model and correlate them with various characteristics of firms. One would want to use *algebraic* values, so the tests in the paper using absolute values or squared deviations will not do for a check of firm-specific effects. I would still be unconvinced by the exercise, though, because I do not think there has been enough modeling of what those firm-specific effects and hence the explanatory variables should be.

My concern with the paper's underlying premise does not presume there *is* an optimal capital structure, but just that to allow rejection of that possibility or to calculate estimates of such optimal structures, the model specified must be consistent with the theory of optimal capital structure. Even to get the industry-specific effects, in general we need the whole model that includes the industry-specific effects but does not exclude other effects. Industry effects need to be part of a coherent model that is consistent with the theoretical reasons for optimal capital structure. I do believe that a variant of the model could allow rejection of the hypothesis that there is *no* optimal capital structure, yet rejection of the alternative or estimates of its parameters does not seem conclusive given the premises.

Since the question of whether and to what extent we can reject a null hypothesis of no optimal capital structure is of interest, I would like to contribute two simple tests.

First, if capital structure were utterly irrelevant, having neither economic nor noneconomic motivation, we could say that all capital structures were equally likely. The ratio of debt to assets for a firm would be a random variable, x, with uniform distribution over the range 0–1. Thus, $f(x) = 1$ for $x = [0, 1]$ and zero otherwise; $F(x) = \int_0^x f(x)dx = x$. For any firm, leverage would then have expected value of .5 and variance 1/12. The average leverage for a sample of N firms would have expected value of .5 and standard deviation of $.289/\sqrt{N}$. One is then tempted to reject the null hypothesis of complete irrelevance (conditional, of course, on the factors determining the sample) by observing the several tables in Robert Taggart's contribution to this volume (table 1.1, Cols. 3 and 6; table 1.2, cols. 1, 2, 4, and 5; table 1.3, cols. 1, 2; table 1.4, col. 1). Only for table 1.1, column 6, which shows book value balance sheet ratios of debt to assets during the 1970s for U.S. manufacturing firms, do we find anything looking like an average of .5. But it turns out even that is not consistent with total irrelevance because of underdispersion in the data. For my own sample of 376 *large* U.S. manufacturing firms examined below, COMPUSTAT book values show their average leverage, defined broadly as total liabilities divided by total assets over the years 1974, 1975, 1976, was .501, but the unbiased and consistent estimate of the variance was .0140, which is far less than .0833. Defined narrowly as total debt divided by total assets, the average COMPUSTAT leverage for my sample is .246 with variance of .01245. This suggests, incidentally, that the well-reported differences in this period between debt-to-assets ratios of about .25 using market values and those of about .50 using book values may reflect sample selection rather than the use of market instead of book values. Evidently, there is at any point in time at least one "fashionable" capital structure, and one might suspect the average has some economic significance.

Second, although for the reasons above I do not believe industry-specific "optimal capital structures" are invariant to the firm in which they are embedded, I do believe such a fixed-coefficient model would allow rejection of the hypothesis that there is only one "fashionable" capital structure.

Let n denote the nth company and j denote the jth of 37 activity categories (20 two-digit manufacturing, 14 nonmanufacturing, miscellaneous, domestic regulated, and foreign categories). Let $A = [a_{nj}]$ be the 376 × 37 matrix with representative element a_{nj}, $a_{nj} = A_{nj}/\Sigma_j A_{nj}$, where A_{nj} denotes the assets of the nth firm in the jth category.

If in fact there is only one "fashionable" capital structure characterized by α such that

$$\alpha_j = \frac{D_{nj}}{D_{nj} + E_{nj}} = \alpha,$$

where D denotes debt and E denotes equity, then observed capital structure will equal the "optimal" or "fashionable" plus error:

$$\frac{D_n}{D_n + E_n} = \sum_j \alpha a_{nj} + e_n,$$

where $\sum_j a_{nj} = 1$, and

$$a_{nj} = \frac{D_{nj} + E_{nj}}{\sum_j (D_{nj} + E_{nj})}$$

and I assume e_n is (close to) a normally distributed random variable with mean zero and the same variance for all n. If there were only one "fashionable" (perhaps "optimal") capital structure, then the model $D/(D + E) = \alpha + e$ is theoretically equivalent to the model $D/(D + E) = \Sigma_j \alpha_j a_j + e$, since the latter reduces directly to the former. Statistically, if we fit the two models, by choosing α and the α_j to minimize the sum of squared residuals, reduction in the sum of squared residuals as we move from the former to the latter model will be insignificant if the null hypothesis is true.

For the 376 companies for which I could obtain complete data, using both COMPUSTAT and data available at the Federal Trade Commission's Line of Business Program, to compute for each company each variable over the 3-year period 1974–76, the [reduction of residual sum of squares as we go from the restricted to unrestricted model/36] divided by [the residual sum of squares for the unrestricted model/339] is under the null hypothesis distributed as F with 36 and 339 degrees of freedom. I have fit the two models, computed the sums of squared residuals, and finally the F-ratio (and equivalently the F-ratio for the model which drops one column from A and fits an intercept). The probability of getting an F as large as observed would be far less than .01 if the null hypothesis were true, for both the broad and narrow definitions of leverage.

Evidently there are significant differences in capital structures. To make progress in understanding this alternative to the null hypotheses (both rejected) of utter irrelevance or only one relevant structure except for random error, we need to specify and test alternative theories of how product-market structure affects optimal capital structures. From the tests above, I am fairly sure there is at least significant variance in "fashionable" capital structures, and I suspect these differences have economic significance, but I await conclusive evidence.

Regarding the paper's profitability results, I have concerns about two major factors that have been left out. As Spence recognizes, it would be desirable to sweep out the variance across firms in normal rates of return. That is, a priori, I would expect a normal rate of return to be higher for some firms than for others, whether one subscribes to CAPM or some other model of equilibrium rates of return.

Second, I think a large part of the explainable (i.e., nonrandom) information in profitability has to do with multimarket interdependence of firms—because of its effects on conjectural variations within markets and on entry conditions across markets. I would expect these factors might be correlated in the sample with included variables, some of which may be irrelevant and yet the expected value of their coefficients will not be zero if they are correlated with the left-out variables. In any case I believe the two excluded considerations are a priori important.

Regarding the regressions of debt to assets on various explanatory variables, (1) I do not think the u_i's estimated can be "optimal" for the reasons above. That is, they are estimated in a model that I do not believe is consistent with theories of optimal structure. (2) I would like to see explicit development of why particular variables would be important, entering them to test various theories of how product market characteristics might explain capital structures that maximize value. For example, an R&D-intensive environment might be an indicator of an environment with a high probability of an undesirable transition to another state. Thus, a strong negative correlation of R&D intensity with leverage could be taken as evidence in favor of the bankruptcy cost theory of optimal structure. Then again, it could be interpreted otherwise as in the contribution of Long and Malitz (chap. 9 "Investment Patterns and Financial Leverage"). We need careful modeling of our statistical tests to sort out these possibilities.

List of Contributors

Alan J. Auerbach
Department of Economics
University of Pennsylvania
160 McNeil Building/CR
Philadelphia, PA 19104

Christopher F. Baum
Department of Economics
Boston College
Chestnut Hill, MA 02167

Fischer Black
Goldman, Sachs and Co.
85 Broad Street
New York, NY 10004

Zvi Bodie
School of Management
Boston University
Boston, MA 02215

John H. Ciccolo, Jr.
Citibank, NA
55 Water Street
New York, NY 10041

Benjamin M. Friedman
Harvard University
Department of Economics
Littauer Center 127
Cambridge, MA 02138

Roger H. Gordon
Department of Economics
University of Michigan
Ann Arbor, MI 48109

Martin J. Gruber
Graduate School of Business
New York University
New York, NY 10003

Patric H. Hendershott
Hagerty Hall
1775 College Road
Ohio State University
Columbus, OH 43210

Roger D. Huang
Faculty of Finance
University of Florida
Gainesville, FL 32611

Michael C. Jensen
Graduate School
  of Management
University of Rochester
Rochester, NY 14627

E. Philip Jones
Graduate School of Business
Harvard University
Soldiers Field Road
Boston, MA 02163

Alex Kane
School of Management
Boston University
704 Commonwealth Avenue
Boston, MA 02215

Michael S. Long
Department of Finance
University of Illinois
Chicago, IL 60680

Robert McDonald
School of Management
Boston University
704 Commonwealth Avenue
Boston, MA 02215

Ileen B. Malitz
Department of Finance
University of Illinois
Chicago, IL 60680

Scott P. Mason
Graduate School of Business
Harvard University
Soldiers Field Road
Boston, MA 02163

Wayne H. Mikkelson
College of Business
    Administration
University of Oregon
Eugene, OR 97403

Franco Modigliani
Sloan School of Management
Massachusetts Institute
    of Technology
Cambridge, MA 02139

Stewart C. Myers
Sloan School of Management
Massachusetts Institute
    of Technology
Cambridge, MA 02139

Eric Rosenfeld
Graduate School of Business
Harvard University
Soldiers Field Road
Boston, MA 02163

John T. Scott
Department of Economics
Dartmouth College
Hanover, NH 03755

Gary Smith
Department of Economics
Pomona College
Claremont, CA 91711

A. Michael Spence
Faculty of Arts and Sciences
University Hall
Harvard University
Cambridge, MA 02138

Robert A. Taggart, Jr.
School of Management
Boston University
704 Commonwealth Avenue
Boston, MA 02215

Jess Barry Yawitz
School of Business
Washington University
St. Louis, MO 63130

Author Index

Subject Index